I0472029

NORTHWESTERN JOURNAL OF TECHNOLOGY AND INTELLECTUAL PROPERTY

EXECUTIVE BOARD

EXECUTIVE EDITORS
Terence Leong, Chris Nofal

EDITOR-IN-CHIEF
Patrick Gibbs

EXECUTIVE ARTICLES EDITOR
Samantha Picans

SUPERVISING NOTE & COMMENT
EDITOR
Kate Nuehring

MANAGING EDITOR
Minar Kim

EXECUTIVE PERSPECTIVES EDITOR
Robin Fagan

PRODUCTION EDITOR
John Lai

DEVELOPMENT EDITOR
Lauren Cohen

ARTICLES EDITORS

Aaron Eisenberg
Tim Hoppe

Joe Lohrum
Alex Ruge

PERSPECTIVES EDITOR

Tiffany Shepard

NOTE AND COMMENT EDITORS

Marissa Maples
John McDonnell

Caroline Olson
Michael Sweeney

Kristen Veresh
Olivia Wang

ASSOCIATE EDITORS

Dargaye Churnet
Joe Drish
Jason Fitterer
Matthew Schultze

Dominique Freyre
Zach Getzelman
Rayiner Hashem

Andrew King
Jared Miller
Sharick Naqi
Allen Wan

STAFF MEMBERS

Jeremy Adler
Shawna Bray
Brandon Bridges
Nikki Buck
Jason Burch
William Staes

Michael Czolacz
Matt Darch
Maria Doukas
Tabrez Ebrahim
Nicholas Fuller
Alessandra Tarcher

Jonathan Gunn
Kyle Hayden
Robert Harrits
Alberto Herrera
Amber Jackson

Sumin Kim
Amanda Leese
Carlos Marin
Natalie Montano
Aisha Pinto
Rui Xu

John Rhine
Liz Samoroukova
Nathan Saper
John Saran
Jessica Schmiege
Mirae Yang

January 2012

VOL. 10, NO. 3

i

NORTHWESTERN
JOURNAL of TECHNOLOGY
AND
INTELLECTUAL PROPERTY

January 2012 | Volume 10 | Number 3

ARTICLES

COMMENTS

Volume 10, Number 3 (January 2012)

Romeo and Juliet Online and in Trouble: Criminalizing Depictions of Teen Sexuality (c u l8r: g2g 2 jail)

By Dawn C. Nunziato[*]

[T]eenagers engaging in sexual activity . . . is a fact of modern society and has been a theme in art and literature throughout the ages.[1]

I. INTRODUCTION

Consider the tales of Alice and Bob, and Carol and Dave, two sets of young lovers. Alice and Bob decide one night, in the midst of their lovemaking, to memorialize the event and take some racy—but not obscene—pictures with Bob's cell phone. Across town, Carol and Dave have the same idea, and Dave takes similar pictures with his cell phone. Bob and Dave decide to share these images with their lovers via text messaging using their cell phones or by uploading them onto their personal computers. Perhaps Bob and Dave take the further step of sharing these images with others.

Fast-forward six months. As a result of his actions, Bob is facing the possibility of life in prison, while Dave's actions are not even plausibly criminal. Wherein lies the difference? Bob and his lover are seventeen years old, while Dave and his lover are eighteen. Because Bob's lover is under the age of majority, Bob is subject to far more severe punishment than is Dave. This anomalous result contravenes our general expectations of our legal system, which imposes gentler punishments on minors than on adults.[2]

Enter the world of "sexting," where prosecutors throughout the United States have invoked child pornography laws to impose harsh penalties on those involved with creating, possessing, or distributing sexually themed images of minors, as Part II discusses. Because the subject of Bob's photographs is seventeen years old, under federal and state child pornography laws Bob can be criminally charged with creating, possessing, and distributing child pornography.[3] In several instances throughout the country, prosecutors have wielded their power to go after minors like Bob who, with the

---

[*] Professor of Law, The George Washington University Law School. The author is grateful to Dean Frederick Lawrence for his generous financial support. The author is also thankful for the helpful comments of Jonathan Lowy, for the excellent editorial assistance of Pat Balakrishnan, and for the superb research assistance of Robert Arcamona, Thomas Hayne, Bridget Rochester, Megan Zaidan, and Kenneth Rodriguez.
[1] Ashcroft v. Free Speech Coalition, 535 U.S. 234, 246 (2002).
[2] *See, e.g.*, N.Y. PENAL LAW §§ 70.00–70.10 (McKinney 2009) (setting lower minimum and maximum prison terms for juveniles); IOWA CODE ANN. § 903.1(1)(a), (3) (West Supp. 2011) (allowing for a juvenile's simple misdemeanor sentence to consist of community service or a fine up to $100, while an adult must pay $50 to $100 or serve up to thirty days in prison).
[3] *See infra* Part III.

help of new technologies such as cell phones, webcams, e-mail, and social networking sites, create and exchange sexually themed images of themselves and their intimate acquaintances.

Bob's conduct—taking and sharing a photograph of a seventeen-year-old girl in a state of undress or engaged in a sexual act—technically falls within most state and federal child pornography laws. However, those laws were created to punish and deter a far different class of conduct—adults' creation and dissemination of images that depict sexual abuse of child victims. The creation and dissemination of true child pornography is a universally condemned act that is appropriately subject to some of the harshest penalties under the law. This Article contends that Bob's conduct, however, is not true child pornography, and the law should not treat it as such. Federal and state child pornography laws should be revised to expressly exempt Bob's conduct from their reach. Although it may be proper to hold Bob liable for violating Alice's privacy if he shares such images without Alice's consent, he should not be subject to the same penalties as a true child pornographer. Moreover, Bob and Alice enjoy a First Amendment right to create and share depictions of themselves engaged in sexual activity to which they legally consent.

Part II of this Article analyzes some recent instances in which minors were threatened with and subject to child pornography charges for sexting. Part III examines the law of child pornography and the stringent constitutional requirements imposed by the Supreme Court upon legislative efforts to proscribe sexually themed content involving minors. Part IV then explores the constitutional rights enjoyed by minors generally and minors' right to engage in sexually themed expression specifically. Part V proposes revisions to state child pornography laws to exempt sexting from their reach. Finally, Part VI contends that while sexting should not be criminally punishable as child pornography, it should be actionable as an invasion of the subject's privacy if the subject did not consent. Further, social networking sites should not be immune from liability for facilitating such invasions of privacy.

II. THE BACK STORY: RECENT SEXTING PROSECUTIONS

Over the past several years, as cell phones with built-in digital cameras and social networking sites facilitating the posting of digital images have become increasingly popular, teenagers (among others) have begun using these technologies with greater frequency. Many of these teens, who have just begun exploring their sexuality, use these technologies to engage in what has become known as "sexting"—the taking and sharing of sexually themed images of themselves or others via their cell phones or using web cams in conjunction with popular social networking sites like MySpace and Facebook. Teens habitually use these technologies to connect with their peers in general by talking, texting, and creating and sharing images, video, and audio. They have also increasingly used cell phones and social networking sites to explore their sexuality by exchanging sexually themed communications of all types. This confluence of sexual coming of age and ever-advancing technologies has changed the means teenagers use to express themselves, but the underlying messages they express are largely the same as those of prior generations and as old as Shakespeare's tale of star-crossed young lovers.

One such means of exploration and communication is sexting. A 2008 survey found that approximately twenty percent of all teenagers have sent or posted nude or semi-nude pictures of themselves, including twenty-two percent of teen girls, eighteen percent of teen boys, and eleven percent of younger teen girls between the ages of thirteen and sixteen.[4] A survey released in December 2009 by the Pew Research Center's Internet and American Life Project (Pew Report) made similar findings, including that fifteen percent of cell phone-owning teenagers ages twelve to seventeen have received a sexually suggestive nude or semi-nude image or video of someone they know via text message.[5] The Pew Report also examined the social contexts in which teenagers engage in such communications and found that sexting occurs most often in the following contexts: exchanges of images solely between two romantic partners; exchanges between partners that are then shared outside the relationship; and exchanges between people who are not yet in a relationship, but where one person hopes to enter into such a relationship.[6] According to the Pew Report:

> [S]exually suggestive images have become a form of relationship currency. . . .
> These images are shared as a part of or instead of sexual activity, or as a way of
> starting or maintaining a relationship with a significant other. And they are also
> passed along to friends for their entertainment value, as a joke or for fun.[7]

As challenging as it may be for many concerned parents, teenagers' use of such technology for general purposes has become an integral part of their creativity, self-actualization, and socialization in today's inter-networked society. But the ability to capture images and video by simply pressing a button on a palm-sized device that is always at hand can create serious problems for both the would-be subject and the photographer or videographer. This is especially true when the images captured are of an embarrassing or intimate nature. The ability to instantaneously capture and share images with others, via cell phones or the Internet, presents a host of new problems. The question becomes how to respond reasonably, effectively, and compassionately to the problems that teenagers' use and misuse of new technologies raise. This Article contends that the response of throwing the book at teenagers—in particular, the draconian book of

---

[4] NAT'L CAMPAIGN TO PREVENT TEEN & UNPLANNED PREGNANCY, SEX AND TECH: RESULTS FROM A SURVEY OF TEENS AND YOUNG ADULTS 1 (2008), *available at* http://www.thenationalcampaign.org/sextech/PDF/SexTech_Summary.pdf. The study makes clear, however, that the survey respondents do not constitute a probability sample, as the respondents were selected from those who volunteered to participate in the marketing company's online surveys.
[5] AMANDA LENHART, PEW RESEARCH CTR., TEENS AND SEXTING: HOW AND WHY MINOR TEENS ARE SENDING SEXUALLY SUGGESTIVE NUDE OR NEARLY NUDE IMAGES VIA TEXT MESSAGING 5 (2009) [hereinafter PEW REPORT], *available at* http://pewresearch.org/assets/pdf/teens-and-sexting.pdf.
[6] *Id.* at 6–8.
[7] Amanda Lenhart, *Teens and Sexting*, PEW INTERNET (Dec. 15, 2009), http://www.pewinternet.org/Reports/2009/Teens-and-Sexting.aspx (internal quotation marks omitted); *see also* PEW REPORT, *supra* note 5. In other key findings, the Report found that there was no gender difference in the sending of sexting images, that older teens are much more likely to send and receive these images, that more intense cell phone users are more likely to receive sext images, and that eighteen percent of teen cell phone owners with unlimited texting plans have received such images compared with eight percent of teens on limited plans and three percent of teens who pay per message. *See* Anne Collier, *Sexting: New Study & the 'Truth or Dare' Scenario*, CONNECT SAFELY (Dec. 15, 2009), http://www.connectsafely.org/NetFamilyNews/sexting-new-study-a-the-truth-or-dare-scenario.html.

child pornography laws—is unduly harsh, unreasonable, and indeed violates these teenagers' (and their parents') First Amendment and privacy rights.

In several states, teenagers engaging in acts of sexting have been arrested for child pornography and related crimes.[8] In some cases, teenagers were threatened with prosecution and faced severe, life-altering sanctions for engaging in such conduct. Although such conduct should not be encouraged, it should not be the subject of child pornography prosecution either. Consider the cases of three girls from Pennsylvania— Marissa Miller, Grace Kelly, and (the pseudonymous) Nancy Doe. About three years ago, when Marissa and Grace were twelve or thirteen, they attended a party where some pictures were taken. Some of these pictures show Marissa and her longtime friend Grace from the waist up.[9] They are wearing opaque training bras and lying side by side, and one of them is talking on the phone while the other is making a peace sign.[10] In another photograph, Nancy Doe is standing outside of a shower with a towel wrapped around her body beneath her breasts.[11] None of these photographs depict sexual activity of any kind, and, while the picture of Nancy Doe depicted her partially nude, the pictures of Marissa and Grace did not. In October 2008, some time after the pictures were taken, school officials discovered these photographs on several students' cell phones.[12] The school officials confiscated the students' cell phones and turned them over to George Skumanick, the District Attorney of Wyoming County, Pennsylvania, who initiated an extensive and ill-conceived criminal investigation into this matter.[13]

In February 2009, District Attorney Skumanick wrote a letter to the parents of Marissa, Grace, and Nancy, as well as to the parents of about twenty other students who were depicted in those photos or found to have the photos on their cell phones.[14] In his letter, Skumanick threatened the students with child pornography charges unless those involved agreed to the equivalent of a guilty plea.[15] This included being placed on probation and attending a re-education program devised to help the girls "gain an understanding of how their actions were wrong" and "what it means to be a girl."[16] In his letter, the District Attorney invited the parents to attend a meeting to discuss the details of

---

[8] Some examples include Alabama, Florida, New Jersey, New York, Michigan, Ohio, Pennsylvania, Texas, Utah, Virginia, Washington, and Wisconsin. *See* Judith Levine, *What's the Matter with Teen Sexting?*, AM. PROSPECT (Jan. 30, 2009), http://www.prospect.org/cs/articles?article=whats_the_matter_with_teen_sexting.

[9] Miller v. Mitchell, 598 F.3d 139, 144 (3d Cir. 2010), *aff'g* Miller v. Skumanick, 605 F. Supp. 2d 634 (M.D. Pa. 2009).

[10] Complaint at 9, *Miller v. Skumanick*, 605 F. Supp. 2d 634 (No. 3:09cv540).

[11] *Miller v. Mitchell*, 598 F.3d at 144.

[12] *Id.* at 143.

[13] *Id.*

[14] *Id.*

[15] *Id.* at 143–44. Skumanick advised the girls and their parents that to avoid charges, they must "finalize the paperwork for [an] informal adjustment," Complaint, *supra* note,10 at 13 (internal quotation marks omitted), which is the equivalent of "a guilty plea in the juvenile-delinquency context allowing for probation before judgment." *Id.* (citing 42 PA. CONS. STAT. ANN. § 6323 (West 2009)).

[16] Miller v. Skumanick, 605 F. Supp. 2d 634, 638 (M.D. Pa 2009) (internal quotation marks omitted); *see also* Shannon P. Duffy, *ACLU Sues NE Pa. DA over Threats Leveled at Teens: Criminal Consequences of 'Sexting' at Issue in Federal Case*, LEGAL INTELLIGENCER, Mar. 26, 2009, at 1; Press Release, Am. Civil Liberties Union, ACLU Sues Wyoming County D.A. for Threatening Teenage Girls with Child Pornography Charges over Photos of Themselves (Mar. 25, 2009), http://www.aclu.org/technology-and-liberty/aclu-sues-wyoming-county-da-threatening-teenage-girls-child-pornography-charg.

the program.[17]   Skumanick informed the parents that while participation in the re-education program was "voluntary," he would file charges against students who did not participate in or successfully complete the program.[18]   He also informed a group of parents and students that he had the authority to prosecute those involved in making available pictures of girls photographed in their underwear, or even of girls photographed wearing bikinis.[19]   The criminal statutes with which the students were charged carry seven-year prison sentences, and juveniles convicted of these charges would have permanent records, since the charges are felonies.[20]   Furthermore, if convicted of such offenses, juveniles over fourteen years of age would be required under the state's version of Meghan's Law to register as sex offenders for at least ten years and to have their names and pictures displayed on the state's sex-offender website.[21]   At the meeting, Skumanick informed the parents that he was prepared to file felony charges against any of their children who refused to agree to his deal within forty-eight hours.[22]

The vast majority of the parties chose to accept the district attorney's deal.[23]   The parents of Marissa Miller, Grace Kelly, and Nancy Doe instead opted to sue the district attorney for, among other things, violating their children's First Amendment rights.[24]   Specifically, the parents alleged that the district attorney violated their children's rights by retaliating against their children for exercising those rights.[25]   Were it not for the legal challenge brought by the parents of Marissa Miller, Grace Kelly, and Nancy Doe, the district attorney would have enjoyed unfettered discretion to threaten dozens of teenagers with child pornography-related charges premised on acts of sexting.[26]

Consider further the case of A.H., a sixteen-year-old Florida teenager, and her seventeen-year-old boyfriend J.G.W., who took digital photographs of themselves naked and engaged in sexual activity.[27]   The couple uploaded these photographs to A.H.'s home computer and e-mailed them to J.G.W., who could then access them on his home computer.[28]   The couple did not further share these images with anyone else.[29]   As a result, both A.H. and J.G.W. faced second-degree felony charges under Florida's child pornography laws, which prohibit individuals from "producing, directing or promoting a

---

[17] *Miller v. Mitchell*, 598 F.3d at 144.
[18] *Id.*
[19] Press Release, Am. Civil Liberties Union, *supra* note 16.
[20] Complaint, *supra* note 10 at 6–7.
[21] *Miller v. Skumanick*, 605 F. Supp. 2d at 638 (citing 42 PA. CONS. STAT. § 9791 (2009)).
[22] Complaint, *supra* note 10, at 12.
[23] *Id.* at 14 ("[E]very parent and minor, except the three families represented in this action, acceded to Skumanick's demands under threat of felony prosecution and accepted the informal adjustment.").
[24] *Id.* at 4.
[25] Miller v. Mitchell, 598 F.3d 139, 147 (3d Cir. 2010). Retaliation for the exercise of constitutionally protected rights "is itself a violation of rights secured by the Constitution [and is] actionable under [42 U.S.C. §] 1983." *Id.* The Third Circuit decision is discussed *infra* at text accompanying notes 206–212.
[26] However, while this case was on appeal, Skumanick was defeated by Jeff Mitchell in the November 2009 election, in the campaign for which Skumanick's prosecutorial decision to pursue this case was an issue. While it is impossible to say if this case was determinative, Skumanick had been in office since 1989 and his defeat was somewhat of a surprise. *See* Robert L. Baker, *Mitchell Upsets DA Skumanick*, WYO. COUNTY PRESS EXAMINER (Nov. 11, 2009), http://wcexaminer.com/index.php/archives/news/7550.
[27] A.H. v. State, 949 So. 2d 234, 235 (Fla. Dist. Ct. App. 2007).
[28] *Id.*
[29] *Id.* at 239–40 (Padovano, J., dissenting).

photograph or representation that they knew to include the sexual conduct of a child."[30] J.G.W. also faced one count of possession of child pornography.[31]

A.H. contested these charges, claiming that criminal prosecution under the state's child pornography statute violated her constitutional rights, including her right to privacy.[32] She maintained that the Florida Constitution protects her right to engage in sexual activity with her boyfriend and that her right to privacy allows her to memorialize these actions in digital images and to share these photographs with her boyfriend.[33] A.H. further claimed that the state's action was unconstitutional on the ground that prosecuting her for felony child pornography was not the least intrusive means of advancing any compelling state interest in preventing such behavior.[34] The court disagreed, holding that the state has a compelling interest in protecting children from sexual "exploitation," regardless of whether the person charged is an adult or a minor (or the "child" herself).[35] The court held that prosecution under the child pornography statute is the least intrusive means of furthering the state's interest and that A.H. did not enjoy a reasonable expectation of privacy under the circumstances to create or disseminate photographs of her consensual sexual activities.[36]

Consider further the case of Phillip Alpert, a high school student who, at the age of seventeen, had been involved in a two-year-long relationship with a sixteen-year-old girl.[37] One night, his girlfriend, with whom he shared many intimacies, e-mailed him a nude picture of herself.[38] The picture depicted neither a sexual act nor an obscene pose, but rather simply showed her standing in front of the camera without clothes on.[39] Unfortunately, Phillip's relationship with his girlfriend did not last. After quarreling one night, Phillip decided to exact revenge on his girlfriend.[40] He used the password she had previously shared with him to access her e-mail account.[41] Phillip then retrieved the nude picture his girlfriend had taken of herself (and had voluntarily sent to him) and sent it to all of her e-mail contacts, totaling about seventy people.[42]

Sending his girlfriend's nude picture to her e-mail contacts without her consent was profoundly unwise. It undoubtedly greatly embarrassed his girlfriend and shocked and surprised the recipients. His actions arguably violated her privacy rights and were actionable as an invasion of her privacy, as this Article discusses below.[43] While Phillip

---

[30] *Id.* at 235 (majority opinion) (citing FLA. STAT. § 827.071(3) (2005)).

[31] *See id.* at 235 n.1 (noting that he was charged under FLA. STAT. § 827.071(5)).

[32] *Id.* at 236.

[33] *Id.* (noting that A.H. relied on FLA. CONST. art. 1, § 23 (1998)).

[34] *Id.*

[35] *Id.*

[36] *Id.* at 235, 238.

[37] Robert D. Richards & Clay Calvert, *When Sex and Cell Phones Collide: Inside the Prosecution of a Teen Sexting Case*, 32 HASTINGS COMM. & ENT. L.J. 1, 17 (2009). The article includes a transcript of the authors' interview with Alpert and his attorney in question-and-answer format. *Id.* at 10–34.

[38] *Id.* at 17.

[39] *Id.*

[40] *Id.* at 8.

[41] *Id.*

[42] *Id.*

[43] *See infra* Part VI (arguing that incidents of sexting in which images are shared without the consent of the subject are actionable under the public disclosure of private fact prong of the common law invasion of privacy tort).

may deserve some form of punishment, the punishment he received does not fit the "crime." After his former girlfriend's parents contacted the authorities, Phillip was arrested and threatened with prosecution for 140 counts of child pornography—one count for each "possession" and another for each distribution of the image, applying each of the two counts to the seventy individual recipients.[44] Prosecutors told him he would spend most of his life in prison if he did not accept a plea.[45]

Faced with the devastating possibility of life in prison, Phillip pled guilty to child pornography charges.[46] He was sentenced to five years probation and is required to register as a sex offender wherever he resides until he turns forty-three years old (and perhaps indefinitely).[47] His name and face now appear on posters describing him as guilty of child pornography.[48] Because he was arrested for a felony, his college expelled him and he has been unable to secure employment (prospective employers apparently do not want to hire him because of his criminal record).[49] Furthermore, Phillip can no longer live with his father because his father's home is too close to the high school Phillip attended, and registered sex offenders cannot live in close proximity to such schools.[50] In short, Phillip's life was devastated by the consequences of his unwise act and by the state's decision to charge him under child pornography laws.

Prosecutors throughout the nation have subjected teens who engaged in similar conduct to the draconian regime of state child pornography laws. In April 2009, for example, a fourteen-year-old New Jersey girl was arrested and charged with possession and distribution of child pornography for posting thirty nude pictures of herself on MySpace to share with her boyfriend.[51] The National Center for Missing and Exploited Children found the photos and informed the local sheriff's department.[52] In March 2004, a fifteen-year-old girl was arrested for taking nude photographs of herself engaged in various sexual acts and posting them on the Internet.[53] Prosecutors charged her with sexual abuse of a child, possession of child pornography, and dissemination of child pornography.[54] In October 2008, a fifteen-year-old girl from Newark, Ohio was charged with felony child pornography for texting nude images of herself to some of her

---

[44] Richards & Calvert, *supra* note 37, at 9, 19.

[45] *Id.* at 20.

[46] *Id.*

[47] Federal law requires states to comply with certain mandates regarding offender registration. The federal Sex Offender Registration and Notification Act, 42 U.S.C. §§ 16901–16962 (2006), requires states to subject all juveniles over the age of fourteen convicted of applicable child pornography or sex offense charges, *id.* § 16911(8), to register as a sex offender for at least fifteen years, *id.* § 16915(a), and to have their names and pictures displayed on the state's sex offender website, *id.* §§ 16914, 16918(a).

[48] *See Sexual Offender/Predator Flyer*, FLA. DEPARTMENT L. ENFORCEMENT, http://offender.fdle.state.fl.us/offender/flyer.do?personId=60516 (last visited Nov. 29, 2011).

[49] Richards & Calvert, *supra* note 37, at 9.

[50] *Id.* at 21.

[51] *See* Beth DeFalco, *NJ Girl, 14, Faces Child Porn Charges After Posting Nude Pics of Herself Online*, ASSOCIATED PRESS, Mar. 27, 2009, *available at* Factivia, Doc. No. APRS000020090327e53r001av; Charles Toutant, *Legislation Would Decriminalize 'Sexting' by Teens*, N.J. L.J., July 27, 2009, *available at* http://www.law.com/jsp/article.jsp?id=1202432466455&slreturn=1.

[52] DeFalco, *supra* note 51.

[53] *Teen Girl Charged with Posting Nude Photos on Internet*, ASSOCIATED PRESS, Mar. 29, 2004, *available at* Factivia, Doc. No. Document APRS000020040329e03t00ivc.

[54] *Id.*

classmates.[55] If convicted, she may have to register as a sex offender for the rest of her life.[56] In Greensburg, Pennsylvania, three girls aged fourteen to fifteen texted nude pictures of themselves to three male classmates aged sixteen to seventeen.[57] School officials seized one of the male students' cell phones for using it in violation of the school's rules and discovered the photos.[58] The girls were "charged with manufacturing, disseminating or possessing child pornography while the boys face[d] charges of possession" of child pornography.[59] In Virginia, two teenage high school students were charged in 2009 with child pornography and related charges after they solicited nude and semi-nude pictures of younger female students to trade among themselves.[60] The list goes on.

In short, many teens in several states are engaging in sexting—as many as fifteen to twenty percent of teens who have a cell phone, according to the latest studies.[61] Prosecuting such conduct under criminal child pornography laws is misguided, unconstitutional, and may harm the very people the laws were designed to protect.

III. CHILD PORNOGRAPHY LAWS AND THE FIRST AMENDMENT

Currently enacted child pornography laws, at both the federal and state level, generally do not exempt cases of sexting from their reach. However, an analysis of the Supreme Court's child pornography jurisprudence shows that applying such laws to typical incidents of sexting is unconstitutional and inconsistent with the government's interests underlying such laws.

Generally, child pornography laws punish the possession, creation, distribution, and receipt of visual depictions of children engaged in sexually explicit conduct. Such laws typically apply across the board to minors and do not exempt minors who are near the age of majority or, indeed, over the legal age to consent to sexual relations.[62] The term "minor" in child pornography laws includes individuals up to age eighteen, although some state laws specify a different age range. In recent years, laws addressing child pornography have become increasingly harsh and expansive in their reach, especially at the federal level.[63] This Article reviews the contours of state and federal child pornography laws and examines the Supreme Court jurisprudence in this area, concluding that applying these laws to instances of sexting does not withstand constitutional scrutiny.

---

[55] See Violet Blue, *When Teens Make Their Own Porn, Who's Being Exploited?*, SFGATE.COM (Jan. 29, 2009), http://articles.sfgate.com/2009-01-29/living/17331420_1_child-pornography-boys-face-charges-nude-photographs.

[56] *Id.*

[57] *See id.*

[58] *See id.*

[59] *Id.* (internal quotation mark omitted).

[60] Bill Starks, *Two Spotsylvania Students Arrested for Child Porn, in Latest 'Sexting' Case*, WUSA9.COM (Mar. 10, 2009, 5:35 PM), http://www.wusa9.com/news/local/story.aspx?storyid=82608&catid=188.

[61] *See supra* text accompanying notes 5–7.

[62] *See infra* text accompanying notes 65–66.

[63] Indeed, the federal Commission on Pornography (unsuccessfully) recommended increasing the age of majority for child pornography laws from eighteen to twenty-one. *See* ATTORNEY GEN.'S COMM'N ON PORNOGRAPHY, FINAL REPORT 623–28 (1986).

A. The Contours of Federal Child Pornography Laws

Congress undertook its first effort to outlaw child pornography with the passage of the Protection of Children Against Sexual Exploitation Act of 1977.[64] The current version of the statute defines "child pornography" as "any visual depiction . . . of sexually explicit conduct" by a minor[65] and defines "minor" to include all those under eighteen years of age.[66] In response to the increased use of personal computers to access sexually explicit content, Congress moved to expand the Act's reach in 1988 and passed amendments to the Act which included criminalizing the transmission of child pornography "by any means including by computer."[67]

The Child Pornography Prevention Act of 1996 (CPPA), provisions of which *Ashcroft v. Free Speech Coalition* struck down,[68] revised and extended the behavior prohibited by the Act.[69] In addition to transporting, distributing, or receiving "any visual depiction" that "involves the use of a minor engaging in sexually explicit conduct,"[70] the CPPA made it a crime to possess computer disks containing three or more images of child pornography.[71] It also extended the federal prohibition of child pornography to sexually explicit images that *appear to depict* minors but were produced without real children, as well as material promoted or pandered so as to convey the impression that it involves minors, regardless of whether it actually involves minors.[72] In 1998, the Protection of Children from Sexual Predators Act modified the federal possession requirement to prohibit possession of a computer disk that contains a single image of child pornography (revising the three-image requirement in the CPPA).[73] After portions of the CPPA were struck down in *Ashcroft v. Free Speech Coalition*, Congress went back to the drawing board in an attempt to remedy the constitutional defects identified by the Court and passed the Prosecutorial Remedies and Other Tools to end the Exploitation of Children Today Act of 2003 (the PROTECT Act).[74] This Act redefined and narrowed the pandering and solicitation provisions of the CPPA to punish only those who actually believe, or intend others to believe, that the subjects of the sexually oriented material at issue are real children.[75] The Supreme Court upheld these provisions of the PROTECT Act in *United States v. Williams*.[76]

---

[64] Pub. L. No. 95-225, 92 Stat. 7 (1978) (current version at 18 U.S.C. §§ 2251–2260A (2006)).
[65] 18 U.S.C. § 2256(8). "Sexually explicit conduct" is defined to include: "actual or simulated—(i) sexual intercourse, including genital-genital, oral-genital, anal-genital, or oral-anal, whether between persons of the same or opposite sex; (ii) bestiality; (iii) masturbation; (iv) sadistic or masochistic abuse; or (v) lascivious exhibition of the genitals or pubic area of any person." *Id.* § 2256(2)(A).
[66] *Id.* § 2256(1).
[67] Child Protection and Obscenity Enforcement Act of 1988, Pub. L. No. 100-690, § 7511(b), 102 Stat. 4181, 4485 (codified as amended at 18 U.S.C. § 2252(a)).
[68] 535 U.S. 234, 258 (2002).
[69] Child Pornography Prevention Act (CPPA) of 1996, Pub. L. No. 104-208, § 121, 110 Stat. 3009, 3009-26.
[70] 18 U.S.C. §§ 2252(a), 2252A(a).
[71] CPPA § 121(3)(a), 110 Stat. at 3009-28 to 3009-29 (codified as amended at 18 U.S.C. § 2252A(a)(5)).
[72] *Id.* § 121(2)(4), 101 Stat. at 3009-27 (codified as amended at 18 U.S.C. § 2256(8)(C)–(D) (2006)).
[73] Protection of Children from Sexual Predators Act of 1998, Pub. L. No. 105-314, § 203, 112 Stat. 2974, 2978 (codified as amended at 18 U.S.C. § 2252A(a)(4)–(5), (d)).
[74] PROTECT Act, Pub. L. No. 108-21, §§ 501–513, 117 Stat. 650, 676–86 (2003).
[75] *See id.* § 503(1), 117 Stat. at 680 (codified as amended at 18 U.S.C. § 2252A(a)(3), (a)(6)).
[76] 553 U.S. 285 (2008).

Punishment of child pornography under federal law carries severe penalties, including a mandatory minimum sentence of five years in prison for any first offense involving trafficking.[77] Additionally, those convicted of child pornography offenses are typically required to register as sex offenders.[78] Federal law provides for severe maximum penalties as well, including a maximum punishment of twenty years for a first offense and double that amount if the defendant has a qualifying prior conviction.[79] The federal government has aggressively prosecuted child pornography offenses under these statutes. For example, over 1,500 defendants faced child pornography and related charges in 2005.[80] In 2007, the Justice Department launched Project Safe Childhood and cracked down even more heavily on child pornography and related offenses.[81]

To the extent that these federal child pornography laws are applied to acts of actual child pornography (typically involving possession, creation, or distribution of images of young children by older male sexual predators, as well as involving or constituting sexual abuse of children), these harsh penalties are appropriate. As the Supreme Court recognized, "[t]he sexual abuse of a child is a most serious crime and an act repugnant to the moral instincts of a decent people."[82] However, to the extent that such laws are extended to incidents of teen sexting, the penalties are disproportionately harsh and unconstitutional as applied. Federal child pornography laws provide no exception for sexually explicit images voluntarily created and shared by older teenagers, despite the fact that under federal law the teenagers may legally consent to engage in sexual activity.[83] Consequently, an individual can legally consent to engage in sexual activity, but face severe criminal punishment for depicting such activity. Protecting sexual activity while criminalizing the depiction and communication of depictions of that activity leads to an anomalous result and presents First Amendment problems.

B. State Child Pornography Laws

The vast majority of states also have child pornography laws that regulate the production, distribution, or possession of child pornography. Like Congress, many state legislatures have amended their statutes to apply to computer, electronic, or digital images.[84] In fashioning their child pornography laws, the majority of states (thirty-two) define a "child" as any person under the age of eighteen,[85] notwithstanding the fact that

---

[77] See 18 U.S.C. §§ 2252(b)(1), 2252A(b)(1).
[78] See 42 U.S.C. §§ 16911, 16913.
[79] 18 U.S.C. §§ 2252(b), 2252A(b).
[80] See Press Release, U.S. Dep't of Justice, Fact Sheet: Department of Justice Project Safe Childhood Initiative (Feb. 15, 2006), http://www.usdoj.gov/opa/pr/2006/February/06_opa_081.html.
[81] See, Jerry Markon, Crackdown on Child Pornography, WASH. POST, Dec. 15, 1997, at A1.
[82] Ashcroft v. Free Speech Coalition, 535 U.S. 234, 244 (2002).
[83] See 18 U.S.C. § 2243(a) (setting the age of consent in federal maritime and territorial jurisdiction at sixteen).
[84] See Karl A. Menninger, II, Cyberporn: Transmission of Images by Computer as Obscene, Harmful to Minors or Child Pornography, 61 AM. JUR. PROOF OF FACTS 3D 51, 87 (explaining that "state laws prohibiting child pornography have phrases or terms clearly including computer-generated images"); see also id. 87–88 nn.17–24 and accompanying text.
[85] These states are Alaska, Arizona, California, Colorado, Florida, Georgia, Hawaii, Idaho, Illinois, Indiana, Iowa, Kansas, Maine, Massachusetts, Michigan, Minnesota, Mississippi, Nebraska, New Hampshire, New Mexico, North Carolina, North Dakota, Oklahoma, Oregon, Pennsylvania, Rhode Island, Texas, Utah,

the vast majority of such states also fix the age of consent to legally engage in sexual activity at sixteen.[86] In contrast, three states define child under their child pornography laws as anyone under the age of seventeen,[87] three other states define child as anyone under the age of sixteen,[88] others provide variable definitions of minor,[89] and the remaining do not explicitly define the age of a minor or child.[90] Yet, other states, while defining minor broadly as anyone under eighteen, provide for enhanced punishment if the minor involved is below a certain age.[91] Some states provide for an affirmative defense if the defendant is not much older than the minor involved,[92] while other states enhance penalties where the adult is significantly older than the minor involved.[93] In contrast, some states' child pornography laws provide for varying penalties that depend on the age

---

Virginia, West Virginia, Wisconsin, and Wyoming. *See* NAT'L DIST. ATTORNEY'S ASS'N, NAT'L CTR. FOR PROSECUTION OF CHILD ABUSE, CHILD PORNOGRAPHY DISTRIBUTION AND PROMOTION STATUTES (2010), *available at* http://www.ndaa.org/pdf/Child%20Pornography%20Distribution%20Statutes%203-2010.pdf [hereinafter CHILD PORNOGRAPHY STATUTES].

[86] Thirty-four states set the age of consent—the minimum age at which an individual can legally consent to engage in sexual intercourse under any circumstances—at sixteen years of age, while another six set the age of consent at seventeen years of age. LEWIN GRP., U.S. DEP'T OF HEALTH & HUMAN SERVS., STATUTORY RAPE: A GUIDE TO STATE LAWS AND REPORTING REQUIREMENTS 5 (2004), *available at* http://aspe.hhs.gov/hsp/08/SR/StateLaws/report.pdf.

[87] These states are Alabama, Arkansas, and Louisiana. CHILD PORNOGRAPHY STATUTES, *supra* note 85, at 6, 10, 63.

[88] These states are Connecticut, Montana, and Vermont. *Id.* at 23–24, 89–90, 139.

[89] These states are Delaware, Ohio, South Carolina, South Dakota, Tennessee, and Washington. *Id.*

[90] Other state codes provide different definitions of minor for different sections. Maryland's code does not define the term minor in § 11-207 (child pornography) but § 11-208 (possession of visual representation of child under 16 engaged in certain sexual acts) defines minor as anyone under sixteen. MD. CODE ANN., CRIM. LAW §§ 11-207, 11-208 (LexisNexis Supp. 2011). It is unclear whether this definition is intended to apply to the section preceding it. Missouri defines a child as anyone under fourteen, but child pornography includes "[a]ny obscene material or performance depicting sexual conduct, sexual contact, or a sexual performance, as these terms are defined in [§] 556.061, and which has as one of its participants or portrays as an observer of such conduct, contact, or performance a minor under the age of eighteen." MO. ANN. STAT. § 573.010(2)(a) (West 2011). In Nevada, minor is not explicitly defined either, but the punishments vary based on the age of the child involved in the pornography. NEV. REV. STAT. ANN. § 200.750 (LexisNexis 2006) ("A person punishable pursuant to NRS 200.710 or 200.720 shall be punished for a category A felony by imprisonment in the state prison: 1. If the minor is 14 years of age or older, for life with the possibility of parole, with eligibility for parole beginning when a minimum of 5 years has been served . . . and shall be further punished by a fine of not more than $100,000. 2. If the minor is less than 14 years of age, for life with the possibility of parole, with eligibility for parole beginning when a minimum of 10 years has been served, and shall be further punished by a fine of not more than $100,000."). New Jersey's statutes are similarly ambiguous, with some sections defining a minor as anyone under eighteen and other sections defining a minor as anyone under sixteen. In New York, some provisions apply to minors under sixteen, others apply to minors under seventeen.

[91] For example, in Texas, sexual conduct with a minor under eighteen is a second degree felony. If the minor is under fourteen, the felony becomes a first degree felony. TEX. PENAL CODE ANN. § 43.25(c) (West 2011). Virginia also defines a minor as anyone under the age of eighteen, but also enhances penalties where the minor is less than fifteen. VA. CODE ANN. § 18.2-374.1(C1)–(C2) (2009).

[92] For example, Texas allows an affirmative defense if the defendant is not more than two years older than the minor involved. TEX. PENAL CODE ANN. § 43.25(f)(3).

[93] Virginia, for example, enhances penalties where the adult is more than seven years older than the minor involved. VA. CODE ANN. § 18.2-374.1(C1)–(C2).

of the minor involved.[94]   State laws also vary in terms of their reach, with some, like Pennsylvania, extending broadly to "nudity ... depicted for the purpose of sexual stimulation or gratification of any person who might view such depiction,"[95] while other states provide for narrower definitions of prohibited expression.[96]

As applied to instances of sexting, the vast majority of state laws—like comparable federal laws—provide no exceptions for sexually explicit images that are voluntarily created and shared by teens, despite the fact that under these state laws, some teens are old enough to legally consent to engage in sexual activity. As under the federal law, this means that an individual can legally consent to engage in sexual activity, yet face severe criminal punishment for creating, possessing, or sharing an image of herself engaged in such activity. Once again, this presents serious First Amendment problems.

To make matters worse, some states have recently specifically amended their child pornography and related laws to expressly cover instances of sexting. Lawmakers in eleven states introduced legislation in 2009 aimed at deterring teens from sexting.[97] Colorado, for example, added "text messages" to the definition of the means to commit "computer dissemination of indecent material to a child"[98] so as to encompass sexting within the reach of this law. Following this trend, Utah recently enacted legislation providing for penalties for minors who distribute pornographic material or who deal in material harmful to a minor.[99] In summary, sexting appears to be within the reach of most state child pornography laws, and some states are expressly revising their laws to make clear that they encompass acts of sexting.

C. Child Pornography Jurisprudence

First Amendment law regarding child pornography has evolved along a somewhat separate course than the law governing obscenity generally. While both areas involve sexually themed works, the Supreme Court has articulated a separate jurisprudence

---

[94] See, e.g., KY. REV. STAT. ANN. § 531.320(2)(a)–(b) (LexisNexis 2008) ("Promoting a sexual performance by a minor is: (a) A Class C felony if the minor involved in the sexual performance is less than eighteen (18) years old at the time the minor engages in the prohibited activity; (b) A Class B felony if the minor involved in the sexual performance is less than sixteen (16) years old at the time the minor engages in the prohibited activity.").

[95] 18 PA. CONS. STAT. ANN. § 6312 (West 2009).

[96] See supra text accompanying notes 90–94.

[97] See 2009 "Sexting" Legislation, NAT'L CONF. ST. LEGISLATURES, http://www.ncsl.org/default.aspx?tabid=17756 (last updated Sept. 1, 2010).

[98] See COLO. REV. STAT. § 13-21-1002(1) (2011) (defining "computer dissemination of indecent material to a child" as "[a] person commits computer dissemination of indecent material to a child when: (a) Knowing the character and content of the communication which, in whole or in part, depicts actual or simulated nudity, or sexual conduct, as defined in section 19-1-103(97), C.R.S., the person willfully uses a computer, computer network, telephone network, data network, or computer system allowing the input, output, examination, or transfer of computer data or computer programs from one computer to another or a text-messaging or instant-messaging system to initiate or engage in such communication with a person he or she believes to be a child; and (b) By means of such communication the person importunes, invites, entices, or induces a person he or she believes to be a child to engage in sexual contact, sexual intrusion, or sexual penetration with the person, or to engage in a sexual performance or sexual conduct, as defined in section 19-1-103(97), C.R.S., for the person's benefit.").

[99] See H.R 14, 2009 Gen. Sess. (Utah 2009).

governing the regulation of sexually themed works with minors as subjects, which constitutes a "related and overlapping category of proscribable speech."[100]

The law of obscenity governs sexually themed works involving subjects of all ages—adults and minors. Indeed, although incidents of sexting have been the subject of child pornography prosecutions, such images might also constitute obscene works under federal or state law. For much of the twentieth century, the Supreme Court struggled to articulate a coherent and workable set of guidelines for distinguishing sexually themed expression protected by the First Amendment from sexually themed expression that constitutes obscenity. Ultimately, in *Miller v. California*, the Supreme Court fashioned a set of guidelines for the regulation of sexually themed works.[101] The three-prong *Miller* test requires a consideration of

> (a) whether "the average person, applying contemporary community standards" would find that the work, taken as a whole, appeals to the prurient interest; (b) whether the work depicts or describes, in a patently offensive way, sexual conduct specifically defined by the applicable state law; and (c) whether the work, taken as a whole, lacks serious literary, artistic, political, or scientific value.[102]

The *Miller* test provides important safeguards for sexually themed speech. *Miller* first makes clear that obscenity is determined using a local, community standard.[103] Specifically, the applicable standard is that of the average member of the community, applying contemporary community standards to assess whether the expression at issue, taken as a whole, appeals to the prurient interest.[104] Second, *Miller* requires that, to regulate obscene content, a regulator (whether the federal, state, or local government) must specifically define which descriptions or depictions of specific sexual acts may be deemed patently offensive under contemporary community standards.[105] This requirement reduces the potential for vagueness within obscenity statutes.[106] Determining whether a work is patently offensive, like determining whether a work appeals to the prurient interest, is judged under the standard of the average member of the local community.[107] The third prong of *Miller* provides that *judges* retain the power to determine whether sexually themed speech has redeeming serious social value (i.e., literary, artistic, political, or scientific value) and, therefore, whether such speech is protected by the First Amendment regardless of its assessment by local communities.[108] Because this determination is ultimately to be made by courts and not jury members, this

---

[100] United States v. Williams, 553 U.S. 285, 288 (2008).

[101] 413 U.S. 15, 24 (1973). These guidelines remain the current standard. *See, e.g.,* Jenkins v. Georgia, 418 U.S. 153, 157 (1974); Pope v. Illinois, 481 U.S. 497, 500–01 (1987).

[102] *Miller v. California*, 413 U.S. at 24 (citation omitted) (quoting Roth v. United States, 354 U.S. 476, 489 (1957)).

[103] *Id.* at 30–32.

[104] *Id.* at 30–31.

[105] *See id.* at 24–25.

[106] *See* Reno v. ACLU, 521 U.S. 844, 873 (1997).

[107] *See* Ashcroft v. ACLU, 535 U.S. 564, 576 n.7 (2002) ("[T]he 'patently offensive' prong of the test is also a question of fact to be decided by a jury applying contemporary community standards.").

[108] *See, e.g.,* Jenkins v. Georgia, 418 U.S. 153 (1974) (reversing jury verdict where film in question was not patently offensive under the Miller standard).

"savings clause" provides a judicial check on local communities' power to determine what sexually themed expression is unprotected by the First Amendment. As the Supreme Court has explained, "the serious value requirement 'allows appellate courts to impose some limitations and regularity on the definition [of obscenity] by setting, *as a matter of law*, a national floor for socially redeeming value.'"[109]

A decade after it set forth the *Miller* standard governing obscene works generally, the Supreme Court articulated a separate test for sexually themed works depicting minors, which are afforded less First Amendment protection. For works involving child pornography, *New York v. Ferber* fashioned a separate test that did not include the speech-protective elements of the *Miller* test.[110] Since its *Ferber* decision in 1982, the Court has continued to advance this separate but related jurisprudence for sexually themed works involving minors in cases such as *Osborne v. Ohio*,[111] *Ashcroft v. Free Speech Coalition*,[112] and recently in *United States v. Williams*.[113]

In *Ferber*, the Supreme Court made clear that First Amendment protection for sexually themed works depicting minors is not governed by the same test as obscene works generally.[114] *Ferber* involved the constitutionality of a New York statute that criminalized the promotion of a "sexual performance by a child."[115] The statute defined child as anyone fifteen years of age or younger[116] and included a detailed and specific definition of sexual performance.[117] Paul Ferber was the proprietor of a Manhattan bookstore specializing in sexually themed works and sold two films to an undercover police officer that depicted young boys masturbating.[118] Ferber challenged the constitutionality of the New York statute, claiming that the works in question were governed by the *Miller* obscenity standard and that the state had no power to criminalize

---

[109] *See Ashcroft v. ACLU*, 535 U.S. at 579 (quoting *Reno*, 521 U.S. at 873). Thus, even if a less "tolerant" community made the determination that a certain edition of *The Joy of Sex* was obscene and unprotected by the First Amendment, *Miller* requires that such determinations be second-guessed by the judicial branch, which has the responsibility for applying this *Miller* savings clause to declare that the expression at issue nonetheless has serious redeeming social value and is therefore protected by the First Amendment. Accordingly, despite the fact that a local jury in Georgia, applying its state obscenity statute, determined that the Academy Award-winning film *Carnal Knowledge* appealed to the prurient interest and described sexual conduct in a patently offensive manner, the Court in that case enjoyed and exercised the power to determine that the work nonetheless enjoyed serious literary value. The Court was therefore able to rescue the film from the jury's classification of it as obscene and unprotected by the First Amendment. *See Jenkins*, 418 U.S. 153.

[110] New York v. Ferber, 458 U.S. 747 (1982).
[111] 495 U.S. 103 (1990).
[112] 535 U.S. 234 (2002).
[113] 553 U.S. 285 (2008).
[114] *Ferber*, 458 U.S. at 764.
[115] *Id.* at 751 (quoting N.Y. PENAL LAW § 263.15 (McKinney 1980)) (internal quotation marks omitted).
[116] *Id.* (noting that the statute defined "sexual performance" as "any performance or part thereof which includes sexual conduct by a child less than sixteen years of age") (quoting N.Y. PENAL LAW § 263.00(1)) (internal quotation marks omitted).
[117] *Id.* (noting that the statute defined "sexual conduct" to include "actual or simulated sexual intercourse, deviate sexual intercourse, sexual bestiality, masturbation, sado-masochistic abuse, or lewd exhibition of the genitals") (quoting N.Y. PENAL LAW § 263.00(3)) (internal quotation marks omitted).
[118] *Id.* at 751–52.

depictions of sexual conduct involving minors that were not legally obscene under *Miller*.[119] The Supreme Court disagreed.

First, the Court rejected Ferber's argument that sexual works involving children can only be banned if the works are obscene under the *Miller* standard.[120] Because the "prevention of sexual exploitation and abuse of children constitutes a government objective of surpassing importance," the state's interest in preventing these harms is distinct from the state's interest in preventing offense from viewing obscene material that the Court credited in *Miller*.[121] The Court observed that the *Miller* standard, which recognizes the state's interest in protecting the "sensibilities of unwilling recipients" from offense brought about by exposure to pornographic materials,[122] "does not reflect the State's particular and more compelling interest in *prosecuting those who promote the sexual exploitation of children.*"[123] While *Miller* primarily concerns offenses based on unwilling exposure to sexually themed expression generally, the state's interest in regulating child pornography primarily centers around drying up the market for child pornography and preventing sexual exploitation and abuse of children by punishing those who commercially promote material that involves the sexual exploitation of children—which is itself a crime. To remove the economic incentive for commercial exploitation of such works and to protect children from sexual exploitation, the Supreme Court recognized that states must be permitted to regulate materials that involve actual sexual exploitation of children under a standard different than that articulated in *Miller*.

Under the standard articulated in *Ferber*, states may prohibit the promotion of sexual conduct involving a minor to dry up the market for the sexual exploitation and abuse of children if (1) such conduct is specifically and narrowly defined by the applicable state law, and (2) the work visually depicts sexual conduct by children at or below a specified age (which, in the case of the New York statute, was fifteen years of age).[124] The Court was careful to emphasize, however, that depictions of nudity, without more, could not be constitutionally prohibited.[125]

Yet, because the state's interest in drying up the material for the sexual exploitation of children is stronger than its interest in protecting adults from being offended by unwilling exposure to obscene works, the safeguards applicable to sexually themed works depicting adults generally do not extend to sexually themed works depicting minors. First, to be proscribable under *Ferber*, the work need not be "taken as a whole," nor must the work "appeal[] to the prurient interest of the average person" or be "patently offensive."[126] Furthermore, under *Ferber*'s test, it is apparently irrelevant whether the material has "serious literary, artistic, political or . . . social value"[127] when determining

---

[119] *Id.* at 760–61.

[120] *Id.*

[121] *Id.* at 757.

[122] *Id.* at 756 (internal quotation marks omitted).

[123] *Id.* at 761 (emphasis added).

[124] *Id.* at 764.

[125] Osborne v. Ohio, 495 U.S. 103, 112, 113–14 (1990) (citing *Ferber*, 458 U.S. at 765 n.18, for the proposition that "depictions of nudity, without more, constitute protected [First Amendment] expression" and holding that the Ohio Supreme Court's limiting construction of the state statute at issue in that case "avoided penalizing persons for viewing or possessing innocuous photographs of naked children").

[126] *Ferber*, 458 U.S. at 761.

[127] *Id.* (internal quotation marks omitted).

whether a work is illegal child pornography. The Court has further distinguished child pornography from obscenity in its decisions regarding private possession. While adults enjoy the right to possess even obscene works in the privacy of their own homes under *Stanley v. Georgia*,[128] the Court made clear in *Osborne v. Ohio* that private possession of child pornography is not similarly protected.[129] Because the state has a compelling interest in "stamp[ing]" out this vice at all levels in the distribution chain" and because such images, even if privately possessed, "permanently record the victim's abuse," the private possession of child pornography is not constitutionally protected.[130]

The Supreme Court further articulated its child pornography jurisprudence in evaluating the constitutionality of the federal Child Pornography Prevention Act of 1996.[131] This Act extended the federal prohibition against child pornography to sexually explicit images that *appear* to depict minors, but that were produced without actual minors, and to material that was promoted so as to convey the impression that it involved minors, even if it actually did not.[132] Extending the definition of child pornography to sexually explicit depictions that appear to be of a minor, the CPPA intended to capture a range of depictions involving virtual child pornography that include computer-generated images of minors, as well as images of actual youthful-looking adults engaging in sexually explicit conduct. Second, the CPPA extended the definition of child pornography to computer-modified images of real children that are made to appear as if the children are engaged in sexual activity, even though no minors were actually engaged in sexual activity.[133] Third, the CPPA extended the definition of child pornography to include any sexually explicit image that is "advertised, promoted, presented, described, or distributed in such a manner that conveys the impression" that it depicts a minor engaging in sexually explicit conduct.[134] This provision was intended to encompass sexually explicit images that are intentionally "pandered" as child pornography,[135] regardless of whether any actual children were depicted in such images. Minor is defined as anyone under the age of eighteen,[136] an age that is above the legal age for marriage in virtually every state and above the age at which persons may consent to sexual relations in most states.[137] The CPPA also provided for severe penalties for violations of these

---

[128] 394 U.S. 557, 568 (1969) (holding that the "mere private possession of obscene material" is not a crime).

[129] *Osborne*, 495 U.S. at 111 (holding that "Ohio may constitutionally proscribe the possession and viewing of child pornography").

[130] *Id.* at 110–11.

[131] *See* Child Pornography Prevention Act (CPPA) of 1996, Pub. L. No. 104-208, § 121, 110 Stat. 3009, 3009-26.

[132] *Id.* § 121(2)(4), 110 Stat. at 3009-28 (codified as amended at 18 U.S.C. § 2256(8)(C) (2006))

[133] *See id.* (extending the definition of child pornography to include material that has been "created, adapted, or modified to appear that an identifiable minor is engaging in sexually explicit conduct").

[134] *Id.* (codified at § 2256(8)(D) (Supp. II 1997) (repealed by PROTECT Act, Pub. L. No. 108-21, § 503(a)(3), 117 Stat. 650, 678 (2003))).

[135] Ashcroft v. Free Speech Coalition, 535 U.S. 234, 242 (2002).

[136] 18 U.S.C. § 2256(1) (2006).

[137] *See id.* § 2243(a) (age of consent in the federal maritime and territorial jurisdiction is sixteen); WILLIAM N. ESKRIDGE, JR. & NAN D. HUNTER, SEXUALITY, GENDER, AND THE LAW 1021–22 (1997) (listing the age of consent for engaging in sexual activity in each state, which shows the age is sixteen or younger in thirty-nine states and the District of Columbia); NATIONAL SURVEY OF STATE LAWS 384–88 (Richard A. Leiter ed., 3d ed. 1999) (stating forty-eight states permit sixteen-year-olds to marry with parental consent).

provisions, including prison terms of up to fifteen years for first-time offenders and up to thirty years for repeat offenders.[138] The Free Speech Coalition, a trade association for the adult entertainment industry and artists specializing in nude and erotic images, challenged several of the definitional changes enacted by the CPPA.[139] The challengers asserted that because the statute banned images that do not involve actual children engaging in sexual performances, it swept too broadly and infringed their First Amendment rights.[140] The Supreme Court agreed.

The Court in *Free Speech Coalition* reviewed and clarified its holding in *Ferber* by explaining that *Ferber* stood for the proposition that the distribution, sale, and production of child pornography could be banned because such acts "were 'intrinsically related' to the sexual abuse of children in two ways."[141] Because the commercial trafficking in child pornography was an economic motive for its production, "[t]he most expeditious . . . method of law enforcement may be to dry up the market for this material by imposing severe criminal penalties on persons selling, advertising, or otherwise promoting the product."[142] Further, the *Ferber* Court held that because pornographic material depicting actual children constituted a permanent record of the child's abuse, the continued circulation of the material would harm the child who participated.[143] The Court explained that, under either of these rationales, the images had a "proximate link to the crime from which it came"[144] and went on to hold that "the creation of the speech is itself the crime of child abuse."[145] In contrast, the Court stated that the first provision of the CPPA challenged by Free Speech Coalition, which prohibited the creation of sexually explicit images using youthful-looking adults or computer-generated images of (imaginary) minors, restricted "speech that records no crime and creates no victims by its production."[146] The Court therefore emphasized that the state's interest in regulating child pornography is primarily one of drying up the market for depictions of child sexual abuse involving actual children—activity that involves an actual crime.[147]

The Court next examined the provision of the statute prohibiting sexually explicit materials that "conve[y] the impression" of depicting minors if the material was promoted or "pandered" in such a way as to suggest that it involved actual minors,[148] even if it did not. Under this provision, it is irrelevant whether the sexually explicit

---

[138] CPPA, Pub. L. No. 104-208, § 121(3)–(5), 110 Stat. 3009, 3009-28 to 3009-30 (1996) (codified at 18 U.S.C. §§ 2251(d), 2252(b), 2252A(b) (Supp. II 1997)). The current statute provides similarly harsh penalties. *See* 18 U.S.C. § 2251(e) (2006) (providing up to thirty years for first-time offenders and up to life for repeat offenders); *id.* §§ 2252(b), 2252A(b) (providing up to twenty years for first-time offenders and up to forty years for repeat offenders).

[139] Because the second extension, involving morphed images, applied to images of actual children, whose interests were implicated by the morphing of their images to make it appear that they were engaged in sexual acts, this extension was not challenged by the plaintiffs in this case.

[140] *Free Speech Coalition*, 535 U.S. at 243.

[141] *Id.* at 249.

[142] *Id.* at 249–50 (quoting New York v. Ferber, 458 U.S. 747, 760 (1982)) (internal quotation marks omitted).

[143] *Id.* at 249.

[144] *Id.* at 250.

[145] *Id.* at 254.

[146] *Id.* at 250.

[147] *Id.* at 254.

[148] *Id.* at 257 (alteration in original).

images actually depict any minors. Even if a work contains no sexually explicit scenes involving minors, it could still constitute child pornography that could be banned if the promotion of the work conveys the impression that it involves actual minors.[149]   In evaluating this provision, the Court acknowledged that its prior precedent recognized that the "pandering" or commercial exploitation of a work factors in the issue of whether the work constituted illegal obscenity.[150]   In *Ginzburg v. United States*, for example, the Court explained that "in close cases evidence of pandering may be probative with respect to the nature of the material in question and thus satisfy the [obscenity] test."[151] However, the Court in *Free Speech Coalition* emphasized that the challenged prong of the CPPA impermissibly went beyond *Ginzburg*'s pandering rationale to criminalize works even absent a context of "commercial exploitation."[152] The majority reasoned that this provision of the CPPA went far beyond prohibiting commercial exploitation because it classified materials falling within this provision as "tainted and unlawful in the hands of all who receive it" simply because the materials were "described, or pandered, as child pornography by someone earlier in the distribution chain."[153] Possession of such material would constitute a crime, even if the material contained no sexual performance by a minor, so long as someone earlier in the distribution chain had promoted the material as containing such a sexual performance.   This provision had the effect of criminally prohibiting the mere possession of sexual explicit materials, regardless of whether they contain sexual performances by a minor.   As a result, the Court had little difficulty finding this provision unconstitutional.

Taken together, *Ferber* and *Free Speech Coalition* make clear that the state has a compelling interest in preventing the sexual abuse of children and that this interest may constitutionally be advanced by targeting those who engage in the commercial exploitation of images involving actual sexual abuse of children or that otherwise have a "proximate link" to the crime of sexual exploitation or abuse of children.[154] The Court emphasized the interest of prosecuting those who commercially promote or participate in the sexual exploitation and abuse of children, as well as drying up the market for such exploitation and abuse.[155] Importantly, the Court also clarified that where the content in question is not a product of sexual abuse or proximately linked to the sexual abuse and exploitation of children (nor legally obscene under *Miller*), such content enjoys full First Amendment protection.[156]

After the Court struck down provisions of the CPPA, Congress went back to the drawing board and attempted to remedy the constitutional defects identified by the Court—in particular, in the CPPA's pandering provision.   The result was the Prosecutorial Remedies and Other Tools to end the Exploitation of Children Today Act

---

[149] *Id.*
[150] *Id.* at 257–58.
[151] 383 U.S. 463, 474 (1966).
[152] 535 U.S. at 258.
[153] *Id.*
[154] *See id.* at 250.
[155] *See id.* at 254.
[156] *See id.* at 251 (*New York v. Ferber*, 458 U.S. 747, 764–65 (1982), made clear that "where the speech is neither obscene nor the product of sexual abuse, it does not fall outside the protection of the First Amendment.").

of 2003, which set forth a revised "pandering and solicitation" provision.[157] In *United States v. Williams*, Michael Williams challenged his conviction for pandering under this provision of the Act, codified at 18 U.S.C. § 2252A.[158] The Court rejected his challenge and upheld the provision.

The Court first acknowledged that this section, which prohibits offers to provide and requests to obtain child pornography, does not require the actual existence of child pornography.[159] Rather, it "bans the collateral speech that introduces such material into the child-pornography distribution network,"[160] which is typically (but not exclusively) a commercial market. Although this section does not require the actual existence of child pornography, the Court nonetheless held that speech falling within the scope of § 2252A could be banned on the ground that "[o]ffers to engage in illegal transactions," like the exchange of child pornography, "are categorically excluded from First Amendment protection."[161] Because an offer to provide or a request to receive child pornography is in fact an offer to engage in an illegal transaction, this collateral speech could be banned so long as the speaker believes, or intends the listener to believe, that the subject of the proposed transaction involves real children.[162]

Several important lessons for the current controversies surrounding sexting may be drawn from the Supreme Court's child pornography jurisprudence. First, the Court has focused primarily on the harm that arises from transactions in content integral to the crimes of sexual exploitation and abuse of children. Second, the Court has focused on the *commercial* or *transactional* nature of the conduct at issue. In the child pornography context, the Court has recognized the government's interest in drying up the commercial, or transactional,[163] market for child pornography. This emphasis on the market for child pornography echoes the Court's emphasis in the obscenity context, in which the Court has determined that criminal prohibitions on *noncommercial* sexually themed speech are

---

[157] *See* PROTECT Act, Pub. L. No. 108-21, § 503(1)(A), 117 Stat. 650, 680 (2003) (codified as amended at 18 U.S.C. § 2252A(a)(3)(B) (2006)) (revising pandering provision to apply to any person who knowingly "advertises, promotes, presents, distributes, or solicits . . . any material or purported material in a manner that reflects the belief, or that is intended to cause another to believe, that the material or purported material is, or contains . . . a visual depiction of an actual minor engaging in sexually explicit conduct"). The Act also provides an appropriately detailed and narrow definition of "sexually explicit conduct," which includes "actual or simulated—(i) sexual intercourse, including genital-genital, oral-genital, anal-genital, or oral-anal, whether between persons of the same or opposite sex; (ii) bestiality; (iii) masturbation; (iv) sadistic or masochistic abuse; or (v) lascivious exhibition of the genitals or pubic area of any person." *Id.* § 502(b), 117 Stat. at 678–79 (codified as amended at 18 U.S.C. § 2256(2)(A)).
[158] 553 U.S. 285, 292 (2008).
[159] *Id.* at 293.
[160] *Id.* at 288.
[161] *Id.* at 297.
[162] *Id.* at 293.
[163] As the Court explained in *Williams*,

> To be clear, our conclusion that all the words in this list relate to transactions is not to say that they relate to *commercial* transactions. One could certainly "distribute" child pornography without expecting payment in return. Indeed, in much Internet file sharing of child pornography each participant makes his files available for free to other participants—as Williams did in this case. . . . To run afoul of the statute, the speech need only accompany or seek to induce the transfer of child pornography from one person to another.

Id. at 295.

unconstitutional.[164] Third, the Court has explained that depictions of nudity alone—even those involving minors—cannot form the sole basis of a child pornography prosecution. Fourth, the Court has been critical of attempts to criminalize the mere depiction of teens engaged in sexual activity—especially when those depicted are at or near the age at which they can legally consent to have sex. The Court has also been critical of attempts to increase the statutory age of "child" for precisely this reason. In criticizing the CPPA's extension of the definition of minor to include all those who are or appear to be seventeen years of age or younger, the Court explained that "[t]he statute proscribes the visual depiction of an idea—that of teenagers engaging in sexual activity—that is a fact of modern society and has been a theme in art and literature throughout the ages."[165] The Court observed that the age established by the CPPA was higher than the legal age at which persons could legally consent to sexual relations, leading to the anomalous result in which an individual could consent to sexual relations yet be criminally prosecuted under the CPPA for depicting such sexual relations.

D. The Constitutionality of Prosecuting Sexting as Child Pornography

A review of the Supreme Court's child pornography jurisprudence makes clear that sexting prosecutions like those described in Part II cannot withstand constitutional scrutiny. First, typical acts of sexting do not depict sexual abuse or exploitation of children—the gravamen of legitimate child pornography claims. The state's interest in prosecuting acts of sexting is not the same as the interest recognized by the Supreme Court of drying up the market for content that constitutes a "proximate link to the crime"[166] of sexual exploitation or abuse of children. Second, acts of sexting typically occur in a noncommercial context, not in commercial or transactional contexts. Third, many incidents of sexting—like the Pennsylvania and Florida cases discussed above— involve mere depictions of nudity or partial nudity, which the Court has held are insufficient to constitute child pornography. Fourth, several instances of sexting, like in Phillip Alpert,[167] A.H., and J.G.W.,[168] involve minors at or near the age of consent, which the Court has made clear are particularly problematic.

In addition, the Supreme Court has determined that minors enjoy First Amendment rights to access and disseminate sexually themed expression of the kind typically involved in sexting communications. Although minors' First Amendment rights are not as extensive as those enjoyed by adults, they are extensive enough to protect the creation and dissemination of semi-nude and nude pictures of oneself that are not child pornography or obscene-for-minors (under properly limited definitions of both terms). Indeed, the act of creating a photograph of oneself, like creating a self-portrait or writing in a diary, is an essential component of an individual's self-expression, the furtherance of which is an essential function of the First Amendment. Part IV contends that

---

[164] See the discussion of *Reno v. ACLU* and the comparison between the Communications Decency Act's provisions and the statute at issue in the *Ginsberg* case *infra* notes 183-202 and accompanying text.
[165] Ashcroft v. Free Speech Coalition, 535 U.S. 234, 246 (2002).
[166] *Id.* at 250.
[167] *See supra* text accompanying notes 37–50.
[168] *See supra* text accompanying notes 27–36.

prosecutions of minors for creating and sharing such images violate the First Amendment rights of the minors involved.

IV. FIRST AMENDMENT RIGHTS OF MINORS

Although minors' First Amendment rights are not as extensive as those enjoyed by adults, the Supreme Court has made it clear that minors enjoy meaningful rights to freedom of expression in general.   As the Court explained in *Erznoznik v. City of Jacksonville*,

> minors are entitled to a significant measure of First Amendment protection, and only in relatively narrow and well-defined circumstances may government bar public dissemination of protected materials to them.
>
> . . . *In most circumstances, the values protected by the First Amendment are no less applicable when government seeks to control the flow of information to minors.*[169]

The Court has also held that minors enjoy meaningful rights to access sexually themed content. This Part first examines the philosophical underpinnings of free speech rights in general and then considers these foundations as applied to minors in particular.   It outlines the general contours of minors' First Amendment rights and examines these rights in relation to sexually themed content.

In considering the contours of minors' free speech rights, it is helpful to return to the philosophical underpinnings and justifications for free speech rights in general and to consider how these translate in the context of minors' interests in free expression. Among the most important justifications for protecting freedom of expression is the integral role this protection plays in self-exploration, self-expression, and self-definition. Although the Court frequently refers to the importance of free speech in establishing the preconditions for democratic self-governance and in advancing the free and open marketplace of ideas,[170] it has also made clear that "[t]he individual's interest in self-expression is a concern of the First Amendment separate from the concern for open and informed discussion."[171] As David Richards explains, the First Amendment rests not only on the value of creating an informed electorate, but also rests "on deeper moral premises regarding the general exercise of autonomous expressive and judgmental capacity and the good that this affords in human life."[172] Similarly, in the words of pre-eminent First Amendment scholar Thomas Emerson, individual self-fulfillment depends upon the development of an individual's capacity for reasoning and emotions, self-exploration, self-expression, and self-definition to form "an integral part of the development of ideas, of mental exploration and of the affirmation of self."[173] This

---

[169] 422 U.S. 205, 212–14 (1975) (emphasis added) (citations and footnote omitted).
[170] *See, e.g.*, Melville B. Nimmer, *Does Copyright Abridge the First Amendment Guarantees of Free Speech and Press?*, 17 UCLA L. REV. 1180, 1187 (1970).
[171] First Nat'l Bank of Boston v. Bellotti, 435 U.S. 765, 777 n.12 (1978).
[172] David A.J. Richards, *Free Speech and Obscenity Law: Toward a Moral Theory of the First Amendment*, 123 U. PA. L. REV. 45, 68 (1974).
[173] Thomas I. Emerson, *Toward a General Theory of the First Amendment*, 72 YALE L.J. 877, 879 (1963).

justification presupposes that adults engage in the active process of self-definition and re-definition, which First Amendment freedoms facilitate. Yet minors, if anything, are even more deeply entrenched in the process of self-exploration and self-definition. Consistent with this justification for First Amendment freedoms, it is important to protect minors' right to express themselves and to access the expression of others, so as to facilitate their process of self-exploration, self-expression, and self-definition.

The Supreme Court expounded upon the self-expression justification for First Amendment freedoms in *Procunier v. Martinez*, in which the Court struck down restrictions on the ability of prisoners to communicate with the outside world.[174] Although prisoners (like minors) enjoy free speech rights that are not as robust as those enjoyed by free adults, the Court emphasized the important role the First Amendment serves in advancing individual self-expression:

> The First Amendment serves not only the needs of the polity but also those of the human spirit—*a spirit that demands self-expression.* Such expression is an integral part of the development of ideas and a sense of identity. To suppress expression is to reject the basic human desire for recognition and affront the individual's worth and dignity. Such restraint may be "the greatest displeasure and indignity to a free and knowing spirit that can be put upon him."
> ... It is the role of the First Amendment and this Court to protect those precious personal rights by which we satisfy such basic yearnings of the human spirit.[175]

Indeed, in expounding on the importance of self-expression to First Amendment freedoms, the Court expressly incorporated the right to access sexually themed expression in the privacy of one's home, which the Court held is protected in Stanley v. Georgia.176 Accordingly, the Court has contemplated that the First Amendment's protections for self-exploration and self-expression incorporate the right to access sexually themed expression.

The Court has also emphasized other important values the First Amendment serves, including access to a wide range of ideas and information that apply not only to adults but to minors as well. As the Court held in the famous *Pico* case, in which it restricted a school board's discretion to remove books from school libraries:

> Our precedents have focused not only on the role of the First Amendment in fostering individual self-expression but also on its role in affording the public access to discussion, debate, and the dissemination of information and ideas. . . .
>
> . . . .

---

[174] 416 U.S. 396 (1974). These regulations "proscribed inmate correspondence that 'unduly complain[ed],' 'magnif[ied] grievances,' 'express[ed] inflammatory political, racial, religious or other views or beliefs,' or contained matter deemed 'defamatory' or 'otherwise inappropriate.'" *Id.* at 396 (alterations in original).
[175] *Id.* at 427–28 (Marshall, J., concurring) (emphasis added) (citations omitted).
[176] Stanley v. Georgia, 394 U.S. 557 (1969) (holding the First Amendment protects an individual's right to view obscene publications in the privacy of his own home).

... [S]tudents must always remain free to inquire, to study and to evaluate, to gain new maturity and understanding.[177]

Similarly, in striking down a public school's decision to suspend minors for wearing black armbands to protest the Vietnam War, the Court explained that "[i]n the absence of a specific showing of constitutionally valid reasons to regulate their speech, students are entitled to freedom of expression."[178] In sum, the First Amendment justification of facilitating individuals' self-expression, self-exploration, and self-definition is of pre-eminent importance, especially as applied to minors, who are entrenched in this self-evolutionary process.

First Amendment protections also facilitate the goals of democratic self-government.[179] Although this justification applies directly only to individuals who have reached the age of majority and are formally capable of voting and engaging in the task of self-government, it applies indirectly to minors as well. During youth, individuals are and should be engaged in the process of acquiring the tools they need to engage in self-government when they do reach the age of majority. Older minors especially must be accorded broad access to a wide variety of content to develop these tools. Striking down efforts to restrict minors' access to violent video game content, Judge Richard Posner explains in *American Amusement Machine Ass'n v. Kendrick*:

> Now that eighteen-year-olds have the right to vote, it is obvious that they must be allowed the freedom to form their political views on the basis of uncensored speech *before* they turn eighteen, so that their minds are not a blank when they first exercise the franchise. ... People are unlikely to become well-functioning, independent-minded adults and responsible citizens if they are raised in an intellectual bubble.[180]

Similarly, the Supreme Court rejected the state's effort to compel students to pledge allegiance to the flag in *West Virginia State Board of Education v. Barnette*, explaining that "educating the young for citizenship is reason for scrupulous protection of Constitutional freedoms of the individual, if we are not to strangle the free mind at its source and teach youth to discount important principles of our government as mere platitudes."[181] Protecting minors' freedom of expression is necessary to allow them to experience and experiment with the freedoms necessary to exercise meaningful rights of self-government. The closer an individual is to the age of majority, the more extensive are her free speech rights. Adolescence marks a transitional period in which individuals should enjoy and experience many of the freedoms that they will come to enjoy fully in adulthood so that they will be better able to meaningfully enjoy those freedoms when they come of age. Our system of free expression should ensure that adolescents are able to inform themselves and contribute to the public discourse even though they cannot yet

---

[177] Bd. of Educ., Island Trees Union Free Sch. Dist. No. 26 v. Pico, 457 U.S. 853, 866–68 (1982) (citations omitted) (internal quotation marks omitted).
[178] Tinker v. Des Moines Indep. Cmty. Sch. Dist., 393 U.S. 503, 511–12 (1969).
[179] *See generally* ALEXANDER MEIKLEJOHN, FREE SPEECH AND ITS RELATION TO SELF-GOVERNMENT (1948).
[180] 244 F.3d 572, 577 (7th Cir. 2001).
[181] W. Va. State Bd. of Educ. v. Barnette, 319 U.S. 624, 637 (1943).

participate in public elections. As the Supreme Court emphasized in *Keyishian v. Board of Regents of the University of New York*, "[t]he Nation's future depends upon leaders trained through wide exposure to [the] robust exchange of ideas" and information.[182]

The Supreme Court has also made clear that older minors enjoy a First Amendment right to engage in and access sexually themed expression, so long as such expression is not obscene, "obscene-for-minors," or child pornography. Although minors' First Amendment rights regarding sexually explicit materials are more limited than adults' rights, they are nonetheless substantial.

Reno v. ACLU is instructive in articulating the contours of minors' First Amendment rights regarding sexually themed expression.[183] The Supreme Court struck down the Communications Decency Act's (CDA) criminal prohibitions on the transmission of indecent messages to minors[184] and on the display of patently offensive messages to minors.[185] The fact that both of these prohibitions were limited by affirmative defenses made available for those who undertook good faith actions to restrict minors' access to the prohibited communications did not save the provisions.[186] In evaluating the constitutionality of these prohibitions, the Supreme Court first compared them to the restrictions at issue in *Ginsberg v. New York*, in which the Court first recognized a category of obscene-for-minors speech that could be regulated under a different standard than obscene speech (for adults).[187]

---

[182] Keyishian v. Bd. of Regents of the Univ. of N.Y., 385 U.S. 589, 603 (1967).

[183] *See* 521 U.S. 844 (1997).

[184] *See* Communications Decency Act of 1996, Pub. L. No. 104-104, § 502, 110 Stat. 56, 133 (current version at 47 U.S.C. § 223(a), (d)–(h) (2006)). The first provision prohibited the knowing transmission of obscene or indecent messages to any recipient under 18 years of age. 47 U.S.C. § 223(a) (Supp. II 1997) ("Whoever—(1) in interstate or foreign communications . . . (B) by means of a telecommunications device knowingly—(i) makes, creates, or solicits, and (ii) initiates the transmission of, any comment, request, suggestion, proposal, image, or other communication which is obscene or indecent, knowing that the recipient of the communication is under 18 years of age, regardless of whether the maker of such communication placed the call or initiated the communication; . . . (2) knowingly permits any telecommunications facility under his control to be used for any activity prohibited by paragraph (1) with the intent that it be used for such activity, shall be fined under title 18, or imprisoned not more than two years, or both.").

[185] The second provision prohibited the knowing sending or displaying of patently offensive messages in a manner that is available to a person under 18 years of age. 47 U.S.C. § 223(d) ("Whoever—(1) in interstate or foreign communications knowingly—(A) uses an interactive computer service to send to a specific person or persons under 18 years of age, or (B) uses any interactive computer service to display in a manner available to a person under 18 years of age, any comment, request, suggestion, proposal, image, or other communication that, in context, depicts or describes, in terms patently offensive as measured by contemporary community standards, sexual or excretory activities or organs, regardless of whether the user of such service placed the call or initiated the communication; or (2) knowingly permits any telecommunications facility under such person's control to be used for an activity prohibited by paragraph (1) with the intent that it be used for such activity, shall be fined under title 18, or imprisoned not more than two years, or both.").

[186] *See id.* § 223(e)(5) (extending affirmative defenses to those who take "good faith, reasonable, effective, and appropriate actions" to restrict access by minors to the prohibited communications and to those who restrict access to covered material by requiring certain designated forms of age proof, such as a verified credit card or an adult identification number or code).

[187] *See* 390 U.S. 629, 636 (1968) (The state "can exercise its power to protect the health, safety, welfare and morals of its community by barring the distribution to children of books recognized to be suitable for adults.") (internal quotation marks omitted).

The *Reno* Court explained that because the CDA's restrictions did not embody similar safeguards to those in the New York statute, it unconstitutionally infringed on minors' (and adults') free speech rights.[188] In *Ginsberg*, the Supreme Court upheld a New York statute that regulated minors' access to content that fell within the statute's definition of obscene for minors.[189] The state statute primarily aimed to restrict the sale of "girlie" magazines to minors. It prohibited the sale of materials considered obscene for minors (although not necessarily obscene for adults) to individuals age sixteen and under.[190] In accordance with the Supreme Court cases that require regulation of obscene speech to include a savings clause,[191] the New York statute exempted from regulation material that has redeeming social importance to minors. Upholding the statute against a constitutional challenge, the Court emphasized that the statute's operation did not usurp parental autonomy to determine what material was suitable for their children in that the statute allowed "parents who so desire [to] purchas[e] the magazines for their children."[192]

Ginsberg therefore stands for the principle that minors' speech can be regulated under a different standard than that applicable to adults' speech, so long as the relevant regulation adheres to certain safeguards. These safeguards include the definitional safeguards set forth in *Miller*[193] tailored to apply to minors, including a savings clause for speech that has redeeming social importance for minors and a patently offensive and prurient interest analysis undertaken in light of contemporary community standards. Requiring a savings clause in this context makes clear that any such regulation must preserve minors' access to expression that has serious literary, artistic, scientific, or political value.[194]

In *Reno*, the Court compared the indecent transmission and patently offensive display provisions of the CDA to those provisions at issue in *Ginsberg* and found that the CDA's provisions were constitutionally infirm.[195] First, the Court held that the CDA was infirm because it defined minor as everyone under eighteen, where the New York statute defined minor as everyone under seventeen.[196] Because the CDA reduced the First Amendment rights of those nearest to the age of majority, it did not meet constitutional muster.[197] The Court's analysis on this point suggests that seventeen-year-old minors' First Amendment rights must be construed as extensively as adults' First Amendment rights, including their right to engage in and access sexually themed expression. Second, while the New York statute was appropriately tailored in line with *Miller* by limiting its definition of "material that is harmful to minors" with the requirement that it be "without redeeming social importance for minors," the CDA failed to provide *any* definition of the

---

[188] *Reno*, 521 U.S. 844.
[189] *Ginsberg*, 390 U.S. at 631–33.
[190] *Id.* at 645–47.
[191] *See* Roth v. United States, 354 U.S. 476, 487 (1957) ("The portrayal of sex, e.g. in art, literature and scientific works, is not itself sufficient reason to deny material the constitutional protection of freedom of speech and press.") (footnote omitted).
[192] *Ginsberg*, 390 U.S. at 639.
[193] *See supra* text accompanying notes 101–109.
[194] *See supra* text accompanying notes 108–109.
[195] Reno v. ACLU, 521 U.S. 844, 864–67 (1997).
[196] *Id.* at 865–66.
[197] *Id.*

81

term "indecent." The CDA also omitted any requirement that the "patently offensive" material covered by § 223(d) lack serious literary, artistic, political, or scientific value.[198] The Court explained that "[t]his 'societal value' requirement, absent in the CDA, allows appellate courts to impose some limitations and regularity on the definition by setting, as a matter of law, a national floor for socially redeeming value."[199]   Third, while in *Ginsberg* the statute's prohibition against sales to minors did not bar parents from purchasing the magazines for their children, under the CDA, "neither the parents' consent—nor even their participation—in the communication would avoid the application of the statute."[200]   Refusing to account for parental discretion on this score disregards the Supreme Court's "consistent recognition of the principle that 'the parents' claim to authority in their own household to direct the rearing of their children is basic in the structure of our society.'"[201]   Finally, the New York statute at issue in *Ginsberg* applied only to *commercial* transactions, whereas the CDA contained no such limitation.[202]

An analysis of *Ginsberg* and *Reno*, together with the Supreme Court's child pornography jurisprudence, indicates that minors enjoy a First Amendment right to communicate and access content that is not proximately linked to actual child abuse or exploitation. This right to communicate encompasses the noncommercial communication of sexually themed material that has societal value for minors and is not obscene for minors. And any attempt by the state to regulate minors' communication of sexually themed content must take care to preserve parents' authority in their own households to determine which sexually themed content their children will have the right to access and exchange.

V. PROPOSED REVISIONS TO CHILD PORNOGRAPHY LAWS TO EXEMPT SEXTING

State and federal child pornography laws do not sufficiently protect minors' free speech rights. Such laws cannot constitutionally be applied to minors engaged in incidents of sexting. These laws should be revised to specifically exempt sexting engaged in by consenting teens, as described in Part I. Non-obscene depictions of nudity or sexual activity created by teens and exchanged voluntarily for noncommercial purposes should be specifically excluded from the definition of child pornography or related crimes. Child pornography and related laws should be amended to exempt sexually themed images that are voluntarily and consensually produced and made available by teens in a noncommercial context.

In 2009, the Vermont Senate took precisely such an approach which should serve as a model to other states and the federal government. The Vermont Senate attempted to amend its Sex Trafficking of Children statute to specifically exclude application to persons eighteen and younger, where the minor photographed is "at least 13 years old, and the child knowingly and voluntarily and without threat or coercion use[s] an electronic communication device to transmit an image of himself or herself to another

---

[198] *Id.* at 865.
[199] *Id.* at 873.
[200] *Id.* at 865.
[201] *Id.* (citing Ginsberg v. New York, 390 U.S. 629, 639 (1968)).
[202] *Id.*

person."[203]   Such legislation would allow prosecutors to send teenage sexting cases to juvenile courts to eliminate the stigma that accompanies child pornography convictions. Such legislation would also prevent prosecutors from labeling juveniles convicted of sexting as sex offenders. Under Vermont's proposed law, even minors convicted of this behavior more than once would not be eligible for sex offender status (although under the legislation they may be prosecuted in a district court rather than family or juvenile court).

Several other states have taken the approach of providing an educational, rather than a criminal law, solution to the problem of sexting. In the wake of a 2009 incident in which prosecutors charged a fourteen-year-old girl with distributing child pornography for posting nude images of herself on her MySpace account, New Jersey legislators proposed alternatives to criminal prosecutions for those engaging in sexting.[204]   Such proposed legislation creates a diversionary program where minors charged with creating or disseminating sexually explicit images can avoid prosecution by completing an educational program focusing on the legal and non-legal consequences (including the effect on relationships and the loss of future job opportunities) of such acts.[205]   Under the proposed legislation, prosecutors have the discretion to divert any minor charged with distribution of nude or sexually explicit images into the program.

States should follow the lead of the Vermont Senate and New Jersey and revise their child pornography and related laws to expressly exempt typical incidents of sexting, consistent with the protections the First Amendment extends to minors communicating non-obscene sexually themed expression that does not constitute a proximate link to sexual abuse or exploitation of children. Congress should follow this lead as well and revise federal child pornography laws to recognize and protect minors' rights to engage in sexually themed communications of the kind described above.

If legislators are unwilling to assume the important but politically unpopular task of revising their child pornography laws to account for the First Amendment rights of minors, then courts construing such laws should recognize and protect these rights. The first appellate court to construe state child pornography laws as applied to sexting did just

---

[203] See Act of June 1, 2009, No. 58, § 2, 2009 Vt. Acts & Resolves 552, 553–54 ("No person shall knowingly: (1) recruit, entice, harbor, transport, provide, or obtain by any means a person under the age of 18 for the purpose of having the person engage in a commercial sex act; (2) compel a person through force, fraud, or coercion to engage in a commercial sex act; or (3) benefit financially or by receiving anything of value from participation in a venture, knowing that force, fraud, or coercion was or will be used to compel any person to engage in a commercial sex act as part of the venture.") (repealed 2011); An Act Relating to Expanding the Sex Offender Registry, S. 125 § 3, 2009 Leg. Sess. (Vt. 2009), available at http://www.leg.state.vt.us/docs/2010/bills/Senate/S-125.pdf ("This section shall not apply if the person is less than 19 years old, the child is at least 13 years old, and the child knowingly and voluntarily and without threat or coercion used an electronic communication device to transmit an image of himself or herself to the person. . . .") (passed in the Senate but not enacted); id. § 4 ("This section shall not apply if the person is less than 19 years old, the child is at least 13 years old, and the child knowingly and voluntarily and without threat or coercion used an electronic communication device to transmit an image of himself or herself to the person.") (passed in the Senate but not enacted); id. § 5 ("This section shall not apply if the person is less than 19 years old, the child is at least 13 years old, and the child knowingly and voluntarily and without threat or coercion, used an electronic communication device to transmit an image of himself or herself to the person.") (passed in the Senate but not enacted).

[204] See Act of Sept. 16, 2011, ch. 128 (N.J.) (to be codified at N.J. STAT. §§ C.2A:4A-71(2), C.2A:4A-71.1(2)); see also Toutant, supra note 51.

[205] Act of Sept. 16, 2011, ch. 128 (N.J.).

that in *Miller v. Mitchell*.[206] In that case,[207] the district attorney threatened to prosecute several teenagers under child pornography laws unless they attended an extensive education program designed by the district attorney.[208] The parents of three of the implicated girls sued the district attorney under 42 U.S.C. § 1983, claiming that this action constituted retaliation against their daughters in violation of the girls' First Amendment rights to appear in the photographs, the girls' right to be free from being compelled to attend the re-education program, and the parents' substantive due process rights to direct their children's upbringing.[209]

The district court ruled in favor of the parents, finding, *inter alia*, that because the pictures were not illegal under Pennsylvania's child pornography law, the only reason to prosecute them would be in retaliation for exercising their constitutional right not to participate in the district attorney's education program.[210] In enjoining the district attorney from initiating criminal charges against the girls in connection with the photographs or their refusal to attend the education program, the district court found that under Pennsylvania law, "plaintiffs make a reasonable argument that the images presented to the court do not appear to qualify in any way as depictions of prohibited sexual acts."[211] The Third Circuit affirmed, holding that the education program required by the district attorney impermissibly violated the daughters' First Amendment right not to engage in compelled speech and the parents' right to raise their children without undue state interference.[212]

In summary, legislatures should revise their child pornography laws to exempt acts of sexting from their reach and ensure that such laws are not used to harm the very people they were designed to protect. Alternatively, courts should construe state child pornography laws consistent with Supreme Court precedent to protect the First Amendment rights of the minors involved and the due process rights of their parents to direct the upbringing of their children free of undue state interference.

VI. PRIVACY NOT PORNOGRAPHY

A. Public Disclosure of Private Facts

In some examples discussed in Part II, nude or sexually themed images of minors, initially created with the subject's permission, were then disseminated or otherwise made available beyond the scope of the subject's consent. This Article contends that, although such incidents do not support criminal child pornography charges, they may nonetheless constitute harmful and actionable invasions of privacy.

Under most states' privacy laws, the transmission of a nude or sexually explicit picture without the subject's consent constitutes an invasion of privacy as a publication of a private "fact."[213] As set forth in the Restatement (Second) of Torts:

---

[206] 598 F.3d 139 (3d Cir. 2010), *aff'g* Miller v. Skumanick, 605 F. Supp. 2d 634 (M.D. Pa. 2009).
[207] *See supra* text accompanying notes 9–26.
[208] *Miller v. Mitchell*, 598 F.3d at 143–44.
[209] *Id.* at 147–48.
[210] *Miller v. Skumanick*, 605 F. Supp. 2d 634.
[211] *Id.* at 645.
[212] *Miller v. Mitchell*, 598 F.3d at 155.
[213] *See infra* note 216 and accompanying text.

One who gives publicity to a matter concerning the private life of another is subject to liability to the other for invasion of his privacy, if the matter publicized is of a kind that

(a) would be highly offensive to a reasonable person, and

(b) is not of legitimate concern to the public.[214]

Although there is a First Amendment defense for the publication of information or images revealing private facts that are "newsworthy" or are otherwise a legitimate matter of public concern, in the overwhelming majority of sexting cases—where one teenager forwards a nude picture of the subject to other friends or classmates, for example—this "newsworthiness" exception would not apply. Furthermore, under the public disclosure of private facts branch of the invasion of privacy tort, truth does not serve as an affirmative defense.[215] The publication of the private facts tort encompasses, for example, making available information about the fact that an individual has a sexually transmitted disease or revealing information about a person's sexual orientation, if such information has not previously been revealed to the public, is not legitimately newsworthy, and if publication of this information would be offensive to a reasonable person. The public disclosure of private fact tort would encompass acts of sexting in which an image is shared without or beyond the subject's consent.

Courts in many jurisdictions have held that the dissemination of nude, semi-nude, or similarly revealing pictures of an individual without or beyond that individual's consent are actionable invasions of privacy as publications of private facts.[216] In *G.J.D. v. Johnson*, for example, the Pennsylvania Supreme Court affirmed an award of compensatory and punitive damages to a woman whose former partner distributed nude pictures of her throughout the community.[217] Similarly, in a case where a plaintiff voluntarily created nude photographs of herself on film and brought the film to

---

[214] RESTATEMENT (SECOND) OF TORTS § 652D (1977).

[215] *See* 62A AM. JUR. 2D *Privacy* § 175 (2011) ("Truth, while a defense to an action of libel, is not a defense to an action for an invasion of the right of privacy.") (footnotes omitted).

[216] *See* York v. Story, 324 F.2d 450 (9th Cir. 1963) (police taking and circulating nude photographs of plaintiff, which were allegedly taken to obtain evidence of bruises from assault, may give rise to an invasion of privacy claim); Daily Times Democrat v. Graham, 162 So. 2d 474 (Ala. 1964) (defendant newspaper liable for publishing photograph of plaintiff's skirt blowing up over her waist at county fair fun house); Taylor v. K.T.V.B., Inc., 525 P.2d 984 (Idaho 1974) (television station that aired footage of plaintiff being arrested and emerging naked from his house could be held liable for invasion of privacy); Wood v. Hustler Magazine, Inc., 736 F.2d 1084 (5th Cir. 1984); Solano v. Playgirl, Inc., 292 F.3d 1078 (9th Cir. 2002); Myers v. U.S. Camera Publ'g Corp., 167 N.Y.S.2d 771 (N.Y. City Ct. 1957) (nudity is a private fact giving rise to damages when shown beyond persons to whom consent is given); Gallon v. Hustler Magazine, Inc., 732 F. Supp. 322 (N.D.N.Y. 1990) (publication of nude photograph without authorization is an invasion of privacy). For academic commentary, see generally Peter B. Edelman, *Free Press v. Privacy: Haunted by the Ghost of Justice Black*, 68 TEX. L. REV. 1195, 1209 n.74 (1990) (noting cases that allowed recovery when defendants published nude or revealing photographs, odd and disfiguring medical conditions, and details from the plaintiff's past life); Patrick J. McNulty, *The Public Disclosure of Private Facts: There Is Life After Florida Star*, 50 DRAKE L. REV. 93, 105–06 (2001); John A. Jurata, Jr., Comment, *The Tort that Refuses to Go Away: The Subtle Reemergence of Public Disclosure of Private Facts*, 36 SAN DIEGO L. REV. 489, 510–30 (1999).

[217] 669 A.2d 378 (Pa. Sup. Ct. 1995).

defendant's photofinishing shop to be developed, the defendant was found liable for invasion of privacy when an employee developed and circulated those photographs to a group of individuals without the plaintiff's consent.[218]   Further, in a case where the plaintiff consented to be photographed nude for the limited purpose of publication in a book, the court held the defendant liable for invasion of privacy because he exceeded the scope of the consent by publishing one of the photographs in a newspaper.[219]   Some courts have held that posting on the Internet video footage of individuals engaging in sexual activity constitutes a violation of the individuals' right to privacy (even where the subject is a public figure, such as Pamela Lee Anderson, who previously consented to making other nude photos available to the public).[220]

Although posting a nude or sexually explicit image of an individual on the Internet would readily satisfy the "public" aspect of the public disclosure of private facts tort, it is less clear whether forwarding such an image to a handful of other acquaintances would satisfy this element.   The case law suggests that, while revealing such images to *one* person does not suffice for *public* disclosure, sharing images with (at least) a handful of others—as occurs in the typical sexting context—would satisfy the publicity requirement. For example, in *Lemnah v. American Breeders Service, Inc.*, the court held that where *only one person* had received the communication (that the plaintiff was fired for drunkenness), there was not the kind of publicity necessary to sustain a public disclosure of private fact claim.[221]   However, in several cases that involved dissemination of private information to (at least) a handful of other people, courts have considered such dissemination to be *public* enough to constitute a valid claim for public disclosure of a private fact.   For example, in *Bolduc v. Bailey*, the defendant accused the plaintiff, a priest, of several criminal and moral offenses.[222]   The defendant communicated these accusations in a series of conversations with fellow members of the plaintiff's religious society.[223]   Even though the defendant did not communicate the accusations to the public at large—only to a limited group—the court found that the complaint properly pled an invasion of privacy for public disclosure of private facts.[224]

Accordingly, individuals who possess sexting images with the subject's initial assent and further disseminate sexting images beyond the subject's initial consent are liable for invading the privacy of the subject, and are properly subject to damages and injunctive relief.   For example, in the case described above in which Phillip Alpert e-mailed nude pictures of his former girlfriend to seventy of her e-mail contacts, Phillip would be liable in an invasion of privacy action brought by his former girlfriend for

---

[218] *See* Lake v. Wal-Mart Stores, Inc., 582 N.W.2d 231, 235 (Minn. 1998) (reversing trial court dismissal of complaint against Wal-Mart and its photo department employees who allegedly distributed nude photos of plaintiffs, and holding that the case could proceed under the privacy theory of public disclosure of private facts, among others).

[219] McCabe v. Village Voice, Inc., 550 F. Supp. 525 (E.D. Pa. 1982) (defendant newspaper liable when plaintiff consented to being photographed nude in the bathtub for publication in a book but not in a newspaper).

[220] Michaels v. Internet Entm't Grp., Inc., 5 F. Supp. 2d 823 (C.D. Cal. 1998).

[221] 482 A.2d 700, 704 (Vt. 1984).

[222] 586 F. Supp. 896, 899 (D. Colo. 1984).

[223] *Id.*

[224] *Id.* at 901.

public disclosure of private facts for sharing this image with a large number of other individuals.[225]

B. Intermediary Liability for Public Disclosure of Private Facts

Individuals who disseminate nude, semi-nude or otherwise sexually explicit images of minors to others without or beyond the subject's consent should be held accountable under the publication of private fact branch of the invasion of privacy tort. However, the subject's ability to sue the disseminator for damages or injunctive relief may provide incomplete relief, especially in circumstances in which the image is made available by a website run by another party such as MySpace or Facebook. Given the current state of the law, it is exceedingly difficult for an individual to hold a website liable in tort for any type of harm resulting from the website's publication of an image. While these social networking sites generally undertake measures to remove such images (once made aware of them), 47 U.S.C. § 230, enacted by the CDA, immunizes such sites from liability for their role in making such images available.[226] Below, this Article argues that § 230(c) should be revised or reinterpreted by courts to reach a more privacy-protective outcome.

In passing the Communications Decency Act of 1996, Congress sought to remedy perceived ills caused by certain types of offensive expression on the Internet using two different approaches. First, the CDA prohibited the transmission of certain types of sexually themed expression on the Internet.[227] These provisions prohibiting the transmission of "indecent" content and prohibiting the display of "patently offensive"[228] content were insufficiently attentive to the First Amendment rights of individuals, and, as discussed above,[229] were quickly struck down by the Supreme Court.[230] Second, Congress also sought to respond to earlier decisions that held websites liable for defamatory content posted by subscribers. Earlier cases treated websites as publishers of information made available by the website's subscribers and held the websites secondarily liable for defamation and related torts. In one early case in particular, *Stratton Oakmont, Inc. v. Prodigy Services Co.*, a website had reserved and exercised editorial control over the content made available by its subscribers.[231] The court in *Stratton Oakmont* held that such control rendered the website a publisher of the defamatory content made available by its subscriber.[232] In response to pleas by website owners to immunize them from liability in such circumstances, Congress passed § 230(c), which both encourages websites to continue to engage in acts of good faith exercises of editorial control—such as by blocking objectionable material[233]—and immunizes them

---

[225] *See supra* text accompanying notes 37–50.

[226] Pub. L. No. 104-104, § 509, 110 Stat. 56, 137 (1996) (codified as amended at 47 U.S.C. § 230 (2006)).

[227] *Id.* § 502, 110 Stat. at 133–34 (codified as amended at 47 U.S.C. § 223).

[228] *See supra* text accompanying note 198.

[229] *See supra* text accompanying notes 195–202.

[230] *See, e.g.*, Reno v. ACLU, 521 U.S. 844 (1997).

[231] No. 31063/94, 1995 WL 323710 (N.Y. Sup. Ct. May 24, 1995).

[232] *Id.* at *4.

[233] 47 U.S.C. § 230(c)(2) (2006) ("No provider . . . of an interactive computer service shall be held liable on account of—(A) any action voluntarily taken in good faith to restrict access to or availability of material that the provider . . . considers to be obscene, lewd, lascivious, filthy, excessively violent, harassing, or otherwise objectionable, whether or not such material is constitutionally protected . . . .").

from liability for publishing or distributing harmful material made available by their subscribers. This provision stipulates that "[n]o provider . . . of an interactive computer service shall be treated as the publisher or speaker of any information provided by another information content provider."[234]

The CDA achieves its purpose to the extent these provisions immunize interactive computer services and websites from liability, like Prodigy, that cannot be expected to control *ex ante* every post made by every subscriber.[235] Since this provision became law, however, countless websites have successfully claimed immunity from a broad range of lawsuits for making available content posted by others—both as an initial matter and after the harmful nature of such content has been asserted by the plaintiff. Indeed, courts have extended § 230(c)'s immunity well beyond defamation, to other state causes of action, such as negligence and gross negligence,[236] nuisance,[237] sending threatening messages,[238] and even statutory violations of the Fair Housing Act and related anti-discrimination violations.[239] Section 230 expressly provides that its immunity does not extend to federal criminal law, including liability for obscenity or for sexual exploitation

---

[234] *Id.* § 230(c)(1). Although the statutory language here refers to "interactive computer service," which is defined as "any information service, system, or access software provider that provides or enables computer access by multiple users to a computer server," courts have held that web sites in general are encompassed by this definition. *See id.* § 230(f)(2).

[235] For example, in an early case involving § 230 immunity, the Fourth Circuit extended broad immunity from liability to AOL for the defamatory post of an AOL subscriber. In *Zeran v. America Online, Inc.*, 129 F.3d 327 (4th Cir. 1997), the court held that AOL was not liable for negligent distribution of defamatory material after an AOL user carried out a malicious hoax on the victim Zeran—even where AOL refused to take down the defamatory material upon learning of it. The plaintiff argued that § 230 leaves intact liability for interactive computer service providers who possess *notice* of defamatory material posted through their services. The court rejected plaintiff's attempts to impose notice-based liability on Internet service providers (ISPs), explaining that:

> By its plain language, § 230 creates a federal immunity to any cause of action that would make service providers liable for information originating with a third-party user of the service. Specifically, § 230 precludes courts from entertaining claims that would place a computer service provider in a publisher's role. Thus, *lawsuits seeking to hold a service provider liable for its exercise of a publisher's traditional editorial functions—such as deciding whether to publish, withdraw, postpone or alter content*—are barred.

Id. at 330 (emphasis added).

[236] *See, e.g.*, Doe v. MySpace, Inc., 528 F.3d 413 (5th Cir. 2008) (upholding MySpace's immunity from negligence and gross negligence liability for failing to institute safety measures to protect minors and for failure to institute policies relating to age verification, in a case in which the Doe's daughter had lied about her age and communicated over MySpace with a man who later sexually assaulted her).

[237] *See, e.g.*, Kathleen R. v. City of Livermore, 104 Cal. Rptr. 2d 772 (Cal. Ct. App. 2001) (upholding the city's immunity from claims of nuisance, *inter alia*, where plaintiff's child downloaded pornography from a public library's computers which did not restrict Internet access to minors).

[238] *See, e.g.*, Delfino v. Agilent Techs., Inc., 52 Cal. Rptr. 3d 376 (Cal. Ct. App. 2006) (upholding immunity from state tort claims arising from an employee's use of the employer's e-mail system to send threatening messages).

[239] *See* Chicago Lawyers' Comm. for Civil Rights Under Law, Inc. v. Craigslist, Inc., 519 F.3d 666 (7th Cir. 2008) (upholding § 230(c) immunity for online services provider Craigslist against Fair Housing Act claims based on discriminatory statements in postings on the classifieds website by third party users). *But see* Fair Hous. Council of San Fernando Valley v. Roommates.com, LLC, 521 F.3d 1157 (9th Cir. 2008) (en banc) (rejecting immunity for the Roommates.com roommate matching service for claims brought under the federal Fair Housing Act and California housing discrimination laws because the website created the questions used for discriminatory practices).

of children,[240] nor does it extend to liability for intellectual property violations.[241] Additionally, the statute explicitly provides that it does not prevent states from enforcing any state law that is consistent with this section.[242] However, in construing § 230 in the context of defenses asserted by Internet service providers and websites, courts have extended this statutory provision unnecessarily broadly and have provided website defendants with immunity for hosting sexually explicit content that is inconsistent with the limited purpose of the statute.

Consider, for example, *Barnes v. Yahoo*, in which the Ninth Circuit extended broad immunity to Yahoo.[243] In 2004, Cecilia Barnes's ex-boyfriend created unauthorized Yahoo profiles of Cecilia and posted nude pictures of Cecilia on those profiles.[244] The profile pages provided Cecilia's work phone number and e-mail address and led viewers to believe that Cecilia was seeking to engage in casual sexual relations.[245] Not surprisingly, strangers began contacting Cecilia at work by phone and e-mail, as well as showing up at her workplace.[246] Cecilia contacted Yahoo several times over the next few months to request that the profile be removed, to no avail.[247] A local television reporter learned of Cecilia's situation and began to prepare a news story on the subject.[248] When the reporter contacted Yahoo on Cecilia's behalf, Yahoo's communications director promised that she would make sure the profiles were removed.[249] When Yahoo still had not acted on its express promise to remove the profiles almost two months later, Cecilia brought suit against the company.[250]

In its decision, the Ninth Circuit held that Barnes' tort claim against Yahoo for negligent undertaking was barred by § 230(c).[251] However, Barnes was also able to assert a contractual claim of promissory estoppel against Yahoo for failing to make good on its express promise to remove the images.[252] Only because Yahoo expressly promised to Barnes that it would promptly remove the offending material, but failed to do so, could Barnes proceed in her action against Yahoo.[253] The Ninth Circuit made clear that absent an express promise on the part of the website hosting such offending content that it would remove such content, a plaintiff's claim will be barred by § 230(c).[254]

---

[240] *See* 47 U.S.C. § 230(e)(1) (2006) ("Nothing in this section shall be construed to impair the enforcement of section 223 or 231 of this title, chapter 71 (relating to obscenity) or 110 (relating to sexual exploitation of children) of title 18, or any other Federal criminal statute.").

[241] *See id.* § 230(e)(2) ("Nothing in this section shall be construed to limit or expand any law pertaining to intellectual property.").

[242] *See id.* § 230(e)(3) ("Nothing in this section shall be construed to prevent any State from enforcing any State law that is consistent with this section. No cause of action may be brought and no liability may be imposed under any State or local law that is inconsistent with this section.").

[243] Barnes v. Yahoo!, Inc., 570 F.3d 1096 (9th Cir. 2009).

[244] *Id.* at 1098.

[245] *Id.*

[246] *Id.*

[247] *Id.*

[248] *Id.* at 1098–99.

[249] *Id.*

[250] *Id.*

[251] *Id.*

[252] *Id.* at 1106.

[253] *Id.* at 1108–09.

[254] *Id.*

The immunity § 230 grants websites for harms arising from their subscribers' speech has been extended too far. Websites like Yahoo and Facebook, presented with notice and clear evidence that the subject of a nude or sexually explicit image did not consent to posting the image (as in the *Barnes v. Yahoo* case), should be required to promptly remove that image or face liability for violating that individual's privacy.[255] A similar regime in the copyright infringement context provides a helpful model. Under the Digital Millennium Copyright Act, a copyright owner who believes his or her material has been infringed may provide notice to a website stating his or her belief that the website is hosting infringing content.[256] Upon receipt of such notice, the website must immediately cease hosting such allegedly infringing content to secure the benefits of the statute's limitations on liability.[257] Unlike § 230, which courts have construed to provide broad immunity to websites regardless of whether they remove the offensive content identified by the subject, the corresponding copyright provisions require the website to act in good faith upon notice to remove the offending content to secure the limitation of liability. Although an obligation to remove such allegedly offensive content, if imposed too broadly, may lead to a chilling of free speech and fair use rights,[258] in the limited context of nude or sexually explicit images that the subject can conclusively establish have been posted without her consent, there is no similar danger that websites' free speech rights will be unduly chilled. In construing § 230, courts should hold that a website that fails to remove such images upon notice and receipt of proper documentation from the subject has participated in the invasion of privacy and is indirectly liable for such conduct. Interpreting the statutory language that "[n]o [service] provider ... shall be treated as the publisher or speaker of any information provided by *another* information content provider,"[259] courts should conclude that when a website refuses to take down the images in a timely manner upon proper request, such material is no longer material that is made available by *another* information content provider, but becomes material made available by the website itself, for which it is liable.

VII. CONCLUSION

As teenagers explore their sexuality and seek to memorialize and exchange information related to their sexual development, their instantaneous ability to

---

[255] Like many U.S. states, the European Union (EU) does not hold ISPs liable so long as they only act as a conduit for information and do not participate in the content selection process. In contrast to the system in the U.S., however, ISPs in the EU are required to remove illegal content upon notification of such. *See* Directive 2000/31, on Electronic Commerce, arts. 12–15, 2000 O.J. (L 178) 1 (EC). If the content is not removed, they can be held liable, as Google was in a recent Italian case involving a video of an autistic boy. Manuela D'Alessandro, *Google Executives Convicted for Italy Autism Video*, REUTERS, Feb. 24, 2010, *available at* http://www.reuters.com/article/idUSTRE61N2G520100224. Here, the defendant successfully claimed that Google should have been on notice when the video became a headline news story, and not waited until police notified them of the illegal content. Furthermore, the EU permits ISPs to voluntarily monitor their sites for illegal content.

[256] 17 U.S.C. § 512(c)(3) (2006).

[257] *Id.*

[258] *See* Jennifer M. Urban & Laura Quilter, *Efficient Process or "Chilling Effects"? Takedown Notices Under Section 512 of the Digital Millennium Copyright Act*, 22 SANTA CLARA COMPUTER & HIGH TECH. L.J. 621(2006).

[259] 47 U.S.C. § 230(c)(1) (emphasis added).

memorialize and share images with others, via cell phones or the Internet, presents a host of new problems to which society must respond intelligently. The recent trend of harshly punishing these teens under the child pornography regime is not an intelligent solution. In light of this wave of prosecutorial overreaching, state and federal child pornography laws should be revised to specifically exempt sexting by minors from the reach of such laws. Child pornography laws were created to punish and deter a far different class of conduct—the conduct of adult pedophiles creating and disseminating images that depict sexual abuse of their child victims in a commercial context—not the conduct of older minors using technology to explore their sexuality and voluntarily exchange images with one another. Non-obscene depictions of nudity or sexual conduct created by teens and exchanged voluntarily among themselves for noncommercial purposes should be specifically excluded from the applicable definitions of child pornography and similar crimes.

Instances of sexting, however, should not necessarily go unpunished, as they may constitute harmful invasions of the subject's privacy. In cases in which nude or sexually themed images of minors, which were initially created with the subject's consent, are disseminated or otherwise made available without or beyond the scope of the subject's consent, such conduct should be cognizable as actionable invasions of the subject's privacy under the publication of private facts branch of this common law tort. The subject should be able to seek relief not only against the individual who made such images available without her consent, but also against a website that continues to host such images after being notified of their presence. Websites that continue to facilitate the hosting of such images after the subject requests their removal should lose their immunity for hosting such content and should be held liable for facilitating the invasion of the subject's privacy.

Copyright 2012 by Northwestern University School of Law
Northwestern Journal of Technology and Intellectual Property

Volume 10, Number 3 (January 2012)

What Really Matters in Spectrum Allocation Design

By Thomas W. Hazlett,[*] Roberto E. Muñoz[**] and Diego B. Avanzini[***]

I. INTRODUCTION

Economists and policy makers have embraced "spectrum auctions."[1] Assigning wireless licenses to high bidders places assets with the most productive firms, reduces rent-seeking costs incurred by comparative hearings or lotteries,[2] and captures license rents for the public treasury. This last benefit potentially increases efficiency, in that funds generated without the use of taxes do not cause tax-distorting social losses. Each tax dollar raised, for instance, is expected to cost society about $0.33 in deadweight loss.[3] Auction dollars, as pure transfers, cost less.

Yet this "public finance bonus" is a delicate matter. Government allocates spectrum, and regulation constrains its use. Wireless licenses generate bids

---

[*] Department of Economics & School of Law, George Mason University, Arlington, Virginia; thazlett@gmu.edu.
[**] Department of Industry, Universidad Técnica Federico Santa Maria, Santiago, Chile; roberto.munoz@usm.cl. Muñoz thanks FONDECYT Project Number 1110837 for supporting (part) of his work.
[***] Senior Fellow, Information Economy Project, George Mason University School of Law, Arlington, Virginia; avanzini@gmail.com. The authors wish to thank George Bittlingmayer, Robert Hahn, Brent Skorup, Bruno Viani, and seminar participants at Georgetown and U.C. Berkeley for valuable insights. The usual disclaimer applies.
[1] "Overall, the auctions have been a tremendous success . . . . Many countries wisely have imitated the FCC auctions; those that have not have suffered from inefficient license assignments and other flaws." Peter Cramton, *Spectrum Auctions*, in 1 HANDBOOK OF TELECOMMUNICATIONS ECONOMICS: STRUCTURE, REGULATION, AND COMPETITION 605, 606 (Martin E. Cave et al. eds., 2002); *see also* Ken Binmore & Paul Klemperer, *The Biggest Auction Ever: The Sale of the British 3G Telecom Licenses*, 112 ECON. J. C74 (2002); Peter C. Cramton, *Money Out of Thin Air: The Nationwide Narrowband PCS Auction*, 4 J. ECON. & MGMT. STRATEGY 267 (1995); Veronika Grimm et al., *Low Price Equilibrium in Multi-unit Auctions: The GSM Spectrum Auction in Germany*, 21 INT'L J. INDUS. ORG. 1557 (2003); Paul Klemperer, *How (Not) to Run Auctions: The European 3G Telecom Auctions*, 46 EUR. ECON. REV. 829 (2002) [hereinafter Klemperer, *How (Not) to Run Auctions*]; Paul Klemperer, *What Really Matters in Auction Design*, 16 J. ECON. PERSP., Winter 2002, at 169; R. Preston McAfee & John McMillan, *Analyzing the Airwaves Auction*, 10 J. ECON. PERSP., Winter 1996, at 159; John McMillan, *Selling Spectrum Rights*, 8 J. ECON. PERSP., Summer 1994, at 145; Patrick S. Moreton & Pablo T. Spiller, *What's in the Air: Interlicense Synergies in the Federal Communications Commission's Broadband Personal Communication Service Spectrum Auctions*, 41 J.L. & ECON. 677 (1998); Eric van Damme, *The Dutch UMTS-Auction* (Ctr. for Econ. Studies & Ifo Inst. for Econ. Research, Working Paper No. 722, 2002); Elmar Wolfstetter, *The Swiss UMTS Spectrum Auction Flop: Bad Luck or Bad Design?* 6 (Ctr. for Econ. Studies & Ifo Inst. for Econ. Research, Working Paper No. 534, 2001) [hereinafter Wolfstetter, *The Swiss UMTS Spectrum Auction Flop*].
[2] *See generally* Thomas W. Hazlett & Robert J. Michaels, *The Cost of Rent-Seeking: Evidence from Cellular Telephone License Lotteries*, 59 S. ECON. J. 425 (1993).
[3] Klemperer, *What Really Matters in Auction Design*, *supra* note 1, at 179.

approximately equal (in a competitive auction) to the present value of the profits expected from owning such licenses.   Policies that increase profits by reducing competition in wireless markets are themselves economically distorting.   Revenues gained by the state cease to be pure transfers and incur social costs of their own.

Many are aware of this conflict and emphasize the importance of rules that promote competition for end users. John McMillan, in one of the first scholarly papers explaining the new wireless license auctions, was careful to note:

> The Act [enabling auctions] downplays revenue as an objective, and by
> its actions also the government showed that revenue was not its overriding
> objective (as, indeed, it should not be). If revenue had been paramount, the
> government could have offered a single monopoly license in each region—at the
> cost, obviously, of creating future inefficiencies.[4]

Yet this important caveat has been only partly heeded. The formal economic literature on wireless auctions focuses not on end-user efficiencies, but on bidding mechanisms. Empirical evaluations are largely rendered on the basis of rent extraction. Auctions resulting in prices exceeding expectations are deemed "successful"; those with surprisingly low prices are "fiascoes" or "disasters." License rents left on the table create social inefficiency, sacrificing a possible public financing bonus.

Were auction policies simply transferring rents for the public treasury, this operative assumption would reflect reality. Yet, rules advanced by economists and widely adopted by policy makers repeatedly cross over the presumed line of demarcation, altering efficiency in output markets. Imposing reserve prices, limiting the number of licenses sold, providing bidding credits for weak competitors, and delaying license assignments are regulatory policies advanced in response to the "low participation" problem encountered at auctions. Economists largely evaluate these measures according to their effectiveness in raising bids, ignoring retail market consequences.

Case studies reviewed in the literature illustrate the inconsistent incorporation of final market welfare effects. Klemperer discusses an interesting Turkish mobile phone license auction, wherein the government mandated that the price for a second national license must equal or exceed the bid by the winner of the first license.[5] That prompted the first licensee to bid aggressively, such that a second operator would not pay the steep entry fee; the result was monopoly market structure. Klemperer identifies this as "the Turkish fiasco."[6]

Alternatively, reserve prices set in Belgium and Greece auctions were applauded for extracting additional government receipts, even though they excluded award of a fourth 3G license in 2001 auctions (only three incumbents' bids met the threshold; i.e., the policy was defended on the grounds that no fourth network would have likely emerged even with a lower reserve price). Of course, with the probability above zero, the expected loss merits consideration. Moreover, even without the entry of a fourth operator, the policy left considerable bandwidth idle (as per the approximately 35 megahertz (MHz) allocated to the marginal licenses in either market). This impedes

---

[4] McMillan, *Selling Spectrum Rights*, *supra* note 1, at 147.
[5] Klemperer, *What Really Matters in Auction Design*, *supra* note 1, at 176.
[6] *Id.* at 178. The Turkish government agreed and undid the monopoly outcome via new rules.

reductions in incumbents' marginal costs, imposing social losses. Such offsets to the revenue-generating gains of the reserve price have not been appropriately incorporated.

As this Article shows, the reserve price policy in the two countries likely resulted in large losses for Belgian and Greek consumers that overwhelmed any possible gains from the public finance bonus. This empirical result, based on the relationship between spectrum inputs and competitive rivalry in retail mobile telephone markets, quantifies the importance of addressing welfare issues in wireless markets in a holistic fashion that looks beyond government revenues. Efficiencies generated by license auctions are evaluated in proper context when auction designs, bidder subsidies, license restrictions, and other policies are evaluated with the response to their incremental auction revenues and to the social costs incurred when radio frequencies are less-utilized, inefficient suppliers win licenses, or multi-year delays reduce entry.

Many regulators have come to the conclusion—correctly, in this Article's view—that burgeoning use of smartphones, tablets, and other devices (including machine-to-machine radios) is driving a "mobile data tsunami" that demands massive new bandwidth. Great productivity is feeding this beast, expanding networks, improving speeds, and accommodating a range of innovative services and applications. The Federal Communications Commission's (FCC) National Broadband Plan issued in March 2010 specifically focuses on the importance of making additional spectrum available for mobile uses. It identifies wireless broadband as a key contributor to U.S. economic growth and an essential platform for the emerging broadband marketplace. Crucially, more inputs are necessary to "ensure that there is sufficient, flexible spectrum that accommodates growing demand and evolving technologies."[7]

This is exactly correct. To maximize consumer welfare, spectrum allocators should avoid being distracted by side issues like government license revenues. By focusing on wireless market efficiency, getting abundant spectrum resources into a competitive marketplace, policy makers can pave the way for low prices, high outputs, and robust innovation. The economic forces unleashed will produce the highest social gains.

Part II offers a simple synopsis of this Article's analysis using "order of magnitude" estimates revealing the big picture—consumer gains in wireless output markets dominate social welfare generated by government extractions for spectrum inputs. Part III then describes the emphasis placed on revenue extraction by economists, noting the inconsistent manner in which efficiency changes in output markets sometimes enter the analysis. Part IV more specifically evaluates the argument that spectrum policy makers should tolerate some inefficiency in wireless markets to produce social gains in public finance. It finds this argument to be implausible given the institutions of the market and the magnitudes of the relevant trade-offs. Part V defines a "regulatory optimum." Part VI offers a conclusion.

II. LICENSE AUCTIONS: TREES IN THE WIRELESS FOREST

Economic research has quantified the incremental trade-offs incurred in particular spectrum allocation choices, as detailed below. The big picture, however, is perhaps best illuminated by simple summary statistics.

---

[7] FED. COMMC'NS COMM'N, CONNECTING AMERICA: THE NATIONAL BROADBAND PLAN 75 (2010).

In the first half of 2009, total U.S. mobile telephone service revenues were approximately $75.8 billion.[8]   Of this, $56.3 billion was for basic subscriptions that include voice service.[9] The remaining $19.5 billion was for data services, primarily text messages (SMS) and high-speed Internet connectivity.[10] Industry sources report 1.16 trillion minutes of use (MOU) for voice services and 740 billion text messages.[11] If the voice revenues (total revenues minus data revenues) are divided by voice minutes, the average price per minute is calculated to be $0.049. If text messages are included in total MOU[12] at the rate of 1 SMS = 1 minute, and total revenues are attributed entirely to voice and text message services, then the average price per MOU (or text message) would be $0.040. This overstates price by attributing high-speed data charges to voice and text, when they properly belong to a third category. In the second half of 2008, messaging (both text and multi-media) accounted for some thirty-six percent of wireless data revenues.[13] Using this metric for the first half of 2009 (1H2009) yields an average price per MOU (counting 1 SMS = 1 MOU) of $0.033.

---

[8] Targeted Information, Cellular Telecomms. & Internet Ass'n, Mid-Year 2009 Survey Results 1 (Oct. 7, 2009) (on file with author).

[9] *Id.* (subtracting the revenues for data services from total revenues).

[10] *Id.* at 2.

[11] *Id.*

[12] Including text messages in the voice minutes total is suggested by the fact that SMS is a substitute for voice calls and pricing structures in the industry imply that looking at voice minutes and revenues separately may distort actual economic outcomes. Of course, using an improper conversion (to add text messages to voice minutes) may also distort the true picture. Setting text messages equal to one MOU in terms of value appears to be a reasonable starting point.

[13] Total wireless data revenues were reported to be $17.5 billion in the second half of 2008, while text messaging revenues (broken out from total data revenue) were $6.3 billion. CELLULAR TELECOMMS. & INTERNET ASS'N, CTIA'S WIRELESS INDUSTRY INDICES, SEMI-ANNUAL DATA SURVEY RESULTS: A COMPREHENSIVE REPORT FROM CTIA ANALYZING THE U.S. WIRELESS INDUSTRY, YEAR-END 2008 RESULTS 112, 114 (2009) [hereinafter CTIA YEAR-END 2008].

FIGURE 1. VOICE MINUTES AND TEXT MESSAGES IN U.S. MOBILE NETWORKS (1991–2008)

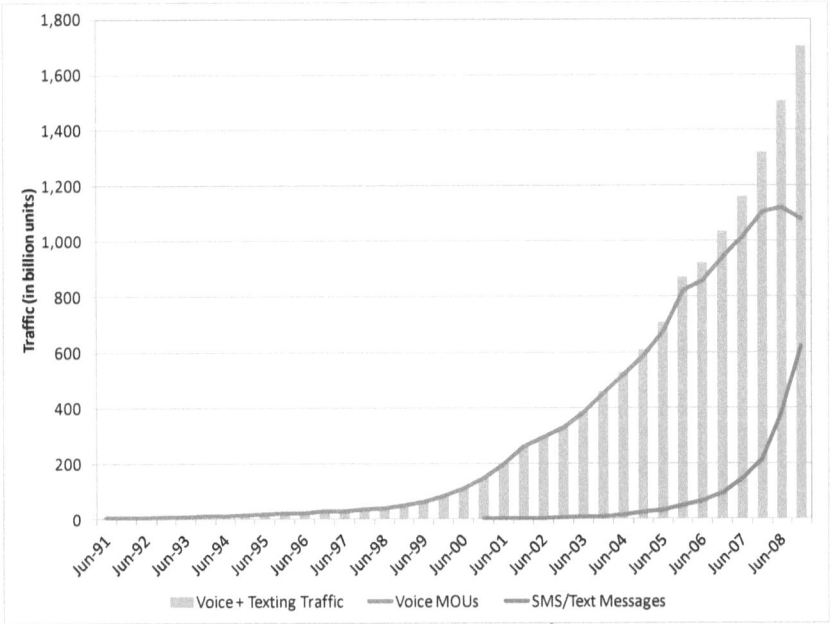

Market data from 1991 forward are available,[14] showing revenues and MOU for the U.S. mobile market. Until recently, complications presented by the voice-data divisions were not an issue. There is now, however, a pronounced trend where mobile subscribers are substituting text messaging for voice minutes.[15]

Making simple adjustments to the data smooths the long-run trend and accounts for the emergence of texting in place of phone calling. The Cellular Telecommunications and Internet Association's data for wireless carrier revenues from 2001 to present are broken out as "voice" or "data." Text message revenues and quantities are also reported. Hence, on the service revenue side, data expenditures are subtracted from total service revenues and text message revenues are then added back in (this excludes revenues for other data services, primarily high-speed Internet access). On the usage side, text messages are added to voice minutes of use at a rate of 1 SMS = 1 MOU.

Figure 2 displays historic prices and outputs. Price is defined as the average revenue (all spending for services by consumers) divided by the number of minutes used. Quantity is defined as the total MOU. The trend in prices is sharply down, and the trend in output is strongly up.

---

[14] These data are published semi-annually by the Cellular Telecommunications and Internet Association, a trade group composed of U.S. wireless carriers. *Id.* at 10–14.

[15] *See supra* Figure 1.

These data appear to assume the shape of a demand curve showing a negative relationship between price and quantity demanded. This is not the case, however. Along a given demand curve, the only variable influencing output is the price of the product. Factors such as supply, quality of service, the price of substitutes, and the availability of complements or substitutes change over time, and much time elapses between the points along the curve in Figure 2—as much as sixteen years.

FIGURE 2. PRICES AND MOBILE VOICE MINUTES OF USE (1992–2008)

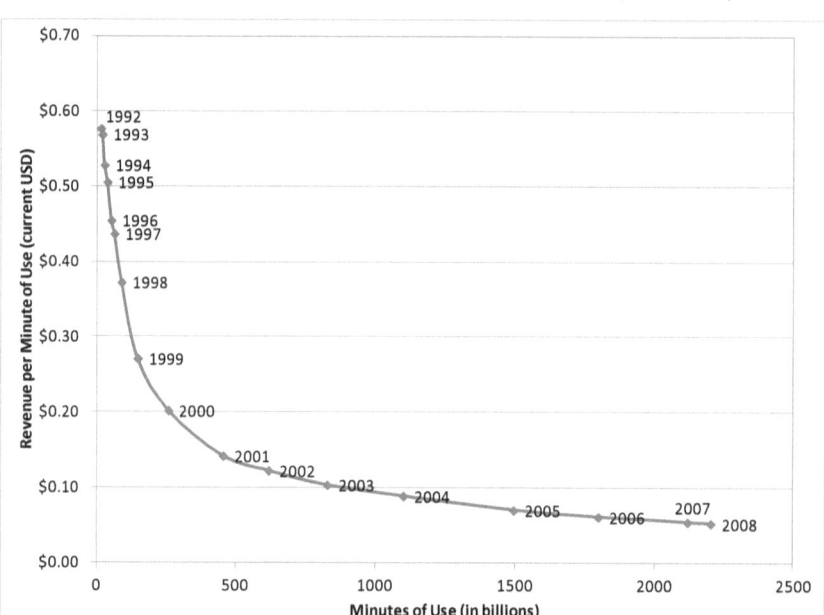

Still, the important mobile market demand drivers (apart from the price of wireless service) are all predicted to influence demand in a positive direction.[16] In the period between 1991 and 2009, service prices fell dramatically, from over $0.50 per MOU to about $0.04, a real decline of over ninety percent.[17] This would be expected to lead to substantial increases in minutes demanded. Indeed, consumption virtually exploded, increasing from 11 billion MOU in 1991 to about 2.3 trillion MOU (excluding text messages) in 2009—a *208-fold* (20,800%) increase. It is likely that price was one of

---

[16] It is also helpful that in an industry with substantial fixed costs, such as mobile telephony, there exists no traditional supply curve. Marginal cost does not determine the quantity offered by firms, and mark-ups over marginal cost are subject to strategic and long-run dynamics not easily captured in two dimensions. In wireless markets it is also the case that capacity available for consumers has been shifting out (increasing) over time, but the impact of this supply effect is captured in (a) lower prices and (b) higher quality service (fewer blocked or dropped calls).

[17] Prices are in current dollars. In constant 2008 dollars, differences are more than forty percent larger (due to inflation). Constant 2008 dollars were obtained using the gross domestic product deflator series from the International Monetary Fund's World Economic Outlook 2011.

many factors encouraging this robust output trend. Demand shifted outwards with rising income, increasing quality of wireless services, broader network coverage, declining size and price of handsets, increasing quality and functionality of handsets and batteries, the introduction of popular mobile applications, and changing social norms regarding the use of mobile phones and network connectivity.

Circumstances here allow us to view the historic price-quantity pairs as lower-bound estimates of current conditions with respect to consumer demand. Were higher prices charged today, quantities demanded would contract but not, presumably, to less than the usage levels observed in previous years when higher prices were, in fact, observed. In essence, the market data from 1991 through 2008 yield information as to the lower bound of the 2009 demand curve, allowing conservative forecasts of the value currently delivered by wireless network services in the United States.

The basic calculation is displayed in Figure 3. Consumer surplus (CS) is the incremental value obtained by customers in a particular market. It is formally defined as what consumers are willing to pay for a good or service minus what they must pay to obtain the product. The area under the "quasi-demand curve" is calculated as a discrete integral, summing each of the incremental CS values associated with a historic price-quantity point (annualized), as prices monotonically fall over time. This method produces slightly lower estimates than taking a continuous integral (for example, using a close-fitting, fourth-order equation). Prices are all in constant 2008 dollars as adjusted by the gross domestic product deflator series from the International Monetary Fund's World Economic Outlook 2011.

FIGURE 3. QUASI-DEMAND CURVE FOR VOICE AND TEXT MOBILE SERVICE (2008)

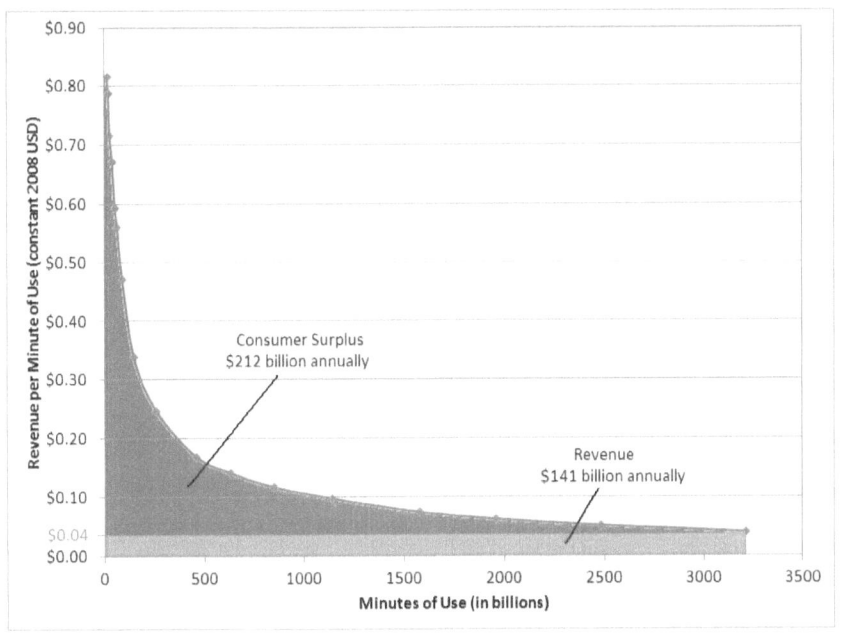

Focusing only on voice revenues—Model 1—deduces a 2008 price (equal to average voice revenue per voice MOU) of 0.0526 and about 2.2 trillion MOU for the year. Consumer surplus, estimated conservatively as described above, is then forecast as $174.1 billion annually (in constant 2008 dollars).[18] Alternatively, by adding text messages to voice MOU (at 1 SMS = 1 MOU)—Model 2—the substitution from phone calls to text messages in recent years is plausibly incorporated. Revenue per MOU falls to $0.0396, with 2008 MOU plus text messages rising to 3.2 trillion.[19] Consumer surplus is then calculated at $211.8 billion (in 2008 dollars).[20]

TABLE 1. ORDER-OF-MAGNITUDE COMPARISON:
AUCTION RECEIPTS VERSUS WIRELESS SERVICE VALUE

Metric		Period	Value	MHz	$/MHz/pop
U.S. Wireless Service Revenues	Total	2009 (annual) (1H2009 x 2)	$151.7 billion	200	2.53
	Voice & Text	2009 (annual) (1H2009 x 2)	$127.1 billion	200	2.12
Consumer Surplus	Model 1	2009 (annual)	$174.1 billion	200	2.90
	Model 2	2009 (annual)	$211.8 billion	200	3.53
FCC Auction Revenues		1994–2009 (lump sum)	$53 billion	>280	< 0.63 (CMRS)

These value magnitudes are important to consider in light of the revenues received by the U.S. government for wireless licenses. Since license auctions began in July 1994, the FCC has collected about $53 billion,[21] a sum that includes many (mostly) non-cellular licenses. The major mobile license (what the FCC generically calls Commercial Mobile Radio Service, or CMRS, licenses) sales have been for personal communications services (PCS) licenses A–F, allocated 120 MHz; advanced wireless services (AWS) licenses A–F, allocated 90 MHz; and 700 MHz licenses, allocated 70 MHz.[22]

Mobile licenses allocating some 230 MHz (nationwide) have been sold via FCC auctions through 2008. All told, however, licenses assigned to mobile operators were

---

[18] This is somewhat above the level of 2008 revenues, indicating a CS-to-revenue ratio that is in line with econometric estimates of consumer surplus in mobile markets. *See* Jerry Hausman, Cellular, 3G, Broadband and WiFi, Shann Memorial Lecture at the University of Western Australia (Mar. 18, 2003). It is below the 2010 consumer surplus estimate produced for the Cellular Telecommunications and Internet Association, the U.S. mobile operators' trade group, by consulting firm Ovum, which estimated 2010 consumer surplus to be $263 billion. ROGER ENTNER, CELLULAR TELECOMMS. & INTERNET ASS'N, THE INCREASINGLY IMPORTANT IMPACT OF WIRELESS BROADBAND TECHNOLOGY AND SERVICES ON THE U.S. ECONOMY: A FOLLOW UP TO THE 2005 OVUM REPORT ON THE IMPACT OF THE US WIRELESS TELECOM INDUSTRY ON THE US ECONOMY 19 (2008).

[19] In fact, SMS revenues in 2008 were approximately ten percent of voice revenues. Basic calling plans must generally be purchased by customers before they can purchase text messages, which are usually bought in packages—200 for $5 per month, unlimited texting for $20, and so on. CTIA YEAR-END 2008, *supra* note 13, at 114.

[20] *See infra* Table 1.

[21] FED. COMMC'NS COMM'N, MOVING FORWARD: DRIVING INVESTMENT AND INNOVATION WHILE PROTECTING CONSUMERS 10 (2009) [hereinafter MOVING FORWARD], *available at* http://www.fcc.gov/fcc-moving-forward-report.pdf.

[22] These were awarded in auctions held 2002–2008; license letters were re-used during that process. In addition to these licenses, other bandwidth can potentially be used to compete with CMRS operators, including those allocated 2.5 GHz frequencies for use in Broadband Radio Services or Educational Broadband Services; General Wireless Services allocated 2.3 GHz spectrum; a license allocated 5 Hz at 1.605 GHz; and satellite telephone licenses permitted to supply terrestrial mobile phone services on an ancillary basis to their main satellite operations.

allocated about 345 MHz. Only about 200 MHz of this total was actually in use at the end of 2008.[23] The 90 MHz allocated to AWS licenses and assigned by auction in September 2006, was still being "cleared" of federal users and was largely off-limits for private operators.[24] Of the 700 MHz spectrum, only the 6 MHz use by Qualcomm's MediaFlo (a mobile television application marketed through mobile phone carriers) had been deployed; the other 64 MHz was held by carriers planning to use the frequencies for advanced systems being developed.[25]

TABLE 2. MOBILE (CMRS) LICENSES AUCTIONED AND IN USE (YEAR-END 2008)

License Sale	Date	Total Revenue (billions)	Nationwide MHz	$/MHz/pop	Implied Value of 200 MHz Nationwide
PCS A, B	Mar. 1995	7.721	60	$0.51	$30.6 billion
PCS C, D, E, F	Dec. 1995–Feb. 2005	not applicable	60	not applicable	not applicable
Nextel @ 1.9 GHz	2004	4.8	10	$1.7	$102 billion
PCS Re-auction	Feb. 2005	2.043	not applicable	$0.98	$58.8 billion
AWS	Sept. 2006	13.7	90	$0.54	$32.4 billion
lower 700 MHz	2002–2003		18	$0.03	$1.8 billion
upper 700 MHz	Mar. 2008	18.957	52	$1.2	$72 billion
Total			**230**		
Mean (excluding lower 700 MHz)					**$59.2 billion**
Total CMRS MHz deployed[26]			**194**		

---

[23] RYSAVY RESEARCH, MOBILE BROADBAND SPECTRUM DEMAND (2008).

[24] Comments of T-Mobile USA, Inc., Relocation of Federal Systems in the 1710–1755 MHz Frequency Band: Review of the Initial Implementation of the Commercial Spectrum Enhancement Act, Docket No. 0906231085-91085-01 (Nat'l Telecomms. & Info. Admin., Aug. 21, 2009).

[25] See infra Table 2. Verizon and AT&T, which own fourth generation (4G) licenses, announced plans to deploy 4G mobile wireless systems with long-term evolution (LTE) networks in the second half of 2010. Christopher M. Larsen et al., Telecommunications Services: Comments by Verizon CTO Indicate Limited Upside to Tower Revs For LTE in '10, PIPER JAFFRAY (2010).

[26] RYSAVY RESEARCH, supra note 23, at 23. Bazelon breaks out the then- (or soon-) available bandwidth for mobile operators as: 50 MHz cellular (800 MHz band), 120 MHz PCS (1.9 GHz band), 29 MHz specialized mobile radio (800, 900, and 1900 MHz bands). This totals 199 MHz. Bazelon also notes availability of 174 MHz (at 2.5 GHz) for wireless services. Coleman Bazelon, Licensed or Unlicensed: The Economic Considerations in Incremental Spectrum Allocations, 47 IEEE COMM. MAG. 110, 112 tbl.1 (2009). See generally Thomas W. Hazlett, Spectrum Tragedies, 22 YALE J. ON REG. 242 (2005). These frequencies, allocated from the early 1960s to licenses assigned for such services as educational video, have been the subject of numerous fragmentation problems as per the regulatory definition of usage rights. Clearwire, a firm receiving investments and partnership agreements from Sprint, Intel, Google, Motorola, Comcast and Time Warner, in addition to equity investments from its 2008 initial public offering, has aggregated many of the licenses and is attempting to build a nationwide wireless broadband network deploying advanced 4G "Wimax" technology. In the third quarter of 2009, it reported 555,000 U.S. customers. Press Release, Clearwire, Clearwire Reports Third Quarter 2009 Results (Nov. 10, 2009), http://corporate.clearwire.com/releasedetail.cfm?ReleaseID=551159. If the 2.5 GHz frequencies were to host viable competitive entry into the mass market for mobile services, this would have a profound impact on the competitive structure of the industry. Given the uncertain nature of this competitive foray, and the

The wireless services supplied using approximately just 200 MHz allocated to mobile phone licenses enabled substantial economic activity. As summarized by the revenue and consumer surplus estimates, the magnitudes dominate license revenues. Even without adjusting for the fact that license revenues are primarily transfers rather than newly created wealth (with the public finance bonus about 0.33), services produce consumer gains of at least $2.90 or $3.50 per MHz per person *per year*. In contrast, license revenues are, at the most (i.e., attributing all federal auction receipts to the 200 MHz in use, when far more than that has been allocated to the licenses sold through 2008), about $0.63 per MHz per person as a *one-time* payment to the government.[27]

The implication is that the yearly gains from using spectrum for consumers (and ignoring profits generated by producers, another source of social benefit) appear to be at least four times the lump sum payments made for licenses. If a real discount rate of five percent is appropriate,[28] then perpetual annual flows are transformed into present values at a rate of twenty-to-one. This implies that the consumer benefit delivered by mobile markets are at least eighty times the magnitude of the receipts captured by FCC license auctions. An apples-to-apples comparison of efficiency gains would then imply that the license revenues must be reduced by two-thirds to reflect the social savings (not merely the transfers) implied by auction receipts. This implies that the efficiencies associated with retail services in mobile markets are about *240 times as large* as those associated with license revenues.[29]

This more than two order of magnitude difference puts spectrum allocation policy into sharp focus. Delicate adjustments that seek to juice auction receipts but also alter competitive forces in wireless operating markets are inherently risky. A policy that has an enormous impact in increasing license revenues need impose only tiny proportional costs in output markets to undermine its social utility. So, for example, a new auction design that (heroically) doubled auction revenues would, if it reduced consumer surplus by just one-half of one percent, produce costs in excess of benefits.

Policy makers and economists have devoted considerable energy to designing and then redesigning spectrum allocation rules and license auction platforms. They have often looked to sales of licenses at high prices as "successes" and sales at low prices as "fiascoes." Economists have justified this enthusiasm for revenue on efficiency grounds: the more money transferred to the government in auctions, the less money the government must raise via taxes. Taxes of the usual sort are highly distortive; firms and

---

difficulty in assessing the scope and value of the bandwidth rights available to operators, the 2.5 GHz spectrum is generally excluded from totals given for the bandwidth available to mobile carriers (as in the 200 MHz estimate for year-end 2008).

[27] Licenses sold at auction are issued for fixed terms, but are renewed indefinitely so long as the licensee complies with perfunctory rules. In effect, licenses are assigned permanently for a lump sum payment.

[28] A five percent real rate is generally appropriate for discounting future flows in cost-benefit calculations. Robert W. Hahn, *The Economic Analysis of Regulation: A Response to the Critics*, 71 U. CHI. L. REV. 1021, 1026–27 (2004). The lower the rate, the higher the present value of the annual consumer surplus flows.

[29] Other economists have found that consumer surplus is similarly one or two orders of magnitude the size of producers' surplus in wireless markets. *See generally* ENTNER, *supra* note 18; Hausman, *supra* note 18; Jerry A. Hausman, *Valuing the Effect of Regulation on New Services in Telecommunications*, 1997 BROOKINGS PAPERS ON ECON. ACTIVITY: MICROECONOMICS 1; Gregory L. Rosston, *The Long and Winding Road: The FCC Paves the Path with Good Intentions*, 27 TELECOMM. POL'Y 501 (2003).

individuals engage in costly activity just to avoid paying them. The rule of thumb is that a dollar of taxes raised by the state results in about one-third of a dollar in distortion costs (in addition to the dollar transferred to the public treasury).[30] By raising a dollar in a license sale, then, one-third of a dollar is saved—under the assumption that government spending remains fixed (does not increase with the spectrum revenue windfall).

Such thinking, and other more political concerns, has pushed spectrum policy and auction rules in the direction of revenue extraction. This has proven costly. Among these costly policies are such measures or strategies as: delays in auctioning licenses, as the government waits until bids will be higher; reserve prices, which leave licenses unsold if minimum bids are not received; bidding credits for weak bidders, intensifying competition with strong bidders; and reducing the number of licenses sold, inducing simple monopoly power.

Indeed, each of the measures in some way seeks to reduce the probability-adjusted supply of spectrum in the mobile market. This is costly in that spectrum is a key input into wireless services. If it is withheld—or delayed, pared back, or restricted in its use— the market cannot fully optimize (or cost minimize) in supplying services. More costly alternatives will be undertaken, such as deploying more expensive technologies, building more infrastructure (base stations, with greater cell splitting), or simply reducing network access through higher prices.

Because the social gains from additional license receipts are relatively tiny, the focus of policy makers interested in maximizing consumer welfare is rightly on the mission of market efficiency. Yet, much spectrum allocation has become distracted. Policies are offered to intentionally create market power, increasing license rents: "[S]ince alternative taxes entail an enormous welfare loss, it is even optimal to accept some deviation from efficiency if this gives rise to more revenue."[31] But because this "deviation from efficiency" raises revenue in the input market while damaging consumer surplus in the output market, this strategy faces a stiff burden. This Article shows that restricting the productive use of radio spectrum is, generally, a relatively expensive means to secure public funds from the first dollar raised. Pursuing such regulatory strategies tends to be penny wise and pound foolish.

III. "SUCCESS" AND "FIASCOES"

[T]he economic theorists advising the Swiss government on its 3G auction favored a multi-unit ascending auction . . . [and] also proposed setting a high reserve price. . . .

But serious reserve prices are often unpopular with politicians and bureaucrats who—even if they have the information to set them sensibly—are often reluctant to run even a tiny risk of not selling the objects, which outcome they fear would be seen as "a failure."[32]

---

[30] Klemperer, *What Really Matters in Auction Design, supra* note 1, at 179.
[31] Wolfstetter, *The Swiss UMTS Spectrum Auction Flop, supra* note 1, at 6.
[32] PAUL KLEMPERER, AUCTIONS: THEORY AND PRACTICE 138 (2004).

A. General Evaluations

Wireless license auctions are typically ranked and evaluated according to receipts raised. This metric is sometimes defined in gross revenues, revenue per capita, or revenue per MHz per capita (reflecting bandwidth allocated to the licenses sold). Higher bids are considered evidence of superior auction design. Table 3 shows results for the European 3G auctions, the "third generation" licenses supporting high-speed data services in addition to voice (1G) and narrowband data (2G) services. The auctions of these licenses in the European Union countries occurred in 2000–2001 and constitute the last major wave of mobile licensing.[33]

Klemperer identifies the British auction as successful, while rating auctions in Austria, the Netherlands, and Switzerland as fiascoes.[34] He concludes that the circumstances separating successful from unsuccessful license assignments demonstrate that: "auction design is not 'one size fits all.' The ascending design that worked very well for the [United Kingdom (UK)] worked very badly in the Netherlands, Italy, and Switzerland because of entry problems, and this was predictable (and predicted) in advance."[35] A similar appraisal of the Swiss auction is offered by Paul Milgrom, who adds a policy prescription: "Swiss authorities could have achieved a higher price if they had wished. The auction rules could have provided that if few bidders entered the auction, the government would sell the spectrum in the form of three licenses, rather than four, to create meaningful competition."[36]

Auctions distribute intermediate inputs. Value is ultimately created via the use of radio spectrum to provide services to end users. The degree to which licenses enable productive use of airwaves is not perfectly correlated with the price of licenses sold, even when the competitive bidding process succeeds in extracting the present value of expected profits.[37] Klemperer notes that "the outcome of an auction is driven by bidders' profits, not by the welfare of consumers or society as a whole," and offers guidance for constructing certain pro-competitive outcomes.[38]

But the conflict between efficiency in output markets and the maximization of input market license sales has generally escaped attention. And the more fundamental question of how rival spectrum policies affect consumer welfare is not systematically addressed in this literature.[39] Output reducing policy conclusions are often reached solely by an examination of how auction bidding is impacted.

---

[33] In 2010, most countries in the European Union were preparing for the auction of 4G licenses which often involve reallocating spectrum from the television band as per the transition to digital television broadcasting. The so-called digital dividend occurs when the move from analog to digital technology effectively reduces the bandwidth required for the same (or greater) terrestrial broadcasting services. *See, e.g.*, Thomas W. Hazlett, Jürgen Müller & Roberto Muñoz, *The Social Value of TV Band Spectrum in European Countries*, INFO, Mar. 2006, at 62.

[34] *See generally* Klemperer, *How (Not) to Run Auctions*, *supra* note 1. The auction in the Netherlands is rated a "miserable failure" in Binmore & Klemperer, *supra* note 1, at C93.

[35] Klemperer, *How (Not) to Run Auctions*, *supra* note 1, at 844.

[36] PAUL MILGROM, PUTTING AUCTION THEORY TO WORK 209 (2004).

[37] Of course, the same is true of output market goods and services. With monopoly power, prices and revenues may increase over competitive levels not due to value-added, but rather due to output restriction.

[38] Klemperer, *What Really Matters in Auction Design*, *supra* note 1, at 177.

[39] There are many treatments of economic efficiency in spectrum policy, but they are largely divorced from the auction literature. *See, e.g.*, WILLIAM J. BAUMOL & DOROTHY ROBYN, TOWARD AN EVOLUTIONARY

TABLE 3. PRICES PAID FOR 3G LICENSES IN EUROPE[40]

Country	Date	$/pop-MHz	Euros/pop
Austria	Nov. 2000	0.604	100
Belgium	Mar. 2001	0.375	45
Denmark	Sept. 2001	0.623	95
Germany	Aug. 2000	3.884	615
Greece	July 2001	0.394	45
Italy	Oct. 2000	1.494	240
Netherlands	July 2000	1.093	170
Switzerland	Dec. 2000	0.12	20
UK	Apr. 2000	4.31	650

The common use of this single metric is curious given the historical economic case for auctions. The primary advantage put forth as a reason to adopt auctions in place of "beauty contests" or lotteries was that competitive bidding distributed licenses to those firms that could use them most productively. This reformed arbitrary awards marked by a rent-seeking process that made socially wasteful investments in pursuit of political

---

REGIME FOR SPECTRUM GOVERNANCE: LICENSING OR UNRESTRICTED ENTRY? (2006); Stuart Minor Benjamin, *Spectrum Abundance and the Choice Between Private and Public Control*, 78 N.Y.U. L. REV. 2007 (2003); Gerald R. Faulhaber, *The Future of Wireless Telecommunications: Spectrum as a Critical Resource*, 18 INFO. ECON. & POL'Y 256 (2006); Gerald R. Faulhaber & David J. Farber, *Spectrum Management: Property Rights, Markets, and the Commons* (AEI-Brookings Joint Ctr. for Regulatory Studies, Working Paper No. 02-12, 2002), *available at* http://www.ictregulationtoolkit.org/en/Document.3629.pdf; Thomas W. Hazlett, *Liberalizing US Spectrum Allocation*, 27 TELECOMM. POL'Y 485 (2003); Thomas W. Hazlett, *The Wireless Craze, the Unlimited Bandwidth Myth, the Spectrum Auction Faux Pas, and the Punchline to Ronald Coase's "Big Joke": An Essay on Airwave Allocation Policy*, 14 HARV. J.L. & TECH. 335 (2001) [hereinafter Hazlett, *Wireless Craze*]; Evan Kwerel & John Williams, *A Proposal for a Rapid Transition to Market Allocation of Spectrum* (Fed. Commc'ns Comm'n Office of Plans & Policy, Working Paper No. 38, 2002), *available at* http://wireless.fcc.gov/auctions/conferences/combin2003/papers/masterevanjohn.pdf; Bruce M. Owen & Gregory L. Rosston, *Spectrum Allocation and the Internet, in* CYBER POLICY AND ECONOMICS IN AN INTERNET AGE 197 (William H. Lehr & Lorenzo M. Pupillo eds., 2002); Gregory L. Rosston & Jeffrey S. Steinberg, *Using Market-Based Spectrum Policy to Promote the Public Interest*, 50 FED. COMM. L.J. 87 (1997); Pablo T. Spiller & Carlo Cardilli, *Towards a Property Rights Approach to Communications Spectrum*, 16 YALE J. ON REG. 53 (1999); Lawrence J. White, *"Propertyzing" the Electromagnetic Spectrum: Why It's Important, and How to Begin*, MEDIA L. & POL'Y, Fall 2000, at 19. An attempt to bridge this gap is found in Thomas W. Hazlett & Roberto E. Muñoz, *A Welfare Analysis of Spectrum Allocation Policies*, 40 RAND J. ECON. 424 (2009).

[40] The source of the information in Table 3 is supplied by regulators in each country. The last column is from Klemperer, *How (Not) to Run Auctions, supra* note 1, at 830.

favors.[41]   Given that licenses were generally reassigned in secondary markets, allowing the price system to select initial licensees afforded clear efficiencies, assigning spectrum rights directly to highest valued users.   This improved market performance and economized transactions, including bargaining costs incurred in license sales. Soon after implementation, auctions were indeed credited with improving spectrum policy, eliminating the time and expense of non-auction assignments.[42]

Next to these economic gains, the diversion of rents to the public treasury was seen as a windfall for government.   These revenues could displace tax funds, reducing economic distortions.[43]   Economists have generally cited all three major sources of greater efficiency: (1) licenses go to the most efficient firms with less transaction cost; (2) rent seeking expense is reduced; and (3) rents to the public treasury replace revenues raised via activity-distorting taxes.[44]

Both economists and policy makers have issued pro forma caveats warning against regulatory approaches that aim to maximize revenues.   But they have generally proceeded with a single-metric approach that credits greater revenues to greater "success" when evaluating auction results. Klemperer argues the case for auctions thusly:

> Even relatively unsuccessful auctions, such as the Netherlands and Italian spectrum auctions, were probably more successful than the "beauty contest" administrative hearings used to allocate third-generation spectrum in several other European countries. For example, the Spanish beauty contest yielded just 13 euros per head of population, but generated considerable political and legal controversy and a widespread perception that the outcome was both unfair and inefficient . . . .[45]

Professor Klemperer's conclusion is surely correct—the efficiencies of competitive bidding compare favorably with those of "beauty contests." But categorizing the Dutch and Italian policies as "relatively unsuccessful"—an assertion based wholly on the fact that license sales prices were low—is a deeply flawed approach to spectrum policy.

The position implicitly assumes that wireless licenses are simply "spectrum" and that a natural resource is being sold to market participants, much like oil leases or timber rights. The analogy is sound in some respects, but faulty in others. One problem lies in

---

[41] Economic analysis of radio spectrum essentially began with Leo Herzel's 1951 call for auctions, followed by Ronald Coase's 1959 analysis. *See* R.H. Coase, *The Federal Communications Commission*, 2 J.L. & ECON. 1 (1959); Leo Herzel, *My 1951 Color Television Article*, 41 J.L. & ECON. 523 (1998); Leo Herzel, Comment, *"Public Interest" and the Market in Color Television Regulation*, 18 U. CHI. L. REV. 802 (1951); *see also* Thomas W. Hazlett, *Assigning Property Rights to Radio Spectrum Users: Why Did FCC License Auctions Take 67 Years?*, 41 J.L. & ECON. 529 (1998); Hazlett & Michaels, *supra* note 2; Thomas W. Hazlett, David Porter & Vernon Smith, *Radio Spectrum and the Disruptive Clarity of Ronald Coase*, 54 J.L. & ECON. (forthcoming Nov. 2011); Evan Kwerel & Alex D. Felker, *Using Auctions to Select FCC Licensees* (Fed. Commc'ns Comm'n Office of Plans & Policy, Working Paper No. 16, 1985), *available at* http://transition.fcc.gov/Bureaus/OPP/working_papers/oppwp16.pdf.

[42] *See generally* CONG. BUDGET OFFICE, WHERE DO WE GO FROM HERE? THE FCC AUCTIONS AND THE FUTURE OF RADIO SPECTRUM MANAGEMENT (1997); WIRELESS TELECOMMS. BUREAU, FED. COMMC'NS COMM'N, FCC NO. 97-353, THE FCC REPORT TO CONGRESS ON SPECTRUM AUCTIONS (1997), *available at* http://wireless.fcc.gov/auctions/data/papersAndStudies/fc970353.pdf.

[43] *See* Cramton, *Spectrum Auctions*, *supra* note 1.

[44] *Id.*

[45] Klemperer, *What Really Matters in Auction Design*, *supra* note 1, at 186.

the fact that the rights that wireless licenses confer are not valued according to substitutes in global commodity markets, but according to expectations of profits in wireless operating markets. These markets (and the profits they generate) are highly sensitive to the policies embedded in the licenses being sold. For example, regulators may increase or decrease license bids by increasing or decreasing the number of licenses assigned, the spectrum allocated to these licenses, the rules governing such licenses, and so on.

The upshot is that the sale of a government-owned commodity (say, oil or timber) generally captures (simply) a transfer price for the public. In spectrum, however, the policies enacted within the spectrum allocation scheme will heavily influence the bids made. Whereas the revenues collected for the standard resource auction are exogenous to the operating market, the revenues collected in the sale of wireless licenses are endogenous. Rules that limit wireless service competition may drive up license prices, but such rules do not leave the operating market unaffected. Quite the reverse; consumers are harmed. Such harms must be explicitly incorporated in an analysis pronouncing spectrum policies "successful" or "fiascoes."

B. Demsetz Auctions

Harold Demsetz proposed an alternative to traditional public utility regulation via a bidding scheme for franchises.[46] In instances where a natural monopoly is obtained, such that one firm could satisfy market demand more cheaply than competitors, a sole provider could be selected by competitive bidding. Specifically, firms' bids would not be cast as payments but in the form of price schedules—the rate at which the company would offer to sell services to consumers. Thus, the market could capture the productive efficiencies of natural monopoly and the allocative efficiencies of market competition.[47]

---

[46] See generally Harold Demsetz, Why Regulate Utilities?, 11 J.L. & ECON. 55 (1968).
[47] See generally WILLIAM J. BAUMOL, JOHN C. PANZAR & ROBERT D. WILLIG, CONTESTABLE MARKETS AND THE THEORY OF INDUSTRY STRUCTURE (1982).

FIGURE 4. DEMSETZ AUCTIONS AND LICENSE PRICES

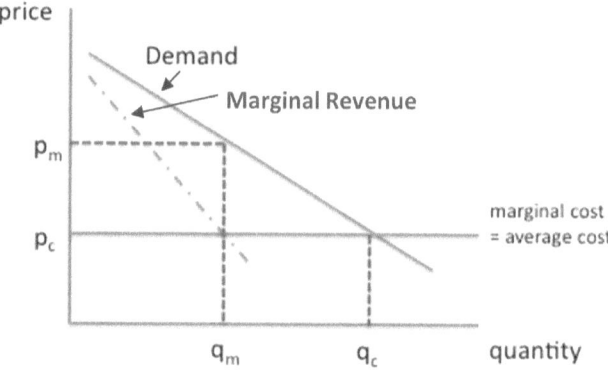

In situations such as the one portrayed in Figure 4, a service franchise (monopoly or otherwise) can operate according to constant marginal costs (equal to average unit costs). If firms bid for one franchise to serve the entire market (defined by the demand curve), and regulators select the lowest price bid,[48] then that price equals p_c, and the firm—mandated by regulation to provide service throughout the life of the franchise at that price—will produce a competitive level of output, q_c. Given that the Demsetz Auction constrains potential monopolists to reveal their long-term retail prices, a competitive outcome obtains. A robust franchise bidding process should not produce any government revenues since no profits are made when the price equals p_c, which equals average cost. Instead, consumer welfare is maximized, albeit with a monopoly supplier.

Were regulators to, alternatively, assign the franchise to the highest price (lump sum payment bid to the government), the economic result markedly changes. The winning franchisee would bid the net present value generated by setting the price to p_m, the rents available from operating as a monopolist restricting output from q_c to q_m. While the government recovers the value of the franchise (rents are transferred to the public treasury), consumers lose the low prices of competition. Moreover, the monopoly prices charged to customers distort economic activity, inducing deadweight losses.

Regulators assigning wireless licenses face this same basic dichotomous policy choice. Importantly, they will not generally be able to avail themselves of a Demsetz Auction to remedy the potential output-restriction problem when licenses are sold for their highest bids. Such an auction requires that the product be stable and well defined, else the firms' price schedule bids cannot be quantitatively ranked.[49] Without such

---

[48] "Price" can be thought of as the lowest price per unit. In reality, however, price will typically consist of an entire schedule of rates (monthly service rates may be lower in one bid, but installation charges higher—or reliability of service lower). Determining which bid implies "the lowest price" will be a non-trivial exercise. On such practical issues, see Thomas W. Hazlett, *Private Monopoly and the Public Interest: An Economic Analysis of the Cable Television Franchise*, 134 U. PA. L. REV. 1335 (1986); Oliver E. Williamson, *Franchise Bidding for Natural Monopolies—in General and with Respect to CATV*, 7 BELL J. ECON. 73 (1976).

[49] *See* discussion *supra* note 48.

transparency, the bids are reduced to competing proposals to be evaluated on the qualitative standards imposed by regulators. This is precisely the "beauty contest" or "comparative hearings" process that competitive bidding was designed to replace.

Mobile wireless networks and services are neither stable nor well-defined; the marketplace is rapidly evolving. Rate regulation for wireless services was abandoned in the United States by federal statute in 1993, having failed to improve prices for consumers even under the cellular duopoly then in place.[50] Demsetz Auctions are not a realistic option compared to pro-competitive policies that avoid franchise monopoly by licensing rival wireless operators.

Spectrum regulators counter market power by issuing multiple licenses and making spectrum inputs available to sustain and enhance network rivalry. This will tend to produce the economic outcome sought in the Demsetz Auction and capture license rents for the public treasury. But tension between efficiency in outputs and value-capture in inputs is a built-in feature. When the focus of the regulator shifts from lower prices for consumers to higher prices for the franchise, economic distortions can easily occur.

C. License Prices and Property Rights

The avoidance of monopoly is well understood. What bears much less notice is that the restrictions embedded into wireless licenses—such as rules limiting services to just voice (1G) or voice and narrowband data services (2G)—constitute analogous output restrictions. Where such legal limitations reduce competitiveness they can make licenses more valuable. These license rents may be captured via competitive bidding for assignment of the rights, but this is a relatively high-cost way to raise public revenues, as it distorts retail wireless markets. When license sales are evaluated on the basis of revenues raised, misleading appraisals result.

It may seem obvious that licenses that are given broader scope—fuller, more complete property rights to the allocated radio waves—would fetch higher prices. Licensees would have more opportunities to productively use frequencies and fewer (if any) restrictions blocking profitable new technologies or business models.

Yet this is not the case.[51] Countries that have instituted decidedly liberal reforms, granting wireless operators qualitatively wider scope to control airwaves, saw prices about sixty percent *lower* than in other markets, all else equal, in a study of thirty-eight mobile license auctions held in twenty-four countries between 1995 and 2001.[52] This result supports the view that by relaxing regulation of the input (spectrum) market, regulators can improve future competitiveness in the output (mobile services) market. The anticipation of greater rivalry produces lower bids.

This result seems counter-intuitive to some because additional property rights are an incremental gain to the owner. With wireless licenses, however, property rights are defined categorically. When regimes alter rights, pro forma rules change for classes of assets (in this case, spectrum use authorizations). Additional rights for one licensee (a

---

[50] Babette E.L. Boliek, *Wireless Net Neutrality Regulation and the Problem with Pricing: An Empirical, Cautionary Tale*, 16 MICH. TELECOMM. & TECH. L. REV. 1, 4 (2009).
[51] *See generally* Thomas W. Hazlett, *Property Rights and Wireless License Values*, 51 J.L. & ECON. 563 (2008).
[52] *Id.* at 564–65.

gain for that licensee) are accompanied by additional rights for current or potential rivals (a loss). The effect of the incremental rights on license value is therefore ambiguous.

What is unambiguous, however, is the direction of change in consumer surplus. Customers gain when market rivalry intensifies, and liberalization (expanded spectrum use rights and increased frequency allotments) strongly drives this market outcome.[53] The effect is visible in license bids. This finding, combined with knowledge about the relative magnitudes of social surplus in the wireless market (i.e., that the gains from efficiency overwhelmingly flow to consumers rather than to firm profits), has important implications. What matters most in spectrum allocation policy is the availability of spectrum bandwidth and broad property rights to productively deploy it—not license revenues.

D. Examples of "Cart Before the Horse" and Vice Versa

Specific examples illustrate how license assignment methods are nested in the spectrum allocation regime. Policies with clear output market efficiency implications are commonly evaluated solely on the basis of how such reforms alter auction receipts. This approach is not universally the case, however, as some policies inflicting inefficiencies are rejected. These latter policies—some of which artificially create market power, making licenses more valuable and bids therefore higher—are sometimes identified as instances in which auction design puts "the cart before the horse."[54]

The appraisal is well put. Yet, there are many instances in which "cart before the horse" reasoning is uncontested. The following arguments by Paul Milgrom, analyzing spectrum auction policies, frame the general approach taken by economists:

> When the likely winner of the auction is not in much doubt, the prospect of incurring unrecoverable costs can depress entry. Spectrum auctions in Germany, Italy, Israel, and Switzerland have all suffered from insufficient entry. . . .
>
> . . . . [W]e show how a seller can structure an auction to encourage entry, increase competition, and promote higher prices.[55]

The problem identified is that demand for licenses is insufficiently intense. In a low demand situation, even if licenses are highly valuable to some parties, these parties are not forced to bid aggressively, and rivalry in the auction is weak. As a result, auction receipts lag. If license auctions are seen as purely a means to an end—enabling productive use of airwaves—"low participation" makes rights distribution *easier*. High demanders outbid others and deploy the rights sold.

Of course, a private asset owner facing this situation would likely employ measures to extract a fuller proportion of value from the buyer. This follows from presumed wealth-maximizing behavior, but a government facilitating access to a valuable resource should, alternatively, strive to maximize social welfare. To achieve that goal, the policy

---

[53] *See* sources cited *supra* note 39.

[54] Klemperer, *What Really Matters in Auction Design, supra* note 1, at 185.

[55] MILGROM, *supra* note 36, at 234.

maker must enable efficiency in the post-auction output market.[56] Promoting measures to generate demand for licenses that compromise such efficiencies put the "cart before the horse." This is seen in the evaluation of the suggested policy remedies, which include first-price auctions, reserve prices, bidding credits, and the withholding of licenses, each considered here.

1. First-Price Versus Ascending-Price Auctions

Paul Klemperer establishes that a simple ascending auction is not an efficient assignment tool due to problems related to collusion and entry deterrence:

> In an ascending auction, there is a strong presumption that the firm that values winning the most will be the eventual winner, because even if it is outbid at an early stage, it can eventually top any opposition. As a result, other firms have little incentive to enter the bidding and may not do so if they have even modest costs of bidding.[57]

Klemperer's solution to the problems associated with the ascending auction format is to make it more robust to collusion and entry-deterring behavior. This is achieved with the Anglo–Dutch design[58] or a first-price sealed-bid auction, which likely generates higher revenues for the auctioneer. Evidence from wireless telephone license auctions suggests that revenues collected in sealed-bid auctions (first- or second-price) generally exceed revenues generated by other formats.[59] But there can be costs associated with such approaches, including the increased probability that a "weak" player will out-bid a "strong" one, displacing a more efficient supplier in the output market. When this happens, higher costs offset some economies gained by more efficient rent extraction in the license auction.

The intended point is not to argue against first-price sealed bids or to dispute the conclusion that these auctions raise higher revenues. Rather, this Article stresses that welfare considerations should be included in the cost-benefit calculus when input or output markets are impacted by regulatory changes. The social losses associated with auction rules designed to encourage participation by weak bidders are particularly pronounced in the U.S. PCS C block auctions, discussed below.

---

[56] This is not merely a normative view, but a result of economic efficiency. A private owner competes with other private owners in the creation or discovery of scarce resources; the value of those resources drives the quest for ownership. In the case of government allocation of radio spectrum, the state assumes monopoly control over valuable natural resources to facilitate productive exploitation. Even where various public interests are pursued, including government-regulated or government-owned spectrum allocations, the welfare-maximizing path is to achieve such objectives in an efficient manner. This implies that the state should not monopolize resources, but seek to enable competitive forces to expand social opportunities.

[57] Klemperer, *What Really Matters in Auction Design*, *supra* note 1, at 172.

[58] *See id.* at 170.

[59] Hazlett, *supra* note 51, at 572.

2. Reserve Prices

The sequential Turkish auctions held in 2000 mandated that the price for the second license equal or exceed the price bid by the winner of the first.[60] This prompted the first auction winner to bid so aggressively that a second operator would not pay the steep entry fee. Klemperer appropriately labels the monopoly output market result the "Turkish fiasco"[61] and a "tale of woe."[62]

Yet the inefficient result is embedded in reserve prices. The purpose of a reserve (or reservation) price is generally to raise bids by blocking the sale of a license when no bid is made exceeding a minimum level set by the regulator. In some instances, then, licenses will remain unsold, yielding less market competition. Moreover, regulators typically allow the bandwidth allocated to the unsold licenses to remain idle—a second source of efficiency loss imposed by reducing the capacity (or, equivalently, raising the opportunity costs) of incumbent wireless operators. Nonetheless, economists ubiquitously advocate such policies,[63] advising governments "to withhold supply and set reserve prices to improve revenues."[64]

The effect of the higher retail prices that may ensue are excluded from the economic analysis, which therefore presents an incomplete, asymmetric evaluation. Empirically, this Article estimates the costs associated with leaving licenses unsold due to reserve prices imposed in Belgian and Greek 3G auctions held in 2001, and finds the miscue of decidedly material magnitude.

It is illustrative that the remedy to the "Turkish fiasco" attempted by Turkish policy makers was not entirely well received in the scholarly literature. When the government moved to moot the monopoly by issuing an additional license, thereby lowering the reservation price *ex post*, the policy shift was challenged on the ground that it undermined confidence in government auction rules.[65]

Regulatory certainty is an important goal, but this Article argues that the policy take-away is virtually the reverse: it is dangerous for governments to commit to policies that exclude competitors so as to encourage higher auction bids. Once that process begins, the state becomes complicit in a scheme to inefficiently restrict output, as in a collusive agreement—indeed, the government structured the market, defined the rules, sold the exclusionary rights created, and cashed the licensee's check paid in advance to exploit the opportunity at hand. Clearly, this is another case of "cart before the horse."

---

[60] Klemperer, *What Really Matters in Auction Design*, *supra* note 1, at 177–78.

[61] *Id.* at 178.

[62] *Id.* at 177.

[63] *See, e.g.*, McMillan, *Selling Spectrum Rights*, *supra* note 1, at 159; Klemperer, *What Really Matters in Auction Design*, *supra* note 1, at 176, 178.

[64] Lawrence M. Ausubel & Peter Cramton, *Vickrey Auctions with Reserve Pricing*, 23 ECON. THEORY 493, 504 (2004).

[65] Klemperer, *What Really Matters in Auction Design*, *supra* note 1, at 177 ("The credibility of reserve prices is of special importance . . . [more competition may be achieved,] but at what cost to the credibility of its future auctions?").

3. Bidding Credits as a "Free Lunch Policy"

Another solution to the "low participation" problem that has gained currency among economists is the use of bidding credits:

> The government could allow any firm to bid on any license, but give the designated firms a price preference. With a preference of, say, 10 percent, a designated firm would win if its bid was no more than 10 percent less than the highest nondesignated-firm bid. This is a free-lunch policy. It would not only address the public-policy goal of increasing the number of licenses won by the designated firms, but it would also actually increase the government's revenue.[66]

This approach received a boost after the FCC's initial use of credits appeared to yield additional revenues.[67] But even before disaster struck in the PCS C and F block auctions in 1996 and 1997, it was deducible that substantial expected costs would be incurred by any mechanism that risked assigning licenses to relatively inefficient suppliers. Indeed, the basic efficiency motivation for adopting license auctions is that competitive bidding awards operating rights to those firms most able to provide high-quality, low-cost service to the public.

Paul Milgrom makes a strong case against beauty contests and lotteries by specifically rejecting the idea that secondary markets correctly adjust for initial awards: "According to a famous result in mechanism design theory—the Myerson-Satterthwaite [(M-S)] theorem—there is no way to design a bargaining protocol that avoids this problem: delays or failures are inevitable in private bargaining if the good starts out in the wrong hands."[68] Bidding credits impose just the inefficiency that the M-S theorem identifies. Yet, such policies are advanced as revenue-raising devices without consideration of inefficiency offsets. The social costs of moving away from market-based awards are implicitly regarded as exogenous to the process.

However, that is not the case, as vividly seen in the U.S. PCS designated-entity fiasco. Small businesses and rural phone companies (qualified designated entities) extended bidding credits and long-term low-interest loans for PCS C (30 MHz) and F (10 MHz) licenses. The result was widespread over-bidding followed by licensee bankruptcies, after which no use was made of the allocated spectrum while court battles (which the government eventually lost) played out over nearly a decade.[69]

As this Article shows below, the social loss associated with an estimated 30 MHz reduction in mobile services spectrum over eight years—a conservative definition of what was incurred—is orders of magnitude larger than any plausible efficiencies associated with rent extraction due to enhanced auction bids. That the U.S. experience can be attributed in large measure to poor implementation, though true, is irrelevant. The rules are endogenous to the handicapping policy. Whatever preferences are crafted,

---

[66] McMillan, *Selling Spectrum Rights*, supra note 1, at 158.
[67] *See* Ian Ayres & Peter Cramton, *Deficit Reduction Through Diversity: How Affirmative Action at the FCC Increased Auction Competition*, 48 STAN. L. REV. 761, 763 (1996).
[68] MILGROM, *supra* note 36, at 21.
[69] *See generally* Robert W. Crandall & Allan T. Ingraham, *The Adverse Economic Effects of Spectrum Set-Asides*, 6 CANADIAN J.L. & TECH. 131 (2007); Thomas W. Hazlett & Babette E.L. Boliek, *Use of Designated Entity Preferences in Assigning Wireless Licenses*, 51 FED. COMM. L.J. 639 (1999).

credits increase weak bidders' chances of winning licenses, which incurs social costs and, occasionally, policy fiascoes inflict much larger costs as well. An optimal spectrum policy would properly account for all of these costs.

4. Withholding Licenses

Economists critical of the Italian 3G auction design have rejected rules intended to render the Italian wireless market structure less competitive. Klemperer writes that the Italian government "stipulated that if there were no more 'serious' bidders ... than licenses, then the number of licenses could, and probably would, be reduced."[70] Klemperer pronounces this policy "fundamentally flawed ... [because] it is putting the cart before the horse to create an unnecessarily concentrated mobile-phone market to make an auction look good."[71] This Article endorses this departure from revenue-maximization—and notes that the departure directly undercuts the curiously universal appeal of binding reserve prices.

E. Costs of Spectrum Allocation or License Assignment Delays

Huge costs have historically been imposed on consumers and businesses by deterring competitive entry or new technologies. For instance, it is estimated that impeding cellular telephone service by a decade cost the U.S. economy about $86 billion in lost productivity.[72] Given that a decade and a half of license auctions have produced about $52 billion in actual receipts for the U.S. Department of the Treasury,[73] this single spectrum policy inefficiency is likely to have cost society five times the claimed public finance efficiencies (assuming $0.33 of lost productivity is averted for every public dollar gained).[74]

1. United Kingdom 3G Delays

In the British 3G auction, Binmore and Klemperer note that a three-year planning phase was used to good effect, improving the policies adopted.[75] Yet the analysis does not consider the loss in service to the public constituted by the waiting period.[76] This Article's simulation, summarized below, suggests that the cost to the UK economy of this three-year delay was approximately $6.5 billion. Considering that the UK 3G auction

---

[70] Klemperer, *What Really Matters in Auction Design, supra* note 1, at 185.

[71] *Id.*

[72] JEFFREY H. ROHLFS ET AL., NAT'L ECON. RESEARCH ASSOCS., INC., ESTIMATE OF THE LOSS TO THE UNITED STATES CAUSED BY THE FCC'S DELAY IN LICENSING CELLULAR TELECOMMUNICATIONS (1991), *available at* http://www.jacksons.net/EstimateofTheLossFromCellularDelay.pdf.

[73] MOVING FORWARD, *supra* note 21, at 11. This total includes $13.7 billion in the 2006 AWS auctions in September 2006, $19.1 billion in the March 2008 700 MHz license auctions, and $19.1 billion in the other sixty-eight auctions held 1994–2008.

[74] Hazlett describes a long list of wireless technologies delayed or deterred by spectrum allocation policies in a section entitled "Silence of the Entrants." Hazlett, *Wireless Craze, supra* note 39, at 375–402.

[75] Binmore & Klemperer, *supra* note 1, at C90.

[76] Similarly, van Damme notes that the Netherlands allocated spectrum for 2G licenses in March 1995, but did not assign such licenses until February 1998, implying that the delay resulted from consideration of the decision to use competitive bidding. van Damme, *supra* note 1, at 5.

raised $34 billion, and assuming social savings of $0.33 per dollar raised, this delay offset around sixty percent of the *entire* public finance dividend.

2. The United States' 3G Delay

The three-year UK 3G rollout constitutes rapid progress, however, compared to 3G licensing in the United States. In 1996, FCC Chairman Reed Hundt proposed a reallocation of ultra high frequency television spectrum, from channels 60 to 69, and licenses were essentially ready to auction by 2000. A congressional statute mandated such—but eight auction postponements occurred through 2004.[77] Economists actually endorsed some of the delays.[78] Finally, with the 700 MHz license auction (FCC Auction No. 73) in March 2008 these licenses were assigned, and, with the turn-off of analog television broadcasting on June 12, 2009, the spectrum was made available for use in alternative (non-television) services.

More generally, U.S. spectrum allocation underwent a "lost decade." Between the allocation of PCS (or 2G) licenses in 1994 and their assignment by auction in 1995–1997, no substantial spectrum allocations for mobile services were made until the AWS license auctions in 2006. In other words, the United States simply missed the 3G licensing round undertaken in the UK and most other advanced economies in 2000–2001, and it did so intentionally, to satisfy policy choices.

In its first spectrum policy initiative, the Bush Administration prepared a March 2001 budget statement that recommended that 3G auctions be delayed until September 2004, calling this "a 'win-win' for all parties involved" and a "good telecom policy."[79] The "win-win" referred to higher receipts for government (as bids were expected to increase over time) and gains for incumbent carriers who requested that new industry capacity be delayed. Only consumer interests and the health of the overall U.S. economy were omitted from the "win-win" analysis.[80]

3. Endemic Spectrum Under-Allocation

The problem of spectrum under-allocation, wherein a regulatory bottleneck blocks the flow of bandwidth to its most highly valued employment, is found in the United

---

[77] Hazlett shows how the argument that the unoccupied spectrum should be preserved to deliver high definition television at some unspecified date in the future, has been used to delay or block new services. Hazlett, *Wireless Craze, supra* note 39, at 466.

[78] Ronald Harstad, Aleksandar Pekec, and Michael Rothkopf filed a Comment with the Federal Communications Commission in January 2001. Ronald M. Harstad et al., Verizon Is Right: Delay Auction No. 31, Comment on DA 01-143 (Fed. Commc'ns Comm'n Jan. 24, 2001). The authors filed another Comment on February 19, 2002, which urged further delay for Auction No. 31. Ronald M. Harstad et al., Thorough Analysis of Package Bidding Procedures Is Still Needed, Comment on DA 02-260 (Fed. Commc'ns Comm'n Feb. 19, 2002). The filings focused solely on the possibility that rent extraction might have been reduced without further delays.

[79] Thomas W. Hazlett, Editorial, *Hostage Standoff: Virtually Worthless UUF TV Stations Strangle Communications Progress*, BARRON'S, Mar. 19, 2001, at 46, 46.

[80] In the interests of *reductio ad absurdum*, this Article abstracts from the numerous other social interests harmed by the intentional policy of delay. Among these are telecommunications equipment manufacturers (shareholders and employees); U.S. businesses using wireless communications as inputs; public safety organizations that rely on wireless networks.

States and many other countries. This restricts the services provided to end users, raises retail prices, and reduces consumer welfare compared to what would be obtained under a more liberal spectrum allocation regime. Yet, perhaps the easiest way to underscore the general problem is to look at a specific country or region where the amount of spectrum allocated to mobile services—the dominant value-generating application in the modern economy—is far below that allocated elsewhere.

Latin America is a region where such endemic under-allocation is visible. On average, countries there allowed only about 100 MHz to be used by mobile operators by 2004. This was far below the allocations in, for instance, the European Union, where countries averaged 266 MHz.[81] The unallocated spectrum did not serve higher-valued uses, but essentially lay idle. And countries with more generous allocations—such as Guatemala, with 140 MHz—exhibited lower prices and higher usage than similar countries that artificially restricted wireless inputs, such as Panama (50 MHz), Honduras (65 MHz), and Nicaragua (85 MHz).[82] Such policy outcomes far outweigh license assignment choices and should be grasped as central to the regulatory analysis.

IV. TAXING LIBERALIZATION

Yet, rather than stress the fundamental mission of improving market access to radio spectrum, much of the policy analysis goes in just the opposite direction. One line of argument in the economics literature has developed that, "just as a competitive telecommunications market contributes to ... welfare, so might high auction revenue, and therefore both objectives should be considered."[83] Hence, some seek to balance the social gains from higher license revenues against the costs of super-competitive pricing resulting from the imposition of suboptimal market structure. And "since alternative taxes entail an enormous welfare loss, it is even optimal to accept some deviation from efficiency if this gives rise to more revenue."[84]

This logic was developed into a policy proposal by Rothkopf and Bazelon, which attempts to extract rents from wireless licensees whose rights are expanded through liberalization.[85] Suppose, for instance, that a cellular phone operator is licensed to deliver analog service but is then awarded the option to use digital technology. The enhanced discretion constitutes an additional property right, and the ownership of that (new) right may confer a windfall gain on the licensee.[86]

Rothkopf and Bazelon are critical of a "Big Bang" proposal by FCC policy analysts,[87] in which existing licensees would be granted use of frequencies in ways not

---

[81] Thomas W. Hazlett & Roberto E. Muñoz, *Spectrum Allocation in Latin America: An Economic Analysis*, 21 INFO. ECON. & POL'Y 261, 261 (2009).

[82] *Id.* at 263 tbl.1.

[83] van Damme, *supra* note 1, at 6.

[84] Wolfstetter, *The Swiss UMTS Spectrum Auction Flop*, *supra* note 1, at 6.

[85] Michael H. Rothkopf & Coleman Bazelon, *Interlicense Competition: Spectrum Deregulation Without Confiscation or Giveaways* (New Am. Found. Spectrum Policy Program, Working Paper No. 8, 2003), *available at* http://www.newamerica.net/files/nafmigration/archive/Pub_File_1329_1.pdf.

[86] Rothkopf and Bazelon assert that expanded rights will unambiguously bestow a "giveaway." *Id.* at 3. Yet, additional rights distributed to a class of licensees may reduce rents, as explained above; the windfall may be positive or negative.

[87] *Id.* at 3–4; *see also* Kwerel & Williams, *supra* note 39, at 4.

specified in their licenses. This would "distribute expanded use rights to incumbents for free or at far below their value."[88] Rejecting "Kwerel and Williams' approach to spectrum management that focuses solely on the efficiency gains associated with distributing the expanded and valuable license rights," Rothkopf and Bazelon devise a way to extract value from incumbents granted new flexibility.[89]

The problem with simply auctioning the new rights is that the incumbents will clearly be the highest bidders. Entry into the auction will be lackluster (given fixed costs of participating), and serious bidding will be rarer still, given the expectation that license rights are worth far more to current networks than to newcomers.

This foreordained outcome might be seen as an opportunity to save resources by assigning rights to incumbents without an auction, a transaction cost-minimizing strategy.[90] Yet, if this approach reduces transfers to the government, license auction revenue will presumably instead be raised by activity-distorting taxes. It is this latter consideration that motivates the policy proposal.

To extract revenues from incumbents receiving new rights, Rothkopf and Bazelon advocate that the regulatory authority withhold some portion of new rights from the market, pitting incumbents against each other in bidding for a reduced number of "windfall rights."[91] Say that there are 100 analog cellular phone carriers in 100 (or fewer) markets, and each could profitably deploy digital technology that is prohibited by current license restrictions. Instead of awarding 100 digital transmission rights (DTR), a lesser number would be issued, with incumbents forced to bid (if they seek to obtain DTR). The point of this restriction is to induce scarcity, driving the market-clearing price of DTR above zero.

In general, the lower the government sets the number, the higher the extraction (equal to the price of DTR) per digital operator. While Rothkopf and Bazelon's proposal provides that additional rights would be released over time, policies to slow assignments would attract bids from those service providers demanding faster access to spectrum. Their proposal "would gradually make spectrum available on a property-rights-like basis,"[92] as opposed to all at once in a "Big Bang."[93]

The rights withheld are valuable to the degree that they improve the efficiency of wireless services; incremental revenues are captured by imposing a loss of efficiency. The magnitude of that social cost, ignored in Rothkopf and Bazelon's proposal, dominates plausible social gains from rent transfers to the public treasury. In fact, considering a base case with two markets, the first auction dollar raised exceeds one dollar in additional social cost.

---

[88] Rothkopf & Bazelon, *supra* note 85, at 4 (internal quotation marks omitted).
[89] *Id.*
[90] *See* Harold Demsetz, *When Does the Rule of Liability Matter?*, 1 J. LEGAL STUD. 13 (1972); R.H. Coase, *The Problem of Social Cost*, 3 J.L. & ECON. 1 (1960).
[91] *See* Rothkopf & Bazelon, *supra* note 85, at 3–4.
[92] *Id.* at 10.
[93] *See Id.* at 3–4.

FIGURE 5. INCUMBENT BIDS FOR A NEW RIGHT

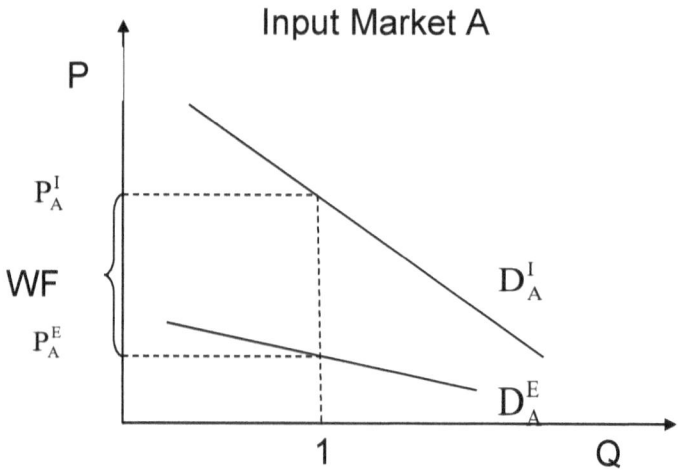

FIGURE 6. INTER-LICENSE AUCTIONS TO INCREASE REVENUE

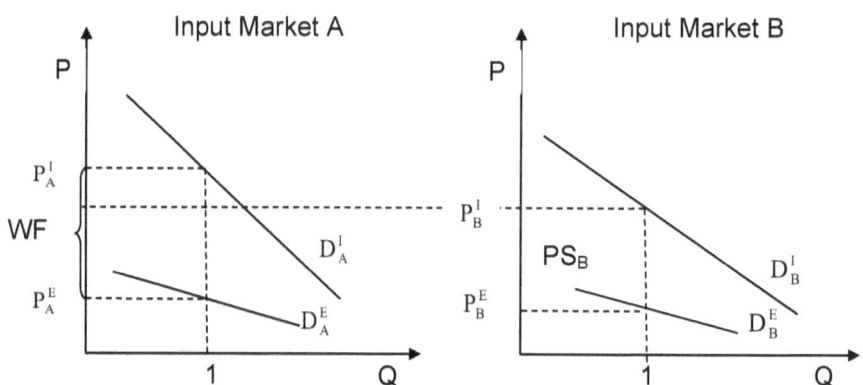

In Figure 5, the basic problem is set forth. An incumbent in Market A, Firm A^I, seeks the right to switch from analog to digital technology. The policy issue is how to award that one new right.[94] The demand curve for such rights dominates the demand expressed by a potential entrant, Firm A^E, given the substantial complementary

---

[94] This Article assumes that wireless license rights are generic and easily defined. Hence, a continuous demand for these rights is postulated. In fact, this is a very favorable assumption for Rothkopf and Bazelon's proposal. This Article also assumes that the spectrum allocation process is unaffected, meaning that the same number of productive rights is released by regulators when incumbents receive windfalls as when they do not. This is, again, highly favorable to the proposal.

118

investments previously sunk by the incumbent. Hence, if an auction were to award one additional right, the price would be bid to just about P_A^E. This means that rents equal to *WF* are retained—a windfall to the incumbent. Rothkopf and Bazelon's solution aims to transfer this private gain to the public by eliminating a license award in another market, Market B. This enables an auction between the incumbents in the rival markets, as pictured in Figure 6.

Now the incumbent in Market A is not bidding against the entrant in Market A, but against the incumbent in Market B. The incumbent in A must bid higher to gain the one new right, as competition for that right is made more intense. Instead of paying approximately P_A^E, the Firm A^E must pay about P_B^I. The windfall to A^I diminishes, and increased rents go to the government. Assuming that incremental revenue ($P_B^I - P_A^E$) equals one dollar, social savings of $0.33 are generated.

This is where the proposal concludes, omitting consideration of the loss imposed on Market B. It must be remembered that these losses are not the artifact of natural limitations with respect to demand, but are manufactured by policy makers imposing legal constraints on productive activities so as to leave some demand unsatisfied. But by excluding the marginal firm (or rights claimant), a social loss exceeding the revenue gained *from the first incremental revenue dollar* results, given that the loss on Firm B^I is greater than $0.33.

And this counts only the loss of producers' surplus. As explained above, consumers' surplus likely exceeds surplus extracted in license bids by at least one order of magnitude. The cost-benefit balance is overwhelmed, tipping against the withholding of spectrum rights over *any* interval. This demonstrates the loss of social efficiency that can result when license revenue extraction is the sole focus of economic analysis.

In the case where there are more than two markets and there are (again) fewer licenses auctioned than incumbents, the comparison is less clear. Suppose that $N - 1$ licenses will be auctioned so that just one incumbent will be deprived of the new right (i.e., $N - N_1 = 1$). The market with the lowest private valuation becomes the relevant margin, setting the license price. Calling A_i the "winning markets" and B the excluded one, as before, Rothkopf and Bazelon's mechanism implies the following necessary (but insufficient) condition for efficiency:

$$\frac{1}{3}\sum_{i=1}^{N-1}\left(P_B^I - P_{A,i}^E\right) > P_B^I + PV(CS_B)$$

where $PV(CS_B)$ represents the present value of consumer surplus lost in market B.

The inequality represents the case where the exclusion of market B is compensated by the social payoff of a less distorting revenue collection mechanism. It is not impossible for this inequality to be satisfied, but it is implausible. First, to escape the very high ratio of consumers' surplus to producers' surplus (shown above to exceed, perhaps, 100-to-1), many licenses must be auctioned for each license withheld; yet expanding rights issued reduces scarcity values and, therefore, revenues. In the limit, this converges with the liberal solution—maximize market competition, worry not about license extractions.

Second, Rothkopf and Bazelon's tactic consciously resists this optimum, creating artificial scarcity to puff up rents (PS) while imposing losses in output markets (PS + CS). Given that CS likely exceeds PS by an order of magnitude or more, this is likely to prove penny wise, pound foolish. Doubling PS—a hugely ambitious target—could be inefficient if CS were reduced by just one percent (an outcome dictated by a CS to PS ratio greater than thirty-three, within the range of plausible estimates).

Third, institutional factors governing market dynamics strongly reinforce this pessimistic conclusion concerning efficiency gains through policy-imposed scarcity. There exists an infinite number of property rights to use radio spectrum in ways not previously specified in restrictive licenses that specify spectrum access with respect to technologies, services, and business models. Which rights would prove socially productive is generally unknown ex ante. Only when applicants petition for permission to change license terms do these new opportunities become visible to the regulator.

The policy of extracting rents from petitioners requesting permission to exploit new wireless property rights directly taxes the discovery process wherein wireless operators innovate in services, technologies, and business models. The object of the rights auction is to obtain full rent extraction; the direct effect of withholding the marginal applicant's rights is to sacrifice the social gains from that deployment entirely. Static losses are entirely a product of public policy, as there is no economic scarcity to be rationed among rival rights holders.

But the spectrum allocation dynamics are likely far more costly. Taxing efficiency-creating discoveries is perverse. Indeed, in intellectual property law, the government awards patents, copyrights, or trademarks to innovators essentially *free of charge* as an inducement to socially productive activity. Regulatory permission to deploy constitutes a barrier to entry; the more effective the system in appropriating innovators' gains, the lower the investment in such activity. Traditionally, spectrum-allocation rigidities have imposed high barriers to innovation, long the subject of normative criticism by economists.[95] Incumbents would be protected by such a system, with competitive entry deterred via tax policy.

V. A REGULATORY OPTIMUM

This Part defines what an optimal regulatory policy might achieve, assuming that an FCC-type spectrum allocation regime exists.[96] It assumes that the regulator pursues

---

[95] *See* Gregory L. Rosston & Thomas W. Hazlett, Comments of 37 Concerned Economists, Promoting Efficient Use of Spectrum Through Elimination of Barriers to the Development of Secondary Markets, WT Docket No. 00-230 (Fed. Commc'ns Comm'n Feb. 7, 2001), *available at* http://www.brookings.edu/~/media/files/rc/reports/2001/02_economists_litan/02_economists_litan.pdf.

[96] Under an FCC-type regime, the government treats radio spectrum as state property and then makes case-by-case determinations as to how spectrum access rules will be crafted. The ostensible aim is to facilitate the efficient deployment of wireless services, and the basic rationale driving this structure is that there would be endemic chaos were there no central allocation mechanism in place. Coase demonstrated the weakness of the argument by showing that rules limiting spectrum access can be imposed as property ownership rules. *See generally* Coase, *supra* note 41. The latter enables resource appropriation choices (including "spillovers") to be determined by asset owners under competitive conditions as opposed to government regulators. The liberalization of allocations for mobile phone licenses, where spectrum use choices tend to be broadly delegated to operators, follows Coase's normative suggestion. Observed results in mobile markets strongly support his intuition as to the efficiency of decentralized property rights. *See* Thomas W. Hazlett, *Optimal Abolition of FCC Spectrum Allocation*, 22 J. ECON. PERSP., Winter 2008, at 103; Hazlett, Porter & Smith, *supra* note 41. Some spectrum regimes—including those in Australia, New Zealand, Guatemala, and El Salvador—have gone further, instituting general liberalization by statute. *See*

policies to maximize social welfare and focus for ease of analysis on the market for wireless telephone service.[97] This goal can be summarized in three objectives: (1) allocate spectrum to promote the most efficient delivery of wireless services; (2) select a mechanism to assign licenses that maximizes social value; and (3) subject to these constraints, distribute licenses so as to maximize the present value of payments to the government.

The first goal concerns decisions made before licenses are assigned; indeed, it encompasses the procedure wherein licenses are created. Here, the regulator constructs a bundle of rights to assign to private parties and establishes rules shaping industry structure and performance, fundamentally determining expected license rents.

A less concentrated market structure tends to increase price competition. Yet, scale and scope economies are pronounced in mobile markets, and dynamic (Schumpeterian) efficiencies may be improved where relatively efficient firms increase market share. Both fixed and variable costs tend to increase when the amount of spectrum assigned to a license is reduced, as happens when additional licenses share a given allocation of bandwidth. Given the costs and benefits of market concentration, this Article's hypothetical regulator designs policies to produce an optimal market structure.

The second goal is to assign licenses such that total welfare is maximized. As van Damme comments, this concept, "market efficiency," can differ from "value efficiency."[98] Because "bidders are guided by shareholder value and not by consumer surplus, . . . at best one can expect an auction to produce an allocation that is 'value efficient.'"[99] Market efficiency might, for example, be improved by auction rules that improve post-auction market structure.[100] Of course, limits on incumbents' bids also have costs, as vividly seen in the U.S. PCS designated entity preferences.

The third goal focuses on raising revenues for public use. This Article's assumptions isolate this process to one of pure rent transfer. In this context, higher revenues are unambiguously preferred to lower revenues. In actual policy-making, however, the assumption is a strong one. It is violated when incremental revenues are extracted by withholding productive rights.[101]

It is worth noting that license auctions are largely independent of the first goal,[102] are useful tools for the second, and are primary mechanisms used to achieve the third.

Hazlett, *supra* note 51, at 582–86. Other countries—notably Norway, the United Kingdom, and the United States—have undertaken regulator-led reforms expanding market spectrum allocation. *See generally* ERIC BASH ET AL., KB ENTERS., SPECTRUM LIBERALIZATION: APPROACHES IN FIVE COUNTRIES—AUSTRALIA, NEW ZEALAND, NORWAY, THE UNITED KINGDOM, AND THE UNITED STATES (2009), *available at* http://kbspectrum.com/wp-content/uploads/2009/10/KBE-Spectrum-Liberalization-FINAL.pdf.

[97] The path taken generalizes easily, as spectrum rights are flexible and can be used to accommodate other wireless services as dictated by consumer demand.

[98] van Damme, *supra* note 1, at 7.

[99] *Id.*

[100] See Richard J. Gilbert & David M.G. Newbery, *Preemptive Patenting and the Persistence of Monopoly*, 72 AM. ECON. REV. 514 (1982), for an excellent discussion of preemptive patenting, directly applicable here.

[101] *See* discussion *supra* Part IV.

[102] It is commonly held that governments allocate more spectrum so that they can auction licenses and raise additional government revenue. *See, e.g.*, Eli Noam, *Spectrum Auctions: Yesterday's Heresy, Today's Orthodoxy, Tomorrow's Anachronism. Taking the Next Step to Open Spectrum Access*, 41 J.L. & ECON. 765 (1998). The evidence is decidedly mixed. Sometimes revenues appear as drivers, but governments

These distinctions are important. This Article argues that the first goal is by far the most important one in terms of its impact on social welfare. This policy defines the amount of spectrum available in the market to provide services and heavily influences final market structure by, among other things, defining the number of available licenses.

The main task of auction design is to assign rights to the most efficient service providers. With market efficiency, this selection process does not conflict with the third goal: maximum revenues for the auctioneer.   High revenues, which have been interpreted as a signal of a well-designed auction, are properly used as a metric when the policy design maximization is subject to the constraint of market-efficiency. And, vice-versa, when the pursuit of high revenues conflicts with market-efficiency, the signal is likely to be highly misleading.

VI. CONCLUSION

> Assigning, or licensing, is the last step in the process of granting a right to use a part of the spectrum and has only limited consequences for economic efficiency in the context of the overall system.[103]

What really matters in spectrum allocation design? The evidence indicates that the answer is two-fold: *spectrum* and *competition* in final markets. This conclusion holds after adjusting for the social savings possible from efficient rent extraction via license auctions.

Yet, the economic analysis of wireless license auctions has focused on revenues extracted from bidders, seeing the "embarrassingly low revenue in the Netherlands," for example, as indicating a fiasco in public policy.[104] It might also be noted that the Dutch succeeded in making 355 MHz available for wireless phone operators, more than any other European Union country. Alternatively, U.S. regulators then made only about 170 MHz of bandwidth available for use in wireless telephone markets—an outcome that merits little scholarly attention despite the "fiasco" it has produced in lost productivity.

Indeed, a decade-long loss of 30 MHz in the U.S. mobile market stemmed from the use of bidding credits in the 1995–1997 PCS auctions—a policy that was praised in the economics literature as a way to boost bid prices in license auctions. The policy did indeed succeed in raising winning bids. But the winners were not efficient providers. Moreover, the revenues went largely uncollected while the spectrum lay idle for years. These policy errors cost consumers in excess of $70 billion, more than all FCC license auction revenues in total, and thereby far out-stripping any social gains from this source of public rent extraction. Such collateral damage of the revenue-enhancement strategy has been unanticipated in policy analysis. It should not be.

---

sacrificed substantial rents for many decades by refusing to auction *any* wireless licenses. Hazlett, Porter & Smith, *supra* note 41. Were revenue a driver of additional allocations, regimes that use competitive bidding to make awards would allocate substantially more spectrum than nations that do not, *ceteris paribus*. While this Article holds that the evidence rejects this, further research on the political economy questions may add useful clarity.

[103] CONG. BUDGET OFFICE, AUCTIONING RADIO SPECTRUM LICENSES 3 box 1 (1992).

[104] Wolfstetter, *The Swiss UMTS Spectrum Auction Flop, supra* note 1, at 6 n.8 (citing Paul Klemperer, *What Really Matters in Auction Design* (Nuffield Coll., Oxford Univ., Working Paper, 2000)).

Spectrum use is assumed to be exogenous to competitive bidding for licenses. If true, rents transferred to government in auctions would, by definition, have no social cost. But policy recommendations that include reserve prices, bidding credits for weak bidders, and a reduction in the number of licenses issued incur expected social costs. These measures thereby breach the assumed line of demarcation. In addition, auction designers have intentionally or unintentionally imposed substantial delays in license assignments, depriving markets of valuable inputs.

This Article does not argue against the use of license auctions; just the reverse.[105] Auctions can be highly useful in eliminating the costs of secondary market recontracting, one of the reasons that random distribution of licenses (as was done by lottery for most cellular permits in the United States) is inefficient. Paul Milgrom's explanation of why it misuses the Coasian analysis to argue for random license assignments is well taken.[106] Yet this efficiency rationale itself conflicts with proposals commonly made with and judging "successes" and "fiascoes" based on prices paid. Policies that alter market structure or the availability of spectrum inputs are not exogenous to spectrum allocation.

By increasing bandwidth allocated to market competitors, promoting rivalry among licensees, and expanding property rights granted to licensees, very large efficiency gains are possible. As shown in this Article's simulations and in empirical research concerning the importance of technological standards, competition liberalization of wireless markets is likely to be the key policy component driving substantial gains in social welfare.[107]

---

[105] One of the authors of this Article argued publicly for FCC license auctions years before Congress enacted reform. *See* Thomas W. Hazlett, *Making Money Out of the Air*, N.Y. TIMES, Dec. 2, 1987, at A35; Thomas W. Hazlett, Editorial, *Dial "G" for Giveaway*, BARRON'S, June 4, 1990, at 12.

[106] MILGROM, *supra* note 36, at 20.

[107] *See generally* Neil Gandal et al., *Standards in Wireless Telephone Networks*, 27 TELECOMM. POL'Y 325 (2003); Peter Grindley et al., *Standards Wars: The Use of Standard Setting as a Means of Facilitating Cartels—Third Generation Wireless Telecommunications Standard Setting*, 3 INT'L J. COMM. L. & POL'Y, Summer 1999, art. 2.

Copyright 2012 by Northwestern University School of Law
Northwestern Journal of Technology and Intellectual Property

Volume 10, Number 3 (January 2012)

Fantasy SCOTUS
Crowdsourcing a Prediction Market for the Supreme Court

By Josh Blackman,[*] Adam Aft[**] and Corey Carpenter[***]

The object of our study, then, is prediction, the prediction of the incidence of the public force through the instrumentality of the courts.[1]

-Oliver Wendell Holmes, Jr.

It is tough to make predictions, especially about the future.[2]

-Yogi Berra

I. INTRODUCTION

Every year the Supreme Court of the United States captivates the minds and curiosity of millions of Americans—yet the inner-workings of the Court are not fully transparent. The Court, without explanation, decides only the cases it wishes. They deliberate and assign authorship in private. The Justices hear oral arguments, and without notice, issue an opinion months later. They sometimes offer enigmatic clues during oral arguments through their questions. Between arguments and the day the Court issues an opinion, the outcome of a case is essentially a mystery. Sometimes the outcome falls along predictable lines; other times the outcome is a complete surprise.

Court watchers frequently make predictions about the cases in articles, on blogs, and elsewhere. Individually, some may be right, some may be wrong. Until recently, there was not a way to pool together this collective wisdom and aggregate *ex ante* predictions for all cases pending before the United States Supreme Court.

Now there is such a tool. FantasySCOTUS.net from the Harlan Institute is the Internet's premier Supreme Court Fantasy League,[3] and the first crowdsourced prediction

---

[*] Josh Blackman is the creator of FantasySCOTUS and President of the Harlan Institute. In August of 2012, Josh will be an Assistant Professor of Law at South Texas College of Law.
[**] Law clerk for a federal judge.
[***] George Mason University School of Law, J.D. (expected May 2012). The authors would like to thank Michael Abramowicz, Ian Ayres, Tom Bell, Aaron Buhl, Miriam Cherry, Orin Kerr, Larry Ribstein, Lawrence Solum, Justin Wolfers, and Todd Zywicki. The authors dedicate this Article to F.A. Hayek and Larry Ribstein.
[1] O.W. Holmes, *The Path of the Law*, 10 HARV. L. REV. 457, 457 (1897).
[2] NASSIM NICHOLAS TALEB, THE BLACK SWAN: THE IMPACT OF THE HIGHLY IMPROBABLE 136 (2d ed. 2010). This quotation has been apocryphally attributed to Yogi Berra. *Id.* at 136 annot.
[3] With 10,000 members and rising, one writer declared FantasySCOTUS the "hottest new fantasy-league game." Bill Mears, *Frustrated with Fantasy Football? Try the Supreme Court*, CNN JUSTICE (Dec. 16,

market for jurisprudential speculation. During the October 2009 Supreme Court Term, over 5,000 members made more than 11,000 predictions for all eighty-one cases decided. Based on these data, FantasySCOTUS correctly predicted the outcome in more than fifty percent of the cases decided, and the top-ranked predictors forecasted seventy-five percent of the cases correctly. This essay explores the wisdom of the crowds in this prediction market and assesses the accuracy of FantasySCOTUS.

Part II provides an overview of the literature about the wisdom of the crowds, crowdsourcing, and prediction markets. By pooling together and aggregating the collective wisdom of many people with expansive knowledge, accurate predictions about future events can be determined to a degree of accuracy unobtainable by individuals. Part III introduces FantasySCOTUS and explains the rules of the game. FantasySCOTUS generated a novel data set with thousands of data points demonstrating how Court watchers viewed the Supreme Court and the decisions of the Justices.

Part IV assesses the accuracy of FantasySCOTUS with internal and external tests. First, to test the power of the wisdom of the crowds, this Article compares the predictions of the FantasySCOTUS "power predictors"—those who made predictions for more than seventy-five percent of the cases—with the FantasySCOTUS "crowd"—those who made predictions for less than seventy-five percent of the cases. The crowd performed worse than the power predictors, but not by much. This result lends support to the wisdom of the crowds theory, wherein a larger pool of predictors with a broader range of knowledge can often predict as well as, if not better than, so-called experts. Additionally, this Article demonstrates how the results are distinguishable from randomized results, such as coin-flips or a million monkeys playing FantasySCOTUS on iPads.

Second, this Article compares FantasySCOTUS predictions to the Supreme Court Forecasting Project's decision tree and experts, finding that the FantasySCOTUS power predictors surpassed.[4] The Forecasting Project's decision-tree relied on past voting data of the Justices to calculate the vote for any given case. The Forecasting Project also assembled a group of expert scholars and practitioners who predicted the same cases. The FantasySCOTUS power predictors predicted 64.7% of the cases correctly, surpassing the Forecasting Project's experts, though the difference was not statistically significant. The decision tree predicted 75% of the cases correctly, which is more accurate than the Forecasting Project's experts, who only predicted 59.1% of the cases correctly. The

---

2009, 2:28 PM), http://www.cnn.com/2009/CRIME/12/16/scotus.journal/index.html; *see also* Josh Blackman, *Asked About FantasySCOTUS.net in an Interview, Justice Breyer Responded: "I Don't Think I Will Bet on It,"* JOSH BLACKMAN'S BLOG (Nov. 30, 2009, 10:30 AM), http://joshblackman.com/blog/?p=2655 (quoting Justice Breyer on the importance of public interest in the Court); Bruce Carton, *Plenty of Fantasy Players on This Bench,* LEGAL BLOG WATCH (Nov. 13, 2009, 11:41 AM), http://legalblogwatch.typepad.com/legal_blog_watch/2009/11/fantasyscoutusnet-the-premier-supreme-court-fantasy-league.html (deeming FantasySCOTUS the "new gold standard in Supreme Court geekery").
[4] Theodore W. Ruger et al., *The Supreme Court Forecasting Project: Legal and Political Science Approaches to Predicting Supreme Court Decisionmaking,* 104 COLUM. L. REV. 1150, 1154–55 (2004). The Forecasting Project developed a sophisticated Super Cruncher algorithm and, utilizing decision trees, predicted how the Justices during the October 2002 Term would decide cases based on certain characteristics of a case—such as circuit of origin, type of case, and the political ideology of the case. *See id.; see also infra* note 5 and accompanying text. To test the power of their model, the organizers of the Forecasting Project assembled a cadre of Supreme Court experts, litigators, and academics to make predictions about the same cases. Ruger et al., *supra,* at 1154–55.

FantasySCOTUS top three power predictors not only outperformed the Forecasting Project's top three experts, but also slightly outperformed the decision-tree algorithm— 75.7% to 75%. This comparison provides insight into the wisdom of the crowds compared to the wisdom of specialized experts, as well as the power of a sophisticated algorithm that can "Super Crunch" the data.[5]

Part V provides an assessment of the limitations of the first version of FantasySCOTUS. As novel as these results are for the first season, FantasySCOTUS' current predictive capabilities are respectable, but not reliable—at best, it was wrong between twenty-five and thirty-five percent of the time. In light of the fact that the Supreme Court typically reverses approximately seventy percent of the cases it considers, these predictions are even less helpful.[6] FantasySCOTUS 1.0 should be understood for what it does. In its current iteration, FantasySCOTUS provides real-time *ex ante* predictions for individual cases. No other product performs this task for every case argued during the term.

Part VI considers whether a Supreme Court prediction market merely mirrors media reports about the cases—that is, whether people make predictions based on coverage about the cases in the news and blogosphere.[7] Using a comprehensive searching process—that considers both old school and new school media, such as popular legal blogs—we found a strong correlation between the amount of media attention and the accuracy of predictions. The power predictors' edge is dulled for cases that receive significant media coverage. For less popular cases that receive less media attention and about which there is less easily accessible information for prospective predictors, the crowd tends to generate less accurate predictions. In contrast, power predictors, who likely perform their own due diligence and research irrespective of media coverage, can better predict even the least noteworthy cases on the docket.

FantasySCOTUS is only two years old, but the implications and applications of this information market are intriguing. Part VII considers the possible future of FantasySCOTUS. First, from a jurisprudential perspective, FantasySCOTUS illuminates public perceptions of how the Supreme Court works as an institution. Specifically, it serves as a comprehensive polling device to provide an honest, albeit unscientific, survey that reflects how a large sample size of Court watchers view the Justices and their legal realist ideological proclivities, particularly in 5–4 decisions. If FantasySCOTUS can accurately reduce each of the Justices to nothing more than a conservative or liberal vote,

---

[5] IAN AYRES, SUPER CRUNCHERS: WHY THINKING-BY-NUMBERS IS THE NEW WAY TO BE SMART 10 (2007) ("Super Crunchers . . . analyze[] large datasets to discover empirical correlations between seemingly unrelated things. . . . Super Crunching . . . is a statistical analysis that impacts real-world decisions.").

[6] In the 2010 Term, the Court reversed seventy-two percent of merit cases before it and seventy-one percent in the 2009 Term. *Stat Pack for October Term 2010*, SUP. CT. U.S. BLOG 4 (June 28, 2011), http://sblog.s3.amazonaws.com/wp-content/uploads/2011/06/SB_OT10_stat_pack_final.pdf [hereinafter *Stat Pack OT2010*]; *SCOTUSblog Final Stats OT09—7.7.10*, SUP. CT. U.S. BLOG 10 (July 7, 2010), http://www.scotusblog.com/wp-content/uploads/2010/07/Final-Stats-OT09-0707101.pdf [hereinafter *Stat Pack OT2009*] (indicating the Supreme Court reversed 71% of its cases during the October Term 2009).

[7] Professor Orin Kerr mentioned this possibility in a 2005 blog post. Orin Kerr, *Tradesports and Supreme Court Nominations*, VOLOKH CONSPIRACY (July 19, 2005, 2:23 PM), http://volokh.com/posts/1121797428.shtml ("As a result, a site [prediction market] like TradeSports would seem to just mirror the collective common wisdom of newspapers and blogs on a question like this. Am I missing something?").

that may have broader implications to the rule of law and objective, detached standards of judging.

From a practical perspective, with more accurate future versions of FantasySCOTUS, attorneys will be able to rely on this program to assist them with litigation decisions involving cases pending before the Supreme Court. As our understanding of judicial behavior improves—perhaps through scanning all filings in PACER (Public Access to Court Electronic Records)—and the program can shift from a pure crowdsourcing technique to a commoditized Super Cruncher information service, a prediction engine can be created for lower courts. An interactive litigation assistant—think of the iPhone's Siri application—could allow attorneys and laymen alike to instantly understand and grasp the law in any given area by simply asking questions.[8] Such technology would be of great value for practicing attorneys, and provide access to justice to people who cannot afford lawyers. This is the promise of law's information revolution, of which we hope FantasySCOTUS is but a first step to the future.[9]

II. IT'S TOUGH TO MAKE PREDICTIONS, ESPECIALLY ABOUT THE FUTURE

The title of this section, apocryphally attributed to Yogi Berra,[10] recognizes the infirmity of the human mind to make predictions about the future: simply put, "we just can't predict."[11] While it is quite difficult for an individual to make predictions about the future, crowds, pooling together their collective knowledge and wisdom, are able to generate accurate predictions about unknowable events. This section explores the wisdom of the crowds, as this phenomenon is known. Prediction markets, which aggregate and assemble this wisdom, are systematic approaches to making informed predictions about the future.

A. The Wisdom of the Crowds

The wisdom of the crowds, popularized by a book by that name,[12] explores how collective knowledge can be pooled together to address problems more efficiently and accurately than decisions from individuals. The beauty of the wisdom of the crowds results from its simplicity; there are no formulas, no self-anointed experts, no normative biases from the creators of the system. Crowds are just people—people who by themselves might not be able to make consistently accurate predictions, but when pooled together generate a level of accuracy unobtainable by individuals.

"The 'wisdom of crowds' is generally more accurate and more objective than the judgment of one uninformed 'expert.'"[13] Perhaps the most popular example of the

---

[8] Josh Blackman, *Siri for the Law*, JOSH BLACKMAN'S BLOG (Nov. 1, 2011, 11:33 PM), http://joshblackman.com/blog/2011/11/01/siri-for-the-law/.

[9] *See* Bruce H. Kobayashi & Larry E. Ribstein, *Law's Information Revolution*, 53 ARIZ. L. REV. 1169 (2011).

[10] TALEB, *supra* note 2, at 136 annot.

[11] *Id.* at 135.

[12] JAMES SUROWIECKI, THE WISDOM OF CROWDS: WHY THE MANY ARE SMARTER THAN THE FEW AND HOW COLLECTIVE WISDOM SHAPES BUSINESS, ECONOMIES, SOCIETIES, AND NATIONS (2004).

[13] Beth Simone Noveck, *"Peer to Patent": Collective Intelligence, Open Review, and Patent Reform*, 20 HARV. J. L. & TECH. 123, 157 (2006) (quoting SUROWIECKI, *supra* note 12, at xv).

wisdom of the crowds is the "ask the audience" lifeline on the game show *Who Wants to Be a Millionaire*. If the contestant on the show is unable to answer a multiple choice question, she can pose the question to the studio audience. Instantly, the votes of each member in the audience are displayed on a screen. For over ninety percent of the questions posed to the crowd, the audience, which possesses a wider swath of knowledge, provided a correct answer where the individual contestant, who possessed a narrower range of information, could not.[14] Indeed, "[u]ncertainty is a painful part of reality; it is only natural that the wisdom of the crowd would be summoned to battle it."[15]

James Surowiecki identifies four factors to determine whether a crowd is *wise*.[16] First, the crowd must possess a diversity of opinions: "[E]ach person should have some private information, even if it's just an eccentric interpretation of the known facts."[17] Second, members of the crowd must make their decisions independently and not be influenced by others.[18] Third, all decisions should be made based only on the information available to the individual, and not based on a single, centralized source of data.[19] Fourth, the manager of the market must possess adequate algorithms to aggregate the predictions and generate accurate results.[20]

F.A. Hayek, in discussing the value of spontaneity and local knowledge, postulated that crowds, acting through markets, are better positioned to make choices than individuals who lack local knowledge.[21] To Hayek, devices such as markets are "orderly structures which are the product of the action of many men but are not the result of human design."[22] Surowiecki aimed to show that Hayek's view on the power of collective knowledge could be applied beyond descriptions of economic systems.[23]

Crowdsourcing, an application of the wisdom of the crowds, was born in a now-famous *Wired* magazine article in 2006.[24] As defined by its creator, "Crowdsourcing is the act of taking a job traditionally performed by a designated agent (usually an employee) and outsourcing it to an undefined, generally large group of people in the form of an open call."[25] Through crowdsourcing, "[h]obbyists, part-timers, and dabblers suddenly have a market for their efforts, as smart companies in industries as disparate as pharmaceuticals and television discover ways to tap the latent talent of the crowd."[26]

---

[14] SUROWIECKI, *supra* note 12 at 3–4.
[15] Note, *Prediction Markets and Law: A Skeptical Account*, 122 HARV. L. REV. 1217, 1217–18 (2009).
[16] SUROWIECKI, *supra* note 12, at 10.
[17] *Id.*
[18] *Id.*
[19] *Id.*
[20] *Id.*
[21] 1 F.A. HAYEK, LAW, LEGISLATION AND LIBERTY: A NEW STATEMENT OF THE LIBERAL PRINCIPLES OF JUSTICE AND POLITICAL ECONOMY, RULES AND ORDER (1973).
[22] Josh Chafetz, *It's the Aggregation, Stupid!*, 23 YALE L. & POL'Y REV. 577, 578 (2005) (quoting HAYEK, *supra* note 21, at 37) (reviewing SUROWIECKI, *supra* note 13).
[23] *Id.* at 578–79.
[24] Jeff Howe, *The Rise of Crowdsourcing*, WIRED, June 2006, at 177.
[25] Jeff Howe, *Crowdsourcing: A Definition*, CROWDSOURCING, http://crowdsourcing.com (last visited Dec. 29, 2011).
[26] Howe, *supra* note 24, at 179.

B. Prediction Markets

Building on the wisdom of the crowds, a prediction market, also known as an information market, encourages people through monetary incentives to aggregate their collective knowledge and information to predict future events.[27]   People buy and sell "contracts," which effectively assign a price to the likelihood of an event happening. Several prominent prediction markets sell contracts to members that yield payments based on the outcome of an uncertain future event,[28] such as the outcome of presidential elections, returns for Hollywood movies,[29] and crime forecasting.[30]   Even "data on past judicial behavior can be used to build prediction models."[31]   The Iowa Electronic Markets, which pools together predictions about the Presidential election, "has yielded very accurate predictions and also outperformed large-scale polling organizations."[32]

In a prediction market, the "market price [for the contracts] will be the best predictor of the event."[33]   The incentive to receive a payoff can "elicit the market's expectations of a range of different parameters."[34]   Prediction markets serve three primary roles: (1) they create "incentives to seek information"; (2) provide "incentives for truthful information revelation"; and (3) generate "an algorithm for aggregating diverse opinions."[35]   F.A. Hayek's writings about markets in general, where the price of goods is based on a range of information from a large group of people, accurately describe the nature of prediction markets.[36]   An important value of prediction markets, beyond creating a fun forum for competitors to test their soothsaying skills, is their value as "predictive tools."[37]

---

[27] Justin Wolfers & Eric Zitzewitz, *Prediction Markets*, J. ECON. PERSP., Spring 2004, at 107, 108 ("[P]articipants trade in contracts whose payoff depends on unknown future events.").

[28] Robert W. Hahn & Robert E. Litan, *Preface* to INFORMATION MARKETS: A NEW WAY OF MAKING DECISIONS xi, xi (Robert W. Hahn & Paul C. Tetlock eds., 2006).

[29] *See* sources cited in Note, *supra* note 15, at 1218 n.6 (citing, for example, FORESIGHT EXCHANGE, http://www.ideosphere.com (last visited Dec. 4, 2011); HOLLYWOOD STOCK EXCHANGE, http://www.hsx.com (last visited Dec. 4, 2011); INTRADE, http://www.intrade.com (last visited Dec. 4, 2011); IOWA ELECTRONIC MARKETS, http://www.biz.uiowa.edu/iem (last visited De. 4, 2011), as examples of prediction markets, as well as Bill Saporito, *Place Your Bets!*, TIME, Oct. 24, 2005, at 76, for general information).

[30] M. Todd Henderson, Justin Wolfers & Eric Zitzewitz, *Predicting Crime*, 52 ARIZ. L. REV. 15, 20 (2010) ("[T]he policy-relevant question is not whether prediction markets are accurate predictors of crime rates, but whether prediction markets yield more accurate crime rate forecasts than alternative approaches.").

[31] Adam M. Samaha, *Judicial Transparency in an Age of Prediction*, 53 VILL. L. REV. 829, 834 (2008); *see also infra* note 131 and accompanying text.

[32] Wolfers & Zitzewitz, *supra* note 27, at 112; *see also* Joyce Berg et al., *Results from a Dozen Years of Election Futures Markets Research*, *in* 1 HANDBOOK OF EXPERIMENTAL ECONOMIC RESULTS 742 (Charles R. Plott & Vernon L. Smith eds., 2008).

[33] Wolfers & Zitzewitz, *supra* note 27, at 108 ("[P]articipants trade in contracts whose payoff depends on unknown future events.").

[34] *Id.* at 109.

[35] *Id.* at 125.

[36] F.A. Hayek, *The Use of Knowledge in Society*, 35 AM. ECON. REV. 519, 520–26 (1945) (noting that a price system permits the transfer of collective value of goods by groups, and that value could not be known by any single member of the group).

[37] Wolfers & Zitzewitz, *supra* note 27, at 112.

III. Crowdsourcing: A Supreme Court Prediction Market

FantasySCOTUS, built on the collective wisdom of its over 5,000 members, is the first and only crowdsourced prediction market for the Supreme Court. The rules for FantasySCOTUS 1.0 were simple.[38] Members could make predictions about cases argued during the October 2009 Term, up until the day the case was decided. When the Supreme Court announced in advance that opinions would be issued, voting was disabled. After an opinion was issued, all future voting for that case was disabled.[39]

Members made predictions based on eleven parameters. First, members predicted whether the Supreme Court would affirm or reverse and remand the lower court's decision. Members were awarded one point for getting the outcome correct. Second, members predicted how the Court would split: 9–0 affirm, 8–1 affirm, 7–2 affirm, 6–3 affirm, 5–4 affirm, 5–4 reverse, 6–3 reverse, 7–2 reverse, 8–1 reverse, 9–0 reverse, or other (including 4–1–4 splits or where less than nine Justices vote). Three points were awarded for correctly predicting the split. Third, for the remaining nine parameters, the members predicted whether each of the nine Justices would vote to affirm or reverse and remand. One point was awarded for each correct prediction. For a single case, members could earn up to thirteen points.

In the event that a case was not decided—for example, if certiorari was dismissed as improvidently granted—no points were awarded. Admittedly, in some cases, the scoring was difficult. In cases where a Justice voted to affirm in part and reverse in part, it was often hard to characterize whether it was an affirmance or reversal. In these cases, the rules provided that the FantasySCOTUS Czar (Josh Blackman) would isolate the most prominent part of the opinion, and determine whether a Justice voted to affirm or reverse on that issue. FantasySCOTUS 2.0 has improved rules that clarify the scoring.[40]

"The success of prediction markets, like any market, can depend on their design and implementation."[41] FantasySCOTUS is not a traditional prediction market. It is free to play,[42] contracts are not sold, and buyers are not matched to sellers.[43] At its core,

---

[38] Josh Blackman, *League Rules*, FANTASYSCOTUS.NET, http://www.fantasyscotus.net/rules.html (last visited Dec. 4, 2011).

[39] On several occasions, due to a technical glitch, members were able to change their predictions after a case was decided but prior to the disabling of the voting feature, and effectively cheated. Those votes were eliminated, and the offenders were banned from FantasySCOTUS. Josh Blackman, *Fantasy Ethics: Cheating on FantasySCOTUS?*, JOSH BLACKMAN'S BLOG (Feb. 25, 2010, 12:05 AM), http://joshblackman.com/blog/?p=4198; *see also* Note, *supra* note 15, at 1222 ("Prediction markets are vulnerable to manipulation, although scholars do not agree on how serious the problem is.").

[40] *League Rules*, FANTASYSCOTUS, http://www.fantasyscotus.net/league-rules/ (last visited Dec. 28, 2011). The rules for FantasySCOTUS 2.0 are somewhat simpler. Rather than asking users to predict the overall outcome, and the split, the league asks users to simply predict whether a given Justice would vote to affirm. Focusing on this level of granularity allows the user to focus on each Justice and the main thrust of the case, rather than viewing the Court as a whole.

[41] Wolfers & Zitzewitz, *supra* note 27, at 120.

[42] Initially, there was no cost for law students and unemployed attorneys. Those who worked in the public sector paid a reduced fee. Those in private practice were asked to pay a nominal fee to help with site maintenance. Midway through the Term, the sign-up fee was eliminated, and everyone could play at no cost.

[43] Some research suggests that prediction markets that do not use real money may actually outperform those that force people to bet with their own wallets. Wolfers & Zitzewitz, *supra* note 27, at 120–21 ("One intriguing question is how much difference it makes whether prediction markets are run with real money or

though, it taps a "diversity of information [that] exists in a way that provides a basis for" predictions.[44] Perhaps FantasySCOTUS could be more accurately labeled a "prediction aggregation mechanism," a term coined by Professor Michael Abramowicz,[45] though for purposes of this essay, we rely on the broader conception of a prediction market.[46]

There are several potential flaws in FantasySCOTUS as a prediction market. First, some "market participants [may] trade according to their desires, rather than objective probability assessments."[47] A study suggests that participants in political markets purchase contracts in a way that reflects their party affiliation.[48] While FantasySCOTUS 1.0 did not request that members identify their ideology—we requested this information in version 2.0, and hope to elaborate on this dynamic in future work—anecdotal evidence suggests that certain members consistently voted in a manner that reflected a particular jurisprudential ideology.

In prediction markets where the "marginal trades are motivated by profits rather than partisanship, prices will reflect the assessments of (unbiased) profit motive."[49] The FantasySCOTUS market, which rewarded members with bragging rights—the grand prize was the coveted "golden gavel trophy"[50]—rather than profits, may be more susceptible to such confirmation bias. Where allowing anonymous users to make predictions without incentives may weaken the accuracy of the prediction market, it may offer the benefit of enabling a more accurate and honest polling of how the Court is perceived.[51] In other words, when not motivated by a desire to win, users may simply vote based on their personal preferences of how the Justices *should* vote—and such data are quite valuable.

Second, the outcomes of Supreme Court decisions are secret. Unlike other prediction markets where people may receive various tips about what will happen (insider trading of sorts), the votes of the Supreme Court are only known by the Justices, and their clerks (in the FantasySCOTUS rules, current clerks are banned from playing). Prediction markets "perform poorly when asked to aggregate closely guarded secret information."[52] Outside of the manner in which the question presented is phrased, discussions during oral arguments, and the questions the Justices pose, there is generally no inside information as

---

with some form of play money. . . . However, we do not yet have sufficient comparative data to know the extent to which money makes predictions more accurate. Indeed, it has been argued that the play money exchanges may even outperform real-money exchanges because 'wealth' can only be accumulated through a history of accurate prediction. . . . One practical advantage of play money contracts is that they offer more freedom to experiment with different kinds of contracts.").

[44] *Id.* at 120.

[45] *See* U.S. Patent No. 7,707,062 B2 (filed May 17, 2007) (discussing a "prediction aggregation mechanism").

[46] *See generally* Miriam A. Cherry & Robert L. Rogers, *Tiresias and the Justices: Using Information Markets to Predict Supreme Court Decisions*, 100 Nw. U. L. Rev. 1141, 1142 (2006).

[47] Wolfers & Zitzewitz, *supra* note 27, at 118.

[48] Robert Forsythe et al., *Wishes, Expectations and Actions: A Survey on Price Formation in Election Stock Markets*, 39 J. Econ. Behav. & Org. 83, 89–93 (1999).

[49] Wolfers & Zitzewitz, *supra* note 27, at 118.

[50] *The October Term 2009 Golden Gavel Trophy*, FANTASYSCOTUS, http://www.fantasyscotus.net/news/the-october-term-2009-golden-gavel-trophy/ (last visited Dec. 28, 2011).

[51] *See infra* Part VII-A.

[52] Note, *supra* note 15, at 1225.

to how the Justices will vote.[53] This is an inherent weakness in FantasySCOTUS—and Supreme Court prediction markets generally—that could not be alleviated, short of someone with personal knowledge leaking information to the public.

Third, general criticisms of prediction markets apply equally to FantasySCOTUS. According to one critical account, "Enthusiasm for 'many minds' arguments has infected legal academia."[54] Academics "now champion the virtues of groupthink, something once thought to have only vices."[55] With respect to legal prediction markets, the criticism is somewhat more acute: "[T]he circumstances in which prediction markets are inaccurate are precisely the circumstances in which law needs them most."[56] Specifically, "the performance of prediction markets is inversely correlated with how valuable their predictions would be."[57] If an event in the future, such as the President's nominee for the Supreme Court "is secret or knowledge about its likelihood is thin, . . . a prediction market will probably not produce accurate information."[58]

Predictors "tend to overvalue small probabilities and undervalue near certainties," and "prediction markets may perform poorly at predicting small probability events."[59] "Most intractable legal informational problems involve a kind of uncertainty—whether secret, idiosyncratic, or catastrophic—not susceptible to aggregation through a market mechanism."[60] Perhaps "information markets can improve knowledge in other areas, and so indirectly improve legal decisionmaking, but this role for information markets in law is considerably more niche-like than recent scholarly enthusiasm would imply."[61] Notwithstanding these potential shortcomings, FantasySCOTUS illustrates that a legal prediction market can be accurate, reliable, and useful to the academic community, and society at large. For a number of cases, where the conventional thinking pointed to one outcome—what some may call a near certainty—FantasySCOTUS was able to discern the "small probability" vote that was generally unforeseen by experts. As FantasySCOTUS develops, these legitimate concerns about prediction markets will hopefully be assuaged.

IV. TESTING THE WISDOM OF FANTASYSCOTUS

In order to assess the predictive power of FantasySCOTUS, we devised two frameworks. The first test was internal. We compared the predictions of the FantasySCOTUS power predictors—those that made predictions for more than seventy-five percent of the cases—with the FantasySCOTUS crowd—those that made predictions for less than seventy-five percent of the cases. With this data we could not conclude that the power predictors were superior to the crowd. In other words, while we were not able

---

[53] *Id.* ("The outcomes that judges would most like to predict are naturally those about which little is already known. In the legal context, thinness of information often results from secrecy.").

[54] *Id.* at 1217.

[55] *Id.*

[56] *Id.* at 1218.

[57] *Id.*

[58] *Id.*

[59] Wolfers & Zitzewitz, *supra* note 27, at 117.

[60] Note, *supra* note 15, at 1238.

[61] *Id.*

to prove that that the crowd was just as good as the power predictors, we were able to reject the alternative hypothesis that the power predictors were simply better.

The second test was external.   We compared the predictions of the FantasySCOTUS power predictors with the experts from the Supreme Court Forecasting Project, which we used as a baseline. With this approach, the diverse power predictor posse, in contrast with the largely homogenous credentialed experts from the Forecasting Project, permitted a statistically significant comparison to determine whether the wisdom of the crowds could trump the experts.   The power predictors outperformed the Forecasting Project's experts, though the results were not statistically significant. Next, we compared the accuracy of the power predictors with the accuracy of the decision tree developed by the Forecasting Project. This approach allowed us to weigh the wisdom of the crowds against the power of Super Cruncher algorithms. In this case, the decision tree surpassed the accuracy of all but the best power predictors.[62]

A. Methodology

Over 5,000 members made nearly 11,000 predictions for all eighty-one cases decided during the October 2009 Term. Predictions consisted of eleven data points: the outcome of the case (affirm or reverse), the split (9–0 affirm, 8–1 affirm, 7–2 affirm, 6–3 affirm, 5–4 affirm, 5–4 reverse, 6–3 reverse, 7–2 reverse, 8–1 reverse, 9–0 reverse, and other, including 4–1–4 splits), and the votes for each of the nine Justices (affirm or reverse and remand). The analysis in this essay only focuses on the outcome of the case. Whether the Court affirmed or reversed the lower court, as opposed to the numerous splits and individual votes of the Justices, is the simplest metric to compare.

Analyzing thousands of data points required focusing on some aspect of the predictions. We decided to focus on the ten most important cases—rather than all eighty-one cases, many of which received very few predictions, and lacked statistical significance—to focus the analysis. Rather than engaging in a debate about what cases were "most important" from a normative perspective, we decided—relying on a crowdsourced approach—that the users would be the best judge of what cases mattered the most. Using the total number of predictions for each case as a measurement of popularity is particularly valuable because it does not require value judgments to determine what data matter most. The metric itself is created directly from the data set with no transformation or processing. For the purposes of the discussion, the top ten most predicted cases will be listed in descending order, from the case with the most predictions to the case with the least predictions.

First, in *Citizens United v. Federal Elections Commission*, the Court held that Congress may not prohibit corporations and unions from making independent expenditures, which are protected speech under the First Amendment.[63] It was by far the most popular case of the Term: 901 members made predictions for *Citizens United*. The second most predicted case was *United States v. Stevens*, in which the Court struck down as unconstitutional a federal statute that criminalized the depiction of animal cruelty.[64] Third was *Maryland v. Shatzer*, where the Court held that police may properly question a

---

[62] *See infra* Table 4.
[63] Citizens United v. Fed. Elections Comm'n, 130 S. Ct. 876 (2010).
[64] United States v. Stevens, 130 S. Ct. 1577 (2010).

suspect who requests a lawyer, is then released, and a couple weeks later waives his right to a lawyer.[65] Fourth was *Johnson v. United States*, in which the Court held that a prior felony does not constitute a violent felony under the Armed Career Criminal Act when the prior felony did not require the government to prove the use of force.[66] Fifth was *Padilla v. Kentucky*, where the Court found that effective assistance of counsel to an undocumented worker requires advising him or her that a guilty plea may lead to a deportation.[67] Sixth, in *Graham v. Florida*, the Court determined that a life sentence without parole for a non-capital juvenile defendant violates the Eighth Amendment.[68] Seventh, in *Bloate v. United States*, the Court interpreted the Speedy Trial Act to not automatically exclude time for preparing pretrial motions; rather, the time is only excluded if the Court finds that such a delay serves justice.[69] Eighth, in *McDonald v. City of Chicago*, the Court held that the individual Second Amendment right to keep and bear arms also applies to the states.[70] Ninth, in *Perdue v. Kenny A.*, the Court found that higher than normal attorney's fees in a civil rights case are permissible only in extraordinary circumstances.[71] Tenth, in *Bilski v. Kappos*, the Court held that the Patent Act covers patentable subject matter that falls outside of the machine or transformation test.[72]

B. Defining the Power Predictors and the Crowd

To internally test the validity of the wisdom of the crowds—and whether crowds can outperform those with certain aptitudes—we focused on two groups of FantasySCOTUS members: the power predictors and the crowd. Power predictors were not selected on the basis of correctness, but rather unknowingly selected themselves by making predictions for more than seventy-five percent of the cases argued during the October 2009 Term (sixty-one out of the eighty-one cases). This group consisted of thirty members. The remaining FantasySCOTUS players—those who made predictions for less than seventy-five percent of the cases—are dubbed the crowd.

We chose not to simply pick the users with the highest accuracy rates because that would make the comparison meaningless. Picking the highest scorers would, by definition, ensure that they performed better than the crowd. Rather, we relied on the percentage of predictions as a measure of how invested users were in their predictions. Users who predicted more cases—the more popular cases as well as the obscure, less popular cases—likely devoted more effort towards predicting cases. FantasySCOTUS'

---

[65] Maryland v. Shatzer, 130 S. Ct. 1213 (2010).

[66] Johnson v. United States, 130 S. Ct. 1265 (2010).

[67] Padilla v. Kentucky, 130 S. Ct. 1473 (2010).

[68] Graham v. Florida, 130 S. Ct. 2011 (2010).

[69] Bloate v. United States, 130 S. Ct. 1345 (2010).

[70] McDonald v. City of Chicago, 130 S. Ct. 3020 (2010); *see also* Josh Blackman & Ilya Shapiro, *Keeping Pandora's Box Sealed: Privileges or Immunities, the Constitution in 2020, and Properly Extending the Right to Keep and Bear Arms to the States*, 8 GEO. J.L. & PUB. POL'Y 1, 17–22 (2010) (discussing *McDonald*); Alan Gura, Ilya Shapiro & Josh Blackman, *Extending the Right to Keep and Bear Arms: The Tell-Tale Privileges or Immunities Clause*, 2010 CATO SUP. CT. REV. 163 (2010).

[71] Perdue v. Kenny A., 130 S. Ct. 1662 (2010).

[72] Bilski v. Kappos, 130 S. Ct. 3218 (2010).

top three power predictors—those who made predictions for 75.7% of the cases—collectively fell only one prediction short of offering predictions for all of the cases.

The composition of the power predictor posse is quite varied, and members fell into five general types of members.[73] First, a number of power predictors had some Supreme Court experience, mostly with writing amicus briefs in law school Supreme Court clinics. The most accomplished player, solo practitioner David Mills,[74] successfully argued and won *Ortiz v. Jordan*.[75] Second, a few power predictors were professors—both of law and political science. One taught as an Associate Professor at Columbia Law School, another as a Political Science Professor at Rice University. Third, the vast majority of power predictors were law students and new attorneys. Most notable among this group was the champion, "Chief Justice" Justin Donoho,[76] who recently graduated from the University of Chicago, worked as a law clerk on the Seventh Circuit, and served as a research assistant to Judge Richard A. Posner.[77] Other top student power predictors attended Southern Illinois School of Law, Vermont Law School, and the University of Tulsa.

Fourth, some power predictors were attorneys who lacked appellate experience. One member in this group has a small general practice firm with his wife in Alabama. Finally, the most interesting group of power predictors consisted of players who had no formal legal training and never attended law school. One of the best players is an actuary who never attended law school and, quite impressively, taught himself constitutional law in high school. He was the "Chief Justice" of the October 2010 Term of FantasySCOTUS.[78] The eighth-ranked player never attended law school and works as an air traffic controller. The eighteenth-ranked player is not a lawyer and earned a degree in Geophysical Engineering from Montana Tech.

Admittedly, our selection of the power predictors is somewhat flawed in that they were selected *ex post*. As a practical matter, we had no other choice. There was no way to select a group of top players *ex ante* in the first season of FantasySCOTUS, when everyone started with a collective score of zero. Similarly, setting the prediction level at seventy-five percent was arbitrary, as we had no other historical baseline to rely on. Any accuracy derived from the increased participation was not deliberate on our part, although incidentally our power predictors effectively overlapped with the top-ranked players.

As our analysis suggests, we can state to a degree of statistical significance that the power predictors' results were not based on chance—that is, predicting that every case the Court hears would be reversed, for example, with hopes of guessing one's way to a high score. For the second season, however, the top performers (those with the most

---

[73] Some, but not all of the power predictors responded to a survey inquiring about who they were and how they made predictions. Some of those who responded requested various degrees of anonymity. For a detailed discussion of who they are and how they made their predictions, see Josh Blackman, *Who Are the FantasySCOTUS Experts and How Do They Make Predictions?*, JOSH BLACKMAN'S BLOG (May 4, 2011, 11:14 PM), http://joshblackman.com/blog/?p=6875.

[74] Mark Curriden, *The Long Shot*, A.B.A. J., Nov. 2010, at 52.

[75] *See* Ortiz v. Jordan, 131 S. Ct. 884 (2011).

[76] *Congratulations to Justin Donoho, the Chief Justice of FantasySCOTUS OT2009*, FANTASYSCOTUS, http://www.fantasyscotus.net/?p=94 (last visited Dec. 28, 2011).

[77] *Id.*

[78] Josh Blackman, *JoshCast: Interview with Jacob Berlove, Chief Justice of FantasySCOTUS OT 2010*, JOSH BLACKMAN'S BLOG (July 5, 2011, 9:01 AM), http://joshblackman.com/blog/2011/07/05/joshcast-interview-with-justice-donoho-chief-justice-of-fantasyscotus-ot-2010/.

accurate predictions) from the first season who returned are designated as repeat power predictors. We are interested to see how repeat performers do. In future work, we will select the next generation of power predictors.

C. Comparing the Power Predictors and the Crowd

We compared the accuracy of the crowd with the accuracy of the power predictors using two tests. First, we compared the outcome accuracy rate of the two tests—that is, whether they correctly predicted that the Court would affirm or reverse a case—as a percentage. This approach allowed us to focus on one clear metric, the outcome. Second, we considered all parameters of the prediction—the outcome, the split, and the votes to the individual Justices—and compared the total scores of the crowd and the power predictors. This approach provides a more comprehensive analysis to see how granular and detailed the accuracy of the crowd is—it is much more difficult to predict the individual votes than to simply predict an overall affirm or reverse outcome. Based on these two approaches, we could not conclude that the power predictors' predictions were superior to those of the crowd, supporting the validity of the wisdom of the crowds.

1. Accuracy of Forecasting the Outcome

Table 1 presents the outcome of each case, the crowd to power predictor ratio, the accuracy of the crowd,[79] whether it was significant,[80] the power predictor accuracy rate, whether it was significant, and the date of oral arguments.

TABLE 1. GENERAL GROUP STATISTICS

Case	Outcome	Crowd-to-Power Predictor Ratio	Crowd		Power Predictor		Number of Predictions	Oral Arguments Date
			Accuracy	Outcome Sig.	Accuracy	Outcome Sig.		
Citizens United	Reverse	24.743	61%	Yes (99%)	71%	Yes (99%)	901	9/9/09
Stevens	Affirm	16.135	83%	Yes (99%)	92%	Yes (99%)	634	10/6/09
Shatzer	Reverse	15.946	50%	No	65%	Yes (90%)	627	10/5/09
Johnson	Reverse	6.868	45%	No	50%	No	299	10/6/09
Padilla	Reverse	7.027	38%	Yes (99%)	35%	Yes (90%)	297	10/13/09
McDonald	Reverse	6.459	66%	Yes (99%)	65%	Yes (99%)	276	3/2/10

---

[79] The accuracy rate, expressed as a percentage, represents the percentage of each group that correctly predicted the outcome of a case.
[80] We calculated whether each of the outcomes—crowd and power predictors—was statistically significant, based on confidence intervals. In statistics, the determination of reliability—that is, how likely the data express a clear outcome (affirm or reverse)—can be specified based on various confidence intervals. The most commonly used intervals, 90%, 95%, and 99%, are sorted in increasing reliability. A 99% confidence level, the gold standard of statistical measures, indicates that the sample results are most reliable. In contrast, 95% and, even more so, 90% confidence intervals express that the data are less likely to be reliable. Each group is independently above the threshold for the Central Limit Theorem. The larger the crowd, the more accurate the results are.

Graham	Reverse	5.486	49%	No	60%	No	240	11/9/09
Bloate	Reverse	5.405	20%	Yes (99%)	32%	Yes (95%)	237	10/6/09
Perdue	Reverse	4.514	57%	Yes (90%)	62%	No	204	10/14/09
Bilski	Affirm	4.270	80%	Yes (99%)	78%	Yes (99%)	195	11/9/09

Due to the novelty of the data set, we created a custom decision rule to determine if each group, as a whole, was correct (or incorrect) above a certain threshold. A confidence interval is a range where the values of the test statistics—in FantasySCOTUS, the affirm or reverse percentage—may differ due to statistical noise.[81] Statistical noise could manifest as uncertainty introduced through sampling.[82] A determination was reliable when the confidence interval did not include 50%, meaning that enough predictions for either affirm or reverse were—for statistical purposes—in agreement with the direction of the outcome such that we could reliably assess the prediction at a given confidence interval. This analysis yields a definitive affirm or reverse decision for the group. Otherwise, the predictions would not be conclusive for affirmation or reversal.

The data suggest several statistically significant trends. First, the number of predictions made roughly tracked the date of oral arguments. The earlier the case was argued, the more predictions were made. Generally, members made predictions following oral arguments. On November 11, 2009 when FantasySCOTUS launched and went viral, *Citizens United, Stevens,* and *Shatzer,* the three cases with the highest crowd-power predictor ratio—which received 901, 634, and 627 predictions, respectively—had already been argued. However, *McDonald,* a landmark Second Amendment case not argued until March 2, 2010—nearly four months after FantasySCOTUS launched—received only 277 predictions. It seems that the number of predictions dropped off over the course of the Supreme Court Term, and web traffic analytics anecdotally support this conclusion.

Cases argued later in the Term had fewer members of the crowd make predictions. Yet the dedicated detail of power predictors voted consistently throughout the Term. Additionally, the accuracy of the predictions seems to indicate that the weakest predictors of the crowd left at an early stage. In this sense, cases argued later in the Term had a more reliable set of predictors.

Second, there was an interesting interplay between the statistical significance of the data and the accuracy of the resulting predictions. Statistical significance must be distinguished from accuracy. Significance refers to how reliable the data are, while accuracy refers to how correct the data are—the difference between precision and correctness.[83] For all cases, in light of the smaller sample size, the power predictor group had a larger confidence interval—meaning more statistical noise and less reliable results. Yet, the power predictor group still provided more accurate results. Conversely, the

---

[81] B.S. EVERITT, THE CAMBRIDGE DICTIONARY OF STATISTICS 86 (2d ed. rev. 2003) ("Confidence interval: A range of values, calculated from the sample observations, that are believed, with a particular probability, to contain the true parameter value.").

[82] *Id.* at 332 ("Sampling error: The difference between the sample result and the population characteristic being estimated. In practice, the sampling error can rarely be determined because the population characteristic is not usually known.").

[83] JOINT COMM. FOR GUIDES IN METROLOGY, INTERNATIONAL VOCABULARY OF METROLOGY—BASIC AND GENERAL CONCEPTS AND ASSOCIATED TERMS 21–22 (2008).

crowd had a smaller confidence interval—less statistical noise and more reliable results—but produced less accurate results. This illustrates the difference between reliability viz. statistical significance and accuracy. The crowd was more reliably wrong, meaning that, while the results were a reliable expression of the crowd's predictions, those predictions were inaccurate. In contrast, the power predictor group was less reliable but more accurate.

The predictions for eight of the ten cases, excluding *Johnson* and *Graham*, were statistically significant. In this context, statistical significance means that the data show a definitive affirm or reverse outcome according to our decision rule. For *Johnson* and *Graham*, which were not statistically significant, the prediction data for affirm and reverse are statistically 50/50—equally likely to generate an affirm or reverse result—and thus were inconclusive. The prediction data for *Padilla* and *Bloate* provide for statistically significant results, yet the ultimate affirm-or-reverse predictions were incorrect. For the remaining six cases, which were decided correctly, the prediction data provide for statistically significant results.

For *Shatzer*, the power predictor group's predictions proved statistically significant, while the crowd's predictions were not statistically significant. This split represents an exception to the rule, because generally, a smaller sample size (power predictors) would not be statistically significant, whereas a larger sample size (crowd) would be statistically significant. Here, the power predictor group (thirty members) was more statistically significant than the crowd (about 590 members). This suggests that, for *Shatzer*, the power predictor group was more reliable—that is, a decisive consensus existed with respect to the affirm or reverse outcome.

2. Accuracy of Forecasting Outcome, Split, and Individual Votes

Members of FantasySCOTUS made predictions for the outcome, split, and individual votes of each Justice. A perfect score was thirteen.[84] Table 2 calculates two averages for each case—the average score for each member of the power predictor group (Power Predictor Average Points) and the average score each member of the crowd (Crowd Average Points). For each average, we calculated the standard deviation.[85] As an additional measure of statistical difference between the two groups, we calculated the Welch's *t*-test.[86] To measure overall performance (that is, how each group performed

---

[84] *See supra* Part III.
[85] The standard deviation for each average reveals how individual scores—that is, the votes of individual members in each group—were distributed around the average. Standard deviation is a common statistic used to measure the spread of data points within a sample. EVERITT, *supra* note 81, at 360. The standard deviation is equal to the square root of the variance. *Id.* For example, if the average score was nine and the standard deviation was one, that would indicate that a certain number of members, within one standard deviation, scored between eight and ten points. A larger standard deviation indicates that there was a greater spread from the average for members in that group as a total.
[86] If two data points are significantly different, that suggests that the difference is not due to statistical noise or randomness. A Welch's *t*-test, using standard deviation, determines whether the two averages were significantly different from each other. We indicated if the results were statistically significant, and whether the confidence level was 90%, 95%, or 99%. *See generally* B.L. Welch, *The Generalization of 'Student's' Problem When Several Different Population Variances Are Involved*, 34 BIOMETRIKA 28 (1947). A *t*-test is a commonly used statistical test to determine if two samples are significantly different through hypothesis testing. A Welch's *t*-test is appropriate in this case, due to its relaxed assumptions, and

over all the cases), we averaged together each individual average from the ten cases—in other words, it is an average of the averages. Based on this average, we calculated the overall standard deviation for each classification.

TABLE 2. AVERAGE SCORES

Case	Crowd		Power Predictor		Significant? (Welch's *t*-test)
	Average Points	Standard Deviation	Average Points	Standard Deviation	
Citizens United	8.62	4.16	9	4.22	No
Stevens	8.17	2.53	8.57	2.23	No
Shatzer	6.9	1.86	8.11	2.55	Yes (99%)
Johnson	6.18	2.41	7.08	2.97	Yes (90%)
Padilla	5.65	2.48	6.08	2.61	No
McDonald	9.17	3.5	9.68	2.99	No
Graham	5.42	3.07	6.49	2.91	Yes (95%)
Bloate	6.56	1.38	6.81	1.58	No
Perdue	6.65	2.86	6.75	2.86	No
Bilski	9.22	3.34	10.68	3.1	Yes (95%)
Avg. of Avg.	7.25	1.43	7.93	1.53	No

¶ 18   For all ten cases, the average member of the power predictor group scored more points than the average member of the crowd. The power predictor average, 7.93 points, was higher than the crowd average, 7.25 points. The biggest difference was in *Bilski*, where the power predictor group scored on average 10.68 points, while the crowd group on average scored only 9.22 points, a difference of 1.46. The case with the least difference was *Perdue*, where the power predictor group scored on average 6.75 points, while the crowd group on average scored only 6.65 points, a difference of 0.1.

¶ 19   While members of the power predictor group scored more points on average, they generally had a higher standard deviation—in other words, a larger point spread—around that average than members of the crowd group. Using *Shatzer* as a typical example, the standard deviation of the power predictor group was 2.55, more than 33% greater than the 1.86 standard deviation of the crowd group. This indicates some uncertainty within the power predictors' forecasts. Perhaps power predictors, convinced of their individual views of the case, are more likely to buck trends and make less conventional predictions about individual Justice behavior. The crowd tends to be more unified in this sense; adhering to conventional views of how the Justices will vote perhaps indicates that crowds are more influenced by media coverage.[87]

---

does not require that the variance within a sample be the same. Without the data set, we could not ensure that the variance would be the same between different samples.

[87] *See infra* Part VI-A.

The Welch's *t*-test in six of the ten cases yielded no significant results. That is, in six of the ten cases the crowd was just as likely as the power predictors to predict the correct outcome. Further, in light of the extensive media coverage of *Citizens United*, *Stevens*, and *McDonald*,[88] any informational advantage the power predictors might have had over the crowd was minimized. For *Shatzer*, *Johnson*, and *Graham*, the difference between the two groups was significant. In these cases, the power predictors may have had insight that the crowd did not—perhaps they gleaned some clue from oral arguments that the media overlooked or discerned how the Justices would vote from the arguments in the briefs.

3. Analysis

The results do not conclusively prove that the power predictors' forecasts were superior to those of the crowd. Although the power predictors generally do better, the crowd is able to make rather strong predictions to bridge the gap. This lends support to the wisdom of the crowds theory, wherein a larger pool of predictors with a broader range of knowledge can often predict as well, if not better, than knowledgeable individuals.

However, this does not hold true for all cases. In the marginal cases, the crowd performs well, but just not as well as the power predictors do. Generally, the power predictors make more informed predictions, although the predictions lack high levels of accuracy.[89] The lack of precision could very well reflect a professional hubris of sorts. With too much knowledge, and perhaps over-confidence, the power predictors may have second-guessed conventional wisdom, and prudence. In contrast, the crowd is more unified in its results, and perhaps influenced by extensive media coverage of the cases.[90] In this respect, the power predictors exhibit some of the flaws particular to experts, and these results demonstrate how a crowd can smooth out these errors.[91] In summary, the power predictors are only better predictors in the marginal case. FantasySCOTUS' wise crowds are about as accurate as the power predictors, meaning individuals who only make a few predictions, when aggregated, were almost as accurate as those who made many predictions.

4. Insulating Results from Randomness

Our statistical modeling, combined with the disparate nature of the Supreme Court docket, helps to mitigate the risk of randomness weakening the reliability of the comparisons and trends. The outcome of one case, generally, will not affect the outcome of a second case (unless they are precedentially related). For example, *United States v. Stevens*, decided early in the Term, had no impact on *Bilski v. Kappos*, decided at the end of the Term. These cases are *independent trials*—the voting in past cases has no impact

---

[88] *See infra* Part VI-A.
[89] Blackman, *supra* note 73 (discussing the sources power predictors rely on to make their decisions).
[90] *Id.*
[91] MICHAEL ABRAMOWICZ, PREDICTOCRACY: MARKET MECHANISMS FOR PUBLIC AND PRIVATE DECISION MAKING 38 (2007) (Aggregated data may "in part cancel out random errors that individuals make in predictions by overweighing or underweighing particular pieces of evidence.").

on the voting in future unrelated cases.[92] Or, to put it another way, flipping a coin once has no impact on flipping the coin a second time.[93]

When comparing a user's performance to a possible random performance—flipping a coin for every prediction—we consider the cumulative results of individual votes, rather than the overall score.[94] In other words, we count the number of times a coin landed on the correct side, rather than the total number of heads or tails. Because the cases are independent due to the different legal doctrines and factual predicates, it is much harder for a user to randomly make predictions to obtain a high score over the course of the entire Supreme Court Term with eighty-one cases decided by the same set of Justices. Specifically, where we presented data we indicated whether they were significant and at what confidence level (90%, 95%, or 99%). With data at these confidence levels, we were able to assert that the result was not due to randomness or chance.

Our methodologies also prevent a statistical "quasi-miracle,"[95] whereby users could randomly predict all of the cases accurately. Assume an infinite number of monkeys were stationed at FantasySCOTUS iPads, randomly making predictions,[96] and obtained a perfect score. A single primate, let's call him Ape Fortas, would need to correctly predict each and every case. The odds of Ape Fortas accomplishing this task are infinitesimally small.[97] Even 5,000 (the number of FantasySCOTUS players) apes mashing away on five-thousand monkey-friendly iPads would not increase the odds of any one player predicting all of the cases correctly. This small sample size is not even close to the same

---

[92] STUART J. RUSSELL & PETER NORVIG, ARTIFICIAL INTELLIGENCE: A MODERN APPROACH 477–79 (2d ed. 2003) (discussing the various forms of independence used in decision making and probability theory).
[93] Formally, coin flips belong to a class of stochastic processes called Bernoulli processes, which use a constant probability of binary outcomes in multiple trials. CHARLES M. GRINSTEAD & J. LAURIE SNELL, INTRODUCTION TO PROBABILITY 96–97 (2d rev. ed. 1998), available at
http://www.dartmouth.edu/~chance/teaching_aids/books_articles/probability_book/amsbook.mac.pdf.
[94] A binomial distribution is the creation of a probability distribution depending on constant probability, the number of trials, and the number of successes to determine the likelihood of conditional outcomes. Michelle Lacey, The Binomial Distribution, YALE U. DEPARTMENT STAT.,
http://www.stat.yale.edu/Courses/1997-98/101/binom.htm (last visited Dec. 28, 2011).
[95] Quasi-miracles are thought of as the logical equivalent of denying the existent of absolutes, i.e. objects always fall towards the ground or a series of a million coin flips will come up heads. For practical purposes, such events are extremely rare, but are an important part of logical statements. See J. Robert G. Williams, Chances, Counterfactuals, and Similarity, 77 PHIL. & PHENOMENOLOGICAL RES. 385, 389 (2008).
[96] The earliest mention of the monkey thought experiment, where one of an infinite number of monkeys, pounding away at typewriters, produces the complete works of Shakespeare, was introduced by Émile Borel, a French mathematician in 1913. Émile Borel, La Mécanique Statique et L'irréversibilité [Static Mechanics and Irreversibility], 3 JOURNAL DE PHYSIQUE THÉORIQUE ET APPLIQUÉE [J. PHYS.] 189 (1913) (Fr.).
[97] Richard Dawkins lays out the probability of writing a twenty-eight character sentence from Shakespeare by a monkey on a typewriter with just the twenty-six letters and the spacebar as $(1/27)^{28}$. RICHARD DAWKINS, THE BLIND WATCHMAKER: WHY THE EVIDENCE OF EVOLUTION REVEALS A UNIVERSE WITHOUT DESIGN 46–47 (3d ed. 1996). The monkey has a 1 in 27 chance of getting each character right, but must get the characters correct in sequence, causing the exponential probability. Id. at 47. In our case, Ape Fortas would face the odds of $(1/2)^{61}$ (sixty-one represents 75% of the eighty-one cases decided). Although this number is much larger than the monkey's odds, it would still be highly unlikely to occur.

order of magnitude to compare with all those prescient prognosticating primates.[98]   The approach we used attempted to insulate the data from logical and statistical problems of randomness.   Further, at the conclusion of the Term we verified that no member of FantasySCOTUS made predictions by selecting reverse for every case, thus confirming that predictions were not made randomly, at least using this strategy.

D. The Supreme Court Forecasting Project

In a path-breaking article, a group of legal and political science "Super Crunchers"[99] developed a decision tree model, based on the prior decisions of the nine Justices, to predict outcomes of Supreme Court cases during the October 2002 Term.[100] The article compared those outcomes to the predictions of a group of experts.[101]   The Project's decision tree did not consider the legal merits of a particular case.   Instead the authors based their model on six variables:[102] (1) the case's circuit, or lower court, of origin; (2) issue area of the case;[103] (3) type of appellant;[104] (4) type of respondent;[105] (5)

---

[98] One programmer was able to recreate the complete works of Shakespeare at random using a few million virtual monkeys. Jesse Anderson, *A Few Million Monkeys Randomly Recreate Shakespeare*, JESSE ANDERSON BLOG (Sept. 23, 2011), http://www.jesse-anderson.com/2011/09/a-few-million-monkeys-randomly-recreate-shakespeare/.

[99] AYRES, *supra* note 5, at 10 ("Super Crunchers . . . have analyzed large datasets to discover empirical correlations between seemingly unrelated things.").

[100] *See* Ruger et al., *supra* note 4.

[101] *See* Ruger et al., *supra* note 4, at 1154–55.

[102] *Id.* at 1163.   The variables the Project utilized were based on the Supreme Court database definitions, which provide coding corresponding to each variable. *Id.* at 1163 n.45. The coding is too extensive to be replicated in the footnotes, but is available on the Supreme Court Database's website. *See* HAROLD SPAETH ET AL., SUPREME COURT DATABASE CODE BOOK: 2011 RELEASE 01, at 1, 12, 14, 20, 27, 35, 44 (2011), *available at* http://scdb.wustl.edu/_brickFiles/2011_01/SCDB_2011_01_codebook.pdf.

[103] *See* SPAETH ET AL., *supra* note 102, at 35. There are too many issue areas to list (fourteen), but as an example, the ten cases discussed above have the following issue areas, as coded in the data available at SUPREME CT. DATABASE, http://scdb.wustl.edu: *Citizens United v. Fed. Elections Comm'n*, 130 S. Ct. 876 (2010) (First Amendment); *United States v. Stevens*, 130 S. Ct. 1577 (2010) (First Amendment); *Maryland v. Shatzer*, 130 S. Ct. 1213 (2010) (criminal procedure); *Johnson v. United States*, 130 S. Ct. 1265 (2010) (criminal procedure); *Padilla v. Kentucky*, 130 S. Ct. 1473 (2010) (criminal procedure); *Graham v. Florida*, 130 S. Ct. 2011 (2010) (criminal procedure); *Bloate v. United States*, 130 S. Ct. 1345 (2010) (criminal procedure); *McDonald v. City of Chicago*, 130 S. Ct. 3020 (2010) (criminal procedure); *Perdue v. Kenny A.*, 130 S. Ct. 1662 (2010) (attorneys); *Bilski v. Kappos*, 130 S. Ct. 3218 (2010) (economic activity).

[104] *See* SPAETH ET AL., *supra* note 102, at 12 (explaining the "petitioner" variable as referring to the party who petitioned the Supreme Court). Again, the types of appellants are too numerous to list (300), but for the ten cases discussed, the types of appellants as coded in the database include: *Citizens United*, 130 S. Ct. 876 (political candidate, activist, committee, party, party member, organization, or elected official); *Stevens*, 130 S. Ct. 1577 (United States); *Shatzer*, 130 S. Ct. 1213 (state); *Johnson*, 130 S. Ct. 1265 (defendant); *Padilla*, 130 S. Ct. 1473 (alien, person subject to a denaturalization proceeding, or one whose citizenship is revoked); *Graham*, 130 S. Ct. 2011 (juvenile); *Bloate*, 130 S. Ct. 1345 (defendant); *McDonald*, 130 S. Ct. 3020 (resident); *Perdue*, 130 S. Ct. 1662 (government official, or an official of an agency established under an interstate compact); *Bilski*, 130 S. Ct. 3218 (inventor, patent assigner, trademark owner or holder).

[105] *See* SPAETH ET AL., *supra* note 102, at 14. Again, the types of respondents are too numerous to list (this variable uses the same coding as types of appellants), but for the ten cases discussed, the type of respondents as coded in the database include: *Citizens United*, 130 S. Ct. 876 (Federal Election Commission); *Stevens*, 130 S. Ct. 1577 (person convicted of a crime); *Shatzer*, 130 S. Ct. 1213 (defendant); *Johnson*, 130 S. Ct. 1265 (United States); *Padilla*, 130 S. Ct. 1473 (state); *Graham*, 130 S. Ct. 2011 (state);

ideological direction of the lower court ruling (liberal or conservative, however nebulously that is defined);[106] and (6) whether the petitioner argued that a law or practice being challenged was unconstitutional.[107]   The decision tree works by starting with a question, such as "Is the lower court decision liberal?," and based on whether the answers to the questions are yes or no, the tree predicts how a Justice would vote.[108]

After members of the project manually coded the value of each of these variables for all cases argued during the October 2002 Term, the model predicted the vote for each Justice based upon the decision tree.[109]   The model scanned for numeric patterns rather than considering the merits of the case, a Super Cruncher algorithm that differs from the way that the experts considered cases.   The trees ultimately yielded an affirm or reverse vote for each case.[110]

To test the accuracy of the decision tree model, the authors vetted and recruited a coterie of reputable Supreme Court followers.   They selected these experts based on factors including writing, experience,[111] appellate practice before the Court,[112] and Supreme Court clerkships.[113]   At the conclusion of the October 2002 Term, the authors compared the results from the Super Crunching decision-tree model[114] and the experts.   Their model predicted 75% of the cases correctly, which was more accurate than their experts (a sample size of three) who only predicted 59.1% of the cases correctly.[115]

The authors provided a number of reasons to explain this result, such as the fact that the model predicted the economic activity cases much better than the experts.[116]   The main factor, unsurprisingly, was the ability of the decision tree to predict the votes of Justices O'Connor and Kennedy.[117]   The Project's authors noted that the "model seems to have captured patterns in [Justice O'Connor's] decisional behavior that the experts did not recognize."[118]   Generally, lawyers can use "their experience along with traditional methods of legal analysis such as logic, analogy, and statutory interpretation to predict

---

Bloate, 130 S. Ct. 1345 (United States); *McDonald*, 130 S. Ct. 3020 (city, town, township, village, or borough government or governmental unit); *Perdue*, 130 S. Ct. 1662 (child, children, including adopted or illegitimate); *Bilski*, 130 S. Ct. 3218 (Department or Secretary of Commerce).

[106] *See* SPAETH ET AL., *supra* note 102, at 27.

[107] *Id.* at 44.

[108] *See, e.g.*, Ruger et al., *supra* note 4, at 1166 fig.1.

[109] *Id.* at 1163–67.

[110] *See id.*

[111] *Id.* at 1168.

[112] *Id.* at 1178 ("The practicing attorneys who participated in [the Supreme Court Forecasting Project] are appellate lawyers who appear regularly before the Supreme Court. Prediction of Supreme Court outcomes, in order to advise clients and develop litigation strategies, is an important element of their professional role."). Unfortunately, the authors did not list the identity of their "experts." The effect that lack of anonymity may have on an expert's willingness to publicly declare her predictions—and thereby open herself up to criticism if the prediction turned out to be incorrect—is unclear.

[113] *Id.* at 1168.

[114] AYRES, *supra* note 5, at 10 (noting that Super Crunching "is statistical analysis that impacts real-world decisions").

[115] *See, e.g.*, Ruger et al., *supra* note 4, at 1171.

[116] *Id.* at 1175. According to the Supreme Court Database codebook, "Economic activity is largely commercial and business related; it includes tort actions and employee actions vis-a-vis employers." SPAETH ET AL., *supra* note 102, at 34.

[117] Ruger et al., *supra* note 4, at 1172–75.

[118] *Id.* at 1173.

case outcomes for their clients."[119] However, statistical models, such as the decision tree used in the Forecasting project "often turn out to be better crystal balls than traditional experts."[120]

E. Comparing the Power Predictors and the Forecasting Project

This section compares the accuracy of the FantasySCOTUS power predictors and crowd with the Supreme Court Forecasting Project's experts and the decision tree. The power predictors predicted 64.7% of the cases correctly, surpassing the Forecasting Project's Experts (59.1%), though the difference was not statistically significant. During the October 2002 Term, the Project's model predicted 75% of the cases correctly, which was more accurate than all but the most accurate power predictors (those who had an average accuracy rate of 75.7%).

1. Of Experts and Crowds

Comparisons between the Forecasting Project's experts and the FantasySCOTUS power predictors are imprecise for several reasons. First, the FantasySCOTUS data set is derived exclusively from a crowdsourced prediction market. We did not develop any predictive model nor did we vet any experts. Unlike the "experts" selected in the Forecasting Project—mostly appellate litigators, former Supreme Court clerks, and professors—the FantasySCOTUS power predictors unknowingly selected themselves by predicting more than seventy-five percent of the cases.

When comparing the power predictors with the Forecasting Project's experts, we are not comparing two similar groups. The former is effectively a crowd, while the latter is a group of specialized experts with largely similar experience and education. Though the subset of only three members reduces the sample size, the composition of the power predictors meets the minimum size required for the statistical measures we used, and can statistically be considered a crowd.[121] Empirically, this selection approximates a normal distribution, and is still valid.

Another manner in which the power predictors differed concerned the scope of cases predicted. In the Forecasting Project, the experts were subject-matter experts—that is, they made predictions in case areas they were familiar with, such as corporate law, criminal law, constitutional law, and so on. Only three of the eighty-three experts in the Forecasting Project made predictions for most of the cases. FantasySCOTUS had a stable thirty-member cadre of power predictors that predicted a majority of the cases, from a noteworthy Second Amendment case to a less popular original jurisdiction water rights case. The power predictors' wide breadth of knowledge and experience—from Supreme Court advocate to actuary—drew from a diverse crowd with a combined wisdom that yielded a respectable accuracy rate.

---

[119] Edward K. Cheng, *Will Quants Rule the (Legal) World?*, 107 MICH. L. REV. 967, 975 (2009).
[120] *Id.*
[121] When using statistics, most measures assume a normal distribution, which is technically very rare. When dealing with groups, however, the central limit theorem states that as the sample size increases, the sample more closely approximates a normal distribution. *See* EVERITT, *supra* note 81, at 64.

2. Analysis

It was impossible to compare FantasySCOTUS' data and the Forecasting Project's data directly. The Forecasting Project looked at the October 2002 Term and FantasySCOTUS considered the October 2009 Term. There were different cases, different arguments, and, perhaps most significantly, different Justices. Indeed, the ability to utilize a significant amount of data concerning that Court's prior decisions was part of the rationale underlying the Project's model, which had an unprecedented consistent membership for nearly a decade.[122]

FantasySCOTUS data are based on the Court's October 2009 Term, which was a brand-new natural court[123] with the addition of Justice Sotomayor and the departure of Justice Souter.[124] Also, the rest of the Court's makeup had changed in the recent past, with the passing of Chief Justice Rehnquist and Justice O'Connor's retirement.[125] Pundits are still trying to figure out the Roberts Court.[126] Any benefits that either the Forecasting Project's decision tree or the experts could gain from experience about the Court likely did not exist for the participants in FantasySCOTUS. In this sense, it was likely harder to predict the October 2009 Term than the October 2002 Term.

Putting aside the temporal disparities, in Table 3 we calculated the overall accuracy ratio as a percentage—which is not dependent on specific terms, cases, or Justices—for the FantasySCOTUS power predictors and crowd, as well as the Forecasting Project's experts and decision tree.[127]

TABLE 3. ACCURACY RATIOS

Group	Correct	Incorrect[128]	Total
FantasySCOTUS Crowd	30 (44.0%)	38 (56.0%)	68 (100%)
FantasySCOTUS Power Predictors	44 (64.7%)	24 (35.3%)	68 (100%)
Forecasting Project Experts' Aggregate Votes	101 (59.1%)	70 (40.9%)	171 (100%)
Forecasting Project Decision Tree	51 (75%)	17 (25%)	68 (100%)

The FantasySCOTUS crowd performed the worst, with an accuracy of 44%. In comparison with the Forecasting Project, the results from FantasySCOTUS power

---

[122] Ruger et al., *supra* note 4, at 1160–61.

[123] "A natural court is a period during which no personnel change occurs." SPAETH ET AL., *supra* note 102, at 30.

[124] *Members of the Supreme Court of the United States*, SUP. CT. U.S., http://www.supremecourt.gov/about/members.aspx (last visited Dec. 28, 2011).

[125] *Id.*

[126] *See e.g.*, Adam Liptak, *The Most Conservative in Decades*, N.Y. TIMES, July 25, 2010, at A1.

[127] The number of cases over which we measured the wins and losses (sixty-eight) is only equal to the number used in the Forecasting Project by coincidence. For example, we removed a number of split outcomes, such as *Free Enterprise Fund v. Public Co. Accounting Oversight Board*, 130 S. Ct. 3138 (2010), which was affirmed in part and reversed in part—an outcome that FantasySCOTUS could not easily predict. We also excluded cases which were carried over to the next term, such as *Harrington v. Richter*, 130 S. Ct. 1506 (2010) (mem.).

[128] For measurement purposes, cases where the same number of users predicted the case would be affirmed and reversed were treated as incorrect to avoid inflating the results. A tie is not a correct prediction.

predictors present a success story, in part. The power predictors, compared to the experts used in the Forecasting Project, predicted a higher percentage of cases correctly—64.7% to 59.1%. This 5.6% difference is not significant enough to draw any broad conclusions about the comparative expertise of the power predictors compared to the Project's experts.[129] If the two groups were to make predictions for the October 2012 Term, for example, we could not rule out the possibility that the Forecasting Project's experts would not outperform the FantasySCOTUS power predictors. These results suggest that further testing could bring the power predictors' results closer to the accuracy rate of the decision tree. The Forecasting Project's decision tree performed better than the FantasySCOTUS power predictors—75% to 64.7%. Comparatively, the FantasySCOTUS power predictors rank between the Forecasting Project's experts and the decision tree Super Cruncher algorithm.

   This comparison demonstrates that in this instance the wisdom of the crowds surpassed specialized experts, yet the Super Cruncher decision tree surpassed the crowd. As Professor Ayres noted, Super Crunchers have the power of "invading and displacing traditional experts," such as the Supreme Court experts the Forecasting Project selected, and, as this analysis shows, even the wisdom of the crowds.[130]

   Only three experts in the Forecasting Project accurately predicted a majority of the cases (more than 50%, thirty-five out of sixty-eight cases). In order to obtain a more accurate analysis and compare similar actors, Table 4 calculates the accuracy of predictions made by the top three Forecasting Project experts, the top three power predictors, as well as the Forecasting Project's decision tree.

TABLE 4. TOP THREE EXPERTS VERSUS TOP THREE POWER PREDICTORS

Group	Correct	Incorrect	Total
The Forecasting Project's Top Three Experts' Aggregate Votes	101 (59.1%)	70 (40.9%)	171 (100%)
The Forecasting Project's Decision Tree	51 (75.0%)	17 (25.0%)	68 (100%)
FantasySCOTUS' Top Three Power Predictors' Aggregate Votes	153 (75.7%)	49 (24.3%)	202 (100%)

   The FantasySCOTUS top triumvirate, who averaged a 75.7% accuracy rate, surpassed the top three Forecasting Project experts, who averaged a 59.1% accuracy rate. These results suggest that the experts who predicted the most cases for the Forecasting Project did not have the predictive prowess the authors were seeking. It is unclear if credentials and pedigree—such as scholarship, Supreme Court practice, and Supreme Court clerkships, the metrics the Forecasting Project selected—sufficiently signal a prognosticator's jurisprudential prescience. From these two data points—the Forecasting Project and FantasySCOTUS—it appears that credentials do not correlate with an ability to predict cases. The FantasySCOTUS top three power predictors not only outperformed the Forecasting Project's top three experts but they also slightly outperformed the

---

[129] At a 90% confidence interval, the margin of error for the power predictors' prediction is 63.7% ± 9.53%. At the low end, the power predictors' accuracy rate is only 54.17%, lower than the Forecasting Project's experts' rate. However, at the high end, the power predictors' accuracy is 73.23%, only 1.77% away from the decision tree's accuracy.

[130] AYRES, *supra* note 5, at 11.

decision-tree algorithm—75.7% to 75%. Justin Donoho, the Chief Justice of FantasySCOTUS, achieved an accuracy rate of 80%, while the second and third place users scored 75% and 72% respectively.

The current iteration of the decision tree, however, suffers from an obvious potential defect: "[I]t cannot handle newly appointed Justices."[131] The Forecasting Project took advantage of a consistent Court, with no new appointments in nearly a decade. During the October 2002 Term the Court had been made up of the same composition of Justices for almost a decade, since Justice Breyer had joined the Court in 1994.[132] The Forecasting Project made note of the natural court's[133] stability as a "unique opportunity for research."[134] That cohort of Justices had developed a stable relationship and voting pattern. In the last seven years, there have been four new appointments, including, most significantly, a new Chief Justice and the replacement of Justice O'Connor's swing vote with Justice Alito's more predictable vote.

While the decision tree was capable of generating an impressive accuracy rate, it might not be able to serve as a viable model for predicting Supreme Court cases year after year with a changing Court. "Even if a model could be constructed that perfectly fit past Supreme Court outcomes, we could not be certain that the model's variables and their relationships would remain useful over time."[135] In contrast, a crowdsourced model is flexible, resilient, and self-evolving. The members of the prediction market naturally take note of the changes in perceptions of the Justices, and adapt accordingly. If Justice Ginsburg were to retire next term, for example, the members may have some uncertainty as to how her successor will vote, but the market would still continue. Further, FantasySCOTUS does not rely on the manual categorization of cases—a subjective process that could insert biases and undue influences into any research. It will be possible in the future to use sophisticated algorithms to Super Crunch data from cases based on precedents, judicial philosophy, and rules of law, rather than on the voting history of a specific set of Justices. This methodology will allow for the prediction of cases, with any composition of Justices or judges, in any court. This evolution will enable the development of sophisticated judicial prediction engines.[136]

V. LIMITATIONS AND VALUE OF FANTASYSCOTUS 1.0

The value of the first season of FantasySCOTUS for the October 2009 Term, or FantasySCOTUS 1.0 as we call it, is quite modest, and should be kept in perspective. The FantasySCOTUS power predictors—those who made predictions for more than

---

[131] Samaha, *supra* note 31, at 834 (citing Ruger et al., *supra* note 4, at 1169–70, 1170 n.67).

[132] Ruger et al., *supra* note 4, at 1154; *see also Members of the Supreme Court of the United States, supra* note 124. This makeup of the Court lasted until the death of Chief Justice Rehnquist and the appointment of Chief Justice Roberts on September 29, 2005. This cadre of the Rehnquist Court, which lasted eleven years, is tied with the 1812–1823 Marshall Court for the longest group of Justices to serve together.

[133] Ruger, et al., *supra* note 4, at 1160 n.38 ("We adopt the commonly accepted definition of 'natural court' as referring to a period of time where the same nine Justices sit together on the Supreme Court without any composition change.") (citing JOAN BISKUPIC & ELDER WITT, THE SUPREME COURT AT WORK 315 n.a (2d ed. 1997)).

[134] *Id.* at 1160.

[135] Samaha, *supra* note 31, at 835.

[136] *See infra* Part VII-C (discussing the evolution of FantasySCOTUS).

seventy-five percent of the cases—were accurate in 64.7% of their predictions. The top three power predictors in FantasySCOTUS scored accuracy rates of 80%, 75%, and 72%, respectively (an average of 75.7%). As novel as these results are for the first season, FantasySCOTUS' current predictive capabilities are respectable, but not reliable—it was wrong, in the best case scenario, between 25% and 35% of the time.

Further, the Supreme Court typically reverses about 70% of the cases it decides each term.[137] During the October 2009 Term, for example, the Court reversed 72% of the cases decided on the merits.[138] In theory, predicting that the Supreme Court would reverse for every case would have yielded a 72% accuracy rate, and a top-three finish (we verified that no member of FantasySCOTUS made predictions in this manner).

FantasySCOTUS 1.0 should be understood for what it does and does not do. The authors of the Forecasting Project recognized that "[w]hat is notable, in light of all the attention focused on the Court, is that few have tried to systematically predict its decisions prospectively."[139] In its current iteration, FantasySCOTUS provides real-time *ex ante* predictions for individual cases. No other product performs this task for every case argued during the Term. Comparing these results to *ex post* aggregate analysis, such as the overall reversal rate of 72%, is imprecise. Simply concluding *ex post* that the Court reversed approximately 72% of all cases argued during a term provides no information about individual cases.

In contrast, FantasySCOTUS generated real-time predictions for every pending case—not just an aggregate overall prediction of what could have been after the Term. Further, the 72% reversal rate provides no information about which 72% of the docket will be reversed. The reversals do not necessarily occur during the first or last cases decided and are distributed throughout the Term, with the reversal granted based on the merits of the case, not the remaining number of cases and outcomes.

To put it another way, armed solely with the 72% aggregate reversal rate, a predictor would have no way *ex ante* of knowing how an individual case will turn out. To say that any individual case has a 72% likelihood of reversal is a statistical fallacy. One would have to know the specifics of the case to make that type of estimate. Comparing *ex post* aggregate trends and *ex ante* predictions fails to account for the independence of each case.

Additionally, the power predictors' accuracy rates of 65% to 75% consist of data points for each case, with an attendant confidence level of at least 90%, or in some cases 95% or 99%. For many of the 25% to 35% of cases that FantasySCOTUS failed to accurately predict, we knew *ex ante* that we lacked sufficient data to make an accurate prediction. For the most part, we were not surprised when the predictions were correct.

---

[137] *See, e.g., Stat Pack OT2010, supra* note 6, at 4 (indicating the Supreme Court reversed 72% of its cases during the October Term 2010); *Stat Pack OT2009, supra* note 6, at 10 (indicating the Supreme Court reversed 71% of its cases during the October Term 2009); *SCOTUSBlog Stat Pack Final Data 6.29.09*, SUP. CT. U.S. BLOG 10 (June 29, 2009), http://www.scotusblog.com/wp-content/uploads/2009/06/full-stat-pack.pdf (indicating the Supreme Court reversed 75.9% of its cases during the October Term 2008).
[138] *Final Stats OT09–7.7.10, supra* note 6, at 2.
[139] Ruger et al., *supra* note 4, at 1154. Also notable is how little attention is paid to attempting to accurately catalogue the past work of the Court, which can be crucial for determining how the Court or individual Justices may resolve a case in the future. *See, e.g.*, Ross E. Davies, Craig D. Rust & Adam Aft, *Justices at Work, or Not: New Supreme Court Statistics and Old Impediments to Making Them Accurate*, 14 GREEN BAG 2D 217 (2011).

Likewise, we were not surprised when the predictions were incorrect, based upon the standard statistical measures of reliability we were able to generate based on the predictions before the Court decided the case.

Consider two cases decided during the October 2009 Term. For *Levin v. Commerce Energy, Inc.*,[140] the data were not significant, and would not yield an accurate prediction. For *Wood v. Allen*,[141] the data were significant, and we were virtually certain that the prediction would likely be accurate. For *Levin v. Commerce Energy*, only fifty-five percent of members predicted that the Supreme Court would affirm the lower court. At a 90% confidence level, the confidence interval was $\pm$ 11.57.[142] Thus, the actual likelihood of an affirmance could be as high as 66.57%, or as low as 43.43%. If the likelihood of an affirmance reaches below 50%, we can no longer be confident that the prediction will be accurate. At the time, in a *Predictions of the 10th Justice* column, we noted that the data were "not strong enough for the [prediction] to be significant."[143] The Court ultimately reversed the lower court 9–0, a minority (forty-five percent) correctly predicting a reversal.

In contrast, *Wood v. Allen* provides an instance where we knew *ex ante* that our predictions would almost certainly be accurate.[144] In the case, 80% of members predicted that the Court would affirm the Eleventh Circuit. At a 99% confidence level, the confidence interval was $\pm$ 11.65.[145] The actual likelihood of an affirmance could have been as low as 68.35%, or as high 91.65%. In either scenario, the confidence at a 99% confidence level that the Court would affirm was greater than 50%. Recognizing this certainty, at the time, we noted that FantasySCOTUS members would be "extremely accurate at predicting the general outcome."[146] We were not surprised when the Justices voted to reverse. With the appropriate confidence interval, we can signal in advance the statistical measures indicating whether the prediction stays above 50% for affirm or reverse, and, if so, the confidence interval at which that prediction stays above 50%. From this, we can determine how reliable, or unreliable, a prediction is.

While a thirty-five percent failure rate is still largely unhelpful—it is doubtful anyone could meaningfully rely on FantasySCOTUS at its present accuracy rate—a larger subscriber base could increase the accuracy. FantasySCOTUS 1.0 had 5,000 members. FantasySCOTUS 2.0—the season that began with the October 2010 Term—has approximately 10,000 members. With developing partnerships with Westlaw and enhanced marketing strategies, we hope to double that number next season. As FantasySCOTUS grows, and more members sign up, with a wider range of views and opinions, our crowd grows, and we can obtain more data points. With more data points, the confidence interval shrinks. Even at higher confidence levels (90%, 95%, and 99%), we expect to see more reliable predictions above 50% to either affirm or reverse.

---

[140] 130 S. Ct. 2323 (2010).

[141] 130 S. Ct. 841 (2010).

[142] Josh Blackman, *FantasySCOTUS.net—Revisiting* American Needle, Graham v. Florida, Comstock, *and* Berghuis, JOSH BLACKMAN'S BLOG (June 2, 2010, 9:35 PM), http://joshblackman.com/blog/?p=4577.

[143] *Id.*

[144] Josh Blackman, *FantasySCOTUS.net Predictions of the 10th Justice: Testing the Wisdom of the Crowds*, JOSH BLACKMAN'S BLOG (Feb. 4, 2010, 10:46 PM), http://joshblackman.com/blog/?p=3951.

[145] *Id.*

[146] *Id.*

FantasySCOTUS 1.0 generated a data set that allowed us to develop an analytical framework to devise a prediction market for the Supreme Court. FantasySCOTUS also provides new insights into predicting Justice behavior. As we continue to gather data, we can see what this information teaches us about the models of judicial decision making, and whether applying different models (such as attitudinal models[147]) yields different types of predictions. In learning about how people predict the Justices will interact, we may learn something about how they actually interact and thus something about the institution of the Court itself.[148] As this technology develops in the future, possibilities of an automated approach to understanding judicial behavior are vast.

VI. IMPACT OF THE MEDIA

FantasySCOTUS, and Supreme Court speculation in general, may pose somewhat of a chicken and egg problem. Are predictions of members organically developed based on the existing precedents and how the Justices interact during oral arguments? Or, do media accounts that describe these precedents and interactions artificially generate predictions in the minds of members? In other words, does FantasySCOTUS "react more than [it] predicts"?[149] This section explores the relationship between the nature of Supreme Court predictions and the impact media coverage plays in these predictions. More specifically, we focus on the benefits of a prediction market, even in light of its potential reactionary tendencies.

Excluding two outlier cases, we found a strong correlation between the amount of media attention and the accuracy of predictions for both the power predictors and the crowd. The power predictors' edge is dulled for cases that receive significant media coverage. For unpopular cases that receive less media attention, and thereby less information for prospective predictors, the crowd tends to generate less accurate predictions. In contrast, the power predictors, who perform their own due diligence and research irrespective of media coverage, can thrive even on the most obscure cases on the docket.

A. Reactionary Prediction Markets

Professor Orin Kerr posed an interesting question about TradeSports, a prediction market that aimed to predict who President Bush would nominate to replace Justice O'Connor. The morning that President Bush announced that Judge John Roberts was his nominee, TradeSports erroneously predicted that Judge Edith Clement—the popular nominee in most media accounts—would be the nominee.[150] Presaging this faulty pick based on media consensus, Kerr wrote:

> The choice of O'Connor's replacement belongs to one man, George W. Bush. A few inside advisors are privy to his thinking, but I think it's fair to assume that neither Bush nor any of his inside advisors are placing any bets on sites like

---

[147] See MAXWELL L. STEARNS & TODD J. ZYWICKI, PUBLIC CHOICE CONCEPTS AND APPLICATIONS IN LAW 406–97 (2009).
[148] See id.
[149] Note, supra note 15, at 1223.
[150] See ABRAMOWICZ, supra note 91, at 38–39.

TradeSports.com. This means that the people who are placing bets presumably are outsiders who are getting their predictions from newspaper articles, blogs, horoscopes, etc., and then placing bets. As a result, a site like TradeSports would seem to just mirror the collective common wisdom of newspapers and blogs on a question like this. Am I missing something?[151]

Commenting on Kerr's post, Michael Abramowicz noted that prediction markets "do not seem to tell participants much more than they could figure out themselves by considering the underlying materials."[152] Do prediction markets merely repeat information in the media?

FantasySCOTUS provides a unique opportunity to test Professor Kerr's idea. In order to consider the impact of media coverage on all of the participants—the crowd and power predictors—we gathered data on the media attention of each case and compared it against the accuracy of predictions. This data helped to answer two questions: first, did the media attention the cases received correlate with the accuracy of the predictions; and second, can the cases that had a statistically significant gap between the crowd's predictions and power predictors' predictions be explained in part by the quantum of media attention?

Even if prediction markets are primarily reactive, they still serve a very important role—aggregation. How can one quantify the "collective common wisdom of newspapers and blogs"?[153] Markets, such as FantasySCOTUS, serve as a clearinghouse of sorts and provide an easy way to assemble the totality of knowledge in the media and elsewhere, even if the predictions merely reflect that consensus. The prediction markets "at least opened up the possibility of accomplishing the task of evidence aggregation,"[154] which is a very important task. On average, the prediction market will "be more accurate than the prediction that the observer independently"—even Professor Kerr—"could derive, because the market will represent an aggregation of the views of a large number of observers."[155] Specifically, this aggregation may "in part cancel out random errors that individuals make in predictions by overweighing or underweighing particular pieces of evidence."[156]

Like unfounded guesses as to who will be the next Supreme Court Justice, where the knowledge is likely restricted to a few people in the Executive Branch, the outcome of Supreme Court cases are known only by the Justices and their clerks. There is no special inside information, known to reporters and supposed experts. Rather, the wise crowd, who are able to read the tealeaves and pick out important questions asked by the Justices, can determine how the Court will decide.

Some research claims that "prediction markets will work better when they concern events that are widely discussed, since trading on such events will have higher entertainment value and there will be more information on whose interpretation traders can disagree."[157] Even if the information surrounding a case is "ambiguous," perhaps

---

[151] Kerr, *supra* note 7.
[152] ABRAMOWICZ, *supra* note 91, at 38.
[153] Kerr, *supra* note 7.
[154] ABRAMOWICZ, *supra* note 91, at 38.
[155] *Id.*
[156] *Id.*
[157] Wolfers & Zitzewitz, *supra* note 27, at 121.

resulting from contentious oral arguments or a longer-than-usual delay in issuing the opinion, this data may result in better predictions because those most skilled in reading between the lines and figuring out the Justice's proclivities can put forth the best guesses.[158]

B. Methodology

In order to assess whether media coverage and prediction accuracy are correlated, the extent of press coverage about a case is relevant. However, other than limited survey data from some power predictors,[159] we had no basis to determine which media sources FantasySCOTUS members relied on to learn about the cases. To solve this problem, we devised an approach to determine media coverage of Supreme Court cases.[160] To reflect the transformation of how Supreme Court cases were covered, we considered two sources of media—old school and new school. First, we looked at coverage in what could broadly be referred to as mainstream media. For this search, two comprehensive databases were utilized: the All News Plus database on Westlaw[161] and the All Legal U.S. News database on LexisNexis.[162] Utilizing sources from both Westlaw and LexisNexis increased the data set's inclusiveness and allowed for normalized results.

Years ago, to learn about a Supreme Court case, one would have to wait for Linda Greenhouse's article in the New York Times the next day or catch Nina Totenberg's spot on National Public Radio. Thanks to the legal blogosphere revolution, that is no longer the case. Many blog authors post instant analyses of oral arguments, opinions, and other developments at the Court within minutes of the breaking news.[163] To consider the impact of coverage in the blogosphere—and sort through the tangled World Wide Web— we searched the "Blogs on Demand" database in Westlaw.[164] This blog database is quite limited and excludes a number of the most popular legal blogs.[165] To focus on the

---

[158] *Id.* ("Ambiguous public information may be better in motivating trade than private information, especially if the private information is concentrated, since a cadre of highly informed traders can easily drive out the partly informed, repressing trade to the point that the market barely exists.").

[159] For a discussion how several power predictors made their decisions, and which resources they relied on, see Blackman, *supra* note 144.

[160] Objectively discerning the media attention given to a Supreme Court case is not an exact science, and there may certainly be room to improve on the method employed.

[161] WESTLAW, WINNING RESEARCH SKILLS: PROFESSIONAL LEGAL RESEARCH 185 (2008), *available at* http://lscontent.westlaw.com/images/banner/SurvivalGuide/PDF08/08WinningResearchSkills.pdf (The All News Plus Wires database (ALLNEWSPLUS) "contains newspapers, magazines, journals, newsletters, government press releases, and transcripts of television and radio shows and congressional testimony . . . plus newswires.").

[162] *Legal US News, All*, LEXISNEXIS, http://w3.nexis.com/sources/scripts/info.pl?7596&GCC (last visited Dec. 28, 2011) ("The ALLNWS file is a group file containing all of the separately searchable online legal newspaper, magazine, and newsletter files.").

[163] *See, e.g.*, Josh Blackman, *Instant Reaction:* Citizens United v. FEC *(Hillary Movie Case)*, JOSH BLACKMAN'S BLOG (Jan. 21, 2010, 10:08 AM), http://joshblackman.com/blog/?p=3771.

[164] *West E-lert Newsletter: Does Westlaw Provide Access to Any Legal or Financial Blogs?*, WESTLAW (May 2009), http://store.westlaw.com/signup/newsletters/westelert/2009-may/article8.aspx ("[T]he Blogs on Demand database (BLOGSOD) . . . contains the full text and abstracts of a variety of financial, legal, and business blogs . . . .").

[165] Among others, it excluded BALKINIZATION, http://balkin.blogspot.com/ (last updated Dec. 4, 2011); INSTAPUNDIT, http://pjmedia.com/instapundit/ (last updated Dec. 4, 2011); PRAWFSBLAWG,

sources that Court-followers read most closely, we augmented the search field to include the blogs listed in the "ABA Journal 4th Annual Blawg 100,"[166] which contains "the best legal blogs as selected by the [*ABA*] *Journal*'s editors" and includes "the best and brightest law bloggers in a variety of categories."[167] To comb through these sources, we programmed a custom Google search engine that searched these 100 sites.[168]

The primary search problem relates to the inconsistent ways authors refer to cases. Take *Citizens United v. Federal Elections Commission*, for example. Some authors call it *Citizens United v. FEC*, others simply *Citizens United*, and still others call it the "Hillary Movie Case." Simply searching for one of these phrases would exclude a number of relevant articles and posts. Further, a case with a common name, such as *United States v. Stevens*, which can be abbreviated as simply *Stevens*, generated a significant number of false negatives, especially in light of the newsworthy retirement of Justice John Paul Stevens.

To minimize inaccurate results, we went through a process of testing multiple search strings and reviewing the results to determine which terms would be most accurate and allow the greatest consistency.[169] Using just the unique party name in a case worked relatively well for *Citizens United*, but we could not replicate that success with cases such as *Stevens* or *Johnson*. In fact, when we just ran the more unique party name, six of the ten cases hit 10,000 search results on the Westlaw All News database,[170] indicating that we exceeded the maximum size of search results permitted on that database.[171]

Utilizing the proximity searches was not particularly helpful; they were either over-inclusive and maximized the search results on the databases (for example, searching for terms in the same sentence), or under-inclusive and did not return a noticeably greater amount of search results (for example, searching for terms within two words of each other). Ultimately, we ran straightforward search strings for each of the cases in all four databases (for example, "citizens united v. federal election commission"). This strategy was under-inclusive for cases such as *Citizens United*, where many commenters did not use the full case name. However, the strategy that provided the most accurate results was

---

http://prawfsblawg.blogs.com/ (last updated Dec. 4, 2011); WALL ST. J.L. BLOG, http://blogs.wsj.com/law/ (last visited Dec. 4, 2011).

[166] Molly McDonough & Sarah Randag, *Our 100 Favorite Blawgs*, A.B.A. J., Dec. 2010, at 33. In the interest of full disclosure, *Josh Blackman's Blog* was selected to this list. *Id.* at 34.

[167] *The 2010 ABA Journal Blawg 100*, A.B.A. J., http://www.abajournal.com/blawg100 (last visited Nov. 13, 2011).

[168] *JoshBlackman.com ABA Blawg 100 Search*, GOOGLE CUSTOM SEARCH, http://www.google.com/cse/home?cx=003923726555708584283:mzan1oszugg (last updated Mar. 7, 2011). *See generally* GOOGLE CUSTOM SEARCH, http://www.google.com/cse/ (last visited Dec. 28, 2011).

[169] A few examples of attempted searches include—with *Citizens United* as an example—["citizens united" /s "federal election commission"]; ["citizens united" /2 "federal election commission"]; ["citizens united"]; and ["citizens united v. federal election commission"]. The search strings tested are too numerous to list. To craft searches that yielded the most accurate search results, we utilized terms and connectors searching in Lexis and Westlaw, with options such as: & (both search terms); or (either search term or both terms); " " (search terms appearing in the same order as in the quotation marks); /n (search terms within n terms of each other (where n is a number from 1 to 255); /s (search terms in the same sentence); and /p (search terms in the same paragraph). WESTLAW, WESTLAW QUICK REFERENCE GUIDE: GETTING STARTED ON WESTLAW 5 (2009), http://store.westlaw.com/documentation/westlaw/wlawdoc/web/rswlcm06.pdf.

[170] *See supra* note 161 and accompanying text.

[171] The six cases that exceeded the maximum results were *Stevens, Johnson, Padilla, Graham, McDonald,* and *Perdue*.

to search for the more common name cases, and we chose to follow the most consistent path.

To further improve the accuracy of the searches, we utilized the date restriction features in Lexis and Westlaw. The custom Google search engine we programmed did not allow for date restrictions. Attempting to focus on the media attention that a participant in FantasySCOTUS would have, we limited the date range from the date the Supreme Court granted certiorari to the date the Supreme Court issued an opinion. We compiled all of the date ranges using the Supreme Court's official docket.[172]

C. Analysis

Table 5 displays the number of results we found in each database for the keyword search between the date certiorari was granted and the date of the opinion. In the final column, we averaged the results.

TABLE 5. NEWS DATABASE RESULTS

Search	Date Range	ALLNWS	ALLNEWS PLUS	BLOG SOD	BLAWG 100	Average
"citizens united v. federal election commission"	8/18/2008[173] –1/21/2010	26	290	5	80	100.25
"united states v. stevens"	4/20/2009– 4/20/2010	19	47	3	59	32
"maryland v. shatzer"	1/26/2009– 2/24/2010	7	28	2	37	18.5
"johnson v. united states"	2/23/2009– 3/2/2010	13	12	0	32	14.25
"padilla v. kentucky"	2/23/2009– 3/31/2010	12	38	1	69	30
"graham v. florida"	5/4/2009– 5/17/2010	16	88	5	83	48
"bloate v. united states"	4/20/2009– 3/8/2010	2	3	0	11	4
"mcdonald v. chicago"	9/30/2009– 6/28/2010	31	212	24	94	90.25
"perdue v. kenny"	4/6/2009– 4/21/2010	50	52	4	26	33
"bilski v. kappos"	6/1/2009– 6/28/2010	113	116	27	92	87

According to the data, *Citizens United*, *McDonald*, and *Bilski* received the greatest average media coverage, while *Bloate*, *Johnson*, and *Shatzer* received the least. To ascertain whether a correlation exists between the media coverage and the accuracy of FantasySCOTUS predictions, it is helpful to scatter plot these data with a best-fit line.

---

[172] *Docket Search*, SUP. CT. U.S., http://www.supremecourt.gov/docket/docket.aspx (last updated Dec. 29, 2011).
[173] This is the date the case was docketed, which we used in lieu of the original date the Supreme Court granted certiorari during the October 2008 Term.

¶98   Figure 2 considers the relationship between the media coverage and the accuracy of the FantasySCOTUS power predictors. Figure 2 plot considers the relationship between the media coverage and the accuracy of the FantasySCOTUS crowd.

¶99   FIGURE 1

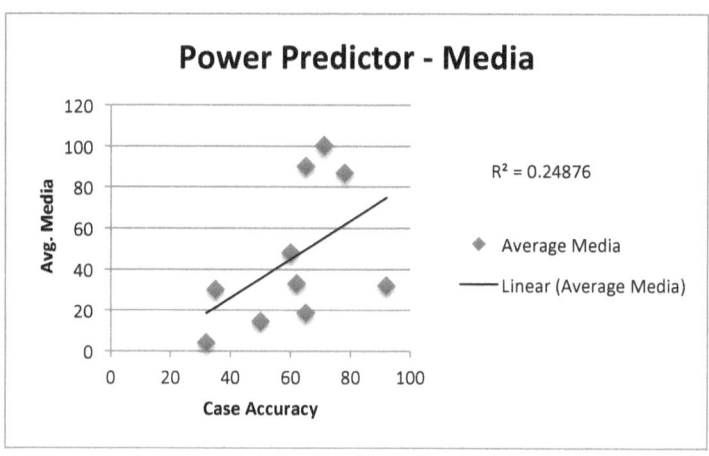

FIGURE 2

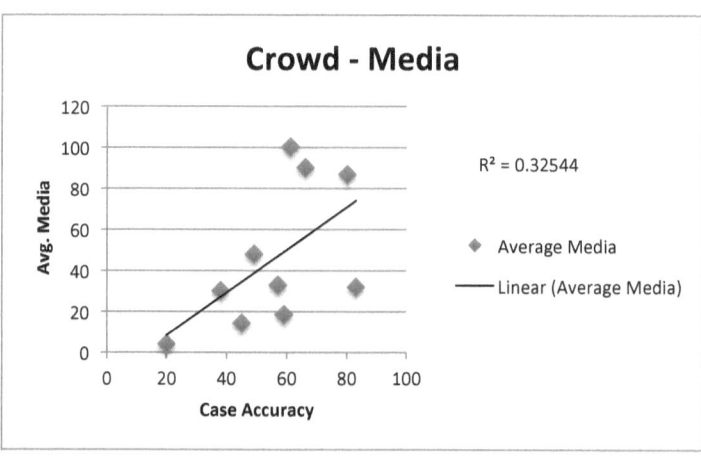

¶100   These scatter plots allow us to draw several conclusions. First, the points slope upward, suggesting that the more media attention a case received, the more accurate the predictions were. However, both the crowd and power predictor best fit lines have very low R^2 values.[174] R^2 ranges between zero and one. As the R^2 value approaches one, we can conclude that the predicted value is closer to the actual value. In other words, the plot has a higher predictive power. As the R^2 value approaches zero, the predictive power decreases, and we cannot say with confidence that the predicted value approximates the actual value. The R^2 values of 0.248 for the power predictors and 0.325 for the crowd are quite low. These values signify that the predictive power of this plot is fairly weak.

However, the crowd trended more closely with the media coverage attention than the power predictors did. Simply put, the accuracy of the crowd improved more with greater media attention relative to the power predictors. The power predictors, in contrast, were able to accurately predict cases even if the media coverage was lacking. Perhaps, the power predictors performed additional research—several members in the survey revealed that they read oral argument transcripts, the briefs, and amici[175]—to hone their results. The crowd, which predicted fewer cases, and likely invested less time into FantasySCOTUS, was perhaps more lackadaisical with their due dilligence, and merely relied on media accounts to form their votes.[176] This would seem to bolster Professor Kerr's theory that prediction markets "do not seem to tell participants much more than they could figure out themselves by considering the underlying materials."[177]

---

[174] R^2 is a statistical measurement, which represents the difference between the actual outcome and the expected outcome, in this case how far away the accuracy of a prediction was based upon the average media hits. EVERITT, *supra* note 81, at 78 (defining coefficient of determination); *see also* Mohan P. Rao & Christian D. Tregillis, *Econometric Analysis*, *in* LITIGATION SERVICES HANDBOOK: THE ROLE OF THE FINANCIAL EXPERT 6.11 (Roman L. Weil et al. eds., 4th ed. 2007) ("R^2 is a summary measure of the goodness of fit of the fitted regression line to a set of data. Formally, R^2 is defined as the ratio of explained sum of squares (variation of estimated Y values about their mean) to total sum of squares (total variation of Y values about their sample mean). R^2 ranges from 0 to 1, where 0 reflects that no variation in the dependent variable is explained by the independent variables and 1 reflects that all of the variation in the dependent variable is explained by the independent variables. Because of the heuristic simplicity of R^2, it is a widely used measure of the goodness of fit of the least squares model. . . . [T]he addition of variables to a model generally will increase its R^2. But a model with a large number of variables and a higher R^2 does not necessarily provide additional understanding of the relation between the key variables of interest and the dependent variable. . . . Further, a model with a large number of variables is harder to interpret.").
[175] Blackman, *supra* note 73.
[176] In Table 6, the difference between the correlations is much smaller, signifying that this observation is potentially attributable to the outliers. Future testing may resolve this quandary.
[177] ABRAMOWICZ, *supra* note 91, at 38.

TABLE 6. AVERAGE MEDIA AND DIFFERENCE FROM POWER PREDICTOR AND CROWD
ACCURACY

Case	Average Media	Power Predictor		Crowd	
		Accuracy	Difference	Accuracy	Difference
Citizens United	100.25	71	29.25	61	39.25
Stevens	32	92	60	83	51
Shatzer	18.5	65	46.5	59	40.5
Johnson	14.25	50	35.75	45	30.75
Padilla	30	35	5	38	8
McDonald	90.25	65	25.25	66	24.25
Graham	48	60	12	49	1
Bloate	4	32	28	20	16
Perdue	33	62	29	57	24
Bilski	87	78	9	80	7
Average	-	-	15.275	-	10.075
Average, omitting outliers	-	-	5.78125	-	1.15625

¶102   The two cases with the greatest difference between media attention and prediction
accuracy were *Stevens* (a difference of 60 for the power predictors and 51 for the crowd)
and *Shatzer* (a difference of 46.5 for the power predictors and 40.5 for the crowd), as
shown in Table 6. These cases were effectively statistical outliers. With only ten cases,
the impact of these outliers significantly impacted the value of R^2, and the predictive
power of the data.

¶103   *Stevens* was particularly problematic because Justice John Paul Stevens, who
coincidentally shares a surname with the respondent in *Stevens*, was still sitting on the
Court during the October 2009 Term. Therefore, any attempt to utilize a proximity
search, such as ["united states" /s Stevens], would return a number of results talking
about the United States and Justice Stevens, but not the desired search, *United States v.
Stevens*. Compounding this problem was Justice Stevens's retirement, which greatly
increased the media attention he received.

¶104   *Shatzer* is a more unique party name, so it is likely that searching the full case name
was somewhat under-inclusive, leading to lower media attention than actually existed.
Given that we are only reviewing the data on ten cases, outliers have a much greater
impact on any potential trends, and excluding them provides a more accurate picture of
any potential correlation between media attention and the accuracy of any predictions.

¶105   We conducted a separate experiment omitting these outliers. Excluding *Stevens*
and *Shatzer*, the average difference for the other eight cases dropped drastically: from
15.275 to 5.78 for the power predictors, and from 10.075 to 1.16 for the crowd. Without
these cases, we generated two new scatter plots using the same methodologies. FIGURE 3
considers the relationship between the media coverage and the accuracy of
FantasySCOTUS power predictors, excluding *Shatzer* and *Stevens*. Figure 4 considers

the relationship between the media coverage and the accuracy of FantasySCOTUS crowd, excluding *Shatzer* and *Stevens*.

FIGURE 3

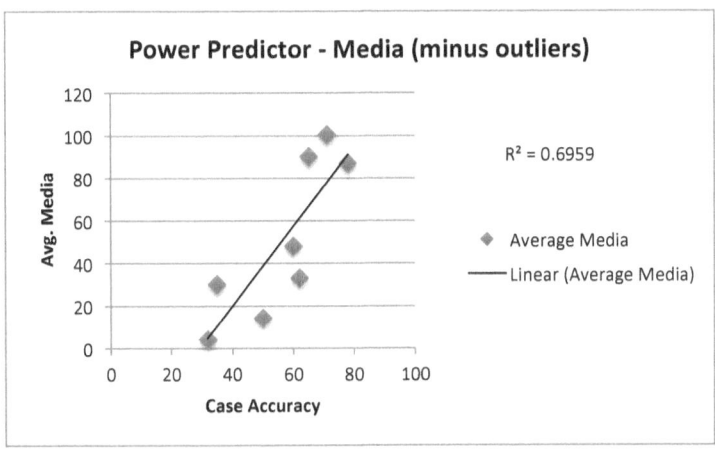

FIGURE 4

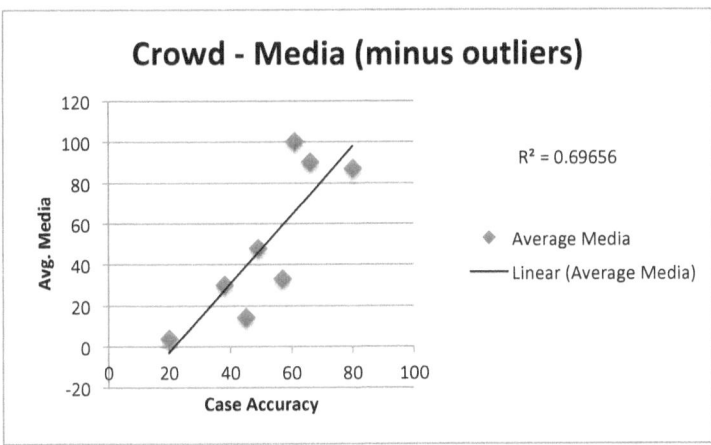

Excluding the outliers, there is a much stronger correlation between the amount of media attention and the accuracy of predictions: there was almost a three-fold increase in the correlation for power predictors between prediction accuracy and media coverage—from 0.25 to 0.69. Further, the correlation is much more similar when comparing the power predictors with the crowd—a difference of only 0.00066. An R^2 value of approximately 0.7, with only eight data points—a relatively small sample size—suggests

159

a relatively strong correlations. The power predictors predicted both of the outlier cases more accurately. Removing those cases narrows the gap between the power predictors and the crowd in terms of correlation.

TABLE 7. AVERAGE MEDIA FOR CASES WITH SIGNIFICANT DIFFERENCES BETWEEN POWER PREDICTORS AND CROWD ACCURACY

Case	Average Media
Shatzer	18.5
Johnson	14.25
Graham	48
Bilski	87

There are relatively few data points using only these ten cases, so analyzing the correlation between media coverage and accuracy is mostly for observational purposes and does not have statistical significance. For comparison, given the sharp drop off in media attention from the first three cases to the last ten, this section considers the top three attention getters compared to the remainder of the cases. Three of the four cases in which the difference between the power predictors' predictions and the crowd's predictions were statistically significant were also the three cases which received the least media attention: *Johnson*, *Shatzer*, and *Graham*, ranked ninth, eighth, and fourth, respectively. The fourth case with a significant difference between power predictor and crowd predictions, *Bilski*, received significant media attention, ranking third out of the ten cases.[178] For *Bilski*, the fact that the power predictors' predictions were still significantly different than the crowd's predictions appears to be an outlier that may be explained by the highly technical nature of the patent case.

Less media attention, and thereby less information for prospective predictors in the crowd, helps to explain the crowd's weaker performance for the less-noteworthy cases. In contrast, the power predictors, who likely perform their own due diligence irrespective of media coverage, can thrive even on the most obscure and neglected cases on the docket. With only four cases with a statistically significant difference, there are too few data points to consider any correlation, but this consideration may yield interesting results in future experiments.

In short, Professor Kerr's thesis accurately observes how prediction markets generate results, but it overlooks an important aspect of these markets. Prediction markets serve a valuable function of aggregating and sorting knowledge and opinions in a unified clearinghouse. This sorting, accomplished independently by the crowd and aggregated by FantasySCOTUS algorithms, is far easier and more accurate than manually combing through and reading the unbounded amount of information printed about every

---

[178] Even though *Graham* had the fourth highest average of media hits and *Bilski* had the third, the jump from third to fourth, a difference of thirty-nine, is the largest jump in the average media hits. The next largest difference is only a fifteen point jump from *Perdue* to *Graham*, and the average difference from case to case is only ten points. Thus, *Graham* is more appropriately grouped with *Johnson* and *Shatzer* in this instance than with *Bilski*.

case in the mainstream media and on blogs. FantasySCOTUS tapped a "diversity of information [that] exist[ed] in a way that provides a basis for" predictions.[179]

VII. IMPLICATIONS OF FANTASYSCOTUS

In this section, we discuss some of the jurisprudential implications of creating a market that accurately predicts how the Court and, more specifically, how nine Justices will vote. This market may have a broader impact on public perceptions of the Court as an institution and its role in furtherance of the rule of law. This Part takes a brief excursion to the future and explores how a sophisticated prediction market can contribute to the evolution of the legal profession.

A. FantasySCOTUS and the Supreme Court as an Institution

FantasySCOTUS provides insights into how the Supreme Court is perceived. While the Supreme Court enjoys a favorability rating of roughly 60%, higher than the other two branches of the federal government, a recent Pew Research Center report suggests that 46% of those surveyed think the Court is too partisan—23% thinks it is liberal, 23% thinks it is conservative.[180] Only 39% believes the Court is "middle of the road."[181] Some polling exists as to how the public perceives certain noteworthy cases— for example, 68% of those surveyed disagreed with *Citizens United*[182]—but no data exist as to how people perceive the individual Justices, and their ideologies. Considering that 72% of those surveyed could not identify the name of the Chief Justice of the United States,[183] such polling of the public at large would probably be impossible, if not futile. In this sense, FantasySCOTUS serves as one of the most comprehensive, albeit unscientific, polling mechanisms to capture perceptions of the Supreme Court as an institution.

While FantasySCOTUS 1.0 did not request that members identify their ideology— we requested this information in version 2.0, and hope to elaborate on this dynamic in future work—anecdotal evidence suggests that certain members consistently voted in a manner that reflected a particular jurisprudential ideology. This bias usually manifests in predictions for Justice Kennedy's often decisive vote in 5–4 decisions. Members who voted for outcomes that could be deemed liberal would align Justice Kennedy's vote with those of Justices Stevens, Ginsburg, Breyer, and Sotomayor. Many of these same members made outlier predictions in a related FantasySCOTUS game to predict Justice Stevens's replacement, selecting long shots like Cass Sunstein or Pam Karlan. These votes were likely based on their personal predilections rather than realistic expectations. In contrast, members who voted for outcomes that could be deemed conservative would

---

[179] Wolfers & Zitzewitz, *supra* note 27, at 120.

[180] *The Invisible Court*, PEW RES. CENTER (Aug. 3, 2010), http://pewresearch.org/pubs/1688/supreme-court-lack-of-public-knowledge-favorability.

[181] *Id.*

[182] News Release, Pew Research Ctr., Obama's Ratings Are Flat, Wall Street's Are Abysmal: Midterm Election Challenges for Both Parties 31 (Feb. 12, 2010), *available at* http://www.people-press.org/files/legacy-pdf/589.pdf.

[183] News Release, Pew Research Ctr., Political Knowledge Update 2 (July 15, 2010), *available at* http://people-press.org/files/legacy-pdf/635.pdf.

align Justice Kennedy's vote with those of Chief Justice Roberts, and Justices Scalia, Thomas, and Alito.

By enabling people to vote their preferences, and thereby express their views of how ideological cases will be decided, FantasySCOTUS can gather how people view the Justices. This collective wisdom of the crowds captures the public coarsening among lawyers and law students—the vast majority of players on FantasySCOTUS—towards the notion that judges of all ideological stripes are independent and decide cases solely based on the law.

These results are perhaps more honest, and sober, as players are voting their actual preferences, anonymously, with the incentive to win by accurately predicting votes. Were the same lawyers—excluding members of the professoriate, perhaps—to be polled formally, even anonymously, it is doubtful they would be so candid about their views of the Justices.[184] Rather, their answers may more likely be driven by platitudes as to what they think they should answer. Ultimately, the perceptions of Court watchers no doubt spill over, and affect the perceptions of the how the public at large views the Supreme Court. Determining an accurate picture of how Court watchers view the Court likely provides a window into how society at large views the Court.

These observations have several potential jurisprudential implications. FantasySCOTUS brings into stark focus that "[w]e are all realists now."[185] Predicting many cases, particularly the 5–4 splits, in a similar fashion to how people predict the outcome of political elections—during the last election, this district voted Republican, so it is likely to vote Republican again during the next election, regardless of the candidate's merits—reduces the judicial process from abstract, objective pronouncements of law to ascertaining the ideological votes of individual Justices. A survey of several power predictors suggested as much—members made predictions based on philosophical and ideological understandings of the Justices, sometimes without any regards to the merits of the actual case. As Prediction Markets grow more sophisticated, questions about the ideological Court, the nature of the judicial process, and the rule of law may become more pronounced.[186]

B. The Legal Prediction Market of Tomorrow

In a prescient 2005 article, Miriam Cherry and Robert Rogers postulated about an information market to predict Supreme Court decisions, named Tiresias, after the clairvoyant prophet of Thebes.[187] The authors remarked that "[t]he ability to know a

---

[184] A recent Pew Research Center Publication found that 39% of those surveyed view the Court as "middle of the road," 23% found the Court conservative, and 23% found the Court liberal. *The Invisible Court, supra* note 180. Overall, 58% of those surveyed have a favorable impression of the Court. *Id.* No data exist as to perceptions of each individual Justice. *Id.* Considering 53% of those surveyed could not name the Chief Justice of the United States, such data are likely impossible to collect among the public at large. *Id.*

[185] LAURA KALMAN, LEGAL REALISM AT YALE, 1927–1960, at 229 (1986).

[186] STEPHEN BREYER, MAKING OUR DEMOCRACY WORK: A JUDGE'S VIEW xiv (2010) ("At the end of the day, the public's confidence is what permits the Court to ensure a Constitution that is more than words on paper. It is what enables the Court to ensure that the Constitution functions democratically, that it protects individual liberty, and that it works in practice for the benefit of all Americans.").

[187] *See* Cherry & Rogers, *supra* note 46.

probable Supreme Court outcome in advance can potentially create monetary value for practitioners, provide guidance for lower courts, and perhaps even influence the Supreme Court itself."[188] Every year, the article notes, "probably hundreds, if not thousands, of civil disputes and criminal prosecutions are settled that contain issues the Supreme Court may resolve that Term."[189] Indeed, in light of the fact that the Court hears about eighty cases each year on a variety of topics, "many with monetary ramifications, the financial value of the Tiresias predictions could be considerable."[190] Over 100 years ago, Oliver Wendell Holmes, Jr. wrote, "[t]he object of our study, then, is prediction, the prediction of the incidence of the public force through the instrumentality of the courts."[191]

FantasySCOTUS takes a first step towards Tiresias, and fulfilling Holmes' observation, by creating a prediction market that could transform how attorneys make decisions. Future iterations of FantasySCOTUS will be more accurate, robust, powerful, and insightful. The software will be able to sense subtle changes in predictions at different stages of the litigation, and incorporate the historical performance of the Justices, and their voting patterns, along with the past success and track records of the power predictors automatically and instantly. In the future, the predictions will likely be accurate enough that people can meaningfully rely on them. Once the information market yields these rates, it could become an invaluable tool for litigation decisions.

Consider two cases—one civil, one criminal—recently decided by the Supreme Court, and how a FantasySCOTUS of the future, with a much higher accuracy rate, could provide helpful legal and litigation assistance for lawyers.

In *AT&T Mobility LLC v. Concepcion*, the Supreme Court found that California courts could not refuse to enforce contracts that prohibit class-action arbitration.[192] The case was argued on November 9, 2010 and decided on April 27, 2011.[193] Assume that before April 27, a Californian is threatening to assemble a class-action arbitration against a company, even though the contract the customer signed prohibits class-action arbitration. The company, following oral arguments in the lead-up to the Supreme Court's decision, is faced with a decision that could cost millions of dollars: risk a California court ordering costly class-action arbitration, or settle the matter and avoid the arbitration.

If the FantasySCOTUS of the future could predict with a degree of certainty that the Court will find that the contracts must be enforced, the company may be hesitant to engage in a settlement, as they will triumph in court. On the other hand, if FantasySCOTUS predicts the Supreme Court will agree with the California courts, and find the agreements unenforceable, the corporation may wish to settle the case, to avoid risky and expensive class-action arbitration. These are practical and tactical litigation decisions attorneys must make. Now, they can make this decision informed by data of

---

[188] *Id.* at 1142.
[189] *Id.* at 1183.
[190] *Id.* at 1184.
[191] Holmes, *supra* note 1, at 457.
[192] 131 S. Ct. 1740 (2011).
[193] *Id.*

what the Court will do, whereas in the past such decisions were made perhaps based on a law firm partner's "gut" instinct.[194]

The stakes in a criminal case could be even greater. Imagine that during an interrogation a suspect was read her *Miranda* rights, did not affirmatively invoke her right to remain silent, and subsequently made an incriminating statement. Assume that *Berghuis v. Thompkins*, which presented just this issue, has been argued before the Court, but not yet decided.[195] The prosecutor offers the defendant a favorable plea bargain that is only on the table for a limited duration; if not accepted, the prosecutor will take the case to trial. If the defendant accepts the plea agreement, she waives all appeal rights.

The defense attorney is faced with a choice. If her client accepts the plea bargain, and the Supreme Court subsequently finds that this interrogation did not result in a violation of *Miranda*, her client will have secured a short sentence, less than what she likely would have received at trial. Alternatively, if her client accepts the plea bargain, and the Supreme Court finds this interrogation did result in a violation of *Miranda*, her client cannot challenge the confession on appeal, and she is stuck in jail; had she gone to trial, the court would have suppressed the evidence, and she would have likely been acquitted without the confession.

If FantasySCOTUS shows that the Court will find a violation of *Miranda* rights in *Berghuis v. Thompkins*, perhaps the attorney should roll the dice and go to trial, hoping the judge will ultimately suppress the evidence, or perhaps her client could challenge it on appeal. If FantasySCOTUS shows that the Court will not find a violation of *Miranda* (the actual outcome of this 5–4 decision), perhaps the attorney should accept the favorable plea bargain, and not risk it. These are real decisions defense attorneys have to make. With the FantasySCOTUS of the future, this decision could be aided by informed predictions and their accompanying statistical measures of certainty.

C. From a Crowdsourced Prediction Market to an Intelligent Litigation Assistant

Admittedly, in its present form, FantasySCOTUS 1.0 is not particularly reliable for making important legal decisions. Further, while the eighty or so cases the Supreme Court decides each year are no doubt quite significant and of broad interest,[196] the 282,307 civil cases commenced in federal district courts[197] and the 56,790 appeals commenced in federal circuit courts in 2010 affect far more people.[198] A prediction market that can provide accurate predictions for the vast number of cases filed and appealed in federal courts each year could prove invaluable to lawyers and non-lawyers

---

[194] *See* AYRES, *supra* note 5, at 12 (With Super Cruncher information, "you don't need to guess, follow rules of thumb, or trust grizzled traditionalists. Increasingly, it is possible to tease out measureable effects of separate attributes to tell you what" approach would work best.).

[195] 130 S. Ct. 2250 (2010).

[196] *See* SUP. CT. R. 10.

[197] JAMES C. DUFF, ADMIN. OFFICE OF THE U.S. COURTS, FEDERAL JUDICIAL CASELOAD STATISTICS MARCH 31, 2010, at 40 tbl.C (2010), *available at* http://www.uscourts.gov/Viewer.aspx?doc=/uscourts/Statistics/FederalJudicialCaseloadStatistics/2010/tabl es/C00Mar10.pdf.

[198] *Id.* at 21 tbl.B, *available at* http://www.uscourts.gov/Viewer.aspx?doc=/uscourts/Statistics/FederalJudicialCaseloadStatistics/2010/tabl es/B00Mar10.pdf.

alike. Building on an idea developed by Professors Kobayashi and Ribstein in *Law's Information Revolution*,[199] a future version of FantasySCOTUS could shift from using a crowdsourced model (it is not likely that enough people will be intimately familiar with the thousands of cases decided in the inferior courts) to an algorithm that can Super Crunch data with an improved decision engine. The model would analyze data from previously decided cases to offer predictions for cases not yet filed.

It would be quite conceivable for a bot to crawl through all of the filings in PACER[200]—which stores every brief, opinion, and order filed in the federal courts, reportedly around 500 million documents[201]—and develop a comprehensive database of all aspects of how each court works. Using sophisticated text-recognition and natural language searches, a database could automatically index all of the cases—eliminating the need for fallible research assistants to laboriously tag cases. The system would note, for example, the parties to the case, the author and nature of a filed brief, the court it is filed with, the judge overseeing the case, the type of case it is, the damages or relief sought, the alleged merits of the case, the timeline of the case, the ultimate resolution of the case, and so on. This process would be instantly performed with every new filing, so the database would always be up to date with the latest jurisprudential and litigation trends, eliminating the need to resort to outdated data sets from the past.

With these data, a prediction engine could determine the various traits of successful and unsuccessful actions of various types, in various courts, under various circumstances. With enough data the prediction engine could provide, *ex ante*, a prognosis of how a case will likely proceed. Telling a client how a case will turn out—usually any client's main concern—is something that attorneys, no matter how well qualified, can only do imprecisely. As Professor Ayres remarked, "[t]rolling through databases can reveal underlying causes that traditional experts"—even pricey, experienced lawyers—"never even considered."[202] If lawyers could ascertain in advance what the likely results of litigation would be, they could "avoid[] disputes altogether"[203] and settle out of court. Even if the dispute cannot be avoided, a realistic prediction of probable damages could yield "ways to contain disagreements amicably and to avoid unnecessary escalation."[204]

But what if the engine could tell an attorney not only what will happen, but also how it should be accomplished? Imagine a program similar to the iPhone's Siri application. Call it *Harlan*. A would-be litigator could tell Harlan the relevant parties, the facts, the merits, and the remedy sought and share any relevant documents.[205] Harlan could generate a roadmap of how the case would be resolved with different judges in

---

[199] Kobayashi & Ribstein, *supra* note 9, at 1201 ("Lawyers might collaborate with computer scientists to develop new computer prediction algorithms," combing through public court records, such as PACER "to predict case results.").

[200] For a present-day tool that combs through PACER, consider RECAP, a crowdsourced program which allows people to "donate the documents they purchase from PACER" to "build a free and open repository of public court records." *About*, RECAP, https://www.recapthelaw.org/about/ (last visited Dec. 4, 2011).

[201] Timothy B. Lee, *Studying the Frequency in Redaction Failures in PACER*, FREEDOM TO TINKER (May 25, 2011, 1:52 PM), http://freedom-to-tinker.com/blog/tblee/studying-frequency-redaction-failures-pacer.

[202] AYRES, *supra* note 5, at 12.

[203] RICHARD SUSSKIND, THE END OF LAWYERS? RETHINKING THE NATURE OF LEGAL SERVICES 184 (2008).

[204] *Id.*

[205] For an example of how a Harlan simulation could provide litigation assistance to lawyers and non-lawyers alike, see Blackman, *supra* note 8.

different courts, and perhaps even recommend an ideal forum (call it fantasy-forum-shopping). Harlan could explain how best to structure the litigation, what types of motions would be most successful, and how to arrange arguments. With advances in artificial intelligence—Google developed cars that drive themselves, and IBM's Watson defeated the Jeopardy world champion[206]—it is not much of a stretch to suggest that Harlan could even draft the briefs (many sections of briefs today are copied from boilerplate anyway), or at least check the persuasiveness of the arguments against other successful arguments already accepted by courts. Harlan would also work wonders for non-lawyers. A person could download the app, talk to *Harlan* in plain language, explain the problem, and listen to possible remedies—that may or may not involve paying a lawyer. Harlan would improve access to justice, at little to no cost.

Such a product would transform the legal profession and our society. This change would require a fundamental rethinking of approaches to legal education,[207] the practice of law, and, broadly speaking, our system of justice. It will likely first be first met with doubt—"computers can't replace human lawyers!" This technology would not be about replacing lawyers (at least not lawyers who adapt[208]); rather, it would provide advocates with information and knowledge to serve clients more effectively and at a lower cost. Next, there will likely be fierce resistance to change from entrenched interests in the form of ethical and regulatory challenges[209]—"computers can't follow the rules of ethics and they will provide ineffective legal assistance to non-lawyers!" These criticisms are fair, but such technology could provide opportunities to improve the quality of representation to all segments of society. Rather than instinctively opposing any change that upsets the status quo, these new technologies should be met with tempered enthusiasm. Reforms to the regulatory regime will come,[210] followed by gradual acceptance of this technology. We hope that FantasySCOTUS will serve as a first step in the evolution from today's time-consuming, customized labor-intensive legal market to tomorrow's on-demand, commoditized law's information revolution.[211]

---

[206] ERIK BRYNJOLFSSON & ANDREW MCAFEE, RACE AGAINST THE MACHINE: HOW THE DIGITAL REVOLUTION IS ACCELERATING INNOVATION, DRIVING PRODUCTIVITY, AND IRREVERSIBLY TRANSFORMING EMPLOYMENT AND THE ECONOMY 316–18 (2011) ("[L]ike the Google autonomous car, Watson the *Jeopardy!* champion supercomputer, and high-quality instantaneous machine translation, then, can be seen as the first examples of the kinds of digital innovations we'll see as we move further into the second half—into the phase where exponential growth yields jaw-dropping results.").

[207] *See* Larry E. Ribstein, *Practicing Theory: Legal Education for the Twenty-first Century*, 96 IOWA L. REV. 1649 (2011).

[208] *See* Blackman, *supra* note 8.

[209] Suits against LegalZoom.com for the unauthorized practice of law—a nebulous and vague term that will likely have to be defined by courts to reflect the development of the legal profession—are the first glimpses of the future of this litigation. Debra Cassens Weiss, *LegalZoom Can Continue to Offer Documents in Missouri Under Proposed Settlement*, A.B.A. J. NEWS (Aug. 23, 2011, 6:32 AM), http://www.abajournal.com/news/article/legalzoom_can_continue_to_offer_documents_in_missouri_under _proposed_settle/; Debra Cassens Weiss, *LegalZoom Sues North Carolina State Bar, Seeks to Register Legal Services Plan*, A.B.A. J. NEWS (Oct. 5, 2011, 5:31 AM), http://www.abajournal.com/news/article/legalzoom_sues_north_carolina_state_bar_seeks_to_register_legal _services_pl/.

[210] *See generally Unlocking the Law Symposium*, TRUTH ON MARKET, http://truthonthemarket.com/unlocking-the-law-symposium/ (last visited Dec. 29, 2011).

[211] *See* BRYNJOLFSSON & MCAFEE, *supra* note 206, at 363; MICHIO KAKU, PHYSICS OF THE FUTURE: HOW SCIENCE WILL SHAPE HUMAN DESTINY AND OUR DAILY LIVES BY THE YEAR 2100, at 312–13 (2011)

VIII. CONCLUSION

The inner-workings of the Supreme Court of the United States are shrouded in secrecy. From the first Monday in October until the last week in June, the Justices operate behind-the-scenes to decide some of the most important issues in our society. Now FantasySCOTUS can provide real-time predictions how the Court will decide these cases. The FantasySCOTUS crowdsourced prediction market provides a novel insight into how Court watchers perceive the decision-making of the United States Supreme Court.

This essay lays the foundation for future research into the predictive power of FantasySCOTUS. Ultimately, the data that serve as the basis for this Article are simply a starting point. As FantasySCOTUS continues to crowdsource new information, we will gain new and deeper insights into the task of predicting Supreme Court cases and modeling judicial behavior. Looking forward, this project is not just a scholarly exposition of a theoretical construct or a discussion of a novel fantasy league that yields respectable, but an analysis of not-yet reliable, Supreme Court predictions. Rather, it is effectively an emerging plan for a legal information service that could transform the way lawyers, and non-lawyers alike, interact with courts in the not-so-distant future.

("When technologies become widely dispersed, such as electricity and running water, they eventually become utilities. With capitalism driving down prices and increasing competition, these technologies will be sold like utilities, that is, we don't care where they come from and we pay for them only when we want them."); SUSSKIND, *supra* note 203, at 32 ("In summary, a commoditized legal service is an IT-based offering that is undifferentiated in the marketplace (undifferentiated in the minds of the recipients and not the providers of the service). For any given commodity, there may be very similar competitor products, or the product is so commonplace that it is distributed at low or no cost."); Kobayashi & Ribstein, *supra* note 9, at 1218 ("[T]he opportunities evident in advances in information technology will make more visible the costs of maintaining the current system of relying on the one-to-one delivery of legal advice and the benefits of moving to a legal information market.").

Copyright 2012 by Northwestern University School of Law
Northwestern Journal of Technology and Intellectual Property

Volume 10, Number 3 (January 2012)

Claiming Nanotechnology: Improving USPTO Efforts at Classification of Emerging Nano-Enabled Pharmaceutical Technologies

By Jordan Paradise[*]

I. INTRODUCTION

Touted as ushering in "the next industrial revolution"[1] over ten years ago, nanotechnology is now positioned to enable tremendous advances in virtually limitless scientific and technological fields. Unique and novel properties at the nanoscale have powered innovations in medicine and health care, environmental remediation, electronics, mechanics, energy, optics, computing and information technology, industrial manufacturing, and a vast array of marketed consumer goods. However, as nanotechnologies advance, so do a barrage of familiar questions that have vexed past technologies such as biotechnology, genetics, and stem cell research: how should knowledge and applications of the science and technology be integrated into marketed products, how will consumers access information about these products, how and to what extent should resulting inventions be protected, and who will serve as the gatekeeper?

The unique and far-ranging properties of nanostructures and nanotechnologies have particularly facilitated breakthroughs in the pharmaceutical and medical device realms. The interface of nanotechnology, biotechnology, and genetics have increased bioavailability, introduced more precise targeted drug delivery and release, decreased adverse side effects, and enabled cutting-edge cancer treatments. Due to the high-stakes characteristics of the pharmaceutical industry—national and multinational corporations, high upfront research and development costs, rigorous clinical trials and data requirements, a thriving generic drug market, and intense competition—patents are particularly critical to innovation and market protection.[2]

Not surprisingly, innovations at the intersection of nanotechnology and medicine have inundated the United States Patent and Trademark Office (USPTO) with the resulting patent applications. Patents that couple genetic sequence information,

[*] J.D.; Associate Professor of Law, Seton Hall University School of Law. E-mail: jordan.paradise@shu.edu. The author would like to thank John Jacobi and David Opderbeck for helpful feedback on drafts. Special thanks also to Katherine Matos, Joseph Jakas, and Ethan Fitzpatrick for excellent research assistance. This Article was generously supported by a summer research stipend from Seton Hall University School of Law.

[1] See, e.g., Press Release, White House, National Nanotechnology Initiative: Leading to the Next Industrial Revolution (Jan. 21, 2000), http://clinton4.nara.gov/WH/New/html/20000121_4.html.

[2] See Jordan Paradise, The Devil Is in the Details: Health Care Reform, Biosimilars, and Implementation Challenges for the Food and Drug Administration, 51 JURIMETRICS J. 279 (2011) [hereinafter Paradise, The Devil Is in the Details]; Jordan Paradise, Reassessing 'Safety' for Nanotechnology Combination Products: What Do 'Biosimilars' Add to Regulatory Challenges for the FDA?, 56 ST. LOUIS U. L.J. (forthcoming Dec. 2011).

biological information, and the enabling properties at the nanoscale for diagnosis, treatment, and long-term patient assessment are the next frontier in health care and medicine. Along with great promise, nanotechnology innovations undoubtedly signal looming patent battles as products reach the market.[3] As the U.S. health care model moves toward targeted and personalized medicine utilizing emerging technological advances, where drugs and medical interventions are tailored to individual biological make-up and genetic propensity, the pharmaceutical industry will need patent protections more than ever to stake out product identity and market share.

Recognizing the scope and commercial importance of nanotechnology, the USPTO has implemented a nanotechnology classification in a laudable effort to foster consistent categorization in the review of patent applications and maintain an organized storehouse of issued patents that involve nanotechnology. Developed in 2004, this classification spans 263 subclasses pertaining to inventions

> related to research and technology development at the atomic, molecular or macromolecular levels, in the length of scale of approximately 1–100 nanometer range in at least one dimension, and that provide a fundamental understanding of phenomena and materials at the nano-scale and to create and use structures, devices and systems that have novel properties and functions because of their size.[4]

As of May 31, 2011, the USPTO reports over 6,930 issued patents and over 8,725 pending patent applications classified as nanotechnology-related inventions.[5] While undoubtedly helpful for internal purposes, the USPTO's nanotechnology classification system merely groups patents together to ease prior art searches undertaken by patent examiners. The classification fails to assess relationships among and between these patents; identify potentially overlapping and infringing claims; and communicate information to critical stakeholders, including industry, consumers, and other regulatory agencies. It also leaves discretion to individual patent examiners to reassess and reclassify previously issued patents (before 2004) to determine if they are appropriate for the recently implemented nanotechnology classification. Problems of overlapping claims and complicated scientific aspects that arise will largely be left to courts to sort out—a clumsy forum for determination of complex patent law issues that arise based on scale, size, and interactions at the nanoscale that transcend previously envisioned physical and chemical boundaries.

Specifically, the USPTO and courts will increasingly face three core problems involving nanotechnology: (1) limitations of and inconsistencies among current definitions of nanotechnology; (2) uncertainty and lack of uniformity in measurement capabilities regarding critical aspects of size, properties, and characteristics at the

---

[3] *See* discussion *infra* Part III-B.

[4] *Class 977 Nanotechnology Cross-Reference Art Collection*, U.S. PAT. & TRADEMARK OFF., http://www.uspto.gov/web/patents/biochempharm/crossref.htm (last updated Mar. 18, 2010).

[5] *USPTO Patent Full-Text and Image Database*, U.S. PAT. & TRADEMARK OFF., http://patft.uspto.gov/netahtml/PTO/search-adv.htm (search "Query" for "ccl/977/$") (search last conducted May 31, 2011); *Patent Application Full Text and Image Database*, U.S. PAT. & TRADEMARK OFF., http://appft1.uspto.gov/netahtml/PTO/search-adv.html (search "Query" for "ccl/977/$") (search last conducted May 31, 2011).

nanoscale; and (3) the role of patent claims to accurately and consistently encapsulate and distinguish the scope of nanotechnology inventions. Although pressing, the first two problems apply across all scientific disciplines and federal regulatory agencies confronted with emerging applications of nanotechnology. This Article touches on these first two problems in a broad context, but it focuses on the third problem as positioned against the function and activities of the USPTO. Given the recent interest of the Supreme Court in questions of patentability and appropriate claim scope of genetic inventions,[6] the time is ripe for the USPTO to extract lessons for nanotechnology. Honing in on U.S. patent law, policy, and the current practice of the USPTO, as well as the effect of judicial review in shaping case law in scientific and technical areas, this Article extracts general lessons and extrapolates those lessons to the emerging realm of nanopharmaceuticals. While courts have yet to confront these issues on a regular basis, one particular case is useful in examining how nanotechnology patents may play out in courts.

This Article utilizes the recent district court case *Elan Pharma International, Ltd. v. Abraxis Bioscience*,[7] which involved a blockbuster nanotechnology cancer treatment, to illustrate inherent problems with the USPTO nanotechnology patent classification system and patent claim scope. Part II discusses the patent system and the USPTO, highlighting statutory provisions relevant to nanotechnology and identifying informative cases that apply and interpret those provisions. Part III examines the USPTO response to nanotechnology, tracing the development of the 977 patent classification system and identifying where clarification is needed from the USPTO and courts as nanopatenting progresses. Part IV discusses *Elan Pharma*, tying it to the three problems identified above and to the scientific and technical aspects of nanotechnology in the pharmaceutical realm. Part IV also analyzes both the Elan Pharma patent involved in the case and the subsequent patent awarded to Abraxis Bioscience following the case and attempts to reconcile the two. Part V suggests a research agenda to assist the USPTO in fulfilling its mission to foster and reward innovation, while also assisting in broader efforts to gather nanotechnology information. These suggestions include improving the existing nanotechnology classification process, increasing feedback and collaboration with other federal agencies relevant to nanotechnology inventions, instituting independent educational programs for patent examiners, and utilizing new pilot peer review pathways for nanotechnology applications to encourage broader dialogue on the scope of patent claims and relationships to already issued patents. Part VI concludes.

II. THE USPTO AND PATENT RIGHTS FOR INVENTIONS

Article I, Section 8, Clause 8 of the Constitution grants Congress the power "[t]o promote the Progress of Science . . . by securing for limited Times to . . . Inventors the exclusive Right to their . . . Discoveries."[8] The USPTO, first established as a governmental bureau in 1802, is now within the Department of Commerce. Congress vested authority in the USPTO to review and award patents within the confines of the U.S. Patent Code[9] and USPTO regulations[10] and to disseminate patent-related

---

[6] *See* discussion *infra* Part II-A-1.
[7] No. 06-438 GMS, 2007 WL 6382930 (D. Del. Dec. 17, 2007).
[8] U.S. CONST. art. 1, § 8, cl. 8.
[9] 35 U.S.C. §§ 1–376 (2006).

information to the public.[11]   This Part describes the traditional role of the USPTO in granting patent protections for inventions, highlights general patent requirements, and discusses legal precedent focusing on advancements in genetics that may pose future challenges for emerging nanopharmaceutical developments.   It also examines the characteristics of pharmaceutical patents given the statutory schemes for generic drug development and approval by the Food and Drug Administration (FDA).

A. Patent Requirements and Case Law

Patent law sets forth four general areas of invention: processes, machines, manufactures, and compositions of matter.[12]   In return for the public disclosure of an invention,[13] the applicant is rewarded with exclusive rights to the invention for twenty years from the date that the application was filed with the USPTO.[14]   The patent then gives the patent holder "the right to exclude others from making, using, offering for sale, or selling the invention throughout the United States or importing the invention into the United States."[15]

Patent law is not technology specific.   The federal patent statute,[16] USPTO regulations,[17] and internal USPTO policies and procedures[18] all apply to nanotechnology-related inventions as they do to inventions in any other technological field.   Absent direction from the USPTO or courts, examiners must review nanotechnology patents by applying the substantive requirements for patentability set out in 35 U.S.C. § 101 (utility), § 102 (novelty), § 103 (nonobviousness), and § 112 (specification) and must assure all other patent requirements in Title 35 are fulfilled.   Due to the evolving nature of the understanding of the science and technologies involved, questions remain about the application by the USPTO and courts of the substantive requirements to nanotechnology, as well as the foundational issue of patentable subject matter.   This Part examines these concerns as linked to specific provisions in the patent law[19] and addresses recent case law that may impact nanotechnology in the future.

---

[10] *Id.* § 2(b)(2).

[11] *Id.* § 2(a)(1), (2).

[12] *Id.* § 101. The USPTO defines process as a "process, act or method, and primarily includes industrial or technical processes"; machine as "need[ing] no explanation"; manufacture as "articles that are made, and includes all manufactured articles"; and compositions of matter as "relat[ing] to chemical compositions and may include mixtures of ingredients as well as new chemical compounds." U.S. PATENT & TRADEMARK OFFICE, GENERAL INFORMATION CONCERNING PATENTS 2–3 (2011), *available at* http://www.uspto.gov/patents/resources/general_info_concerning_patents.pdf. These four categories "taken together include practically everything that is made by man and the processes for making the products." *Id.*

[13] 35 U.S.C. § 112.

[14] *Id.* § 154(a)(2). Where a patent application was submitted prior to June 8, 1996, the term of exclusive rights extends seventeen years from the application filing date. MPEP § 2701 (8th ed. Rev. 2, May 2004).

[15] 35 U.S.C. § 154(a)(1).

[16] *Id.* §§ 1–376.

[17] 37 C.F.R. §§ 1–150 (2010).

[18] *See, e.g.*, MPEP (8th ed. Rev. 8, July 2010).

[19] This examination of patent law is admittedly only a cursory snapshot of the core provisions and case law in the interest of length.

1. Patentable Subject Matter

As the Supreme Court has identified through case law spanning over a century, the threshold question for determining patentability is whether the invention claims "laws of nature, physical phenomena, and abstract ideas."[20] If the claimed invention falls into one of these three broad categories, it is outside the scope of patentable subject matter as a foundational determination before even reaching issues of utility, novelty, nonobviousness, and specification. Anything falling within these three categories is "part of the storehouse of knowledge of all men . . . free to all men and reserved exclusively to none."[21] Supreme Court case law tracing back to 1874 instructs that merely removing natural sources from a naturally occurring material does not make it a new composition of matter or article of manufacture worthy of patent protection because the primary characteristics and functioning of the product do not significantly differ from what already exists in nature.[22] Case law involving abstract ideas teaches that the USPTO cannot issue patents for principles in the abstract, which are akin to fundamental truths.[23] There must be some tangible process tied to the formula or idea that moves it into the realm of patentability.[24]

Two recent high profile Supreme Court decisions tackling these boundaries of patentability:[25] the Federal Circuit's highly anticipated July 29, 2011 decision regarding

---

[20] Diamond v. Chakrabarty, 447 U.S. 303, 309 (1980).

[21] Funk Bros. Seed Co. v. Kalo Inoculant Co., 333 U.S. 127, 130 (1948).

[22] Am. Wood-Paper Co. v. Fibre Disintegrating Co., 90 U.S. (23 Wall.) 566, 584 (1874). Subsequent cases exploring similar questions of physical phenomenon and products of nature relating to claimed inventions for compositions of matter or articles of manufacture include *Funk Brothers Seed Co.*, 333 U.S. 127 (combinations and mixtures of root nodule bacteria were not patentable where they served as packaging function and bacteria still performed in their natural way); *Cochrane v. Badische Anilin & Soda Fabrik*, 111 U.S. 293 (1884) (synthetic version of alizarine, a dye already existing in nature, imbued with a brighter hue was not patentable subject matter because it was a known product of nature); *Merck & Co. v. Olin Mathieson Chemical Corp.*, 253 F.2d 156 (4th Cir. 1958); *General Electric Co. v. De Forest Radio Co.*, 28 F.2d 641 (3d Cir. 1928) (ductility and high tensile strength of purified tungsten making it pliable at room temperature were characteristics given by nature, not the inventor, and thus not patentable); *In re Merz*, 97 F.2d 599 (C.C.P.A. 1938) (purified ultramarine dye unpatentable even though produced with new process creating brighter hue); *In re Marden* (*Marden II*), 47 F.2d 958, 959 (C.C.P.A. 1931) (patent for purified vanadium exhibiting increased ductility and malleability denied because it was a product of nature and "nothing more or less than vanadium freed from all of its impurities"); *In re Marden* (*Marden I*), 47 F.2d 957 (C.C.P.A. 1931) (purified uranium with increased ductility not patentable because it was a purified form of a product of nature; the court found the process, but not the composition, patentable); and *Ex parte Latimer*, 1889 Dec. Comm'r Pat. 123 (holding that purified pine needle fiber derived from *Pinus australis* was not patentable as a new article of manufacture for use in textiles).

[23] Gottschalk v. Benson, 409 U.S. 63, 67 (1972) (citing Le Roy v. Tatham, 55 U.S. (14 How.) 156, 175 (1852)).

[24] The chronological trilogy of cases on this point are *Gottschalk*, 409 U.S. 63 (algorithm to convert binary-coded decimal numerals into pure binary code not patentable because not a process but an abstract idea); *Parker v. Flook*, 437 U.S. 584, 590 (1978) (claiming process for monitoring conditions during catalytic conversion process in petrochemical and oil-refining industries not a patentable process because "post-solution activity" does not alone transform an unpatentable principle into a patentable process); and *Diamond v. Diehr*, 450 U.S. 175 (1981) (claims to previously unknown method for molding raw, uncured, synthetic rubber into cured precision products using a mathematical formula to complete some of the steps with a computer is patentable, as it patents an industrial process rather than the mathematical formula).

[25] These two cases are *Bilski v. Kappos*, 130 S. Ct. 3218 (2010), and *Laboratory Corp. of America Holdings v. Metabolite Laboratories*, 548 U.S. 124 (2006) (per curiam). Bilski involved patent claims

the patentability of genetic sequences[26] and the recent grant of certiorari to examine whether diagnostic tests that correlate results and patient health are phenomena of nature[27] pose questions for nanotechnology patents. Although outside the scope of this Article, this collection of cases signals past and present struggles by courts and the USPTO to apply bright-line rules to determine whether a claimed invention is not patent eligible as a law of nature, physical phenomenon, or abstract idea. This is surely informative for nanotechnology as patenting trends continue; aside from litigation involving allegations of patent infringement for a nanotechnology patent, there may also be challenges to USPTO (and Patent Board of Appeals) determinations of ineligibility that make their way to the Federal Circuit and Supreme Court. To be sure, nanotechnology products and inventions will inevitably cross all scientific and technical areas that have thus far raised questions in terms of patentable subject matter and laws of nature, physical phenomenon, and abstract ideas.

2. Utility

In addition to enumerating the four technological categories of patentable subject matter, § 101 also requires that an inventor show that the claimed invention is "useful." As discussed in the context of patentable subject matter, "[w]hoever invents or discovers any new and useful process, machine, manufacture, or composition of matter, or any new and useful improvement" may obtain a patent, subject to the conditions of the application

---

related to the interaction of commodities buyers and sellers and methods of hedging against the risk of price fluctuations using a mathematical formula. *Bilski*, 130 S. Ct. at 3223. The Federal Circuit had previously applied the machine-or-transformation test and found the invention is not patentable subject matter. *In re* Bilski, 545 F.3d 943, 964 (Fed. Cir. 2008). The court held that "[a] claimed process is surely patent-eligible under § 101 if: (1) it is tied to a particular machine or apparatus, or (2) it transforms a particular article into a different state or thing." *Id.* at 954. In *Metabolite*, the majority ultimately dismissed the writ of certiorari as improvidently granted following oral arguments. *Metabolite Labs.*, 548 U.S. at 125. The patent claim covered not only the action of assaying body fluid samples to measure homocysteine levels, but also the action of correlating the assay result to a vitamin deficiency. *Id.* at 129 (Breyer, J., dissenting). However, the strong dissent by Justice Breyer foreshadows future attention from the Court. Examining precedent and the scope of the patent claim, Breyer concluded that the patent was invalid as an unpatentable natural phenomenon. *Id.* at 137 (citing *Flook*, 437 U.S. at 588 n.9).

[26] Ass'n for Molecular Pathology v. U.S. Patent & Trademark Office, 653 F.3d 1329 (Fed. Cir. 2011). The panel reversed the district court's decision that the composition claims to "isolated" DNA molecules claiming *BRCA1* and *BRCA2* genes cover patent-ineligible products of nature under 35 U.S.C. § 101 because the molecules as claimed do not exist in nature. *Id.* at 1334, 1342. It reversed the decision that the method claim to screening potential cancer therapeutics via changes in cell growth rates is directed to a patent-ineligible scientific principle and affirmed the decision that method claims directed to "comparing" or "analyzing" DNA sequences are patent ineligible, reasoning that they include no transformative steps and cover abstract mental steps and are thus patent ineligible. *Id.* at 1334.

[27] The Supreme Court granted certiorari on June 20, 2011. Prometheus Labs., Inc. v. Mayo Collaborative Servs., 628 F.3d 1347 (Fed. Cir. 2010), *cert. granted*, 131 S. Ct. 3027 (2011). The patents at issue in *Prometheus* claim blood level measurement and assessment methods coupled with correlation of patient blood levels, patient health, and proper dosage of thiopurine drugs for treatment of "gastrointestinal and non-gastrointestinal autoimmune diseases." Prometheus Labs., Inc. v. Mayo Collaborative Servs., 581 F.3d 1336, 1339 (Fed. Cir. 2009). The Federal Circuit originally held the claims patentable and valid in 2009 based on the machine-or-transformation test. *Id.* The Federal Circuit upheld that decision in December 2010. *Prometheus Labs.*, 628 F.3d at 1347.

requirements.[28]   An inventor must show that the invention has a specific, substantial, and credible utility where credibility is measured from the perspective of one skilled in the art.[29]   This inquiry also ties into the § 112 specification assessment, discussed below, which requires a description of how to make and use the invention.   Given the fact that the USPTO rarely invokes the utility requirement as grounds for denying a patent (and accused infringers rarely hinge a legal defense on it),[30] it is similarly unlikely to be a hurdle for nanotechnology patents.   By its very nature, nanotechnology introduces characteristics and functions not observed at the macro scale or micro scale that lead to new uses based on those characteristics and functions.   Both the National Nanotechnology Initiative (NNI) definition and the USPTO definition instruct that the size is not the only aspect to be considered; the novel features that result, as well as the ability to control and manipulate at that size, are also critical.[31]

3. Novelty

Novelty is generally described as what it does not include.   An invention is not novel if it was: (1) known or used by others, patented, or described in a printed publication prior to the invention by the patent applicant;[32] (2) in public use or on sale for over a year prior to the date of the application;[33] (3) abandoned by the inventor;[34] (4) patented for more than a year prior to the U.S. application in a foreign country;[35] (5) described in another patent;[36] (6) not invented by the applicant (as in the case of theft);[37] or (7) made by a person other than the applicant or assignee.[38]   Case law offers that "there can be no hard and fast rule" to determine novelty and each case must be examined on a case-by-case basis;[39] but, essentially, an invention must accomplish something new to satisfy the substantive novelty requirements.

Claims based on the novel properties of nanotechnology inventions often distinguish new claims from prior art due to the different features, characteristics, and properties at the nanoscale that did not exist at the macro scale.   Nanotechnology inventions often exhibit unexpected, size-dependent properties that result in the very novelty of the invention.   For example, gold nanoparticles (approximately 13 nm in diameter) have fluorescent properties not present at a larger scale, and their ability to bind to DNA make them excellent sensors to detect and image life-threatening viruses and bacteria.[40]   One such detection system reports ten times the sensitivity and 100,000 times

---

[28] 35 U.S.C. § 101 (2006).
[29] Utility Examination Guidelines, 66 Fed. Reg. 1092, 1097 (Jan. 5, 2001).
[30] MARTIN J. ADELMAN ET AL., CASES AND MATERIALS ON PATENT LAW 181 (1st ed. 1998).
[31] See discussion infra Part III.
[32] 35 U.S.C. § 102(a).
[33] Id. § 102(b).
[34] Id. § 102(c).
[35] Id. § 102(d).
[36] Id. § 102(e)(2).
[37] Id. § 102(f).
[38] Id. § 102(g)(2).
[39] Union Carbide Co. v. Am. Carbide Co., 181 F. 104, 106 (2d Cir. 1910).
[40] KEWAL K. JAIN, THE HANDBOOK OF NANOMEDICINE 69–70 (2008).

the specificity of genomic detection systems currently in use.[41]   Because the nanotechnology definition implemented by the USPTO requires size-dependent properties to be included in the 977 Class,[42] patent applicants must include some indicia of inclusion into that size range that results in a novel property exhibited by the claimed invention.

Two century-old cases demonstrate courts' long-standing view regarding novelty and are relevant to nanotechnology. Both cases involve a new form of an already known man-made substance that gave the invention an increased commercial or therapeutic value. In one, the inventor laid claim to a man-made substance, calcium carbide, in crystalline form when it was previously only available in a man-made amorphous form.[43] The Second Circuit held that a "[m]ere change of form in and of itself does not disclose novelty"[44] but could be based on superior efficiency, durability, purity, or other comparative aspects that gave the invention commercial benefit.[45] Similarly, the Seventh Circuit held that aspirin—a purified, crystallized version of acetyl salicylic acid (a man-made substance)—was patentable because, although it is chemically the same, after it is heated with acetic anhydride to produce a crystallized form, it holds a tight bond while passing through the acidic fluids of the stomach and releases effectively in the intestines. This increases the therapeutic effect.[46]   The court noted that "a chemical formula is simply the symbolical expression of the composition or constitution of a substance . . . . That is to say, two substances, having the same chemical formula, may differ widely, as to impurities, upon qualitative analysis."[47] Subsequent cases have echoed this view.[48]

4. Nonobviousness

Logically tied to concepts of novelty, patent applications can also be rejected by patent examiners on grounds of obviousness, where patent examiners conduct a comparison of the invention to what is already in the public domain, termed the prior art. If the patent examiner determines that the differences between the scope and content of subject matter in the application and the prior art renders the subject matter as a whole obvious at the time of invention to a "person having ordinary skill in the art," it will be deemed obvious and unable to acquire patent protection.[49]

In a recent trend, the USPTO and the Federal Circuit have construed obviousness by applying the "teaching, suggestion, or motivation" (TSM) test. Under this test, an invention is obvious if the "the prior art, the problem's nature, or the knowledge of a person having ordinary skill in the art reveals some motivation or suggestion to combine

---

[41] So-Jung Park et al., *Array-Based Electrical Detection of DNA with Nanoparticle Probes*, 295 SCIENCE 1503 (2002).
[42] *See* discussion *infra* Part III.
[43] *Union Carbide*, 181 F. at 105.
[44] *Id.* at 106.
[45] *Id.* at 106–07.
[46] Kuehmsted v. Farbenfabriken of Elberfeld Co., 179 F. 701 (7th Cir. 1910).
[47] *Id.* at 703–04.
[48] *See, e.g.*, Lori Andrews & Jordan Paradise, *Genetic Sequence Patents: Historical Justification and Current Impacts*, *in* MAX PLANCK INST. FOR THE HISTORY OF SCI., LIVING PROPERTIES: MAKING KNOWLEDGE AND CONTROLLING OWNERSHIP IN THE HISTORY OF BIOLOGY 137, 151–52 (Jean-Paul Gaudillière et al. eds., 2009) (discussing cases addressing the issue of gene patenting).
[49] 35 U.S.C. § 103(a) (2006).

the prior art teachings."[50]   The Supreme Court clarified the scope of the TSM test in *KSR v. Teleflex*, holding that the narrow, rigid manner of evaluating obviousness under the TSM test is inconsistent both with § 103 and with the Court's precedent.[51]   Referencing the 1966 case *Graham v. John Deere Co. of Kansas City*,[52] the Court reiterated the need for an expansive and flexible approach in which the inquiry is not limited to the TSM test, but considers whether the improvement to the prior art is more than "the predictable use of prior art elements according to their established functions."[53]   Although the Court stated that the TSM test "captured a helpful insight" that a patent is nonobvious merely because each element of the patent was independently known in the prior art, it should not become a rigid and mandatory formula.[54]   The USPTO, the Board of Patent Appeals and Interferences, and the Federal Circuit will be attempting to apply this expansive view of the obviousness inquiry to all areas of invention in the coming years.[55]

The USPTO appears to maintain the position that claim limitations related to size or scale are insufficient to overcome prior art.[56]   The USPTO relies on the 1955 U.S. Court of Customs and Patent Appeals case of *In re Rose*[57] to support its position that the nonobviousness requirement is not fulfilled by the mere nanoscale "miniaturization" of already-patented products.[58]   *In re Rose* involved claims to an apparatus and methods of packaging, handling, and storing lumber where the claimed invention related merely to a difference in size from that in the prior art.[59]   Analogizing to this case, merely scaling down to the nanoscale would conflict with *In re Rose*.

However, where a patent application also provides a novel use and utility (and fulfills all other patentability requirements) in addition to identifying and claiming a difference in scale, it would be eligible for patent protection. Of course, this also depends

---

[50] KSR Int'l Co. v. Teleflex Inc., 550 U.S. 398, 399 (2007).

[51] *Id.* at 400.

[52] 383 U.S. 1 (1966).

[53] *KSR*, 550 U.S. at 417. The Court stated:

> Often, it will be necessary for a court to look to interrelated teachings of multiple patents; the effects of demands known to the design community or present in the marketplace; and the background knowledge possessed by a person having ordinary skill in the art, all in order to determine whether there was an apparent reason to combine the known elements in the fashion claimed by the patent at issue. To facilitate review, this analysis should be made explicit. As our precedents make clear, however, the analysis need not seek out precise teachings directed to the specific subject matter of the challenged claim, for a court can take account of the inferences and creative steps that a person of ordinary skill in the art would employ.

Id. at 418 (citations omitted).

[54] *Id.* at 418, 419.

[55] For a discussion of the case's relevance to nanotechnology, see Matthew J. Dowd et al., KSR International Co. v. Teleflex Inc.: *Another Small Issue for Nanotechnology?*, 4 NANOTECHNOLOGY L. & BUS. 293 (2007).

[56] *In re* Rose, 220 F.2d 459 (C.C.P.A. 1955).

[57] *Id.*

[58] R. Scott Roe, Note, *Nanotechnology: When Making Something Smaller is Nonobvious*, 12 B.U. J. SCI. & TECH. L. 127, 130 (2006) (citing Vivek Koppikar et al., *Current Trends in Nanotech Patents: A View from Inside the Patent Office*, 1 NANOTECH. L. & BUS. 24, 28 (2004)).

[59] *In re* Rose, 220 F.2d at 463 ("Appellant argues that this claim recites that the package is of appreciable size and weight so as to require handling by a lift truck whereas [the prior art references'] packages can be lifted by hand. We do not feel that this limitation is patentably significant since it at most relates to the size of the article under consideration which is not ordinarily a matter of invention.").

on the scope of the claims present in prior art patents and whether a size range that covered the nanoscale was specifically claimed in the prior art patent that covered the nanotechnology invention for which a patent is sought.[60] The USPTO has indicated that patent applicants would be more likely to avoid rejection on obviousness grounds if they affirmatively provide both a statement that the prior art did not recognize that the reduction of the disclosed invention to nanoparticle size would have specific benefits and recite a standard deviation from average particle size.[61]

Case law also establishes that a product claim is not obvious unless the process for making that product is also obvious.[62] This relates to the level of ordinary skill in the art, as measured from the date of the invention. Courts have examined this in the context of crystalline drug forms.[63] For nanotechnology, inventors should explicitly set forth that the methods for making the nano-sized invention were not obvious because the methods to scale it either top-down or bottom-up did not exist at the time of the prior art.[64]

Anticipation is another facet of obviousness that has been discussed in the context of nanotechnology. A patent claim is deemed "anticipated" by the prior art "if each and every limitation is found either expressly or inherently in a single prior art reference."[65] Despite a finding of novelty based on the newfound properties grounded in changes in size, patent claims may face "inherency" rejections where the claimed invention focuses on the inherent properties at the nanoscale.[66] The doctrine of inherency allows the examiner to locate similar art and argue that the claimed property is inherently or necessarily possessed in that prior art because it "necessarily flows from the teachings of the applied prior art."[67] This strong reliance on nanoscale properties may complicate the patent examination process, as searching prior art for size and property limitations is not an easy task where inventions span numerous scientific fields. As a result, many examiners are inclined to reject the application for inherency.[68] For example, a substantially identical structure or composition may establish a prima facie case of obviousness, even if the claimed nanotechnology characteristic is not disclosed or claimed in the prior art.[69] However, as discussed in Part III, the USPTO nanotechnology classification aims to ameliorate some of these problems.

---

[60] Part II-B, *infra*, discusses this in terms of literal infringement and the reverse doctrine of equivalents.

[61] *USPTO Holds Second Nanotechnology Customer Partnership Meeting*, USPTO CONNECTION (Moazzam Latimer LLP, McLean, Va.), May 2004, at 3, http://www.moazzamlaw.com/dev/Vol1-Issue1.pdf [hereinafter *Second Nanotechnology Meeting*].

[62] Jeremy M. Stipkala, *Overcoming Obviousness When Patenting Nanotechnology Inventions*, 23 NATURE BIOTECHNOLOGY 677, 677 (2005).

[63] *Id.* (citing *In re* Irani, 427 F.2d 806 (C.C.P.A. 1970)).

[64] *Id.* at 678.

[65] Celeritas Techs., Ltd. v. Rockwell Int'l Corp., 150 F.3d 1354, 1361 (Fed. Cir. 1998).

[66] Nikolas J. Uhlir, Note, *Throwing a Wrench in the System: Size-Dependent Properties, Inherency, and Nanotech Patent Applications*, 16 FED. CIR. B.J. 327, 342 (2007).

[67] *Id.* at 343–44.

[68] *Id.* at 339–41.

[69] *Id.*

5. Specification

In addition to showing the utility, novelty, and nonobviousness of the claimed invention, the applicant must also include a specification.[70] This specification must include a written description that provides the manner and process of making and using the invention in such concise, exact terms as to "enable any person skilled in the art" to make and use it.[71] Pursuant to this section, the applicant also must set forth the best mode of carrying out the invention and must sufficiently disclose the invention.[72] As the second paragraph of § 112 mandates, the specification section must conclude with "one or more claims particularly pointing out and distinctly claiming the subject matter" of the invention.[73] This two-paragraph section offers the public the general knowledge included in the patent in return for the exclusive patent rights to the invention being awarded to the inventor.[74] Patent examiners use the specification to interpret the scope of the claims and relationship to the prior art.

The Federal Circuit recently visited the scope of the written description requirement in *Ariad Pharmaceuticals, Inc., v. Eli Lilly & Co.*[75] Ariad and its research partners discovered the activation mechanisms of the NF-kB protein in human cells in response to certain diseases such as AIDS and various cancers, and they identified how the protein subsequently binds to other cells in the human body and causes the cells to produce proteins that fight infections.[76] The proteins produced by NF-kB are harmful when produced in such excess.[77] Ariad filed a patent for methods to reduce binding of NF-kB to limit the negative impacts of excess protein production.[78] However, when it submitted its patent application, Ariad had not finalized the listed techniques it claimed could effectively reduce NF-kB binding. On review, the Federal Circuit examined the state of jurisprudence regarding written description.

The court addressed two primary issues in *Ariad*: (1) whether § 112 contains a written description requirement separate from the enablement requirement; and (2) if so, the scope of that written description requirement.[79] The court provided a lengthy analysis

---

[70] 35 U.S.C. § 112 (2006) ("The specification shall contain a written description of the invention, and of the manner and process of making and using it, in such full, clear, concise, and exact terms as to enable any person skilled in the art to which it pertains, or with which it is most nearly connected, to make and use the same, and shall set forth the best mode contemplated by the inventor of carrying out his invention. The specification shall conclude with one or more claims particularly pointing out and distinctly claiming the subject matter which the applicant regards as his invention.").

[71] *Id.*

[72] *Id.* The best mode requirement pertains to the best mode as contemplated by the inventor at the time of invention.

[73] *Id.*

[74] *See* Rebecca S. Eisenberg, *Patents and the Progress of Science: Exclusive Rights and Experimental Use*, 56 U. CHI. L. REV. 1017, 1022 (1989).

[75] 598 F.3d 1336 (Fed. Cir. 2010). For a thoughtful analysis of the case, see Joseph Jakas, Comment, *Encouraging Further Innovation:* Ariad v. Eli Lilly *and the Written Description Requirement*, SETON HALL L. REV. (forthcoming 2012).

[76] Ariad Pharm., Inc. v. Eli Lilly & Co., 560 F.3d 1366, 1369–70 (Fed. Cir. 2009).

[77] *Ariad Pharm.*, 598 F.3d at 1340.

[78] *Id.* at 1355. These techniques included manipulating NF-kB inhibitors, using an NF-kB molecule that did not have the ability to produce the harmful proteins, or using decoy molecules to bind to NF-kB binding sites. *Id.* at 1356.

[79] *Id.* at 1342.

of the history and interpretation of § 112, looking to the statute and relevant court precedent. The Federal Circuit determined that the two requirements were, indeed, separate and that the written description requirement should be applied to original claims.[80] The court further held that an inventor must specifically show "possession [of the claimed invention] as shown in the disclosure" upon filing of the patent application.[81] Thus, an inventor would not satisfy the requirement by describing a broad method and listing a few ways to accomplish that method. Without a more detailed description, the inventor fails to possess the full scope of the claimed invention.

Although how lower courts will interpret and apply this decision remains unclear and somewhat controversial, the Federal Circuit's decision in *Ariad* may have an impact on nanotechnology patents that claim a broad range of sizes. After *Ariad*, an inventor must show in the disclosure of the invention that she was able to produce the size within the range being claimed. To accomplish this, the inventor should disclose separate species within the claimed range rather than general description of a broad category. The inventor should also be specific about the effects of the invention, linking the disclosed structure and size to the desired function of the claimed invention. The core failure of the Ariad patent is that it merely predicted how certain claimed techniques would have the desired effects of reducing binding before actually achieving those effects as a result of the research. Nanotechnology inventions could have similar issues with the possession requirement if they disclose unfinished (yet informative) research findings to claim an invention not yet completed.

B. Critiques of Nanotechnology Patenting

Academics[82] and practitioners[83] alike have written on the topic of nanopatenting, focusing much of their discussion on the scope of claims and the approach to claim

---

[80] The court parsed out the statute as: the specification must contain (1) a written description of the invention and (2) a written description "of the manner and process of making and using [the invention] in such full, clear, concise, and exact terms as to enable any person skilled in the art . . . to make and use the same." *Id.* at 1344.

[81] *Id.* at 1351 (internal quotation marks omitted).

[82] *See, e.g.*, Indrani Barpujari, *The Patent Regime and Nanotechnology: Issues and Challenges*, 15 J. INTELL. PROP. RTS. 206 (2010); Diana M. Bowman & Graeme A. Hodge, *A Small Matter of Regulation: An International Review of Nanotechnology Regulation*, 8 COLUM. SCI. & TECH. L. REV. 1 (2007); K. Eric Drexler & Jason Wejnert, *Nanotechnology and Policy*, 45 JURIMETRICS J. 1 (2004); Frederick A. Fiedler & Glenn H. Reynolds, *Legal Problems of Nanotechnology: An Overview*, 3 S. CAL. INTERDISC. L.J. 593 (1994); Ernest J. Getto et al., *Nanotechnology: Will Tiny Particles Create Large Legal Issues?*, SCITECH LAW., Summer 2009, at 6, 6; Dennis S. Karjala, *Protecting Innovation in Computer Software, Biotechnology, and Nanotechnology*, 16 VA. J.L. & TECH. 42 (2011); Mark A. Lemley, *Patenting Nanotechnology*, 58 STAN. L. REV. 601 (2005); Thomas M. Mackey, *Nanobiotechnology, Synthetic Biology, and RNAi: Patent Portfolios for Maximal Near-Term Commercialization and Commons for Maximal Long-Term Medical Gain*, 13 MARQ. INTELL. PROP. L. REV. 123 (2009); Glenn Harlan Reynolds, *Nanotechnology and Regulatory Policy: Three Futures*, 17 HARV. J.L. & TECH. 179 (2003); Douglas J. Sylvester & Diana M. Bowman, *Navigating the Patent Landscape for Nanotechnology: English Garden or Tangled Grounds?*, in BIOMEDICAL NANOTECHNOLOGY: METHODS AND PROTOCOLS 359 (Sarah J. Hurst ed., 2011); Georgios I. Zekos, *Patenting Abstract Ideas in Nanotechnology*, 9 J. WORLD INTELL. PROP. 113 (2006).

[83] *See, e.g.*, Laurie A. Axford, *Patent Drafting Considerations for Nanotechnology Inventions*, 3 NANOTECHNOLOGY L. & BUS. 305 (2006); Raj Bawa, *Nanotechnology Patenting in the US*, 1

drafting.[84] The claims are critical during review by examiners to determine scope and whether an invention has an adequate written description. Similar to arguments raised regarding the emergence of biotechnology and genetic technologies at the end of the last century and the beginning of the twenty-first century,[85] some contend that the proliferation of nanotechnology patents may create a patent thicket due to overlapping claims.[86]

Due to the nature of broad claim drafting, nanotechnology-related patents are likely to literally infringe traditional product patents with broad claims and no reference to scale. However, many scholars posit that the reverse doctrine of equivalents may preclude a finding of literal infringement where the claimed invention is sufficiently different from the previously patented product, despite the fact that the accused claimed invention literally infringes the accuser's patent claims.[87] The reverse doctrine of equivalents was espoused by the Supreme Court in *Graver Tank & Manufacturing Co. v. Linde Air Products Co.*:

> [W]here a device is so far changed in principle from a patented article that it performs the same or a similar function in a substantially different way, but nevertheless falls within the literal words of the claim, the doctrine of equivalents may be used to restrict the claim and defeat the patentee's action for infringement.[88]

Two requirements must be satisfied for the reverse doctrine of equivalents to apply: the accused product must literally infringe the accuser's patent claims while also being "sufficiently different" from the patented product.[89]

Both Congress and the Federal Circuit have supported the basic principles of the reverse doctrine of equivalents set out by the Supreme Court. In enacting § 112 in 1952,

---

NANOTECHNOLOGY L. & BUS. 31 (2004); Dowd et al., *supra* note 55; Drew Harris et al., *Strategies for Resolving Patent Disputes Over Nanoparticle Drug Delivery Systems*, 1 NANOTECHNOLOGY L. & BUS. 372 (2004); Koppikar et al., *supra* note 58; John Josef Molenda, *The Importance of Defining Novel Terms in Patenting Nanotechnology Inventions*, 1 NANOTECHNOLOGY L. & BUS. 174 (2004); Sean O'Neill et al., *Broad Claiming in Nanotechnology Patents: Is Litigation Inevitable?*, 4 NANOTECHNOLOGY L. & BUS. 29 (2007).

[84] *See Nanotechnology Gold Rush Yields Crowded, Entangled Patents*, PRNEWSWIRE (Apr. 21, 2005), http://www.prnewswire.com/news-releases/nanotechnology-gold-rush-yields-crowded-entangled-patents-54373177.html. For example, Stephen B. Maebius, chair of the Nanotechnology Industry Team at Foley & Lardner LLP, advised companies filing nanotech patents to draft claims of intermediate scope rather than broad claims in response to court determinations in a number of biotechnology patents that held such broad claims invalid. *Id.*

[85] *See* Michael A. Heller & Rebecca S. Eisenberg, *Can Patents Deter Innovation? The Anticommons in Biomedical Research*, 280 SCIENCE 698, 698 (1998) (citing Garrett Hardin, *The Tragedy of the Commons*, 162 SCIENCE 1243 (1968)).

[86] *See, e.g.*, Lemley, *supra* note 82; Sylvester & Bowman, *supra* note 82.

[87] *See, e.g.*, Lemley, *supra* note 82; Terry K. Tullis, *Application of the Government License Defense to Federally Funded Nanotechnology Research: The Case for a Limited Patent Compulsory Licensing Regime*, 53 UCLA L. REV. 279 (2005); Andrew Wasson, *Protecting the Next Small Thing: Nanotechnology and the Reverse Doctrine of Equivalents*, 2004 DUKE L. & TECH. REV. 0010, *available at* http://www.law.duke.edu/journals/dltr/articles/2004dltr0010.

[88] Graver Tank & Mfg. Co. v. Linde Air Prods. Co., 339 U.S. 605, 608–09 (1950).

[89] Texas Instruments, Inc. v. U.S. Int'l Trade Comm'n, 846 F.2d 1369, 1371 (Fed. Cir. 1988).

Congress imposed "requirements for the written description, enablement, definiteness, and means-plus-function claims that are co-extensive with the broadest possible reach of the reverse doctrine of equivalents."[90] The Federal Circuit said that the reverse doctrine of equivalents and § 112 "spring from the same roots and very often take account of the same factors and considerations"[91] and the Supreme Court said that § 112 is "an application of the doctrine of equivalents in a restrictive role."[92] Given this view that the 1952 amendments codified the reverse doctrine of equivalents, the Federal Circuit has never relied upon the reverse doctrine of equivalents to affirm a decision of noninfringement independently of a § 112 analysis.[93] Some predict that, although the reverse doctrine of equivalents has existed only in theory for the last sixty years, it may be a successful defense for nanotechnology patent holders against claims of literal infringement.[94] Unique properties at the nanoscale may perform a similar function as chemicals, materials, or processes at the micro scale or macro scale, but operate in a substantially different manner. For example, nanocrystals diffuse at different rates given extremely small changes in size. Recent breast cancer research reports that the time for a 100 nm nanocrystal particle to reach tumor cells was two and a half times that of 20 nm particles (389 minutes as compared to 158 minutes).[95] One can assume that much larger particles, in the range of traditional pharmaceuticals, take much longer to reach a target site because of biological interactions. This has enormous implications for pharmaceutical development and pharmacokinetics, in that the purpose (i.e., drug delivery) remains the same, yet the rate of diffusion and biological and pharmacological interactions may differ dramatically.

Many of these projections remain untested because patent litigation targeted to nanotechnology has been limited thus far. However, future cases are likely to attack issues of patentability under § 101 in the context of genetic sequence patents, as well as the specific application of the core substantive requirements. The USPTO, the agency actively reviewing and issuing nanotechnology patents, is presently tackling many of these questions. If genetics are a litmus test for emerging medical technologies, then developments and inventions in nanotechnology (and nanopharmaceuticals specifically) will soon be appearing in court dockets. Part III provides an overview of the USPTO's efforts to gather information and classify inventions that utilize nanotechnology.

---

[90] Tate Access Floors, Inc. v. Interface Architectural Res., Inc., 279 F.3d 1357, 1368 (Fed. Cir. 2002). However, their application differs as to the timing of the inquiry. Whereas a § 112 analysis is made during examination of the patent application or during a court's determination of patentability, the reverse doctrine of equivalents serves as a defense to a claim of literal infringement where a court's inquiry is focused on the alleged infringing product's characteristics.
[91] Texas Instruments, 846 F.2d at 1372 (Davis, J., concurring in part).
[92] Warner-Jenkinson Co. v. Hilton Davis Chem. Co., 520 U.S. 17, 28 (1997).
[93] Tate Access Floors, 279 F.3d at 1368.
[94] See, e.g., M. Veronica Mullally & David R. Winn, Patenting Nanotechnology: A Unique Challenge to IP Bar, N.Y. L.J., July 6, 2004, at t2.
[95] Masaaki Kawai et al., Dynamics of Different-Sized Solid-State Nanocrystals as Tracers for a Drug-Delivery System in the Interstitium of a Human Tumor Xenograft, 11 BREAST CANCER RES. R43 (2009), http://www.biomedcentral.com/content/pdf/bcr2330.pdf.

III. THE USPTO NANOCLASSIFICATION

The term nanotechnology encompasses an array of technologies at the nanoscale, where "nanoscale" refers to measurements less than 100 nm (i.e., 10^{-9} m; one billionth of a meter). The NNI's definition of nanotechnology involves three inter-related (and inseparable) aspects:

> [(1)] Research and technology development at the atomic, molecular or macromolecular levels, in the length scale of approximately 1–100 nanometers,

> [(2)] Creation and use of structures, devices and systems that have novel properties and functions because of their small and/or intermediate sizes, and

> [(3)] Ability to be controlled or manipulated on the atomic scale.[96]

To earn the term nanotechnology, a particle or material must possess unique physical, chemical, or biological properties at the nanoscale that make that particle or material function in a manner that can be harnessed and controlled to utilize those unique properties. As discussed above, the USPTO has adopted a variation of the NNI definition for nanotechnology, keying in on the 1 to 100 nm range.[97] Nanobiotechnology merges nanotechnology and biotechnology and is described as "a field that applies the nanoscale principles and techniques to understand and transform biosystems . . . and which uses biological principles and materials to create new devices and systems integrated from the nanoscale."[98] Nanomedicine is an important facet of research and development, which, according to the National Institutes of Health, "refers to highly specific medical intervention at the molecular scale for curing disease or repairing damaged tissues, such as bone, muscle, or nerve."[99] There is widespread research activity in biomolecule and biomimetic devices, biosensors, molecular motors, biomolecular fabrics, engineered enzymes and proteins, and drug discovery and delivery.[100] The pharmaceutical and medical device industries, two of the most patent-motivated industries, are at the forefront of nanotechnology research and development.

One source reports that the USPTO began issuing nanotechnology-related patents as early as 1976.[101] However, it was not until the infusion of federal research funding for nanotechnology research and development that the unifying term nanotechnology made

---

[96] ENVTL. PROT. AGENCY, NANOTECHNOLOGY: AN EPA RESEARCH PERSPECTIVE, FACTSHEET 1 (2007), *available at* http://epa.gov/ncer/nano/factsheet/nanofactsheetjune07.pdf.

[97] *See supra* pp. 3–4.

[98] Mihail C. Roco, *Nanotechnology: Convergence with Modern Biology and Medicine*, 14 CURRENT OPINION IN BIOTECHNOLOGY 337, 337 (2003).

[99] *Nanomedicine Overview*, NAT'L INST. OF HEALTH COMMON FUND, http://commonfund.nih.gov/nanomedicine/overview.aspx (last updated Jan. 1, 2011).

[100] Alan L. Porter et al., *Refining Search Terms for Nanotechnology*, 10 J. NANOPARTICLE RES. 715, 718 (2008).

[101] Tyson Winarski, Esq. & Elizabeth Stoker-Townsend, *Nanotechnology Thriving on Patents*, INTELL. PROP. TODAY, Apr. 2005, at 26 (citing the National Science Foundation). However, the first patent within the USPTO patent classification system was filed in September 1975 and issued in August 1978. Injectable Compositions, Nanoparticles Useful Therein, & Process of Mfg. Same, U.S. Patent No. 4,107,288 (filed Sept. 9, 1975).

its way into the scientific and technical literature and into patent applications for inventions. In response to a surge of nanotechnology inventions, the USPTO embarked on a multi-phase project to systematically identify nanotechnology-related patents, patent applications, and research publications to ultimately develop a method of classification to capture the breadth of nanotechnology.[102]   The USPTO's goals in developing a nanotechnology classification system were to construct a uniform framework to standardize the terminology, create an effective system for disclosure and cross-referencing, assist inventors and examiners in identifying and reviewing relevant prior art, and decrease inadvertent patent infringement.

A. Development of the "977" Class

The USPTO initiated the 977 classification project in November 2001, recognizing that patent examiners assessing nanotechnology patent applications were increasingly confronted with challenges relating to their level and type of training and the multidisciplinary features of nanotechnology.   These challenges included a lack of familiarity with the underlying science and technologies, the utilization of complex and often new terminology, and the expanse of the scientific literature.   These difficulties increased the risk that examiners were not equipped to assess the scope of the invention and previous inventions and increased the risk that relevant publications would be overlooked during examination.[103]   The USPTO recognized that the broad range of technological specialty areas and prior art reflected in the applications increased the likelihood that separate patent examiners would contemporaneously issue overlapping or even conflicting patents.[104]

Cognizant of these challenges facing examiners, the USPTO initiated the nanotechnology classification project. This multi-phase project proceeded incrementally in three core phases. The first was defining and setting the scope of nanotechnology for USPTO purposes; the second was creation of a cross-reference digest; and the third was the development of the 977 classification system.   To develop a classification of nanotechnology patents and to cross-reference the patents and supporting documents, the USPTO established a definition for purposes of "searching for, identifying, and classifying documents" related to nanotechnology.[105] The USPTO arrived at a definition of nanostructure "to mean an atomic, molecular, or macromolecular structure that: (a) [h]as at least one physical dimension of approximately 1–100 nanometers; and (b) [p]ossesses a special property, provides a special function, or produces a special effect

---

[102] 35 U.S.C. § 8 provides authority to the USPTO to classify patents. It reads: "The Director may revise and maintain the classification by subject matter of United States letters patent, and such other patents and printed publications as may be necessary or practicable, for the purpose of determining with readiness and accuracy the novelty of inventions for which applications for patents are filed." *Id.*

[103] *See* Barnaby J. Feder, *Tiny Ideas Coming of Age*, N.Y. TIMES, Oct. 24, 2004, at WK12.

[104] *See, e.g.*, EROSION, TECH., & CONCENTRATION GRP., NANOTECH'S "SECOND NATURE" PATENTS: IMPLICATIONS FOR THE GLOBAL SOUTH 8 (2005), http://etcgroup.org/upload/publication/54/02/com8788specialpnanomar-jun05eng.pdf [hereinafter NANOTECH'S "SECOND NATURE" PATENTS].

[105] Vance McCarthy, *USPTO Poised to Ring in a New Era of Simplified Search and Better Visibility for Nano Patents*, NANO SCI. & TECH. INST. (Dec. 20, 2005), http://www.nsti.org/news/item.html?id=35.

that is uniquely attributable to the structure's nanoscale physical size."[106] The USPTO then established five categories of inventions involving nanotechnology: (1) nanostructures and chemical compositions; (2) devices that include at least one nanostructure; (3) mathematical algorithms; (4) methods or apparatuses for making, detecting, analyzing or treating nanostructure; and (5) specified uses of nanostructures.[107]

The agency next organized a task force consisting of twenty-five internal patent professionals from USPTO technology centers and the classification office to develop a list of nanotechnology-related terms used by inventors that would assist in the identification of nanotechnology publications within the existing patent database. The task force developed 150 search terms to be employed to sketch out trends and concepts emerging from the patented inventions relating to nanotechnology. To garner input from the larger community of consumers of nanoproducts, the USPTO also invited the public to a series of Nanotech Partnership Meetings[108] through a Nanotechnology Customer Partnership initiative. The initiative was envisioned by the USPTO as "a forum to share ideas, experiences, and insights between individual users and the USPTO."[109] To further inform the process, the USPTO also initiated a trilateral discussion on the topic of effective and consistent international review of nanotechnology applications and development of classes and subclasses for nanotechnology inventions with the European Patent Office and Japanese Patent Office.[110]

As a result of these efforts, the USPTO in August of 2004 established a nanotechnology cross-reference digest—designated Class 977, Digest 1. This cross-reference digest operated by gathering all nanotechnology publications in a single place, replacing the inefficient keyword searches of prior art in multiple scientific fields by examiners.[111] The Office of the Commissioner of Patents provided that the new 977 cross-reference digest would (1) "[f]acilitate the searching of prior art related to Nanotechnology"; (2) "[f]unction as a collection of issued U.S. patents and published pre-grant patent applications relating to Nanotechnology across the technology centers"; and (3) "[a]ssist in the development of an expanded, more comprehensive, nanotechnology cross-reference art collection classification schedule."[112]

The important efficiency outcome of the cross-reference digest was to weed out prior art that was not actually developed by nanotechnology or did not actually contain nano-sized materials. For a variety of reasons, including the massive federal funding initiative supporting nanotechnology research and development as well as misunderstandings about nanotechnology, many inventors, scientists, and companies (often inaccurately) describe their research, inventions, or resulting products as involving

---

[106] U.S. PATENT & TRADEMARK OFFICE, CLASSIFICATION DEFINITIONS: CLASS 977, NANOTECHNOLOGY 1 (2010) [hereinafter CLASS 977 DEFINITIONS], *available at* http://www.uspto.gov/web/patents/classification/uspc977/defs977.pdf.
[107] *Id.*
[108] McCarthy, *supra* note 105.
[109] *Nanotechnology Customer Partnership Meeting*, U.S. PAT. & TRADEMARK OFF., http://www.uspto.gov/patents/init_events/nanotech.jsp (last updated July 4, 2009).
[110] *Second Nanotechnology Meeting*, *supra* note 61.
[111] NANOTECH'S "SECOND NATURE" PATENTS, *supra* note 104, at 8; McCarthy, *supra* note 105.
[112] Memorandum from the Office of the Comm'r for Patents to Patent Prof'l Emps., Nanotechnology Digest and Forthcoming Nanotechnology Cross-Reference Art Collection (XRAC)—Class 977 (Aug. 25, 2004), http://www.uspto.gov/web/offices/pac/dapp/opla/documents/nanotechdig.pdf.

or containing nanotechnology. For example, a keyword search of the prefix nano in the USPTO patent database returns tens of thousands of results where the majority of these patents are not technically nanotechnology as defined and classified by Class 977, Digest 1. Creating a nano-specific definition and class requirements has aided the USPTO in identifying and assessing prior art by eliminating irrelevant prior art from the start. However, the classification is also constrained by the USPTO's definition of nanotechnology.[113]

The USPTO next converted the single digest to a nanotechnology classification schedule with 263 cross-reference art collection subclasses,[114] facilitating the routing of patent applications to examiners with particular expertise. The USPTO based these classes on international patent classes available, as well as prior experience. In November 2005, the USPTO Classification Order 1850 officially abolished Class 977, Digest 1 and established the Class 977 and the cross-reference art collection Subclasses 700 through 963.[115] Each contained subclass definitions and a search note.[116]

While there is no centralized nanotechnology art unit within the USPTO centers, the 977 Class assists in locating applications and distributing among art units.[117] The lack of a nanotechnology art unit means that, to date, the USPTO has not assigned a group of "nano" examiners because of the diversity of nanotechnology inventions. When an application is submitted to the USPTO, it is distributed to one or more of the existing art units and linked subclasses such as "chemistry: molecular biology and microbiology" (Class 435) or "drug, bio-affecting and body treating compositions" (Class 424) based on the patent claims, and then filtered to the 977 classification as a cross-reference tool. In tandem with creation of the 977 classification, the USPTO has partnered with outside professionals and experts to train and educate patent examiners on nanotechnology terminology and concepts.[118]

B. Nanopharmaceutical Subclassifications

The 977 classification is comprised of 263 subclassifications: 700 through 963. Subclassifications 700 to 838 encompass various forms of a "nanostructure."[119] Subclassification 839 is reserved for mathematical algorithms "specifically adapted for

---

[113] See discussion supra notes 106–107 and accompanying text.
[114] Charles R. Eloshway, Nanotechnology-Related Issues at the United States Patent and Trademark Office, COMMUNITY RES. & DEV. INFO. SERVICE 5 (Dec. 2006), ftp://ftp.cordis.europa.eu/pub/nanotechnology/docs/iprworkshop_eloshway_en.pdf.
[115] David J. Robeson, Nanotechnology and the USPTO, NAT'L ASS'N PAT. PRAC. 3 (2006), http://www.napp.org/disclosure/linked_files/Nanotechnology%20and%20the%20USPTO_05.01.2006.pdf.
[116] CLASS 977 DEFINITIONS, supra note 106.
[117] Where Science and Law Meet: Nanotechnology and Intellectual Property Issues, NAT'L CANCER INST. 3 (Oct. 2006), http://nano.cancer.gov/action/news/featurestories/monthly_feature_2006_oct.pdf [hereinafter Where Science and Law Meet].
[118] Feder, supra note 103; Patent Office Struggles to Stay Ahead of Nanotech Industry, ELECTRO IQ (Apr. 20, 2004), http://www.electroiq.com/index/display/nanotech-article-display/269406/articles/small-times/legal/2004/04/patent-office-struggles-to-stay-ahead-of-nanotech-industry.html.
[119] U.S. PATENT & TRADEMARK OFFICE, CROSS-REFERENCE ART COLLECTIONS: CLASS 977 NANOTECHNOLOGY 1–3 (2010), available at http://www.uspto.gov/web/patents/classification/uspc977/sched977.pdf [hereinafter CLASS 977 SCHEDULE].

modeling configurations or properties of [a] nanostructure";[120] subclassifications 840 to 901 encompass "manufacture, treatment, or detection of [a] nanostructure";[121] subclassifications 902 to 962 encompass "specified use of [a] nanostructure";[122] and subclassification 963 is reserved for miscellaneous.[123]

The subclassifications within the 977 class most relevant to nanomedicine and pharmaceutical development are those that fall into subclassifications 904 through 926. These are specified uses of nanostructure for "medical, immunological, body treatment or diagnosis," divided into areas such as "drug delivery" (977/906), "mechanical repair performed/surgical" (977/908), "therapeutic or pharmaceutical composition" (977/915), "vaccine" (977/917), and "topical chemical" (977/926).[124] A particular patent will first list its primary classifications and subclassifications and then list the 977 cross-reference classifications and subclassifications. As of May 31, 2011, the 977/904 through 977/926 classifications consist of a total of 896 patents, many of which are listed in multiple subclassifications based on the substance of their claims.[125]

---

[120] *Id.* at 3.
[121] *Id.* at 4.
[122] *Id.*
[123] *Id.* at 5.
[124] *See infra* Figure 1.
[125] This count was retrieved using a specific methodology to eliminate duplicate patents listed in multiple sub-classifications. *USPTO Patent Full-Text and Image Database, supra* note 5 (search "Query" for "ccl/977/904 or ccl/977/905 or ccl/977/906 or ccl/977/907 or ccl/977/908 or ccl/977/909 or ccl/977/91$ or ccl/977/920 or ccl/977/921 or ccl/977/922 or ccl/977/923 or ccl/977/924 or ccl/977/925 or ccl/977/926").

FIGURE 1. USPTO NANOTECHNOLOGY SUBCLASSIFICATIONS 977/902 THROUGH
977/926[126]

```
977/902:  Specified Use of Nanostructure
    977/903:  For conversion, containment, or destruction of hazardous material
    977/904:  For medical, immunological, body treatment, or diagnosis
        977/905:  Specifically adapted for travel through blood circulatory system
        977/906:  Drug delivery
            977/907:  Liposome
        977/908:  Mechanical repair performed/surgical
            977/909:  Obstruction removal
            977/910:  Strengthening cell or tissue
            977/911:  Cancer cell destruction
            977/912:  Cancer cell repair
            977/913:  Stem cell therapy implantation
        977/914:  Protein engineering
        977/915:  Therapeutic or pharmaceutical composition
            977/916:  Gene therapy
            977/917:  Vaccine
        977/918:  Immunological
        977/919:  Dental
        977/920:  Detection of biochemical
            977/921:  Of toxic chemical
            977/922:  Of explosive material
        977/923:  Cell culture
        977/924:  Using nanostructure as support of DNA analysis
        977/925:  Bioelectrical
        977/926:  Topical chemical (e.g., cosmetic or sunscreen, etc.)
```

Patents for various FDA-approved and marketed pharmaceutical products have been classified in the 977 cross-reference system. For example, within the *Orange Book*[127] listing for Depocyt, an FDA-approved nanoparticle formulation of cytarbine for treatment of lymphomatous meningitis, the patent and exclusivity references include U.S. Patent No. 5,455,044 (method for treating neurological disorders).[128] In the patent itself, the primary classification is 424/450 (drug, bio-affecting, and body-treating compositions; preparations characterized by physical form; liposomes), followed by 977/907 (nanotechnology; specified use of nanostructure for medical, immunological, body treatment or diagnosis; specifically adapted for travel through blood circulatory system; liposome), 977/911 (nanotechnology; specified use of nanostructure for medical, immunological, body treatment or diagnosis; mechanical repair performed; surgical; cancer cell destruction), and 977/915 (nanotechnology; specified use of nanostructure for medical, immunological body treatment, or diagnosis; therapeutic or pharmaceutical composition). Similarly, the *Orange Book* listing for Estrasorb, an FDA-approved micellar nanoparticle estrogen delivery system for topical treatment of menopausal hot flashes, lists U.S. Patent No. 5,629,021 (micellar nanoparticles) within the patent and

---

[126] CLASS 977 SCHEDULE, *supra* note 119.
[127] The *Orange Book* is a publication of the Food and Drug Administration that lists patent and exclusivity information for pioneer and generic drugs. The searchable electronic version is available at *Orange Book: Approved Drug Products with Therapeutic Equivalence Evaluations*, U.S. FOOD & DRUG ADMIN., http://www.accessdata.fda.gov/scripts/cder/ob/default.cfm (last updated Oct. 28, 2011).
[128] Method for Treating Neurological Disorders, U.S. Patent No. 5,455,044 (filed May 14, 1993).

exclusivity references.[129] This patent's primary classification is 424/489 (drug, bio-affecting and body treating compositions; preparations characterized by physical form; particulate form), followed by 977/915 (nanotechnology; specified use of nanostructure for medical, immunological, body treatment or diagnosis; therapeutic or pharmaceutical composition) and 977/926 (nanotechnology; specified use of nanostructure for medical, immunological body treatment or diagnosis; topical chemical).

However, the underlying patents for many pharmaceutical products utilizing nanotechnology that have been approved by the FDA and are currently on the market have not been classified by the USPTO as nanotechnology.[130] As discussed below, there may be a variety of reasons for this, including the particular claim drafting, date of patent application, or other special circumstances relating to product development and commercialization. For example, many of the FDA-approved drugs utilizing nanotechnology were approved well before the USPTO implemented the 977 classification system.[131]

As the Appendix illuminates, the development of such a nanotechnology classification system, while proactive on the part of the USPTO, suffers from a number of limitations. The first major limitation is the USPTO's cut-off at 100 nm or less particle size. As described below, the first litigation involving an FDA-approved nanodrug was based on a preexisting patent that had not been classified by the USPTO in their nanotechnology classification because the claims regarding particle size exceeded the 100 nm ceiling (and the patent application was filed well before 2004). In fact, Abraxane, one of the first marketed nanodrugs and the subsequent product at issue in the litigation described in Part IV, has a 130 nm mean particle size;[132] the claim drafting moved that into the 977 classification based on the use of the phrase "less than about 200 nm" coupled with examples provided within the patent specification within the 50–220 nm range, which begins below 100 nm.[133] Because of broad claiming, many patents that have been awarded may be inaccurately excluded from the nanotechnology classification. In reality, nanomedicine products resulting from such patents could be deemed nano for FDA purposes (the Center for Drug Evaluation and Research within the FDA defines

---

[129] Micellar Nanoparticles, U.S. Patent No. 5,629,021 (filed Jan. 31, 1995).

[130] These products were identified using a two-pronged search methodology: a search of the relevant scientific literature reporting on research and development in nanopharmaceuticals and the FDA's website providing information on FDA-approved drugs, *Drugs@FDA Database*, U.S. FOOD & DRUG ADMIN., http://www.accessdata.fda.gov/scripts/cder/drugsatfda/index.cfm (last visited Dec. 20, 2011). Where a product was identified in the scientific literature as a nanopharmaceutical, the FDA database was used to retrieve that product's approval information. Searches were conducted from January 2011 through May 2011. The Appendix references all scientific sources.

[131] The Appendix provides information both from the scientific literature and the FDA on FDA-approved nanotechnology pharmaceutical products. Of the twenty-six products identified in the Appendix, only three of them have patents listed in the *Orange Book* that have been classified by the USPTO as qualifying for the 977 nanotechnology classification (i.e., Abraxane, DepoCyt, and Estrasorb).

[132] *See* ABRAXIS BIOSCIENCE, ONCOLOGIC DRUGS ADVISORY COMMITTEE MEETING BRIEFING PACKAGE: ABRAXANE (Aug. 4, 2006), http://www.fda.gov/ohrms/dockets/ac/06/briefing/2006-4235B2-01-01AbraxisBioscience-background.pdf.

[133] Compositions & Methods of Delivery of Pharmacological Agents, U.S. Patent No. 7,820,788 B2 col. 38 l. 22 (filed Oct. 26, 2006).

nanoscale material as having a particle size of less than 1,000 nm)[134] and not for USPTO purposes (defining nano as having a particle size of 100 nm or less). Other drug products may deviate from the 100 nm ceiling depending on the size of the actual nanodrug product compared to the total size of the particle containing the drug product and any encapsulating material or adjuvant.

The second limitation is that the USPTO began the classification project in 2004, without installing a uniform mechanism to retroactively reclassify existing patents into the new 977 classification system. Retroactively classifying already-issued patents into the new classification system was encouraged, though not required: "While every effort has been made to make the subclasses as complete as possible, the agency encourages patent examiners to classify newly issuing patents as well as previously published patent documents into the Class 977 cross-reference art collection subclasses . . . ."[135] An individual examiner may take the initiative to reclassify an already issued patent, but time constraints and meager salaries counsel otherwise. This may cause problems down the road in litigation, as Part IV illustrates.

The third limitation is that the information, once the patent is placed in the class and given a subclassification for cross-referencing, is not tracked or otherwise effectively utilized to identify patterns that may be playing out in the resulting marketed products or relationships to other issued patents. The USPTO's efforts serve as an example for other federal agencies in terms of gathering information relevant to nanotechnology and categorizing nano-specific features that could be useful in the future as more becomes known about the potential products, uses, and risks of nanotechnology. This information would be particularly useful to regulatory agencies overseeing the resulting products, such as the FDA. For example, as the Appendix reflects, there is often a disconnect between scientific research findings, information provided to the FDA for approval purposes, and what is actually presented to the public about the nanotechnology involved in commercial products. Utilization and effective linking of this information among agencies could serve as a mechanism to fill in the information gaps currently confronting other relevant agencies.

Despite the nascent state of patent litigation involving the scale or characteristics of nanotechnology, the scholarly literature has identified several concerns that will emerge as patenting continues that tie into the three limitations described above. The first major concern is that overlapping claims will result from broad claiming of scale in early patents coupled with more precise scale claims linked to particular properties and functions in later patents. For example, early patent claims may conflate the macro, micro, and nanoscale in a manner that is problematic for later inventions that identify and harness something present at a range in the nanoscale but not at the micro or macro scale. Another concern is the convergence of technologies at the nanoscale, in that overlapping patents and claims may cross multiple technologies, with many issued before nano was a widespread word. Many of these concerns will abate given the USPTO's classification

---

[134] OFFICE OF PHARM. SCI., CTR. FOR DRUG EVALUATION & RESEARCH, MANUAL OF POLICIES AND PROCEDURES, § 5015.9 REPORTING FORMAT FOR NANOTECHNOLOGY-RELATED INFORMATION IN CMC REVIEW 3 (2010), *available at* http://www.fda.gov/downloads/AboutFDA/CentersOffices/CDER/ManualofPoliciesProcedures/UCM2143 04.pdf [hereinafter NANOTECHNOLOGY MAPP].
[135] *Class 977 Nanotechnology Cross-Reference Art Collection, supra* note 4.

system as patenting moves forward, although questions will arise with regard to inventions submitted and patents issued prior to the development of the classification system. In performing the cross-listing classifications, the USPTO is merely putting issued patents into those 263 subclasses and not making determinations on claim scope and potential infringement from one patent to the next, except as part of the evaluation of prior art.

Part IV explores how the limitations in the USPTO's classification system play out in the courtroom by describing litigation involving a blockbuster nanotechnology-enabled treatment for cancer. This litigation highlights the problems posed by nanotechnology: the limitations of current definitions of nanotechnology; the critical aspects of size, properties, and characteristics at the nanoscale; and the importance of specificity in the scope of claim drafting. While this case is the first of its kind, the influx of nanotechnology patent applications into the USPTO over the last decade (as well as the thousands of issued patents classified as nanotechnology by reviewers for prior art purposes) suggests that similar litigation targeting the scope of nanotechnology claims will be forthcoming.

IV. "NANOTECHNOLOGY" IN COURT: *ELAN PHARMA V. ABRAXIS BIOSCIENCE*

Nanotechnology-specific issues have yet to loom large in the context of patent litigation. A targeted search of legal cases identifies very few patent disputes resulting in litigation that relate to the nano-size or characteristics of the invention at the nanoscale.[136] Most cases that include a reference to nano consist of non-patent allegations, including breach of contract, licensing issues, or trademark or copyright issues regarding a company name or product.[137] However, one high profile case in the realm of nanobiotechnology, *Elan Pharma v. Abraxis Bioscience*,[138] is particularly on point and instructive. The case exemplifies problems regarding scale range and lack of uniformity in patent claim drafting, the relationship between earlier non-nanotechnology classified patents and later nanotechnology classified patents, and the struggle in the courtroom by judges and juries to provide resolution to thorny scientific and technical issues. The case and the relevant patents are described below.

A. The Patent Litigation

Elan Pharma v. Abraxis Bioscience involved Abraxane, the Abraxis Bioscience blockbuster drug for treatment of breast cancer, approved by the FDA in 2005 for treatment of metastatic breast cancer and marketed widely. Sales generated $314.5 million in 2009.[139] Abraxane, the alleged infringing product, is the albumin formulation of paclitaxel, a cancer-fighting agent that has been used in FDA-approved drugs, such as

---

[136] A search of Westlaw state and federal cases retrieved forty-four cases. Search conducted June 2011.

[137] However, cases involving nanotechnology that do not utilize the term nanotechnology will not be identified by a search of case law resources, nor will litigation that has not progressed to the stage of reporting in an official reporter.

[138] Elan Pharma Int'l Ltd. v. Abraxis Bioscience Inc., No. 06-438 GMS, 2007 WL 6382930 (D. Del. Dec. 17, 2007).

[139] Jessica Merrill, *Celgene Moves into Solid Tumors with $2.9 Billion Abraxis Acquisition*, PINK SHEET: PRESCRIPTION PHARMACEUTICALS & BIOTECHNOLOGY, July 5, 2010, at 11.

Taxol, for years.[140]   In addition to allowing the faster administration of the drug (thirty minutes as opposed to three hours for the previous formulation, Taxol), the albumin-bound formulation "eliminates the need for a solvent that can be toxic and also means greater doses of paclitaxel can be given before side effects become intolerable."[141]

The jury determined that Abraxane infringed on several of Elan's patent claims in U.S. Patent No. 5,399,363 ('363 Patent),[142] issued by the USPTO in 1995. The Elan '363 Patent claimed anticancer compositions in the form of "surface modified nanoparticles" in "crystalline" form that "exhibit reduced toxicity and/or enhanced efficacy."[143]   The Elan Patent specifically claimed:

> Particles consisting essentially of 99.9% by weight of a crystalline medicament useful in treating cancer susceptible to treatment with said medicament, said medicament having a solubility in water of less than 10 mg/ml, and having a non-crosslinked surface modifier adsorbed on the surface thereof in an amount of 0.1–90% by weight and sufficient to maintain an average effective particle size of less than 1000 nm . . . .[144]

The court determined that the scope of the nanoparticles as claimed required that "90% of the particles have a number average particle size of less than 1000 nanometers."[145]   Other key terms construed by the court were "surface modifier," defined as "a substance that modifies the surface properties of the crystalline medicament,"[146] and "non-crosslinked," defined as "the individually adsorbed molecules of the surface modifier are essentially free of intermolecular crosslinkages."[147]

While it was not identical to the Elan Patent, Elan argued that Abraxane infringed because "more than one particle" out of over 61 trillion nanoparticles in the product were "entirely crystalline" and "non-crosslinked surface modifiers."[148]   Abraxis argued that Abraxane's eight percent crystalline form did not require that any specific particle be entirely crystalline,[149] but did acknowledge that the human serum albumin, which is captured by the '363 Patent's definition of "surface modifier," is adsorbed on the surface

---

[140] The drug ingredient is named paclitaxel; one brand name drug product is called Taxol. *See Paclitaxel,* DRUGS.COM, http://www.drugs.com/international/paclitaxel.html (last visited Dec. 19, 2011).

[141] Merrill, *supra* note 139, at 12.

[142] Verdict Form at 1, *Elan Pharma,* No. 06-438 GMS, 2008 WL 2556294. The jury, however, did not find willful infringement of the '363 Patent. *Id.* at 5. The jury also found Elan's patent 5,834,025 and the '363 patent not invalid for lack of enablement, failure of written description, or inequitable conduct. *Id.* at 2–4.

[143] Surface Modified Anticancer Nanoparticles, U.S. Patent No. 5,399,363 (filed July 1, 1992) col. 1 l. 45–50. The listed patent assignee is the Eastman Kodak Company, who licensed the technology to Elan Pharma for development.

[144] *Id.* at col. 14 l. 7–14. The abstract reads: "Dispersible particles consisting essentially of a crystalline anticancer agent having a surface modifier adsorbed on the surface thereof in an amount sufficient to maintain an effective average particle size of less than about 1000 nm." *Id.* at [57].

[145] Order Construing the Terms of U.S. Patent Nos. 5,399,363 and 5,834,025 at 3, *Elan Pharma.* 06-438 GMS, 2007 WL 6137001 (internal quotation mark omitted).

[146] *Id.* at 2 (internal quotation marks omitted).

[147] *Id.* (internal quotation marks omitted).

[148] Defendant Abraxis Bioscience, Inc.'s Opening Brief in Support of Its Motion for Judgment as a Matter of Law of Noninfringement, Invalidity, Inequitable Conduct, and Its Motion for New Trial at 5–6, 12, *Elan Pharma,* No. 06-438-GMS, 2008 WL 2856297 (internal quotation marks omitted).

[149] *Id.* at 2.

of Abraxane to prevent crosslinking.[150]   The jury found a sufficient number of the Abraxane medicament particles were entirely crystalline and thus infringed the '363 Patent.

The outcome of the 2008 Delaware district court case was a jury verdict of $55.2 million to Elan Pharma for Abraxis' infringement of the '363 Patent issued in 1995.[151] The monetary damages amount reflects a six percent royalty on the sales of Abraxane during the infringement period of January 7, 2005 to June 13, 2008.[152]   In June 2010, Celgene acquired Abraxis Bioscience for approximately $2.9 billion in cash and stocks;[153] the acquisition was finalized in October 2010.[154]   Celgene also agreed to pay Elan a one-time licensing fee of $78 million when it acquired Abraxis under terms that Elan will not "receive any additional payments for sales of [Abraxane], or any other [nab]-Paclitaxel product."[155]   It is not clear what terms were negotiated among the parties regarding the relationship between the '363 Patent and the pending patent applications at the USPTO covering the Abraxane product and technology. Part IV-B discusses the two key patents in more detail.

Subsequent to the litigation, the USPTO granted Abraxis two patents for its nanoparticle technology on October 26, 2010[156] and April 12, 2011.[157]   Celgene plans to initiate a marketing campaign aimed at increasing Abraxane drug sales to $1 billion by the year 2015.[158]   Celgene anticipates that Abraxane will retain patent protection and large profits until 2023,[159] likely based on calculations involving the licensing deal from Elan, which resulted from this litigation, coupled with the recently issued patent for certain aspects of the technology. Five other drugs are currently in development based on the nanoparticle technology in Abraxane, including drugs in Phase III clinical trials for treatment of first-line non-small cell lung cancer and pancreatic cancer.[160]

Notably, this case illustrates the limitation inherent in the definition of nanotechnology as under 100 nm. The USPTO has not classified the Elan Patent in the 977 cross-reference nanotechnology classification, likely because the patent broadly claims nanoparticles "under 1000 nm" which, while including particle size under 100 nm, also includes the 101–999 nm range as well.

---

[150] Plaintiff Pharma International Ltd.'s Opening Claim Construction Brief at 5–6, *Elan Pharma*, No. 06-438-GMS, 2008 WL 2856297.

[151] William F. Prendergast & Heather N. Schafer, *Nanocrystalline Pharmaceutical Patent Litigation: The First Case*, 5 NANOTECHNOLOGY L. & BUS. 157, 157 (2008).

[152] Verdict Form, *supra* note 142, at 5.

[153] Andrew Pollack, *Prominent Drug Chief to Sell Abraxis BioScience to Celgene for $2.9 Billion*, N.Y. TIMES, July 1, 2010, at B3; Press Release, Celgene Corp., Celgene to Acquire Abraxis BioScience Inc. (June 30, 2010), http://ir.celgene.com/phoenix.zhtml?c=111960&p=irol-newsArticle&ID=1442901.

[154] Press Release, Celgene Corp., Celgene Completes Acquisition of Abraxis (Oct. 15, 2010), http://ir.celgene.com/phoenix.zhtml?c=111960&p=irol-newsArticle&ID=1483257.

[155] *Elan and Celgene Enter into Settlement and License Agreement Related to ABRAXANE*, BUSINESS WIRE, Feb. 24, 2011, *available at* http://www.businesswire.com/news/home/20110224007229/en/Elan-Celgene-Enter-Settlement-License-Agreement-Related.

[156] '788 Patent.

[157] Compositions & Methods of Delivery of Pharmacological Agents, U.S. Patent No. 7,923,536 B2 (filed Apr. 12, 2010).

[158] Merrill, *supra* note 139, at 11.

[159] *Id.* at 12.

[160] *Id.* Other investigations include refractory invasive bladder cancer and malignant melanoma.

B. The Patents

The 1995 Elan Patent and the subsequently issued Abraxis Biosciences patents illustrate what is sure to be an increasingly problematic aspect of nanotechnology patenting—claim scope and drafting. Both patents claim characteristics and interactions of serum albumin and Taxol, an anti-cancer agent. The relationship between the two patents warrants a brief primer.

Taxol (paclitaxel) is a molecule that contains many non-polar (hydrophobic) carbon rings that share electrons equally, causing the solubility of Taxol in water to be significantly reduced and inhibiting its effectiveness as a cancer therapy.[161] The protein serum albumin, a molecule having both hydrophobic and hydrophilic properties, can be used as a surface modifier to enhance the solubility of Taxol. Non-polar domains interact with Taxol, and the polar (hydrophilic) domains interact with water.[162] Due to its dual nature, albumin will self-assemble on a Taxol particle and create a shell of albumin, coating the Taxol particle, whereby hydrophobic Taxol is insulated from water and other Taxol particles.[163] The albumin thus prevents the aggregation of multiple Taxol particles and enhances the solubility in water.[164] Both the Elan Patent and the Abraxane Patents rely on the Taxol and serum albumin interaction at the nanoscale.

1. The Elan '363 Patent

The Elan '363 Patent is drafted extremely broadly. Claim 1 covers any particles that have an average size of less than 1,000 nm and are composed of one of the named poorly water-soluble anti-cancer medications and any adsorbed surface coating.[165] Claim 1 gives specific examples of the types of medication and includes Taxol in this list.[166] The use of Taxol for the specific purpose of an anti-cancer agent is stated in Claim 5.[167] Beginning with Claim 12 of the '363 Patent, the different types of surface modifiers are listed.[168] Claim 12 is especially broad because it covers any surface modifier that is "a surfactant."[169] Surfactants are an entire class of small molecules that have both hydrophobic and hydrophilic properties. Claim 15 goes on to state other specific surface modifiers including bovine serum albumin,[170] which contains hydrophobic and hydrophilic domains.

This patent is not classified by the USPTO as within the 977 nanotechnology cross-reference system, due to both procedural and substantive reasons mentioned in Part III. On the procedural side, there is no retroactive classification of issued patents into the 977

---

[161] For a primer on hydrophobic and hydrophilic interactions, see BRUCE ALBERTS ET AL., MOLECULAR BIOLOGY OF THE CELL 57–58 (4th ed. 2002).

[162] Toru Takagishi, *Amphiphilic Polymers (Binding Properties for Small Molecules), in* 1 POLYMERIC MATERIALS ENCYCLOPEDIA 228, 228 (Joseph C. Salamone ed., 1996).

[163] A.G. Garro et al., *Reversible Exposure of Hydrophobic Residues on Albumin as a Novel Strategy for Formulation of Nanodelivery Vehicles for Taxanes*, 6 INT'L J. NANOMEDICINE 1193, 1193 (2011).

[164] *Id.*

[165] *See* '363 Patent col. 14 l. 7.

[166] *Id.*

[167] *Id.* at col. 14 l. 35.

[168] *Id.* at col. 14–15.

[169] *Id.* at col. 14 l. 68.

[170] *Id.* at col. 15 l. 5.

cross-reference system. Individual patent examiners may initiate reclassification. Coupled with examiner discretion, the Elan Patent was filed back in 1992 and issued in 1995.[171] Its expiration is quickly approaching, likely making it an unpopular candidate for reclassification energy.

On the substantive side, the USPTO's definition of nanostructure may limit inclusion of certain patents including the Elan Patent. Based on physical dimension requirements alone, the Elan particles could simply be too large. The '363 Patent claims surface modified particles in crystalline form in the range of less than 1,000 nm,[172] less than 400 nm,[173] and less than 300 nm.[174] While each of the three claimed particle sizes may be within the 1–100 nm range, they might not be. Examples in the patent that illustrate the invention identify the smallest final particle size to be 240 nm.[175]

2. The Abraxis '788 Patent

Unlike the Elan Patent, the Abraxis Patent has been classified as a nanotechnology patent by the USPTO. The patent's primary classification is denoted as 530/350 and the nanotechnology subclassification is 977/779 (nanotechnology; nanostructure; within specified host or matrix material; possessing nano-sized particles, powders, flakes, or clusters other than simpler atomic impurity doping); 977/906 (nanotechnology; specified use of nanostructure; drug delivery); and 977/911 (nanotechnology; specified use of nanostructure; for medical, immunological, body treatment, or diagnosis; mechanical repair performed; surgical; cancer cell).[176]

The scope of the '788 Patent is much narrower, but it appears that there is some overlap with the '363 Patent regarding the nanoparticle composition. Claim 1 of the Abraxis Patent claims

> A pharmaceutical composition for injection comprising paclitaxel and a pharmaceutically acceptable carrier, wherein the pharmaceutically acceptable carrier comprises albumin, wherein the albumin and the paclitaxel in the composition are formulated as particles, wherein the particles have a particle size of less than about 200 nm, and wherein the weight ratio of albumin to paclitaxel in the composition is about 1:1 to about 9:1.[177]

There are eleven subsequent claims.

In '788, the only anti-cancer compound claimed is paclitaxel,[178] the only surface modifier is human serum albumin,[179] and the average particle size is limited to less than 200 nm.[180] As compared to the Elan '363 Patent, there are arguably areas of overlap.

---

[171] Id. at [22], [45].
[172] Id. at col. 14 l. 14.
[173] Id. at col. 14 l. 29.
[174] Id. at col. 14 l. 31.
[175] Id. at col. 8 l. 28, col. 9 l. 63.
[176] '788 Patent. This Part analyzes the earlier issued patent, as the later patent ('536 Patent) is subject to a terminal disclaimer.
[177] Id. at col. 38 l. 17–24.
[178] Id. at col. 38 l. 18.
[179] Id. at col. 38 l. 25.
[180] Id. at col. 38 l. 22.

Taxol (paclitaxel) was specifically mentioned as a possible anti-cancer compound in the '363 Patent. The average particle size of less than 200 nm in the '788 Patent would fall within the average particle size of less than 1,000 nm (and less than 400 and 300 nm) in the '363 Patent, and bovine serum albumin was specifically mentioned as a surface modifier in the '363 Patent.[181]

FIGURE 2. COMPARISON OF KEY CLAIMS IN THE '363 AND '788 PATENTS

Patent Claims	'363 Patent[182]	'788 Patent[183]
Particle Size & Ranges	"Average effective particle size" of < 1,000 nm; < 400 nm; < 300 nm	"particle size [of paclitaxel and albumin] of less than about 200 nm"
Agents	"anti-cancer agents"; claims taxol among others	paclitaxel
Surface modifiers	Any surface modifier that is a "surfactant"; claims bovine serum albumin among others	human serum albumin
Indications	"anticancer agent"	Cancer, arthritis, restenosis
Route of Administration	"administer[ed] to a mammal"	Various, including intravenous, orally, etc.

C. Reconciling the '363 and '788 Patents

A comparison of the two patents described in Parts IV-A and IV-B illustrate the problems that courts, the USPTO, and industry will face as nanotechnology development pushes forward. This Part raises a number of comparative points in order to frame Part V; this is not intended to be an exhaustive analysis of the patents, and the author acknowledges that this is a cursory look rather an in-depth examination.

The particle range of the claims is significant to the discussion of the novel properties that emerge at the nanoscale. In the '363 Patent, all examples provided within the patent exceed 240 nm; in the '788 Patent, all examples provided in the patents are within the range of 50 to 220 nm, a range starting squarely under the 100 nm outer bounds range set forth by the USPTO. Another critical aspect that came to light in the litigation is the surface modifier form; the '363 Patent claims non-crosslinked surface modifiers that include those in "crystalline form." This was at the heart of the litigation regarding Abraxane's mechanism of action and drug form. The patents seemingly overlap in a number of regards: both claim in the size range greater than 200 nm, both claim either the agent Taxol or paclitaxel, and both claim a form of serum albumin as an agent, though the '536 Patent claims are limited to cancer, arthritis, and restenosis.[184]

In contrast to the Elan Patent, the Abraxis Patent claims average particles sizes less than 200 nm[185] and example preparations provide an average range for the particle rather than a final particle size as presented in the Elan Patent. For instance, Example 12 of the Abraxis Patent describes preparation of particles "in the range 50–220 nm."[186] While it is

---

[181] Cf. infra Figure 2.
[182] '363 Patent col. 14–15.
[183] '788 Patent col. 38.
[184] '536 Patent col. 37.
[185] See supra Figure 2.
[186] '788 Patent col. 19 l. 20.

unclear, perhaps the claim is drafted so that the nanoparticle size is sufficiently small to impart special diffusion properties not present at the scale offered in the Elan Patent.

Additionally, the distinction between bovine serum albumin and human serum albumin may or may not be significant. Claim 2 of the '788 Patent covers *human* serum albumin[187] (HSA) as the surface modifier, rather than the *bovine* serum albumen (BSA) claimed in the '363 Patent.[188] HSA and BSA share seventy-six percent identical amino acids and approximately eighty-seven percent of the amino acids are either identical or have similar chemical properties.[189] This degree of sequence homology suggests that HSA and BSA are interchangeable for constitution of soluble nanoparticles that do not aggregate, though it is unclear if this is the case when utilized in a human.

Parts III and IV argue that the USPTO nanotechnology classification, while a laudable effort, is not performing as well as it could to quell the impending problems that will confront the patent system. Part V details a research agenda of possible steps that could improve outcomes for nanotechnology patenting.

V. A RESEARCH AGENDA

This Article presents three core challenges facing the USPTO and reviewing courts as nanotechnology develops and litigation emerges: (1) limitations of and inconsistencies among current definitions of nanotechnology; (2) uncertainty and lack of uniformity in measurement capabilities regarding critical aspects of size, properties, and characteristics at the nanoscale; and (3) the role of patent claims in accurately and consistently encapsulating and distinguishing the scope of nanotechnology inventions. Keying in on the third problem, this Part suggests mechanisms to more effectively utilize the 977 classification system, learning from experience and case law in other scientific and technological areas, scholarly criticisms of the patent system as applied to nanotechnology, and the Abraxane litigation and related patents.

A. Improve the Internal 977 Process

The lowest-hanging fruit is, of course, to recommend that the USPTO reassess the 977 classification system and develop improvements to the system. These improvements can come in two forms: substantive and procedural. One major substantive improvement

---

[187] *Id.* at col. 38 l. 25.

[188] *See* '363 Patent col. 16 l. 8.

[189] These results were reached utilizing both the European Bioinformatics Institute EMBOSS Needle online tool and the protein sequence database on the National Center for Biotechnology Information's website. EMBOSS is a bioinformatics tool that can be used to create an optimal alignment between two proteins that have similar, but not identical, amino acid sequences. The program uses the Needleman-Wunsch algorithm and a pre-determined scoring matrix to create the alignment; the resulting optimal alignment is displayed graphically along with the percentage of identical and chemically similar amino acids between the two proteins. *See EMBOSS Needle: Pairwise Sequence Alignment*, EUR. BIOINFORMATICS INST., http://www.ebi.ac.uk/Tools/psa/emboss_needle/ (last visited Dec. 19, 2011). First, users should obtain the protein sequences for HSA and BSA. *E.g.*, *Protein Database*, NAT'L CTR. FOR BIOTECHNOLOGY INFO., http://www.ncbi.nlm.nih.gov/protein/ (last visited Dec. 19, 2011) (accessed by searching for "178344" and "3336842," the unique identifiers for HSA and BSA, respectively, and clicking "FASTA"). Users should then paste the resulting sequences into EMBOSS (one in "first protein sequence" and the other in "second protein sequence") to compare the two sequences. *EMBOSS Needle: Pairwise Sequence Alignment, supra*.

would be to revisit the definition and qualifications for inclusion into the 977 classification. As evidenced in the pharmaceutical realm, many products utilizing nanotechnology may exceed the rigid 100 nm ceiling and are, in fact, legitimately nanotechnology as a scientific and technical matter. This is the stance recently taken by the FDA's Center for Drug Evaluation and Research and the Research Office of Pharmaceutical Science (CDER). In May 2010, CDER jointly issued an internal Manual of Policies and Procedures (MaPP) instructing drug reviewers to capture relevant information pertaining to "nanomaterial-containing drugs" and to organize data into a nanotechnology database.[190] This MaPP describes the terms nanomaterial and nanoscale material as involving "[a]ny materials with at least one dimension smaller than 1,000 nm."[191] The 1 to 1,000 nm range included in CDER's conception of nanoscale as compared to both the NNI and USPTO definitions extending from 1 nm to 100 nm implies that the FDA has determined, as many scientists have argued for years, that nanotechnology is not necessarily capped at 100 nm, as the size-dependent novel properties vary with the material, environment, and interactions.[192]

On the procedural side, a second improvement would be to tackle retroactive classification of patents applications submitted before 2004. The USPTO should establish an internal task force to discuss such an action, particularly identifying priority sub-classifications and proper scope and application of the retroactivity. For example, patents that have expired would be less of a priority as challenges to those patents would not be forthcoming. The task force should also consider prioritizing scientific and technical areas with the most active patent litigation.

B. Collaborate with Other Agencies

Inextricably tied to the first suggestion regarding internal improvements, the USPTO should also strive to improve not only the internal functioning of the 977 classification system, but also its interoperability with other relevant regulatory agencies. Although useful within the USPTO, this system of classification and wealth of nanotechnology-specific information could be more broadly shared and utilized by other relevant administrative agencies as they tackle the inherent challenges of nanotechnology and nanomedicine specifically. The USPTO should develop mechanisms to collaborate with other agencies, specifically the FDA, to extend the utility of their information-gathering and classification efforts. For purposes of this Article, the FDA is a prime example of a regulatory agency that would benefit from improvements in the USPTO process and joint collaboration efforts. Given the close relationship between patents and pharmaceutical development, enhanced feedback mechanisms between the FDA and USPTO would assist in a variety of ways.

Perhaps most helpful would be active collaboration between the USPTO and FDA regarding patent disclosures for purposes of listings in the *Orange Book*. As a key resource for generic drug companies in developing bioequivalent versions of pioneer

---

[190] NANOTECHNOLOGY MAPP, *supra* note 134, at 1.
[191] *Id.* at 3.
[192] *See* Paradise, *Reassessing 'Safety' for Nanotechnology, supra* note 2.

drugs,[193] the *Orange Book* provides all relevant patents that the generic sponsor must consider when developing the generic drug and filing for FDA approval. The Appendix reveals that very few nanodrugs disclose patents that have been classified by the USPTO as nanotechnology, suggesting an apparent disconnect between the information presented to the FDA and information presented to the USPTO or, as discussed earlier, a difference in defining nanotechnology. As a means to more effectively track nano-specific features and outcomes of nanodrugs, some type of feedback mechanism or cross-reference system between the two agencies would bolster transparency and foster uniformity in the drug industry with regard to information disclosure in the patent application process and eventual FDA application for market approval.

The USPTO should also build on the actions of other agencies in providing guidance to industry on nanotechnology issues. The FDA would be an ideal ally for the USPTO in this respect, as the FDA has possibly been the most proactive agency in terms of identifying regulatory challenges to the existing oversight system.[194] The FDA has thus far formed a multi-center task force,[195] instituted a drug specific internal policy,[196] published draft guidance for industry,[197] solicited public comments through public meetings,[198] and partnered with research institutions to examine particular aspects of nanotechnology.[199] In particular, development by the USPTO of a document similar to the FDA's draft guidance to industry may be especially helpful to patent applicants when contemplating whether to specifically describe their inventions in the nanoscale range. A "how to" for applicants would assist in more uniformity at the inventor and claim level.

C. Provide Training and Resources for Examiners

Any critique of the USPTO necessarily entails some treatment of patent examiner expertise, credentials, and performance. As nanotechnology is a confluence of

---

[193] The requirements and framework of the generic drug approval process is found in 21 U.S.C. § 355(j) (2006). A showing of bioequivalence requires "the absence of a significant difference in the rate and extent to which the active ingredient or active moiety in pharmaceutical equivalents or pharmaceutical alternatives becomes available at the site of drug action when administered at the same molar dose under similar conditions in an appropriately designed study." 21 C.F.R. § 320.1(e) (2010).

[194] *See* Paradise, *Reassessing 'Safety' for Nanotechnology, supra* note 2.

[195] U.S. FOOD & DRUG ADMIN., NANOTECHNOLOGY TASK FORCE, NANOTECHNOLOGY: A REPORT OF THE U.S. FOOD AND DRUG ADMINISTRATION NANOTECHNOLOGY TASK FORCE 20–21 (2007), *available at* http://www.fda.gov/downloads/ScienceResearch/SpecialTopics/Nanotechnology/ucm110856.pdf.

[196] NANOTECHNOLOGY MAPP, *supra* note 134.

[197] Draft Guidance for Industry: Considering Whether an FDA-Regulated Product Involves the Application of Nanotechnology, 76 Fed. Reg. 34,715 (June 14, 2011); *see also FDA Draft Guidance Questions and Answers*, U.S. FOOD & DRUG ADMIN., http://www.fda.gov/ScienceResearch/SpecialTopics/Nanotechnology/ucm258391.htm (last updated June 9, 2011); News Release, U.S. Food & Drug Admin., FDA Takes 'First Step' Toward Greater Regulatory Certainty Around Nanotechnology (June 9, 2011), http://www.fda.gov/NewsEvents/Newsroom/PressAnnouncements/ucm258377.htm.

[198] Consideration of FDA-Regulated Products that May Contain Nanoscale Materials, 73 Fed. Reg. 46,022 (Aug. 7, 2008).

[199] *Nanotechnology Partnerships at FDA*, U.S. FOOD & DRUG ADMIN., http://www.fda.gov/ScienceResearch/SpecialTopics/Nanotechnology/ucm208110.htm (last updated July 22, 2010).

disciplines, very few patent examiners have advanced degrees in nanotechnology.[200] Acknowledging the high turnover of patent examiners, less than ideal wages, and heavy workloads, the USPTO can take certain actions to address issues with delivery of information to patent examiners. First, the USPTO should contract with disinterested outside parties to train and educate patent examiners on nanotechnology and nanotechnology patent drafting. In November 2004, the USPTO established a working group consisting of outside lawyers and scientists to provide guidance to key figures as the USPTO began training examiners in nanotechnology concepts and terminology.[201] It is unclear how this working group has been utilized to date. Other sources report that some select law firms that supply counsel to the nanotechnology industry are hosting educational sessions for patent examiners. For example, Burns, Doane, Swecker & Mathis, LLP began a monthly forum to provide nanotechnology education to examiners.[202] Such arrangements raise potential conflicts of interest and should possibly be avoided by the USPTO.

The USPTO should pursue partnerships with the NNI, which is the federal vehicle for nanotechnology funding and development. Placed within the National Science and Technology Council as a national coordinating entity for nanotechnology research, development, and education, the NNI is made up of twenty-five federal agencies.[203] The NNI serves as coordinating entity for agencies dealing with nanotechnology and fosters collaborative efforts in research and education among the agencies.[204] A direct partnership between NNI and the USPTO in training and resources would help feed cutting-edge research findings and processes into patent examiners for consideration when reviewing patent applications and classifying them.

D. Utilize the Patent Peer Review Pilot Program

The USPTO implemented a pilot program to gather information on peer-reviewed publications and research in the public domain to locate "prior art that might not otherwise be located by the USPTO during the typical patent examination process."[205] The original pilot program began in 2007 and lasted two years,[206] returning evidence that the public is "capable of contributing to the location of prior art of value to the examiner during the examination process."[207] The scope of the initial pilot program was limited to patent applications in computer-related arts.[208] The project was then expanded to include patent applications in Class 705, "Data Processing: Financial Business Practice,

---

[200] See, e.g., Where Science and Law Meet, supra note 117, at 3.
[201] Feder, supra note 103.
[202] Patent Office Struggles to Stay Ahead of Nanotech Industry, supra note 118.
[203] NAT'L SCI. & TECH. COUNCIL, SUBCOMM. ON NANOSCALE SCI., ENG'G, & TECH., NATIONAL NANOTECHNOLOGY INITIATIVE STRATEGIC PLAN 1 (2011), available at http://www.nano.gov/nnistrategicplan211.pdf.
[204] See, e.g., id. at 35.
[205] Peer Review Pilot FY2011, U.S. PAT. & TRADEMARK OFF., http://www.uspto.gov/patents/init_events/peerpriorartpilotindex.jsp (last updated May 31, 2011).
[206] Id.
[207] Id.
[208] Id.

Management, or Cost/Price Determination."[209] Out of the total 189 applications accepted into the program, thirty applications had at least one claim rejected based on prior art contributed by the public.[210] In fifteen of those thirty applications, the patent examiner did not find the prior art used to ultimately reject the claim.[211]

The USPTO expanded the program again in October 2010, which will continue through September 2011.[212] As described by the USPTO:

> In addition to statistical data on participation rates and the number of prior art references found and utilized by the USPTO, this pilot will be evaluating the effectiveness of the process more closely as it relates to patent examination efficiency and quality and peer participation behaviors. This pilot will test whether a peer review process is a viable addition to the normal processes of the USPTO and as an option for applicants to choose among the other products offered by the USPTO.[213]

Although the additional pilot program expansion includes several patents areas, including several primary drug classifications, the 977 classification is not included. Several of the drug classifications, however, may implicate an overlap with nanotechnology, such as 424/514 (Drug, Bioaffecting and Body treating compositions).[214] As previously discussed, many drugs utilizing nanotechnology are currently on the market or in research and development stages.

The USPTO should consider using the peer review pilot as a mechanism to gather nanotechnology-specific information and prior art from stakeholders outside the USPTO. Particularly cueing in on nanopharmaceuticals, the USPTO should select a set of nanotechnology subclassifications to present as the next phase of the pilot program.

VI. CONCLUSION

Nanotechnology is no longer a forecast. It has arrived in basic consumer products, environmental remediation, electronics, mechanics, energy, optics, computing and information technology, industrial manufacturing, and health care and medicine. The resulting innovations and inventions are beginning to inundate the USPTO, an agency still trying to grapple with the patent ramifications of genetics over a decade after the completion of the Human Genome Project. The USPTO's newly created 977 nanotechnology classification aims to organize nanotechnology patents into relevant sub-classifications for ease in prior art searches and uniformity in cross-referencing. The USPTO system installs a collection of patents and patent applications that share the

---

[209] John Doll, *Extension and Expansion of Pilot Concerning Public Submission of Peer Reviewed Prior Art*, 1333 OFF. GAZ. PAT. & TRADEMARK OFF. 103 (2008), http://www.uspto.gov/web/offices/com/sol/og/2008/week33/TOC.htm#ref13

[210] David J. Kappos, *A New Pilot Program Concerning Public Submission of Peer Reviewed Prior Art*, 1361 OFF. GAZ. PAT. & TRADEMARK OFF. 230, 230 (2010), http://www.uspto.gov/web/offices/com/sol/og/2010/week52/TOC.htm#ref15.

[211] *Id.*

[212] *Peer Review Pilot FY2011*, *supra* note 205.

[213] Kappos, *supra* note 210, at 235.

[214] *Eligible Classes and Subclasses for the Peer Review Pilot 2011*, U.S. PAT. & TRADEMARK OFF., http://www.uspto.gov/patents/init_events/class_subclasses_FY2011pilot.jsp (last updated Jan. 4, 2011).

common feature of falling within the nanotechnology penumbra—inventions at the nanoscale that exhibit unique features because of their 1–100 nm size. Despite the laudable effort, the classification system suffers from serious shortcomings.

¶81   This Article argues that as nanotechnology development and patenting progresses, three core problems will continue to raise challenges for the USPTO and courts: (1) limitations of and inconsistencies among current definitions of nanotechnology; (2) uncertainty and lack of uniformity in measurement capabilities regarding critical aspects of size, properties, and characteristics at the nanoscale; and (3) the role of patent claims to accurately and consistently encapsulate and distinguish the scope of nanotechnology inventions. Careful examination of *Elan Pharma v. Abraxis Bioscience*[215] helps to illustrate these three inherent problems and the related shortcomings of the USPTO nanotechnology patent classification system. Tying this case to U.S. patent law and policy, case precedent, and practice of the USPTO, we can extract lessons to apply to the emerging realm of nanopharmaceuticals.

¶82   Drawing from this analysis, a variety of adjustments would serve to assist the USPTO in fulfilling its mission to foster and award innovation while also facilitating effective information gathering to feed into regulation of the resulting products and inform any ensuing patent infringement litigation. These include improvements to the existing nanotechnology classification process, increasing feedback and collaboration with other federal agencies relevant to nanotechnology inventions, instituting independent educational programs for patent examiners, and utilizing the pilot peer review system for nanotechnology applications to encourage broader dialogue on the scope of patent claims and relationships to already issued patents.

---

[215] No. 06-438 GMS, 2007 WL 6382930 (D. Del. Dec. 17, 2007).

Appendix: FDA-Approved Drugs Utilizing Nanoscale Properties or Materials

Product	Indications[i]	Company[ii]	Formulation Description	Original NDA Approval[iii]	U.S. Patent No.[iv]	977 Nano subclass
Zoladex	Anti-cancer drug[v]	AstraZeneca	Polymer rods used as nanocarrier[vi]	12/29/89*	7,118,552; 7,220,247; 7,500,964	None
Adagen	Immunodeficien cy disease[vii]	Sigma Tau	PEG-adenosine deaminase[viii]	3/21/90*	None	None
Tricor *(discontinued)*	Lipid regulation[ix]	Abbott	Nanocrystalline fenofibrate[x]	12/31/93[xi]	5,145,684; 6,277,405; 6,375,986[i]; 6,652,881; 7,037,529; 7,041,319; 7,276,249; 7,320,802	[i] 773; 896
Doxil	Anti-cancer drug for metastatic ovarian and breast cancers, and HIV-related Kaposi's sarcoma[xii]	OrthoBiotech Products, LP	Liposomal doxorubicin[xiii]	11/17/95*	None	None
Abelcet	Fungal infections[xiv]	Sigma Tau	Amphotericin B/lipid complex[xv]	11/20/95*	5,616,334; 6,406,713	None
DaunoXome	HIV-related Kaposi's sarcoma[xvi]	Gilead	Nano-sized drug for treatment of solid tumor[xvii]	4/8/96*	None	None
Feridex	*In vivo* imaging of liver tumors[xviii]	AMAG Pharms Inc.	Iron nanoparticles[xix]	8/30/96*	5,248,492	None
Amphotec	Fungal infections[xx]	Aldopharma USA	Amphotericin B/lipid colloidal dispersion[xxi]	11/22/96*	None	None
Gastromark	Used for improved imaging of abdominal structures[xxii]	AMAG Pharms Inc.	Nano-sized contrast agent[xxiii]	12/6/96*	None	None
Ambisome	Fungal infections[xxiv]	Astellas	Liposomal Amphotericin B[xxv]	8/11/97	5,874,104; 5,965,156	None

Product	Indications[i]	Company[ii]	Formulation Description	Original NDA Approval[iii]	U.S. Patent No.[iv]	977 Nano subclass
Renagel	Chronic kidney disease[xxvi]	Genzyme	Crosslinked poly(allylamine) resin[xxvii]	10/30/98	5,496,545; 5,667,775; 6,509,013; 6,733,780; 7,014,846; 7,459,151	None
Depocyt	Treatment of lymphomatous meningitis	Pacira	Liposomal cytarabine[xxviii]	4/1/99 (accelerated approval)	5,455,044[i]; 5,723,147	[i] 907; 911; 915
Rapamune	Immunosuppress ant for prevention of organ rejection	Wyeth	Nanocrystalline sirolimus[xxix]	9/15/99	5,100,899; 5,145,684; 5,212,155; 5,403,833; 5,989,591	None
Visudyne	Age-related macular degeneration[xxx]	QLT	Liposomal verteporfin[xxxi]	4/12/00	5,095,030; 5,707,608; 5,756,541; 5,770,619; 5,798,349; 6,074,666	None
Copaxone	Multiple sclerosis[xxxii]	TEVA	Copolymer of alanine, lysine, glutamic acid, and tyrosine[xxxiii]	2/12/02*	5,981,589; 6,054,430; 6,342,476; 6,362,161; 6,620,847; 6,939,539; 7,199,098	None
Somavert	Acromegaly[xxxiv]	Pharmacia & Upjohn	PEG-HGH[xxxv]	3/25/03	5,350,836; 5,681,809; 5,849,535; 5,958,879; 6,057,292; 6,583,115	None
Emend (Aprepitant)	Prevents nausea and vomiting induced by chemotherapy	Merck & Co.[¥]	Nanocrystalline aprepitant[xxxvi]	3/26/03	5,145,684; 5,538,982; 5,719,147; 6,048,859; 6,096,742; 6,235,735; 7,214,692	None

Product	Indications[i]	Company[li]	Formulation Description	Original NDA Approval[iii]	U.S. Patent No.[iv]	977 Nano subclass
Estrasorb	Menopausal therapy[xxxvii]	Graceway	Estradiol in micellar nanoparticles[xxxviii]	10/9/03	5,629,021	773; 915; 926
Abraxane	Anti-cancer drug for treatment of metastatic breast cancer[xxxix]	Abraxis Bioscience	Albumin-bound paclitaxel[xl]	1/7/05	5,439,686; 5,498,421; 6,096,331; 6,506,405; 6,537,579[i]; 6,749,868; 6,753,006; 7,820,788[ii]; 7,923,536[iii] ; RE41,884[iv]	[i] 729; 773; 775; 896; 906; 915 [ii] 779; 906 [iii] 779; 906; 911 [iv] 700; 904
Triglide	Lipid regulation[xli]	SkyePharma	Nanocrystaline fenofibrate[xlii]	5/7/05	6,696,084	None
MegaceES	Eating disorders[xliii]	Par Pharm	Nanocrystalline megesterol acetate[xliv]	7/5/05	5,145,684; 6,592,903; 7,101,576	None
Emend (fosa-prepitant dime-glumine)	Prevents nausea and vomiting induced by chemotherapy	Merck & Co.[v]	Nano-sized drug molecules	1/25/08	5,512,570; 5,538,982; 5,691,336; 5,716,942; 7,214,692	None

Special thanks to Research Assistant Ethan Fitzpatrick, Ph.D., a Seton Hall University School of Law second year law student, for constructing this Appendix. These products were identified by a two-pronged search methodology: a search of the relevant scientific literature reporting on research and development in nanopharmaceuticals and the FDA's website providing information on FDA-approved drugs. *See Drugs@FDA Database*, U.S. FOOD & DRUG ADMIN., http://www.fda.gov/Drugs/InformationOnDrugs/ucm135821.htm (last updated June 18, 2009). Where a product was identified in the scientific literature as a nanopharmaceutical, the FDA database was used to retrieve that products approval information. Searches were conducted January 2011 through May 2011. The references below provide all scientific sources identified in the search.

Roman numerals indicate a direct link between a specific patent (in the "U.S. Patent No." column) and the USPTO classifications within that patent (in the "Classification" column).

*Approval letters not available.

¥ Uses Elan Corporation's NanoCrystal Technology.

[i] Drug indications were identified utilizing the approval letters posted at the FDA's drug search database. *Search by Drug Name, Active Ingredient, or Application Number*, U.S. FOOD & DRUG ADMIN., http://www.accessdata.fda.gov/scripts/cder/drugsatfda/index.cfm (last visited Dec. 19, 2011). Where the original approval letters were not available at the drug search database, the table notes this with an asterisk in the "Original NDA Approval" column and secondary sources for indications are identified in that drug's informational row.

[ii] Company information was accessed using the FDA's drug search database. *Id.*

[iii] New Drug Applications (NDAs) are submitted to and approved by the FDA.

[iv] Patent information was accessed using the FDA's electronic listings of the *Orange Book: Approved Drug Products with Therapeutic Equivalence Evaluations*, U.S. FOOD & DRUG ADMIN.,http://www.accessdata.fda.gov/scripts/cder/ob/docs/querytn.cfm (last visited Dec. 19, 2011).

[v] K.K. Jain, *Advances in the Field of Nanooncology*, BMC MED., Dec. 13, 2010, at 1, 4 tbl.1, *available at* http://www.biomedcentral.com/1741-7015/8/83.

[vi] *Id.*

[vii] Volker Wagner et al., *The Emerging Nanomedicine Landscape*, 24 NATURE BIOTECHNOLOGY 1211, 1214 tbl.2 (2006).

[viii] *Id.*

[ix] *Id.* at 1215 tbl.2.

[x] *Id.*

[xi] Original NDA was approved December 31, 1993. Subsequent NDAs have been approved and the drug formulation based on the original NDA was discontinued. Patent information reflects currently active formulation and NDA for Tricor.

[xii] Rakesh K. Jain & Triantafyllos Stylianopoulos, *Delivering Nanomedicine to Solid Tumors*, 7 NATURE REVS. CLINICAL ONCOLOGY 653, 654 tbl.1 (2010).

[xiii] *Id.*

[xiv] Wagner et al., *supra* note vii, at 1214 tbl.2.

[xv] *Id.*

[xvi] Jain & Stylianopoulos, *supra* note 11, at 654 tbl.1.

[xvii] *Id.*

[xviii] Wagner et al., *supra* note vii, at 1215 tbl.2.

[xix] *Id.*

[xx] *Id.* at 1214 tbl.2.

[xxi] *Id.*

[xxii] Pilar Rivera Gil et al., *Nanopharmacy: Inorganic Nanoscale Devices as Vectors and Active Compounds*, 62 PHARMACOLOGICAL RES. 115, 118 (2010).

[xxiii] *Id.*

[xxiv] Wagner et al., *supra* note vii, at 1214 tbl.2.

[xxv] *Id.*

[xxvi] *Id.* at 1215 tbl.2.

[xxvii] *Id.*

[xxviii] *Id.* at 1214 tbl.2.

[xxix] *Id.* at 1215 tbl.2.

[xxx] *Id.* at 1214 tbl.2.

[xxxi] *Id.*

[xxxii] *Id.*.

[xxxiii] *Id.*

[xxxiv] *Id.*

[xxxv] *Id.*

[xxxvi] *Id.* at 1215 tbl.2.

[xxxvii] *Id.* at 1214 tbl.2.

[xxxviii] *Id.*

[xxxix] Jain & Sylianopoulus, *supra* note xii, at 654 tbl.1.

[xl] *Id.*

[xli] Wagner et al., *supra* note vii, at 1215 tbl.2.

[xlii] *Id.*

[xliii] *Id.*

[xliv] *Id.*

Copyright 2012 by Northwestern University School of Law
Northwestern Journal of Technology and Intellectual Property

Virtual Inequality: Challenges for the Net's Lost Founding Value

By Jonathon W. Penney[*]

I. INTRODUCTION

Freedom, liberty, and autonomy were the ideals heralded by cyberspace's first generation of thinkers—the cyber-libertarians like John Parry Barlow—who helped forge the early technological and intellectual foundations for "cyberspace."[1] These ideas were, says Lawrence Lessig, the "founding values of the Net."[2] Not surprisingly, these foundational values have received much attention from scholars. In his famous *Declaration of the Independence of Cyberspace*, Barlow proclaims to speak with "no

---

[*] Policy Fellow at the Citizen Lab, Munk School of Global Affairs, University of Toronto. The author is especially indebted to Greg Lastowka for his insights and advice. The author would also like to thank Dan Hunter, Julian Dibbell, Tom Boellstorff, Biella Coleman, and fellow panellists James Grimmelmann, and Nic Suzor at the 2009 State of Play IV Conference at New York School of Law, for their helpful comments.

[1] Like other articles, this Article uses "cyberspace" to refer not just to the Internet, but to all related computer systems, networks, and wireless communications. *Cf.* RICHARD A. CLARKE & ROBERT K. KNAKE, CYBER WAR: THE NEXT THREAT TO NATIONAL SECURITY AND WHAT TO DO ABOUT IT 70 (2010); Duncan B. Hollis, *An e-SOS for Cyberspace*, 52 HARV. INT'L L.J. 373, 374 n.1 (2011). As for first-generation thinkers, see, for example, John Perry Barlow, *A Declaration of the Independence of Cyberspace*, ELEC. FRONTIER FOUND. (Feb. 8, 1996), https://w2.eff.org/Misc/Publications/John_Perry_Barlow/barlow_0296.declaration.txt, *as reprinted in* CRYPTO ANARCHY, CYBERSTATES, AND PIRATE UTOPIAS 27 (Peter Ludlow ed., 2001); *see also* JACK GOLDSMITH & TIM WU, WHO CONTROLS THE INTERNET? ILLUSIONS OF A BORDERLESS WORLD 10, 13 (2006) (writing that Dibbell and Barlow promoted "a new frontier, where people lived in peace, under their own rules, liberated from the constraints of an oppressive society and free from government meddling," a vision shared by other cyberspace pioneers who "believed that the Internet might transcend territorial law and render the nation-state obsolete"); FRED TURNER, FROM COUNTERCULTURE TO CYBERCULTURE: STEWART BRAND, THE WHOLE EARTH NETWORK, AND THE RISE OF DIGITAL UTOPIANISM (2006); Julian Dibbell, *A Rape in Cyberspace or How an Evil Clown, a Haitian Trickster Spirit, Two Wizards, and a Cast of Dozens Turned a Database into a Society*, VILLAGE VOICE, Dec. 21, 1993, *as reprinted in* 1994 ANN. SURV. AM. L. 471 (describing how a virtual Internet community reacted to an unruly participant by creating a self-governance scheme).

[2] Wen Stephenson, *The Values of Code (and Code): An E-mail Exchange with Lawrence Lessig, the Author of* Code and Other Laws of Cyberspace, ATLANTIC ONLINE (Dec. 13, 1999), http://www.theatlantic.com/past/docs/unbound/digicult/lessig.htm ("I don't think it is an issue of values. I like the values of John Perry Barlow and Esther Dyson (emphasizing the freedom and creativity of the Net). I think the difference between us comes from a difference in experience. I've spent my professional life learning how law learns to regulate; I'm therefore skeptical of arguments that presume law can't learn. I view my work as building on the values Barlow and Dyson spoke of—as well as the insights of people like Mitch Kapor ('architecture is politics') and William Mitchell (author of *City of Bits*)—to tell a story that more realistically captures the threats that should make one work harder to defend the founding values of the Net, as well as the values from our tradition that the Net might threaten.") (quoting Lawrence Lessig).

greater authority than that with which liberty itself always speaks."[3] Lessig's deeply influential text, *Code: Version 2.0*, explains that the "challenge for our generation" is to "protect liberty" in cyberspace in the face of "architectures of control."[4] Likewise, Yochai Benkler centers his influential work, *The Wealth of Networks*, almost entirely on concepts of human freedom.[5] He begins with the solemn pronouncement: "Information, knowledge, and culture are central to human freedom and human development."[6] The first generation of legal scholarship about the Internet—or "cyberlaw scholarship"—was deeply influenced by such cyber-libertarian ideas and, thus, often explored innovative ways to preserve liberty, self-government, and autonomy in cyberspace from coercion.[7]

Few scholars today focus on equality as a founding value of the Internet that ought to be achieved or preserved. It is indeed doubtful that many scholars ever acknowledged its existence. As Anupam Chander has noted, "[c]oncerns for equality and distributive justice [in cyberlaw scholarship] are greatly neglected."[8] But neglect devolves to downright omission in the emerging body of scholarship addressing the unique legal complexities of virtual worlds.[9] Given the prominence of liberty in cyberlaw scholarship and the neglect of distributive justice concerns, one might infer that liberty is (in Lessig's terms) the only founding value of the Internet. Thus, Jack Balkin offers a persuasive account of liberty in this context,[10] but no one has focused on virtual equality.

This Article aims to fill the void, tackling equality justice issues in the cyberlaw context. Parts II and III of this Article offer an account of equality and its importance to

---

[3] Barlow, *supra* note 1, at 28.

[4] LAWRENCE LESSIG, CODE: VERSION 2.0, at xv (2006).

[5] YOCHAI BENKLER, THE WEALTH OF NETWORKS: HOW SOCIAL PRODUCTION TRANSFORMS MARKETS AND FREEDOM (2006).

[6] *Id.* at 1.

[7] *See, e.g.*, I. Trotter Hardy, *The Proper Legal Regime for "Cyberspace,"* 55 U. PITT. L. REV. 993, 1019–25 (1994) (advocating self-help, custom, and contract to regulate cyberspace); David R. Johnson & David G. Post, *And How Shall the Net Be Governed?: A Meditation on the Relative Virtues of Decentralized, Emergent Law*, in COORDINATING THE INTERNET 62, 65 (Brian Kahin & James H. Keller eds., 2d prtg. 2000) (arguing for a decentralized system of Internet governance); David R. Johnson & David Post, *Law and Borders—The Rise of Law in Cyberspace*, 48 STAN. L. REV. 1367, 1367–75 (1996) (noting possibilities of internal regulation of Internet through competing rule sets); Henry H. Perritt, Jr., *Cyberspace Self-Government: Town Hall Democracy or Rediscovered Royalism?*, 12 BERKELEY TECH. L.J. 413, 419 (1997) (contending that, as a general rule, "self-governance is desirable for electronic communities"); David G. Post, *Governing Cyberspace*, 43 WAYNE L. REV. 155, 159–161 (1996) (arguing for a metaphor of cyberspace as separate space); Joel R. Reidenberg, *Governing Networks and Rule-Making in Cyberspace*, 45 EMORY L.J. 911, 912 (1996) (arguing that "attempts to define new rules for the development of [cyberspace] rely on disintegrating concepts of territory and sector, while ignoring the new network and technological borders that transcend national boundaries"); Joel R. Reidenberg, *Lex Informatica: The Formulation of Information Policy Rules Through Technology*, 76 TEX. L. REV. 553 (1998) (arguing for a "Lex Informatica" which would regulate cyberspace through technological devices).

[8] Anupam Chander, *The New, New Property*, 81 TEX. L. REV. 715, 718–19 (2003). Those who have addressed concerns about equality in cyberspace usually give it passing importance, at least in comparison to the attention given to ideas of freedom and liberty. For example, Benkler discusses equality only in relation to its importance to liberal theories of justice; but not as something inherent to the "wealth" of networks. *See* BENKLER, *supra* note 5.

[9] Elsewhere, this author has referred to this body of scholarship as "New Virtualism." *See* Jonathon W. Penney, *Privacy and the New Virtualism*, 10 YALE J.L. & TECH. 194, 195–200 (2008).

[10] Jack M. Balkin, *Virtual Liberty: Freedom to Design and Freedom to Play in Virtual Worlds*, 90 VA. L. REV. 2043 (2004).

cyberspace, including online communities, arguing that equality ought to be understood as a founding value of cyberspace as much as liberty and freedom. Part III then offers a wide-ranging account of the different forms of inequality in cyberspace, particularly in online communities. Part IV offers proposals to address this inequality. Among other things, this Article argues that unlike other founding values such as liberty and autonomy, which are usually defined by the amount of freedom from coercion a person might have in cyberspace, equality is relative—it is measured against the relationships among people, rather than against an abstract ideal. This Article also argues that when inequities arise in online communities, it may be a foundational cyberspace value that ought to be dealt with within those communities, rather than imposed from without.

Of course, this Article recognizes that these ideas hearken back, somewhat, to first generation cyberlaw scholarship, which advocated the autonomy of virtual worlds. But the difference is that this Article does not suggest that online communities be fully autonomous or that real-space laws are inapplicable. Rather, it suggests that equality might be best left to citizens of online communities to define and defend. Thus, an ideal legal regime might include real-space laws that require virtual worlds to simply promote equality, but leave the definition of equality, and its defense, to members of online communities.

II. THE HISTORY OF A LOST FOUNDATIONAL VALUE OF CYBERSPACE

A. Equality in the Beginning

Not surprisingly, scholars often begin a discussion of cyberspace values with John Perry Barlow's 1996 *Declaration of the Independence of Cyberspace*.[11] Barlow was, after all, speaking in the name of "liberty"[12] at an important moment in the development of cyberspace (Julie Cohen calls it "the dawn of the Internet age"[13]). He was also speaking as a founding member of the Electronic Frontier Foundation—one of the first organizations to promote and defend online civil liberties. His words thus echoed, perhaps better than those of anyone else, the sentiment of many of the Internet's founders about the importance of freedom and liberty to cyberspace.[14] Cohen's words resonated to the extent that Barlow's ideas influenced an entire generation of lawyers who were themselves pioneering something new: an emerging body of cyberlaw scholarship,

---

[11] Barlow, *supra* note 1, at 27.

[12] *Id.* at 28.

[13] Julie E. Cohen, *Cyberspace As/And Space*, 107 COLUM. L. REV. 210, 216 (2007).

[14] RICHARD S. ROSENBERG, THE SOCIAL IMPACT OF COMPUTERS 600 (3d ed. 2004) ("John Perry Barlow, a founding member of the Electronic Freedom [sic] Foundation, a leading online civil liberties organization published, online of course, 'A Declaration of the Independence of Cyberspace.' It captures much of the strong feeling that the early founders and aficionados of the Internet had about that new technology."); *see also* GOLDSMITH & WU, *supra* note 1, at 10, 13 (writing that Dibbell and Barlow promoted "a new frontier, where people lived in peace, under their own rules, liberated from the constraints of an oppressive society and free from government meddling," a vision shared by other pioneers of cyberspace who "believed that the Internet might transcend territorial law and render the nation-state obsolete"); TURNER, *supra* note 1, at 261 (writing that the "techno-utopians" had "conjured up visions of a disembodied, peer-to-peer utopia . . . a return to a more natural, more intimate state of being").

which, like Barlow's *Declaration*, aimed to preserve liberty and autonomy in cyberspace.[15]

Few would quibble with Lessig's statement that liberty and freedom were foundational values of cyberspace[16] or blame him and other cyberlaw scholars, such as Yochai Benkler and David Post, for doing their best to promote these ideals.[17] This Article argues there is more to it than that. Equality was also a founding value of cyberspace. Though scholars now only occasionally speak its name, it was there in the beginning, heralded—just like freedom and liberty—in many of the early foundational texts that have helped to shape, define, and understand cyberspace.[18]

Take Barlow's *Declaration*. Though it proclaimed the importance of "liberty" and became a "rallying call" to a certain libertarian ethic for an entire generation of "computer enthusiasts, hackers, and cypherpunks,"[19] his *Declaration* also envisioned equality as a part of cyberspace's idealized project: "We are creating a world that all may enter without privilege or prejudice accorded by race, economic power, military force, or station of birth."[20] In fact, notions of universalism and equality run throughout the *Declaration*, as elsewhere Barlow declares cyberspace a home for "all the sentiments and expressions of humanity"—no matter if "debasing" or "angelic"—where "anyone, anywhere" is entitled to speak freely.[21] Barlow even rejects traditional concepts, such as property, that contribute to inequities, promising cyberspace to be more "fair" than the "world" created by real-space governments.[22] Barlow's celebration of cyberspace's potential for complete equality even prompted one of the *Declaration*'s first critics to accuse him of implicitly invoking Marxist ideology.[23]

---

[15] *See generally* sources cited *supra* note 7. *See also* Penney, *supra* note 9, at 196 ("The simplicity and revolutionary character of [Barlow's] ideas was appealing—so appealing that many early 'cyberlaw' scholars followed Barlow to argue that traditional laws ought not apply to the virtual worlds of cyberspace, that they be left alone to formulate their own legal rules and norms.") (footnotes omitted).

[16] *See* Stephenson, *supra* note 2 (quoting Lawrence Lessig).

[17] *See generally* BENKLER, *supra* note 5; LESSIG, *supra* note 4; DAVID G. POST, IN SEARCH OF JEFFERSON'S MOOSE: NOTES ON THE STATE OF CYBERSPACE (2009).

[18] Does it make any sense to say that cyberspace has "foundational" texts that have helped define it, like the *Federalist Papers* helped define the U.S. Constitution? Lessig, for example, has spoken explicitly of "cyberspace's Constitution." Lawrence Lessig, Lecture at the American Academy in Berlin, Germany: Cyberspace's Constitution (Feb. 10, 2000), *available at* http://www.lessig.org/content/articles/works/AmAcd1.pdf. So might there also be influential texts, like Lessig's own *Code as Law*, essential to understanding that constitution's meaning and scope? Aimée Hope Morrison has recently expressed a similar sentiment about Barlow's *Declaration*. Aimée Hope Morrison, *An Impossible Future: John Perry Barlow's 'Declaration of the Independence of Cyberspace,'* 11 NEW MEDIA & SOC'Y 53, 54 (2009) (describing Barlow's declaration as "one document among many that attempts at once to define and delimit the arena of electronic interaction, commerce and information popularly designated as 'cyberspace'").

[19] COLIN J. BENNETT, THE PRIVACY ADVOCATES: RESISTING THE SPREAD OF SURVEILLANCE 49 (2008) ("Barlow's 'A Declaration of the Independence of Cyberspace' became a rallying call for a generation of young computer enthusiasts, hackers, and cypherpunks . . . . [T]his philosophy is deeply rooted in a particular interpretation of the American political tradition and an absolutist reading of the First Amendment to the U.S. Constitution.").

[20] Barlow, *supra* note 1, at 29.

[21] *Id.*

[22] *Id.* at 29–30.

[23] Reilly Jones, *A Critique of Barlow's "A Declaration of the Independence of Cyberspace,"* 8 EXTROPY, no. 2, 1996, *available at* http://sociology.morrisville.edu/readings/cyberculture/Barlow-Declaration-

But equality and egalitarian aims were claimed as part of cyberspace's cultural fabric even before the *Declaration*. Another early cyberspace manifesto is "Cyberspace and the American Dream: A Magna Carta for the Knowledge Age," published in 1994[24] and "coauthored by information-age luminaries such as [Alvin] Toffler, George Gilder, and Esther Dyson."[25] Dyson, an early cyber-libertarian like Barlow, is today described as "one of the most influential and powerful women in the high-tech sector."[26] Similarly influential and widely quoted,[27] the cyber "Magna Carta" heralded the "egalitarian explosion" promoted by cyberspace and the value of "universal access to personal computing."[28] Even William Gibson's fictional novel *Neuromancer*, which coined the term cyberspace to help describe a dystopian future, held out some promise for greater equality in the disembodied world of cyberspace.[29]

But equality was also a concern among some early cyberlaw scholars. Dan Burk, for example, was writing about inequalities between "information-rich" and "information-poor" countries in 1993, three years before Barlow first declared cyberspace's independence.[30] Lessig noted the importance of equality in his widely influential text *Code and Other Laws of Cyberspace*:

> We stand on the edge of an era that demands we make fundamental choices about what life in [cyberspace] . . . will be like. These choices will be made; there is no nature here to discover. And when they are made, the values we hold sacred will either influence our choices or be ignored. The values of free speech, privacy, due process, and equality define who we are. If there is no government to insist on these values, who will do it?[31]

Lessig's campaign against a *laissez-faire* approach to cyberspace governance included a concern for equality. Similarly, over half a decade before *The Wealth of Networks*, Yochai Benkler argued that the dynamism of the "digital environment" offered a means

---

Critique_by_Jones.pdf ("If cyberspace is institutionalized as its own *unlimited* sovereign, then its jurisdiction will grow at the expense first of other institutions, and if successful, at the expense of everyone outside of cyberspace. Hence Barlow initiates a new version of Marx's class struggle.").

[24] Esther Dyson, George Gilder, George Keyworth & Alvin Toffler, *Cyberspace and the American Dream: A Magna Carta for the Knowledge Age*, PROGRESS & FREEDOM FOUND. (Aug. 1994), http://www.pff.org/issues-pubs/futureinsights/fi1.2magnacarta.html.

[25] NICK DYER-WITHEFORD, CYBER-MARX: CYCLES AND CIRCUITS OF STRUGGLE IN HIGH-TECHNOLOGY CAPITALISM 34 (1999).

[26] LAURA LAMBERT, THE INTERNET: A HISTORICAL ENCYCLOPEDIA, BIOGRAPHIES 88 (Hilary W. Poole ed., 2005).

[27] MARGARET WERTHEIM, THE PEARLY GATES OF CYBERSPACE: A HISTORY OF SPACE FROM DANTE TO THE INTERNET 296 (1999) (noting that the manifesto was "widely quoted" and "based on the ideas of a group that included Esther Dyson and Alvin Toffler").

[28] Dyson, Gilder, Keyworth & Toffler, *supra* note 24.

[29] *See* CHRIS WOODFORD, THE INTERNET: A HISTORICAL ENCYCLOPEDIA, ISSUES 255 (Hilary W. Poole ed., 2005) ("When writer William Gibson coined the word cyberspace in his 1984 novel *Neuromancer*, he promised disabled people a brave new world of equality, a 'bodiless exultation' free from the 'prison of flesh.'").

[30] Dan L. Burk, *Patents in Cyberspace: Territoriality and Infringement on Global Computer Networks*, 68 TUL. L. REV. 1, 50–51 (1993) (demonstrating concern about "neo-colonization" and the "disparity between 'information-rich' and 'information-poor' nations").

[31] LAWRENCE LESSIG, CODE AND OTHER LAWS OF CYBERSPACE 220 (1999).

to reconcile economic productivity with social equality.[32]   Though not as frequently proclaimed as freedom or liberty, these texts show equality was an important—even foundational—value to cyberspace and its future.

B. Equality's Unequal Treatment

So how did concerns for "equality and distributive justice" in cyberlaw scholarship become "greatly neglected"?[33] This is a difficult question to answer, though there are a few potential explanations. The first is the emergence of concern over the "digital divide" in the late 1990s. The term was popularized by several reports of the U.S. Department of Commerce's National Telecommunications and Information Administration (NTIA) in 1999. The digital divide refers to the gap between those who have access to information and technology, and those who do not.[34] By the late 1990s, the digital divide was the most debated equality issue for cyberspace and information technology.[35]   Ironically, the U.S. government's interest in the digital divide and egalitarian concerns about access to information technology likely turned cyber-libertarians and first generation cyberlaw scholars off equality issues. The NTIA was central to the Clinton administration's policy initiative on the issue.[36] Cyber-libertarians deeply disliked the agency because it pushed hard for the Telecommunications Act of 1996, which included the Communications Decency Act. These actions prompted

---

[32] Yochai Benkler, *The Battle over the Institutional Ecosystem in the Digital Environment*, COMM. ACM, Feb. 2001, at 84, 88 ("The point is that simply copying the settlement from the economy of stuff to the economy of information is unnecessary. In that portion of our lives increasingly occupied by information, we can be free in a richer sense and more egalitarian in the distribution of wealth while maintaining or increasing productivity.").

[33] Chander, *supra* note 8, at 718–19.

[34] DAVID TREND, WELCOME TO CYBERSCHOOL: EDUCATION AT THE CROSSROADS IN THE INFORMATION AGE 10 (Henry A. Giroux ed., 2001) ("As increasing amounts of commercial and cultural activity are shifting to the Internet, the distance between the connected and the unconnected may well be creating a new global information proletariat. That unconnected world knows little about modems, satellites, computer laptops, or the Internet. Although it is rarely, if ever, discussed in the discourse of digital culture, more than half the people in the world do not even have telephone service. Indeed, on many levels the vast expansion of information technology has created what the U.S. Commerce Department has termed a *digital divide*."); *see also* David J. Gunkel, *Second Thoughts: Toward a Critique of the Digital Divide*, 5 NEW MEDIA & SOC'Y 499, 501 (2003) ("The origin of the term 'digital divide' remains uncertain and ambiguous. Recent publications and studies routinely reference 'Falling Through the Net: Defining the Digital Divide,' the third in a series of reports published by the US Department of Commerce's National Telecommunications and Information Administration."); Brian D. Loader, *Introduction* to CYBERSPACE DIVIDE: EQUALITY, AGENCY, AND POLICY IN THE INFORMATION SOCIETY 3, 3–4 (Brian D. Loader ed., 1998).

[35] *See* Peter K. Yu, *Bridging the Digital Divide: Equality in the Information Age*, 20 CARDOZO ARTS & ENT. L.J. 1, 2 (2002) ("This gap between the information-haves and have-nots is commonly referred to as the *digital divide*. Since the mid-1990s, the digital divide has received considerable attention in international forums, in presidential debates, and among corporate leaders.") (footnotes omitted).

[36] *See* Gunkel, *supra* note 34, at 501 (noting the NTIA's role in authoring the U.S. government's key reports on the subject); Amy Lynne Bomse, Note, *The Dependence of Cyberspace*, 50 DUKE L.J. 1717, 1745–46 (2001) ("Despite its largely laissez-faire approach to technology, the Clinton administration in 1999 took an active role in addressing the issue of uneven access. At the behest of President Clinton, the Commerce Department held a Digital Divide Summit to address the problem through a government–private sector partnership.").

Barlow to issue the *Declaration*, calling President Clinton "that great invertebrate in the White House."[37] Though the cyber-libertarians *did* care about equal access, they saw the government's newfound interest in the digital divide as a foil for more intrusion into cyberspace. This certainly did not help the cause of equality in the eyes of cyberlaw writers.

A second, and perhaps more important, explanation is that egalitarian concerns simply did not align with the libertarian ethic that most first generation cyberlaw scholarship came to exemplify. As noted, this early work was deeply influenced by the ideals of influential cyber-libertarians like Barlow, Dibbell, and Dyson, preserving and promoting liberty as its primary object. Cyber-libertarians believed they were forging a new space, and their most urgent priority was to keep the government out.[38] Equality, in many cases, was overlooked as a secondary concern;[39] it was something that would flow naturally from the New World of cyberspace once liberty and freedom were guaranteed.[40] The Internet was a flattener, an equalizer.[41] Not surprisingly, cyber-libertarians simply did not take the digital divide seriously; for them, it was merely an "imperfection[]," a "passing phase[]" on cyberspace's inevitable march toward universality.[42] Thus, Louis Rossetto, founder of *Wired* magazine, called it "laughable" that there exists a problem of "info-haves and have nots"; properly understood, it was merely a question of haves and "have-laters."[43]

A third, and related, explanation concerns broader attitudes about technological neutrality. Internet is technology, and technology is often understood as neutral.[44] That is, as a technology, the Internet is value-neutral because it is instead infused with the values, and the social, political, and economic contexts, of those who use it.[45] Mirroring

---

[37] Barlow, *supra* note 1, at 27.

[38] DAVID BELL ET AL., CYBERCULTURE: THE KEY CONCEPTS 45 (2004) ("The nation-state and government in general represent for cyberlibertarians the single biggest threat to liberty, self-expression, and individual prosperity.").

[39] *Id.* at 46 (noting the cyber-libertarians "seem unable to address significant questions about access, the digital divide and the distribution of power and economic resources."); TREND, *supra* note 34, at 10 ("While occasionally acknowledging that the Internet replicates existing relations of commerce, popular spokespeople for the electronic frontier, such as Mitch Kapor, John Perry Barlow, and Benjamin Wolley, generally overlook the imperialistic, logocentric implications of this new space, as well as the way the 'real' world continues to define who people are and what they can do.").

[40] For example, Toffler is famous for the argument that "technology would destroy inequality and hence make the redistributive arm of the state obsolete." Ashley Dawson, *Surveillance Sites: Digital Media and the Dual Society in Keith Piper's* Relocating the Remains, POSTMODERN CULTURE, Sept. 2001.

[41] *See* TURNER, *supra* note 1, at 1; Nicholas Negroponte, *Being Digital—A Book (P)review*, WIRED, Feb. 1995, *available at* http://www.wired.com/wired/archive/3.02/negroponte_pr.html (writing that the Internet would "flatten organizations, globalize society, decentralize control and help harmonize people").

[42] Bomse, *supra* note 36, at 1728–29 (noting the view of "digital libertarians").

[43] Louis Rossetto, *Responses to the Californian Ideology*, HYPERMEDIA RES. CENTER, http://www.hrc.wmin.ac.uk/theory-californianideology-responses1.html (last visited Nov. 27, 2011) ("The utterly laughable Marxist/Fabian kneejerk that there is such a thing as the info-haves and have-nots . . . displays a profound ignorance of how technology actually diffuses through society."); *see also* Bomse, *supra* note 36, at 1727.

[44] Philip T. Shepard, *Technological Neutrality and the Changing Normative Context of Applied Science Research, in* NEW DIRECTIONS IN THE PHILOSOPHY OF TECHNOLOGY 163, 164–65 (Joseph C. Pitt ed., 1995).

[45] Lori Gruen, *Technology, in* TECHNOLOGY AND VALUES: ESSENTIAL READINGS 423, 426 (Craig Hanks ed., 2010); Shepard, *supra* note 44, at 164–65.

neutrality in liberal theory,[46] equality advocacy in technology would require an abandonment of that inherent state of neutrality. Of course, technological neutrality is not an uncontroversial view, but it is nevertheless common.[47] Right or wrong, a belief in this kind of neutrality may have helped to marginalize any concerns about equality; or at least those concerns about distributive justice that went beyond traditional debates about access to the Internet and information technologies.

A final explanation for the neglect of equality issues in cyberlaw scholarship, or at least a neglect of in-depth analysis, concerns what Orin Kerr calls the problem of internal (or virtual) and external (or real) perspectives of cyberlaw.[48] A "virtual" perspective means approaching disputes from the perspective of a person "internal" to cyberspace.[49] With the virtual perspective, the person is often understood as a virtual person, or an avatar, inhabiting the contours of cyberspace. Likewise, a "real" perspective refers to the perspective of someone "external" to the virtual community—an ordinary computer-user sitting at her desk in real space, with cyberspace understood as a physical, external global communications network.[50] Interestingly, any cyberlaw scholars that have taken the time to address egalitarian concerns have stuck to externalist issues: concerns about the digital divide among rich and poor countries and the importance of universal access to computers, software, and connectivity to promoting equality.[51] Though some anthropologists have explored issues of inequality *within* virtual worlds,[52] cyberlaw scholars have offered no similar exploration. Few, if any, such scholars have written about inequality online or proposed any cyber-legal ideas to promote equality. And internal perspectives on equality in cyberspace have been entirely ignored in the cyberlaw literature.

---

[46] Louis P. Pojman & Robert Westmoreland, *Introduction* to EQUALITY: SELECTED READINGS 1, 1 (Louis P. Pojman & Robert Westmoreland eds., 1997) (Equality "is one of the basic tenets of almost all contemporary moral and political theories that humans are essentially equal, of equal worth, and should have this ideal reflected in the economic, social, and political structures of society.").

[47] Gruen, *supra* note 45, at 426; Shepard, *supra* note 44, at 165 ("A great many people seem to go on taking some vague notion of technological neutrality for granted."); *see also* Tomas A. Lipinski, *The Myth of Technological Neutrality in Copyright and the Rights of Institutional Users: Recent Legal Challenges to the Information Organization as Mediator and the Impact of the DMCA, WIPO, and TEACH*, 54 J. AM. SOC'Y FOR INFO. SCI. & TECH. 824 (2003) (providing a legal context).

[48] Orin S. Kerr, *The Problem of Perspective in Internet Law*, 91 GEO. L.J. 357, 359–61 (2003).

[49] *Id.* at 357.

[50] *Id.*

[51] *See, e.g.*, Burk, *supra* note 30, at 50–51 (expressing concern about "neo-colonization" and the "disparity between 'information-rich' and 'information-poor' nations"); Lawrence Lessig, *Open Code and Open Societies: Values of Internet Governance*, 74 CHI.-KENT. L. REV. 1405, 1417 (1999) (discussing the importance of "universal standing" and equal access to software in the Open Source Movement, which produces what Lessig admits is a kind of "formal equality"—equality of access but not equality of result—but Lessig feels it is something nevertheless worth preserving).

[52] *See, e. g.*, TOM BOELLSTORFF, COMING OF AGE IN SECOND LIFE: AN ANTHROPOLOGIST EXPLORES THE VIRTUALLY HUMAN 225–30 (2008); Mikael Jakobsson & T.L. Taylor, *The Sopranos Meets* EverQuest: *Social Networking in Massively Multiplayer Online Games*, FINEART FORUM, Aug. 2003, *available at* http://mjson.se/doc/sopranos_meets_eq_faf_v2.pdf. Due to the fact that the virtual worlds of Second Life, EverQuest, and World of Warcraft have become more of cultures and virtual worlds than simply video games, this Article does not italicize the titles of the virtual worlds. *See* BOELLSTROFF, *supra*, at 255

C. Situating Equality: Some Preliminary Comments

A.   Equality, Distributive Justice, and Cyberspace

Before discussing equality in cyberspace further, it is helpful to explore the general concept of equality itself. Equality is a central, perhaps fundamental, value in contemporary moral, political, and legal thought. It is often used as a basic measure of what is just and legitimate, and helps define the baseline for fair treatment of individuals: "It is one of the basic tenets of almost all contemporary moral and political theories that humans are essentially equal, of equal worth, and should have this ideal reflected in the economic, social, and political structures of society."[53]   Indeed, as Jeremy Waldron recently noted, the idea of equality has played an essential role in Western thought on social, political, legal, and economic organization for nearly two thousand years.[54] Contemporary legal and political theory is no different. The only theories of justice taken seriously today, as Will Kymlick points out, are egalitarian, meaning that they take equality as a foundation.[55]

But saying that equality is an important concept does little to help understand what it means in application. At the outset, the basic idea of equality should not be confused with equality as a political or legal objective; there is voluminous scholarship on the latter subject, but figuring out the basic idea of equality is often neglected.[56]   This is unfortunate, as clear thinking about the basic idea of equality is necessary to think about equality as a policy aim. Part of the problem is the illusion that there is a consensus regarding the basic notion of equality. Kymlicka defines equality as requiring that citizens be entitled to "equal concern and respect."[57] Most people would probably agree with this highly abstract description of equality. But there is deeper disagreement about what equality requires in more concrete situations: re-distribution of wealth, acknowledgment of people's differences, adopting a difference-blind approach, and so on. Scholarship has gravitated toward equality as a policy goal, likely as a means to give some context to these questions.

But these seeming policy disagreements tend to elide a deeper dispute about two conceptions of equality: formal and substantive equality. Formal equality requires that all people be treated exactly the same—treat like cases alike.[58] This notion of equality is often associated with a libertarian political philosophy, emphasizing liberty and sameness

---

[53] Pojman & Westmoreland, *supra* note 46, at 1.

[54] Jeremy Waldron, *Basic Equality* 1 (N.Y. Univ. Sch. of Law Pub. Law & Legal Theory Research Paper Series, Working Paper No. 08-61, 2008) ("That humans are all one another's equals, and that this makes a difference to how we ought to deal with each other and how we ought to organize ourselves legally, politically, socially and economically—this has been one of the enduring themes in Western thought for at least the past two thousand years.").

[55] WILL KYMLICKA, CONTEMPORARY POLITICAL PHILOSOPHY: AN INTRODUCTION (1990).

[56] Waldron, *supra* note 54, at 1–2.

[57] KYMLICKA, *supra* note 55, at 4.

[58] ROBIN L. WEST, RE-IMAGINING JUSTICE: PROGRESSIVE INTERPRETATIONS OF FORMAL EQUALITY, RIGHTS, AND THE RULE OF LAW 107 (2003) (discussing the "basic ideal of formal equality" as treating like cases alike in terms of Equal Protection jurisprudence).

of treatment.[59]   Substantive equality generally requires equality of result rather than of treatment[60] and is closely linked to the idea of distributive equality, or distributive justice. Substantive equality recognizes that, to achieve equality of result, it may be necessary to address issues of distributive equality by redistributing resources to account for people's differences in ability and socioeconomic standing.[61]   Perhaps the most famous work on distributive equality is John Rawls's *A Theory of Justice*.[62]   Rawls aims to achieve true equality by constructing an entire theory of egalitarian justice based on distributive equality.[63]   For many theorists, distributive equality is an essential component of achieving equality.[64]

D. Dimensions of Virtual Equality and Inequality

¶17   Though equality is a complex concept, forms of inequality in cyberspace are identifiable and have significant impact. This subsection discusses two dimensions of virtual equality, what this Article refers to as the Digital Divide 1.0 and the Digital Divide 2.0. The Digital Divide 1.0 is essentially the traditional account of global inequalities between technology haves and have-nots. The Digital Divide 2.0 involves inequalities online as well as inequalities caused by an interaction between real space and cyberspace. While the first dimension has received much scholarly treatment, both cyberlaw and otherwise, the second dimension has received little treatment, if any. These dimensions of inequality are by no means exhaustive, but provide a good starting point.

1. Digital Divide 1.0: National and Global Inequality

¶18   The term digital divide, as noted above, refers to the division between those who have access to information technology like the Internet and those who do not.[65] Concern regarding this issue grew in the 1990s, particularly as it became apparent that the utopian future described by advocates of information technology[66] was not going to materialize.

---

[59] *Id.* at 134 (noting that "formal equality [has been] embraced by a wide range of liberal and libertarian commentators"); MICHEL ROSENFELD, JUST INTERPRETATIONS: LAW BETWEEN ETHICS AND POLITICS 157 (1998) (discussing formal equality as being consistent with libertarian theories of justice).
[60] There are different approaches to substantive equality, but this is a commonly cited standard. *See* ROSENFELD, *supra* note 59, at 157; Catherine Barnard & Bob Hepple, *Substantive Equality*, 59 CAMBRIDGE L.J. 562, 564 (2000) ("These limitations of the principle of formal or procedural equality have led to attempts to develop concepts of substantive equality.... Apparently consistent treatment infringes the goal of substantive equality if the results are unequal.").
[61] ROSENFELD, *supra* note 59, at 121 ("[S]ubstantive equality . . . properly incorporates differences."); Robin West, *Equality Theory, Marital Rape, and the Promise of the Fourteenth Amendment*, 42 FLA. L. REV. 45, 61 (1990).
[62] JOHN RAWLS, A THEORY OF JUSTICE (1971).
[63] *See generally id. See also* AMY GUTMANN, LIBERAL EQUALITY 119 (1980) (discussing Rawls's work as "the most remarkable contemporary attempt to situate the concept of equality within a comprehensive theory of egalitarian justice").
[64] Richard J. Arneson, *Equality, in* THE BLACKWELL GUIDE TO SOCIAL AND POLITICAL PHILOSOPHY 85, 95–97 (Robert L. Simon ed., 2002) (discussing many theorists of distributive equality, including both Ronald Dworkin and John Rawls).
[65] *See* BELL ET AL., *supra* note 38, at 61–63; *see also* Loader, *supra* note 34.
[66] *See, e.g.,* Barlow, *supra* note 1, at 28, 30 (declaring that people of cyberspace will "create a civilization of the Mind" that is "more humane and fair" than the physical world, and describing that world as free of

With the gap between information technology haves and have-nots growing, social scientists instead turned to more practical matters, such as the steps needed to narrow this digital divide.[67] The first step was to document the gap, which became a priority of the Clinton administration in the 1990s.[68]

The digital divide concerns socioeconomic inequality, both on a national and global level.[69] For example, the final report issued by the U.S. government under the Clinton administration in late 2000 showed that significant gaps remained in the digital divide, but there were improvements in terms of connectivity and Internet access among previously underrepresented groups.[70] Although the digital divide may be closing in America, in other countries, particularly poorer ones, it is not.[71]

Traditional discussion of the digital divide is entirely concerned with "external" matters from a cyberlaw perspective. That is, the digital divide debate is about physical global communications, particularly the Internet, and addressing the problem that some people have access to information technology while others do not. Since the 1990s, this

---

the "Governments of the Industrial World"); Dyson, Gilder, Keyworth & Toffler, *supra* note 24 (writing of a new cyberspace "constituency-to-come" that will bring about the "creation of a new civilization, founded in the eternal truths of the American Idea"); *see also* GOLDSMITH & WU, *supra* note 1, at 10, 13 (discussing cyberlibertarian writers who spoke of "a new frontier, where people lived in peace, under their own rules, liberated from the constraints of an oppressive society and free from government meddling," a vision shared by other cyberspace pioneers who "believed that the Internet might transcend territorial law and render the nation-state obsolete").

[67] Alain Rallet & Fabrice Rochelandet, *ICTs and Inequalities: The Digital Divide*, *in* INTERNET AND DIGITAL ECONOMICS: PRINCIPLES, METHODS AND APPLICATIONS 693, 693 (Eric Brousseau & Nicolas Curien eds., 2007) (noting the digital divide debate arose in part out of criticisms of a common but "naïve" vision in the 1990s that "[v]irtual space" could be a "substitute for physical space"); Loader, *supra* note 34, at 3 ("Until fairly recently the euphoria surrounding the advent of the Internet as a means of enabling 'many-to-many' communication across the globe might easily have led one to believe that if people were not already 'online' then they very soon would be. . . . Talk amongst the technologically elite of advanced capitalist societies of joining the Information Superhighway is a discourse which has little meaning in many regions of the globe where even intermediate telecommunications are underdeveloped."). *See generally* Gunkel, *supra* note 34 (for a discussion of inception and evolution of the debate about the digital divide).

[68] Bomse, *supra* note 36, at 1745–46; Yu, *supra* note 35, at 3 ("During the Clinton Administration, the Department of Commerce conducted four detailed surveys on the digital divide in the United States.").

[69] Gunkel, *supra* note 34, at 503 ("It is not until 1999 that the term appears in NTIA's 'Falling Through the Net.' In this report, 'digital divide' is defined as 'the divide between those with access to new technologies and those without.' In this way, 'digital divide' names a form of socioeconomic inequality demarcated by the level of *access* that one has to IT.") (citation omitted).

[70] U.S. DEP'T OF COMMERCE, FALLING THROUGH THE NET: TOWARD DIGITAL INCLUSION (2000), *available at* http://search.ntia.doc.gov/pdf/fttn00.pdf; Yu, *supra* note 35, at 3 ("The final report, which was released shortly before the end of the Administration, showed an increasing number of Americans using computers and the Internet. . . . The report also found a rapid increase in Internet access 'among most groups of Americans, regardless of income, education, race or ethnicity, location, age, or gender.'"); *see also* Andrew Leigh & Robert D. Atkinson, *Clear Thinking on the Digital Divide*, POL'Y REP. (Progressive Policy Inst., Washington, D.C.), June 2001, at 1 ("Historical comparisons suggest that while the current gaps in computer ownership and Net access have risen over the past few years, they will soon begin to narrow as most Americans adopt these technologies.").

[71] Yu, *supra* note 35, at 4 ("Although the report showed that the digital divide in the United States is closing, the same is not true for the less developed countries.") (footnote omitted). *See generally* JAN A.G.M. VAN DIJK, THE DEEPENING DIVIDE: INEQUALITY IN THE INFORMATION SOCIETY (2005); INFORMATION TECHNOLOGY POLICY AND THE DIGITAL DIVIDE: LESSONS FOR DEVELOPING COUNTRIES (Mitsuhiro Kagami et al. eds., 2004).

perspective on the digital divide has been the focal point of sustained public debate, which continues today.[72] Yet, something new still might be said.

2. Digital Divide 2.0: Virtual Inequality

The digital divide is certainly about equality in virtual worlds, but only insofar as they are aspects of the Internet and other communications networks with global reach. The digital divide does not only concern the *physical* aspects of cyberspace. One innovation of "New Virtualist" scholarship[73] is its understanding that the virtual and external perspectives in cyberlaw are both relevant and interdependent, providing for more thorough and nuanced analysis. This subsection explores how the digital divide and virtual worlds interact in terms of inequality by setting out how the digital divide creates significant inequalities within cyberspace. In other words, a complete picture of virtual equality requires an interdependent approach to this perspective.

One way of thinking about this interdependency is to consider how real-world capacities impact the virtual-world experience. Take time lag, for instance. Lag occurs when the technological capacity of hardware, software architectures, models, Internet connectivity, and computing hardware significantly limits the capacity of virtual worlds to deliver real-time experiences. Often, this means delays in loading graphics, user-interface, application program interfaces; in the case of virtual worlds, it means delays in loading landscapes, avatars, terrain, and architecture.[74] Lag is a synchronization problem which can seriously impact the quality of an online experience, reducing not only the "sense of realism" but even basic usability.[75] According to Richard Bartle, lag is a hardware issue as well as a geographical one.[76] Simply put, people with slower computers or unreliable Internet connectivity will experience more lag; but even with the fastest, most modern hardware, a user will still experience significant lag if there are

---

[72] Yu, *supra* note 35, at 2 ("Since the mid-1990s, the digital divide has received considerable attention in international forums, in presidential debates, and among corporate leaders.") (footnotes omitted). *See generally* BARBARA MONROE, CROSSING THE DIGITAL DIVIDE: RACE, WRITING, AND TECHNOLOGY IN THE CLASSROOM (2004); KAREN MOSSBERGER ET AL., VIRTUAL INEQUALITY: BEYOND THE DIGITAL DIVIDE (2003); United Nations Conference on Trade and Development, New York and Geneva, 2006, *The Digital Divide Report: ICT Diffusion Index 2005*, U.N. Doc. UNCTAD/ITE/IPC/2006/5 (May 10, 2006) (detailing the continued global digital divide); KAREN MOSSBERGER ET AL., *From the Digital Divide to Digital Citizenship, in* DIGITAL CITIZENSHIP: THE INTERNET, SOCIETY, AND PARTICIPATION 95 (2008); Arik Hesseldahl, *The U.N. Will Not Bridge the Digital Divide*, FORBES (Feb. 25, 2005, 10:00 AM), http://www.forbes.com/2005/02/25/cx_ah_0225tentech.html (discussing a United Nations world summit attended by 1,700 information technology experts and the United Nation's efforts and "plan of action" to bridge the information and communications technology digital divide); sources cited *supra* note 71.

[73] *See infra* note 82 and accompanying text.

[74] *See, e.g.*, BOELLSTORFF, *supra* note 52, at 103–04 (discussing the client–server architectural limits of Second Life's technology which causes significant lag problems).

[75] WILLIAM R. SHERMAN & ALAN B. CRAIG, UNDERSTANDING VIRTUAL REALITY: INTERFACE, APPLICATION, AND DESIGN 243 (2003); *see also* RICHARD A. BARTLE, DESIGNING VIRTUAL WORLDS 105 (2003); BOELLSTORFF, *supra* note 52, at 102–03 (discussing the frequency of complaints about in-world lag among Second Life users).

[76] BARTLE, *supra* note 75, at 105; *see also* SHERMAN & CRAIG, *supra* note 75, at 243 ("[T]wo primary ways to reduce latency [or lag] are to (1) send information from the input devices to the computer as quickly as possible and (2) reduce the amount of time it takes to generate the computer graphics image.").

great distances between the user and a virtual world (such as a user in Australia connecting to a server located in the United States).[77]

This is where the digital divide comes in. As noted, it has both a national and global dimension. Part of this layering, however, is social rather than just geographical.[78] In global terms, the developed world retains a vast majority of the access to information technology, while Internet connectivity is variable and "very limited in sub-Saharan Africa, the Middle East, Latin America, and South Asia."[79] Given these realities, the digital divide is a source of significant inequalities of virtual-world experience. This inequality applies not only to individuals with no connectivity, but also to those who have some connectivity but experience significant lag due to geographical or technological factors. Finally, technological limits in poorer regions can create inequalities *between* virtual worlds. While virtual worlds located on American servers are generally stable, those located in parts of Asia suffer from significant server insecurities, where hacking and theft of virtual property are common.[80] In this way, the digital divide contributes a kind of virtual-world inequality—of experience—caused by real-world factors.

Mapping out these points gives a sense of the different layers of equality and makes it easier to identify inequalities. It also links the basic idea of equality—which was an important founding value to cyberspace—to the more policy-laden idea of distributive equality.[81] Concerns of distributive justice largely figure into the discussion of virtual inequalities. Virtual inequalities refer to forms of inequality that have emerged in virtual communities. Though some virtual inequalities have primarily virtual causes, many are linked to real-world challenges of distributive justice, both on a regional and global level.

III. EQUALITY AND DISTRIBUTIVE JUSTICE IN CYBERSPACE

This Part explores the dimensions of virtual inequality, the forms of inequalities that have emerged in cyberspace. The approach here is paradigmatic of an emerging body of second-generation scholarship that addresses the unique legal problems posed by modern virtual worlds. This body of work, referred to elsewhere as the New Virtualism,[82] examines, among other things, how the influences of real space—be it

---

[77] BARTLE, *supra* note 75, at 105 ("Lag happens.").

[78] Rallet & Rochelandet, *supra* note 67, at 693 ("The digital divide has not only a geographical dimension but also an important social side."); *see also* ENCYCLOPEDIA OF COMMUNITY: FROM THE VILLAGE TO THE VIRTUAL WORLD 405–06 (Karen Christensen & David Levinson eds., 2003).

[79] Yu, *supra* note 35, at 4; *see also* PIPPA NORRIS, DIGITAL DIVIDE: CIVIC ENGAGEMENT, INFORMATION POVERTY, AND THE INTERNET WORLDWIDE 41, 233 (3d prtg. 2003) (noting that developed countries constitute roughly eighty percent of the world's information technology market and that there is a lack of Internet access in the noted regions).

[80] *See* EDWARD CASTRONOVA, SYNTHETIC WORLDS: THE BUSINESS AND CULTURE OF ONLINE GAMES 2 (2005) (noting that in Asia people have "lost virtual items because of game-server insecurities and hacks" and that the police have even been called to deal with these problems).

[81] "Distributive justice" is used here in the same sense as used by John E. Roemer, who writes that the central question of distributive justice is "how a society or group should allocate its scarce resources or product among individuals with competing needs or claims." JOHN E. ROEMER, *Introduction* to THEORIES OF DISTRIBUTIVE JUSTICE 1, 1 (1996).

[82] *See* Penney, *supra* note 9, at 195–99; Jonathon W. Penney, *Understanding the New Virtualist Paradigm*, 12 J. INTERNET L. 3, 3–4 (2009) [hereinafter Penney, *New Virtualist*] (discussing the three "key innovations of the New Virtualist scholarship"). Examples of "New Virtualism" scholarship include James

221

governmental, commercial, or socioeconomic factors—impact law, code, and other aspects of virtual communities.

Essentially, first-generation cyberlaw scholarship, as discussed above, primarily focuses on preserving liberty, autonomy, and self-government in cyberspace.[83] However, one of the assumptions upon which this early work rests is the idea that virtual worlds embody separate and unique spaces with defined borders that set off virtual worlds from real space of the real world.[84] Important changes in the years since have shown this assumption to be incorrect.[85] Popularization brought with it increased interest from regulators and e-commerce as corporate interests proliferated online and states around the world proposed laws to control the Internet and its virtual spaces.[86] In other words, there are no immutable borders that kept the outside world from influencing cyberspace and virtual worlds.

By contrast, rather than conceiving of cyberspace and virtual worlds as separate and distinct solitudes, New Virtualist scholarship approaches cyberlaw problems—like equality and distributive justice—from both an internal perspective and an external one. Virtual communities are interconnected with real-world challenges; so, understanding the former requires studying the latter. This Article's discussion of virtual inequalities follows this approach by examining how both real-world and virtual-world distributive justice issues create and influence inequalities in virtual communities.

Grimmelmann, *Virtual Power Politics*, *in* THE STATE OF PLAY: LAW, GAMES, AND VIRTUAL WORLDS 146 (Jack M. Balkin & Beth Simone Noveck eds., 2006) (exploring software design through lens of virtual world politics); Balkin, *supra* note 10 (discussing "virtual liberty" in virtual worlds and the boundaries between cyberspace and real space); Richard A. Bartle, *Virtual Worldliness: What the Imaginary Asks of the Real*, 49 N.Y.L. SCH. L. REV. 19 (2004); James Grimmelmann, *Virtual Worlds as Comparative Law*, 49 N.Y.L. SCH. L. REV. 147 (2004) (approaching the law within virtual worlds as comparative legal study); Dan Hunter, *Cyberspace as Place and the Tragedy of the Digital Anticommons*, 91 CALIF. L. REV. 439 (2003) [hereinafter Hunter, *Cyberspace as Place*] (arguing that the metaphor of cyberspace legitimizes the imposition of private property-like regimes on virtual spaces, precluding their common use and enjoyment); Kerr, *supra* note 48 (exploring the "problem of perspective" in cyberlaw); F. Gregory Lastowka & Dan Hunter, *The Laws of the Virtual Worlds*, 92 CALIF. L. REV. 1 (2004) [hereinafter Lastowka & Hunter, *Virtual Worlds*] (arguing that items in virtual worlds ought to have property protection as much as items in non-virtual worlds); F. Gregory Lastowka & Dan Hunter, *Virtual Crimes*, 49 N.Y.L. SCH. L. REV. 293 (2004) (exploring whether destruction of virtual property can or ought to be conceived as criminal activity); Tal Z. Zarsky, *Information Privacy in Virtual Worlds: Identifying Unique Concerns Beyond the Online and Offline Worlds*, 49 N.Y.L. SCH. L. REV. 231 (2004) (discussing possible questions raised by virtual worlds for real-world laws).

[83] *See generally* sources cited *supra* note 7.

[84] Penney, *New Virtualist*, *supra* note 82, at 3.

[85] *Id.* at 4 ("As it turned out, the original virtualists were wrong. The developments of the ensuing decade would show that the borders between real space and cyberspace were neither clear nor impermeable.").

[86] *Id.* ("Increasing public use and popularity of the Internet and its cyberspaces and virtual worlds brought more attention and scrutiny from real space state regulators and law enforcement officials. New laws were proposed, and new means of controlling this supposed new frontier of cyberspace were propagated and enforced, reaching into the presumably impenetrable borders of cyberspace. Increasing electronic commerce and commodification also played a role in blurring borders between cyber and real space.") (footnotes omitted).

A. Virtual Economies and the Emergence of Class Inequality

1. Technology, Wealth, and Virtual Class Disparity

Virtual worlds are supposed to be distinct from real space.[87] That is what Barlow's *Declaration* envisioned. Yet, those who have studied virtual worlds often note what Ed Castronova calls a "blurring," where real-world tendencies bleed into the realm of virtual worlds.[88] One such form of blurring is the emergence of monetary systems within virtual worlds. EverQuest's platinum pieces and Second Life's "Linden dollars," which are convertible from U.S. dollars, are two prominent examples.[89] Such in-world currencies are not only a big reason for the popularity of these virtual worlds, but also promote in-world creation, expression, and innovation through financial incentive.[90] In Boellstorff's terms, Second Life's ethic of "creationist capitalism" fuses creativity to labor, production, and consumption.[91]

But with the introduction of monetary systems (including labor, production, and consumption) comes forms of inequality—particularly class status. This is no different in virtual worlds.[92] Again, Second Life offers a good example, with the emergence of an "elite" class—the property owners and "content creators" who embodied the ideal of Second Life's "creationist capitalism" political economy.[93] This class of users was "treated differently by other[s]," not only by other virtual world residents, but by the operators of the world itself—they often were given more opportunities to influence virtual world design, and sometimes were offered jobs.[94]

Most interestingly, not only do these privileged classes exist in virtual worlds, but other users have developed a kind of class consciousness about their inequality of status.[95] Sandra, a Second Life resident, expresses an almost class consciousness about this state of affairs:

---

[87] BOELLSTORFF, *supra* note 52, at 225 (noting how virtual worlds are often inaccurately seen as places of "untrammeled freedom" where people are free to re-invent themselves at will); FRIEDRICH VON BORRIES ET AL., SPACE TIME PLAY: COMPUTER GAMES, ARCHITECTURE AND URBANISM: THE NEXT LEVEL 148 (2007) ("Those unfamiliar with the workings of virtual worlds are often tempted to regard them merely as collective hallucinations. But their inhabitants' fictional actions have real consequences . . . .").

[88] CASTRONOVA, *supra* note 80, at 149 (noting the appearance of monetary systems and commodities in virtual worlds to be an example of blurring the distinction between the virtual and the real).

[89] *Id.* at 19 (discussing "real money" system in EverQuest); BOELLSTORFF, *supra* note 52, at 211–15 (discussing "money and labor" in Second Life, in terms of "creationist capitalism," an ethic the author says best describes Second Life's political economy).

[90] CASTRONOVA, *supra* note 80, at 64 (discussing EverQuest's "reward structures"); JOHN PALFREY & URS GASSER, BORN DIGITAL: UNDERSTANDING THE FIRST GENERATION OF DIGITAL NATIVES 124 (2008) (discussing the case of Anshe Chung, a Second Life land baroness, and the role of financial incentives in fostering UCC or "digital creativity").

[91] BOELLSTORFF, *supra* note 52, at 209.

[92] Mikael Jakobsson, *Rest in Peace, Bill the Bot: Death and Life in Virtual Worlds*, in THE SOCIAL LIFE OF AVATARS: PRESENCE AND INTERACTION IN SHARED VIRTUAL ENVIRONMENTS 63, 73 (Ralph Schroeder ed., 2002) ("The concept of social status can thus also be used in virtual worlds, and it is as important in understanding a virtual society as it is in any ordinary society.").

[93] BOELLSTORFF, *supra* note 52, at 226.

[94] *Id.* at 226–27 (internal quotation mark omitted).

[95] *Id.* at 227.

> They need to upgrade the platform so that people like me have more things to play with. But instead they say fuck the people who don't own businesses and tons of land in [Second Life]. They give those people everything they want because they feed [Linden Lab] tons of cash every month. . . . They don't care about us . . . . Second Life is no different from real life. The rich get richer while the poor stay poor.[96]

So as with world economies, virtual economies can lead to disparities of wealth, power, and distribution of property and privilege. Yet Sandra's comments also reveal something about the root causes of these disparities, speaking to the ability of Second Life members who are privileged in real space to perpetuate their wealth and power in virtual space.

2. Open and Closed Virtual Economies and Real-Space Wealth

Indeed, the emergence of such class inequalities in a virtual world like Second Life is not entirely unforeseeable. One unique aspect of Second Life is its virtual economy, an in-world economy which involves exchange among community members in Linden dollars. Also known as an "open" virtual economy, Second Life members can convert actual U.S. dollars into Lindens for in-world use.[97] Though Second Life defines Linden dollars as a fictional in-world currency, it is fully exchangeable in U.S. dollars and therefore accessible to anyone with any real-world currency.[98] And a currency exchange, called the LindenX, measures the fluctuating Linden-to-USD exchange rate.[99] Though this "openness" allows real-world wealth to facilitate virtual commerce, it also allows that same wealth to carry real-world inequalities of power and privilege into the virtual community.

Sandra's comment about a privileged class of community members speaks to the emergence of these virtual inequalities. This privileged class "feeds" Linden Labs by investing real money into Second Life, in return for preferential treatment. Central to the way real-world wealth translates into wealth and power in Second Life is virtual landownership. Second Life's economy is centered on property, and land sales are a key source of income for many residents.[100] But to own land, a member must not only purchase a "premium account," but also pay a monthly landowning fee to Linden Labs that increases with the size and character of the member's virtual parcel.[101] These are not necessarily paltry sums—though Boellstorff notes a basic land usage fee of $10, further blocks of land can be purchased for an additional range of land fees from $5 for small

---

[96] *Id.* (third alteration in original) (quoting Sandra, a Second Life resident).
[97] *See id.* at 211–12 (noting that Second Life activities could be financed by real-world money and labor with credit card purchases of Linden dollars, and that Second Life was unique among virtual worlds as permitting work for wages, free exchange, and intellectual property rights); Viktor Mayer-Schönberger & John Crowley, *Napster's Second Life?: The Regulatory Challenges of Virtual Worlds*, 100 Nw. U. L. REV. 1775, 1789 (2006).
[98] *See* BOELLSTORFF, *supra* note 52, at 212.
[99] *See id.*; Mayer-Schönberger & Crowley, *supra* note 97, at 1789.
[100] BOELLSTORFF, *supra* note 52, at 215–16 (noting "[t]he economic system of Second Life, however, was predicated on property" and noting that real estate transactions are the most "lucrative" form of work in Second Life).
[101] *Id.* at 216.

blocks to $195 for larger ones.[102] The impact of real-world wealth is clear: Second Life members with sufficient real-world wealth can cover the costs to finance large-scale virtual land purchases. In other words, Second Life members can easily leverage real-world wealth into virtual world wealth, power, and privilege. In fact, real estate in Second Life is concentrated in a small group of wealthy landowners, known as land barons.[103]

Though Second Life is unique in that it is an open virtual economy, real-world wealth can create inequality even in those virtual worlds with closed economies. Closed economies refers to virtual worlds that allow for exchange but do not have a currency that is exchangeable into real-world dollars. Sony's EverQuest is a massive multiplayer online game (MMOG) with a virtual economy that includes the exchange of virtual items without a real-money conversion.[104] Despite being closed to currency exchange, real-world wealth nevertheless has an important impact. In particular, EverQuest members can use real-world markets to exchange virtual items. Despite Sony's "bitter opposition,"[105] people were actually purchasing, exchanging, and auctioning virtual objects and weapons used in EverQuest on real-world e-commerce sites like eBay and Yahoo.[106] Castronova's groundbreaking work on "virtual economies," such as EverQuest, illustrates the significance and volume of exchange—sometimes greater than the GNP of many actual countries.[107] The volume of real-money transactions for virtual items was so significant that Sony changed its mind, and founded its own online exchange forum to make money off the trades.[108]

Such real-world exchange of wealth can lead to in-world disparities among users. Most apparent is the notion of "cheating" the rules of the virtual world by using real-world wealth to gain virtual world power and prestige.[109] For example, normally it takes

---

[102] *Id.*

[103] David Kirkpatrick, *Coldwell Banker's Second Life*, FORTUNE (Mar. 23, 2007, 3:48 AM), http://money.cnn.com/2007/03/22/technology/fastforward_secondlife.fortune/index.htm ("A small number of land barons mostly control real estate in Second Life . . . and we thought we could bring real estate to the masses.") (quoting a vice president of Second Life) (internal quotation marks omitted); BOELLSTORFF, *supra* note 52, at 216–17 (discussing a group of successful land barons who have purchased whole islands).

[104] Mayer-Schönberger & Crowley, *supra* note 97, at 1787 & n.55.

[105] *Id.* at 1807.

[106] *Id.* at 1788.

[107] Edward Castronova, *On Virtual Economies* 3 n.2 (Ctr. for Econ. Studies Ifo. Inst. for Econ. Research, Working Paper No. 752, 2002) (discussing the notion of virtual world GDP); Edward Castronova, *Virtual Worlds: A First-Hand Account of Market and Society on the Cyberian Frontier* 31–33 (Ctr. for Econ. Studies Ifo. Inst. for Econ. Reseach, Working Paper No. 618, 2001) (discussing virtual world GNP and noting that "[a]ccording to GNP data from the World Bank[,] Norrath is the 77th richest country in the world, roughly equal to Russia").

[108] Mayer-Schönberger & Crowley, *supra* note 97, at 1807 ("Sony Online Entertainment has already had to reverse its negative stance towards player-to-player auctions of virtual objects. After long and bitter opposition to the sale of *EverQuest* objects on eBay and IGE, Sony Online Entertainment saw that market demand and revenue opportunities of virtual object sales were too great to ignore. In July 2005, Sony launched Station Exchange, a site which its Senior Vice President and CFO, John Needham, characterized as 'SOE-bay.'") (footnotes omitted).

[109] JULIAN DIBBELL, PLAY MONEY: OR, HOW I QUIT MY DAY JOB AND MADE MILLIONS TRADING VIRTUAL LOOT 14–15 (2006) (discussing how regular members of the *Dark Ages of Camelot* MMOG "hate[d]" real-world purchase of virtual objects, which is akin to "pulling out a real twenty-dollar bill in the middle of a

time and experience to amass special virtual items, but those with enough disposable wealth could acquire those items effortlessly through real-world purchases allowing them to "level up" in power and prestige faster. Moreover, purchase of such items confers a measure of power—using their privileged virtual status in EverQuest acquired via real-world transactions, players have new powers to confer similar wealth and status on others of a lower level (a status similar to being of a lower class), those they feel are worthy to move up the *EverQuest* socioeconomic hierarchy.[110]

3. Virtual Class Disparities

Real-world wealth and distributive inequality can bleed into virtual worlds, bringing those very same inequalities in virtual contexts. And, like the real world, those class disparities can become entrenched. This is certainly apparent in Second Life. Boellstorff observes that many residents of Second Life complain about the "preferential treatment" given to this class of virtual world residents.[111] A group of wealthy property owners—who invested the most real money and, through exchange, created the most virtual world wealth—receive special status in the governance of the virtual world (often being directly consulted by Linden Labs).[112] Further, as landowners, this elite class had additional means to perpetuate their wealth—in Second Life, the only way to create permanent objects is to own land.[113] Real-world wealth is consolidated and perpetuated by the creation of virtual world disparities. The result is not insignificant: the creation of elites with privilege and influence not held by other virtual world members; a permanently stratified virtual class system.

There is also the emergence of a privileged class in virtual worlds with a competitive orientation like EverQuest. Here, real-world wealth can confer special status in a way that undermines the "rules" of the game, as well as the labors of regular users. This privileged gaming class also has advantages beyond a competitive advantage—it can confer status and wealth on other players by transferring virtual world currency or scarce items.

A final interesting dimension to these virtual inequalities is how they re-entrench real-world disparities of wealth. As Julian Dibbell notes, outgoing World of Warcraft players can make money by selling off high-demand virtual items on real-world markets.[114] And presumably, many of these items can be purchased from those very same real-world e-commerce markets. Virtual-world economies, like the real-world economies that influence them, lead to social and economic classes with disparities of wealth, power, and privilege.

Monopoly game and giving it to another player in exchange for Boardwalk and Park Place"); *see also* Mayer-Schönberger & Crowley, *supra* note 97, at 1787.

[110] *See* Jakobsson & Taylor, *supra* note 52 (describing how author Taylor, a more experienced EverQuest user, had amassed enough in-world money, or "platinum pieces," to be able to confer on Jakobsson higher status, by sharing some wealth and more powerful weapons).

[111] BOELLSTORFF, *supra* note 52, at 227.

[112] *Id.*

[113] *Id.* at 215 ("The economic system of Second Life, however, was predicated on property. Only by owning property could residents build objects with permanence: this was an economic model in which property made the virtual 'real.'").

[114] DIBBELL, *supra* note 109, at 12–13.

B. Inequality of Virtual Expression

Real-world problems of distributive justice (unequal distribution of wealth and resources) also play a role in creating inequalities in virtual expression. There is an emerging recognition that virtual worlds can play a unique role in fostering cultural expression and diversity. A key, if not central, part of this contribution is user-created content (UCC).[115] The idea that virtual game worlds constitute a form of cultural expression is not new,[116] but UCC takes the creative expression in virtual worlds to a new level because, often, such content is created not to "win" the game, but for its own sake.[117] That is, creativity and expression for the sake of creativity and expression. Second Life, for example, is Linden Lab's virtual world built by Second Life members. The community offers the complete "architecture of modern societies" with "clothing, buildings, vehicles, and opportunities for starting online businesses."[118] According to Second Life's website, an average of one million members log into the virtual community from around the globe.[119] A big part of Second Life's attraction is its incentives for user creativity—its terms of service and end-user agreements confer intellectual property on users for their virtual world creations.[120]

UCC offers some hope for those who believed, like Barlow and Benkler had, that virtual worlds will offer a dynamic new frontier for creative expression.[121] UCC in

---

[115] Mira Burri-Nenova, *User Created Content in Virtual Worlds and Cultural Diversity*, in GOVERNANCE OF DIGITAL GAME ENVIRONMENTS AND CULTURAL DIVERSITY: TRANSDISCIPLINARY ENQUIRIES 74, 75–78 (Christoph Beat Graber & Mira Burri-Nenova eds., 2010), *available at* http://ssrn.com/abstract=1316847 (discussing how some user-generated content falls within the United Nations' definition of "cultural expression"); PALFREY & GASSER, *supra* note 90, at 114–15; JONATHAN L. ZITTRAIN, THE FUTURE OF THE INTERNET—AND HOW TO STOP IT 146–47 (2008).

[116] *See* Jack M. Balkin, *Law and Liberty in Virtual Worlds*, 49 N.Y.L. SCH. L. REV. 63, 69 (2004) ("Should we understand the developing technologies and social practices of designing and playing games, including the cooperative features of play that I have called the freedom to design together, as a new medium for the communication of ideas? I think the arguments are quite compelling. Courts already recognize much simpler games—so-called first person shooter games—as artistic creations entitled to First Amendment protection.").

[117] *See* John Baldrica, *Mod as Heck: Frameworks for Examining Ownership Rights in User-Contributed Content to Videogames, and a More Principled Evaluation of Expressive Appropriation in User-Modified Videogame Projects*, 8 MINN. J.L. SCI. & TECH. 681, 687 (2007); Burri-Nenova, *supra* note 115, at 76.

[118] Mayer-Schönberger & Crowley, *supra* note 97, at 1787.

[119] Linden Lab, *The Second Life Economy in Q3 2011*, SECOND LIFE (Oct. 14, 2011, 2:38 PM), http://community.secondlife.com/t5/Featured-News/The-Second-Life-Economy-in-Q3-2011/ba-p/1166705.

[120] Burri-Nenova, *supra* note 115, at 80–81 ("In other games, content creation may very well be possible but is not allowed. In yet a third category of games, UCC is not only allowed but builds the core of the game—its very mission and function is to facilitate the creation of content within the game environment, as well as to enhance the possibilities of sharing (including trading) the created content. The infamous example of this in fact rather small category of games, is Linden Lab's *Second Life*, which is a 'world created by its Residents,' where players can build basically anything from scratch through the process of atomistic construction.") (footnotes omitted); BOELLSTORFF, *supra* note 52, at 212 ("At the time of my fieldwork, Second Life was known as one of the only virtual worlds that freely allowed one to work for wages inworld, as well as permitting free currency exchange and full intellectual property rights . . . .").

[121] Barlow, *supra* note 1, at 27; BENKLER, *supra* note 5, at 297 ("As online games like Second Life provide users with new tools and platforms to tell and retell their own stories, or their own versions of well-trodden paths, as digital multimedia tools do the same for individuals outside of the collaborative storytelling platforms, we can begin to see a reemergence of folk stories and songs as widespread cultural practices. And as network connections become ubiquitous, and search engines and filters improve, we can begin to

227

virtual worlds, for example, can provide a means for the limitless expression Barlow pronounced in his *Declaration*. UCC is available to all members of a virtual community equally, at least in theory. It thus helps to render cyberspace—or a given virtual world—a home for equality of expression, welcome to "all the sentiments and expressions of humanity," no matter if "debasing" or "angelic."[122] Though again, this depends on the virtual world itself. If the virtual world is wired by way of the Internet (or some other global communications network), there is also universal access to UCC in that virtual world and, thus, universality of expression.

1. Intellectual Property and User-Created Content

Of course, the real picture is not nearly that rosy. Though UCC may hold out some promise for complete equality of expression in virtual form, in reality, several factors contribute to inequalities. The first, and most often cited, is inequality of treatment of virtual expression. That is, virtual worlds, and their designers and operators, tend to incentivize certain forms of virtual expression, while deterring—or even censoring—others. Some kinds of discrimination between forms of virtual expression is expected, particularly in MMOGs, where UCC related to game advancement will be privileged in comparison to other players.[123] However, in less game-oriented virtual worlds, like Second Life, the differential treatment seems less warranted. In fact, scholars like Jack Balkin have analyzed such discrimination of speech in terms of free expression, proposing regulation that might help preserve speech in certain kinds of more publicly oriented virtual worlds.[124] This Article takes a slightly different angle, exploring in more depth how real-space inequalities of wealth, property, and power play out in a virtual world context. The focus is on the creation of intellectual property rights for UCC. This is one of Second Life's unique features—its terms of service and end-user license agreement confer intellectual property to users for their virtual world creations.[125] In fact, this feature is often cited as a reason for Second Life's popularity and its users' creative drives.

Yet, there is another side to this coin. Recognition of such rights can lead to greater commodification of virtual-world expression, privileging certain kinds of commercial expression over more creative forms.[126] Additionally, intellectual property rights confer on owners a powerful means to potentially suppress expression. In other digital contexts, scholars view intellectual property rights as a serious threat to freedom of expression.[127] This is no different in virtual worlds. As Balkin notes:

---

see this folk culture emerging to play a substantially greater role in the production of our cultural environment.").

[122] Barlow, *supra* note 1, at 29.

[123] Burri-Nenova, *supra* note 115, at 100 (discussing how UCC is often tied to gaming objectives in MMOGs and other game-oriented virtual worlds).

[124] *See generally* Balkin, *supra* note 10.

[125] *See* BOELLSTORFF, *supra* note 52, at 212.

[126] Balkin, *supra* note 10, at 2064 ("Letting players possess copyrights in virtual items significantly increases real-world commodification of virtual worlds, and makes it all the more likely that the law will regulate what goes on in virtual worlds. By allowing players intellectual property rights in virtual items, the makers of *Second Life* are essentially inviting the law into their virtual world.").

[127] Yochai Benkler and Lawrence Lessig provide two classic examples. *See* Yochai Benkler, *Free as the Air to Common Use: First Amendment Constraints on Enclosure of the Public Domain*, 74 N.Y.U. L. REV.

Strong intellectual property rights in real space are a burden on freedom of expression, although in many cases an acceptable burden. Strong intellectual property rights in virtual worlds, however, are a positive nuisance, and they may greatly inhibit the freedom to play as well as the freedom of players to design parts of the virtual world.[128]

This concern about restrictions of expression takes on a dimension of distributive inequality—and inequality of expression—when intellectual property rights become concentrated in the hands of a wealthy few. This is certainly the case in the real world, where large corporations hold the copyrights to vast amounts of commercial art and music, leveraging those rights to control expression by limiting use of copyrighted work.[129] Already, intellectual property claims are emerging in virtual worlds, as demonstrated by the suit Eros, an adult entertainment company in Second Life, brought against another community member for creating virtual adult sex toys that violate its copyright.[130] In many ways, Eros and similar entities embody the powerful creationist class Boellstorff talks about as the elite of Second Life.[131] Though this may not be a pervasive problem at present, users like Eros, particularly Second Life members who have real-world assets to finance their virtual world endeavors, constitute a privileged class of content creators who will create disparities of virtual expression by exerting greater control over the UCC of others and over the platforms for UCC.[132]

2. Expression, Distributive Justice, and the Digital Divide

A second way real-world distributive justice issues create inequality of virtual expression concerns the disparities in opportunity and technological capacity for UCC. Relevant here is the digital divide. The digital divide, as noted above, is concerned with equality and virtual worlds insofar as they are aspects of communications networks with global reach. It also impacts the equality of expression *within* virtual worlds on two levels. The first is on an individual level. Lack of proper access or connectivity seriously limits virtual world members' capacity for UCC. Of course, such connection problems may limit access to the virtual world altogether, but not necessarily. Often, UCC requires

---

354, 394–400 (1999) (discussing copyright and other intellectual property as part of an "enclosure movement" that threatens freedom of speech and diversity of expression); LAWRENCE LESSIG, THE FUTURE OF IDEAS: THE FATE OF THE COMMONS IN A CONNECTED WORLD (2001).

[128] Balkin, *supra* note 10, at 2064–65. *See generally* Hunter, *Cyberspace as Place, supra* note 82 (arguing that the metaphor of cyberspace legitimizes the imposition of private property-like regimes on virtual spaces, precluding their common use and enjoyment).

[129] LESSIG, *supra* note 127, at 183 ("The pattern here is extremely common. Copyright holders vaguely allege copyright violations; a hosting site, fearing liability and seeking safe harbor, immediately shuts down the site. The examples could be multiplied thousands of times over, and only then would you begin to have a sense of the regime of control that is slowly emerging over content posted by ordinary individuals in cyberspace. Yahoo!, MSN, and AOL have whole departments devoted to the task of taking down 'copyrighted' content from any Web site . . . .").

[130] First Amended Complaint—Injunctive Relief Sought and Demand for Jury Trial, Eros, LLC v. Leatherwood, No. 8:07-CV-01158-SCB-TGW (M.D. Fla. Oct. 24, 2007), http://docs.justia.com/cases/federal/district-courts/florida/flmdce/8:2007cv01158/202603/11/0.pdf.

[131] BOELLSTORFF, *supra* note 52, at 226.

[132] For another example of what Dan Hunter calls the problem of the "Digital Anticommons," see Hunter, *Cyberspace as Place, supra* note 82, at 500.

a more advanced level of technological capacity from users—put simply, a computer and an Internet connection that can support graphically intensive applications and scripting. In many regions, people simply do not have that capacity. Burri-Nenova has recognized this point in relation to UCC. The claim that UCC necessarily promotes cultural diversity

> is not true because of the barriers existing to entering the game space. As the usual hindrances, one can list here the access to infrastructure, broadband, hardware, media literacy and the costs related to playing a certain game (especially MMOGs), which should not be underestimated. These thresholds may be too high to overcome, in particular for players coming from developing countries or poor parts of society in developed countries, thus making the overall picture already one of discrimination and privileged access.[133]

By comparison, members of virtual worlds from western countries where connectivity is less of a problem, or where people typically have greater technological capacity, have likewise greater opportunities for virtual expression. This is inequality of virtual expression on an individual level.

There is also a broader concern about equality of cultural expression. UCC, as an independent or practical creative act, can help promote cultural expression and diversity, both in virtual worlds as well as real ones. Indeed, the Organisation for Economic Co-operation and Development Working Party has recognized UCC's potential to boost "availability and diversity of (local) content in diverse languages."[134] However, if UCC can promote cultural diversity by being an expression of a user's culture and there is a lack of diversity in the people using virtual worlds and creating content, then the full potential of UCC will never be realized. If the disparity of access and proper connectivity to virtual worlds does not change—and virtual world participation remains something solely for people from a handful of developed western nations—inequalities of cultural expression within virtual worlds will remain. UCC that arises from certain cultures, classes, and linguistic expressions will dominate in the virtual world, while other UCC will suffer. That is, the kind of world that Second Life, as a virtual community, invites its users to create may be like a virtual monoculture that remains unwelcoming and does not provide users of different backgrounds with many opportunities for expression. Here, lack of access to virtual world participation results in a number of forms of virtual inequality, both in terms of the ability to contribute UCC expression and in terms of the quality of in-world experience.

C. Cyber-security and Inequality

A final emerging aspect of virtual inequality concerns cyber-security. Cyberspace is increasingly being recognized as a "domain of military action;" so, focus on cyber-

---

[133] Burri-Nenova, *supra* note 115, at 100.
[134] Org. for Econ. Co-operation & Dev. [OECD], Comm. for Info., Computer & Commc'ns Policy, *Participative Web: User-Created Content*, at 36, OECD Doc. DSTI/ICCP/IE(2006)7/FINAL (2007), *available at* http://www.oecd.org/dataoecd/57/14/38393115.pdf; *see also* Burri-Nenova, *supra* note 115, at 99.

security is growing.[135] Responding to a range of new threats posed by cyberspace,[136] governments around the world have ramped up cyber-warfare and security capabilities, treating it like the traditional strategic zones of land, sea, and air.[137] Emerging threats in this domain range from lone hackers, to state-supported cyber-warfare, to organized cyber-crime and transnational terrorism.[138] Thus, security threats can be low scale as well as well organized and well funded.[139]

Yet cyber-security, like other forms of security, is largely dependent upon resources. The capacity to secure cyberspace, or defend oneself in it, is not just a matter of technological capacity, but is a matter of other social, political, and economic factors too.[140] On a national level, cyber-security requires, among other things, "collective action"; this involves not just awareness and action by governments, but broader "cyber cultur[al]" practices among populations that promote security.[141] This, of course, requires stable access to Internet connectivity, information and communication technologies, and related resources, which not all countries have. This leaves certain regions at a greater risk to large-scale (even catastrophic) cyber-attack, economic exploitation, and weakened technological competitiveness.[142]

Similar factors cause inequalities on an individual level. Without stable Internet connectivity or access to related technologies, people are less likely to adopt best practices for proper cyber-security, such as purchasing firewalls and anti-virus software and keeping them up to date. This leaves them, like states, at the mercy of the aforementioned threats. But even where there is stable connectivity, there are other challenges. Indeed, even in wealthy countries like the United States where Internet and ICT access is not a widespread problem, there remains a significant knowledge gap on cyber-security matters.[143] Moreover, where best practices have been adopted and entrenched, challenges emerge so quickly that gaps in awareness remain.[144] This leaves some individuals' personal information, located on the margins of these knowledge gaps by virtue of their own wealth, resources, and technical knowledge, highly vulnerable to data loss and exploitation.

And, finally, there is the matter of virtual world experience. This was discussed earlier in relation to other contexts like the digital divide and UCC, but cyber-security

---

[135] Ronald Deibert & Rafal Rohozinski, *Control and Subversion in Russian Cyberspace, in* ACCESS CONTROLLED: THE SHAPING OF POWER, RIGHTS, AND RULE IN CYBERSPACE 15, 31 (Ronald Deibert et al. eds., 2010) (discussing how advanced filtering systems and Internet controls have grown out of an increasing focus on cyber-security by governments and militaries).

[136] NAT'L RESEARCH COUNCIL & NAT'L ACAD. OF ENG'G, TOWARD A SAFER AND MORE SECURE CYBERSPACE 3 (Seymour E. Goodman & Herbert S. Lin eds., 2007) [hereinafter SAFER CYBERSPACE] ("A very broad spectrum of actors, ranging from lone hackers to major nation-states, poses security risks to the nation's IT infrastructure.").

[137] Deibert & Rohozinski, *supra* note 135, at 31. *See generally* SAFER CYBERSPACE, *supra* note 136.

[138] SAFER CYBERSPACE, *supra* note 136, at 3.

[139] *Id.*

[140] ZEINAB KARAKE SHALHOUB & SHEIKHA LUBNA AL QASIMI, CYBER LAW AND CYBER SECURITY IN DEVELOPING AND EMERGING ECONOMIES 214 (2010) (discussing how securing cyberspace is "not simply a technological question," but one involving many other factors).

[141] *Id.* at 214–15; *see also* SAFER CYBERSPACE, *supra* note 136, at 9.

[142] SAFER CYBERSPACE, *supra* note 136, at 3.

[143] *Id.* at 9.

[144] *Id.*

impacts virtual experience too. The rush to secure and, to a certain extent, militarize cyberspace has also encouraged the proliferation of tools for online censorship.[145] Often, those located in poorer, less democratic countries suffer greater levels of filtering, which obviously impacts the richness of online experience.

IV. ADDRESSING VIRTUAL INEQUALITIES

¶ 48   Accepting that equality is an important value to cyberspace, then the inevitable question is: what is the best way to address the inequalities previously discussed? Concerning the Digital Divide 1.0, as well as inequities in online communities due largely to real-world distributive justice challenges and lack of access to Internet and ICT, the solution is likely straightforward, but neither easy nor cheap: national and international access to Internet connectivity and information communication technologies can be improved by more engagement by international governmental and non-governmental organizations and greater foreign aid from wealthier countries.[146]

¶ 49   On the Digital Divide 2.0, inequalities largely arise in online communities, though real-world distributive justice challenges are often interconnected with these issues. This Article argues that addressing virtual inequalities is something that should be left to virtual communities themselves, both to their members and to their designers and operators, at least to the extent possible. This view harkens back somewhat to first generation cyberlaw scholarship—following the cyber-libertarians—which often argued, wrongly, that traditional laws could not and should not apply to cyberspaces.[147] Scholars like Lessig, Goldsmith, and Wu have since shown that this argument and its assumptions are deeply flawed.[148] Cyberspaces are not immune to control and regulation.

¶ 50   But it seems, in some ways, the pendulum has swung too far. Today, scholars feel free to ruefully dismiss the ideas of the cyber-libertarians—as Orin Kerr does when he says that nowadays few people take them "seriously"[149]—as if self-governance does not remain a live issue both in virtual and real space. Indeed, Goldsmith and Wu overstate their case when they say that "notions of a self-governing cyberspace are largely discredited."[150] The idea of cyber-libertarians that is discredited is not the notion of self-government, but the notion that the nature of cyberspace would render it resistant to any form of state control, making self-government inevitable. Conceding that self-

---

[145] Deibert & Rohozinski, *supra* note 135, at 31.

[146] The United Nation's Special Rapporteur on free expression, in his recent report, makes a number of recommendations on point concerning access to Internet and "necessary infrastructure," including calling on all states to work to guarantee "universal" Internet access. Special Rapporteur on the Promotion & Protection of the Right to Freedom of Opinion & Expression, *Promotion and Protection of All Human Rights, Civil, Political, Economic, Social and Cultural Rights, Including the Right to Development: Report of the Special Rapporteur on the Promotion and Protection of the Right to Freedom of Opinion and Expression, Frank La Rue*, Human Rights Council, ¶ 85, U.N. Doc. A/HRC/17/27 (May 16, 2011), *available at* http://www2.ohchr.org/english/bodies/hrcouncil/docs/17session/A.HRC.17.27_en.pdf.

[147] *See* sources cited *supra* note 7.

[148] GOLDSMITH & WU, *supra* note 1; Orin S. Kerr, *Enforcing Law Online*, 74 U. CHI. L. REV. 745, 751–52 (2007) (reviewing GOLDSMITH & WU, *supra* note 1); LESSIG, *supra* note 31, at 6 ("Values that we now consider fundamental will not necessarily remain. Freedoms that were foundational will slowly disappear.").

[149] Kerr, *supra* note 148, at 751.

[150] GOLDSMITH & WU, *supra* note 1, at 14.

government of cyberspace is not inevitable, as time has shown, is not to say that self-governance cannot or should not work in any part of cyberspace. Cyberspace governance is not an all-or-nothing proposition. The Internet and the virtual worlds it hosts are too diverse and dynamic to suggest otherwise.

Thus, a case-by-case approach is preferable to virtual world governance.[151] Since such issues are not all-or-nothing, some concerns need to be regulated by traditional real-world regulators; but other issues might be best addressed by virtual world communities themselves. In this case, there are good reasons for leaving concerns about virtual inequality to virtual world designers and community members. Part V sets out these reasons.

V. LEAVING VIRTUAL INEQUALITY IN CYBERSPACE

As the case-by-case method requires, this Article's argument that virtual inequalities should be left to virtual communities to address is *specific* to equality—both as an idea and how it works in virtual contexts—and is based on a number of contextual factors, including the nature and autonomy of virtual communities, the "power to leave," the persistence of real-world distributive inequality, and the problem of enforcement.

A. The Nature and Autonomy of Virtual Communities

A primary reason for leaving concerns about virtual inequalities to online communities to police is the nature and autonomy of the communities themselves. This point has two parts. First, aspects of virtual worlds themselves may render online communities incompatible at the outset with concerns about equality, whether formal or substantive. That is, virtual worlds come in a vast range of diverse forms, with different rules, objectives, and means of interaction with other members. And, in many cases, forms of inequality are *essential* to the very nature of the virtual world. Inequality, in some ways, has been "integral to virtual worlds."[152] From older text-based games with forms of status to more modern MMOG virtual worlds like World of Warcraft, inequalities and the ability for users to climb higher in the social hierarchy are often the warp and woof of what these virtual worlds are about.[153] But the same could also be said for less gaming-oriented worlds like Second Life. Boellstorff writes that Second Life's "ethic" is oriented around an ideology of "creationist capitalism," which fuses creativity to labor, production, and consumption.[154] If he is right, then the emergent class inequalities in Second Life were likely more than foreseeable—they may have even been intentional, as part of Linden Lab's aim to create a virtual world pervaded by social stratification, competition, and creative impulse.[155]

---

[151] David Post appears to take a similar approach in his recent text, in giving reasons for forms of cyberlaw governance in each context he analyzes, including domain names and virtual worlds. *See* POST, *supra* note 17, at 142–86.
[152] BOELLSTORFF, *supra* note 52, at 226.
[153] *Id.*
[154] *Id.* at 209.
[155] *Id.* at 227 ("While there was no single criterion for becoming a more privileged resident, Linden Lab did structure the world so as to have social classes within it, and this structure became more elaborate as my fieldwork progressed.").

The point is that if lawmakers impose certain equality norms on virtual worlds, the result could be quite destructive; these foreign norms have the potential to destabilize the entire ethic and structure of the virtual communities that the equality protections would aim to serve. From this angle, if there are potentially intolerable forms of inequality in a virtual space, it is best to let communities address those in consultation with world designers and moderators.

A second related point concerns the complexities of equality. The basic idea, explained above, should not be confused with equality as a policy objective.[156] Nor should it be seen as simple, as there is much disagreement on the basic idea, once getting past trite statements like equality requires "equal concern and respect."[157] Indeed, these points of disagreement raise a fundamental issue about the concept of equality itself: the distinction between *formal* and *substantive* equality.

As explained above, formal equality requires that all people are treated equally in the sense that they are treated exactly the same—treat like cases alike.[158] This notion of equality pervades first generation cyberlaw scholarship, which believes cyberspace is supposed to deliver a kind of universalism where differences among people would not matter and all would be treated the same—creating a world where, in Barlow's words, "all may enter without privilege or prejudice accorded by race, economic power, military force, or station of birth."[159] The Internet would, said Negroponte, "flatten organizations, globalize society, decentralize control, and help harmonize people."[160] Indeed, formal equality is often associated with libertarian political philosophy to which Barlow, Dibbell, Dyson, and other cyber-libertarians subscribed.[161]

Substantive equality, by contrast, requires equality not of treatment, but result.[162] To achieve equality of result, a substantive equality approach takes into account people's differences.[163] Interestingly, many critics of first generation cyberlaw scholarship use notions of substantive equality in this way—particularly as concerns for distributive justice—to attack early ideas of cyberspace sovereignty and cyberspace's ability to promote democratic values.[164] Lessig, too, in advocating what he called "universal

---

[156] Waldron, *supra* note 54, at 1–2.

[157] KYMLICKA, *supra* note 55, at 4.

[158] WEST, *supra* note 58, at 107 (discussing the "basic ideal of formal equality" as treating like cases alike in terms of Equal Protection jurisprudence).

[159] Barlow, *supra* note 1, at 27–28.

[160] Negroponte, *supra* note 41; *see also* TURNER, *supra* note 1, at 1.

[161] *See supra* note 59 and accompanying text.

[162] *See supra* note 60 and accompanying text.

[163] *See supra* note 61 and accompanying text.

[164] The most prominent of these critics is Neil Netanel. *See* Neil Weinstock Netanel, *Cyberspace Self-Governance: A Skeptical View from Liberal Democratic Theory*, 88 CALIF. L. REV. 395, 406 (2000) ("[C]yberians give insufficient weight to the distributive function of liberal government. Liberal ideals can be realized only if the incidents of citizenship are distributed among all citizens. Yet opportunities to communicate, process information, and even gain access to cyberspace are vastly unequal. The cyberian vision lacks a vehicle to provide such citizenship resources to those who currently lack them. Without state intervention, therefore, cyberspace self-governance will, at best, resemble the Athenian democracy of the privileged few, not participatory liberalism."); *see also* Timothy Wu, *When Law & the Internet First Met*, 3 GREEN BAG 2D 171 (2000).

standing" offered by "open-evolution," which treats all people equally and is thus open to objection on substantive equality grounds.[165]

Libertarians would likely say the best approach is formal equality. Others would say substantive equality. The point is there is no right answer. *Choosing* which conception of equality to promote requires a fundamental choice about the kind of society an individual wants to promote. As Kent Greenawalt writes, "what counts" is not the concept of equality but "the standards one uses to decide . . . what treatment is appropriate."[166] Whether a community strives for equality of treatment (formal equality) or equality of result (substantive equality) is relevant to whether equality ought to be defined locally, as self-governance would allow in a virtual community. Since defining equality requires a choice between different visions of the fabric of the community, it seems much more prudent to leave this definition to the community itself.

B. The Power to Leave (and the Power to Re-enter)

A second reason why inequalities can be left to virtual communities to police is what this Article refers to as the power to leave: a unique component of choosing and exploring virtual worlds, it is the capacity for users to enter and exit freely, often anonymously.[167] Put another way, a member who feels that virtual inequalities are intolerable can opt to disconnect from the community.[168] The nature of virtual worlds magnifies the power to leave. Unlike countries of the real world, where laws and territoriality tie individuals to certain geographical regions and social strata, virtual worlds, with their ephemeral rules and anonymity, allow "ease of exit" if the circumstances in the world become intolerable.[169] Alternative virtual worlds—and the relatively low cost of establishing a virtual world—increase the freedom to leave in comparison to real space.[170] In other words, because a person generally chooses the virtual world they enter, there is an added level of *liberty* (for example, the liberty to leave that world) that is not available to those who suffer the effects of inequality in real space.

However, there are objections to this. First, as T.L. Taylor teaches, it is not easy to simply walk away from online communities: "What happens in virtual worlds often is just as real, just as meaningful, to participants" as offline interactions.[171] People form meaningful online relationships—with other individuals and entire communities—that, at times, can carry over into real space.[172] Sometimes virtual personas can be more

---

[165] Lessig, *supra* note 51, at 1417.

[166] Kent Greenawalt, *How Empty Is the Idea of Equality*, 83 COLUM. L. REV. 1167, 1167 (1983).

[167] Netanel, *supra* note 164, at 425–26. The classic study of the power to leave political systems or voice dissent is Hirschman's 1970 text. *See generally* ALBERT O. HIRSCHMAN, EXIT, VOICE, AND LOYALTY: RESPONSES TO DECLINE IN FIRMS, ORGANIZATIONS, AND STATES (1970).

[168] Netanel, *supra* note 164, at 425–26.

[169] *Id.* at 425.

[170] *Id.* at 425–26 ("[E]xit . . . is much easier and less costly in cyberspace than in real space. A cyberspace dissenter need only discontinue visiting a forum and find, or fairly cheaply establish, an alternative one more closely aligned with the dissenter's views or preferences. Losers in real world plebiscites, in contrast, can usually avoid the result only if they endure the cost and disruption of physically moving to another jurisdiction.").

[171] T.L. TAYLOR, PLAY BETWEEN WORLDS: EXPLORING ONLINE GAME CULTURE 19 (2006).

[172] *Id.* at 54.

important to people than their offline daily lives.[173] In other words, migration from world to world is not necessarily cost-free—community bonds are sundered and relationships are broken to exercise the power to leave.

There is certainly something to this point. People *do* form meaningful connections to virtual communities and get used to the norms of those spaces. But perhaps there is an empirical premise underlying this objection that is not entirely sound. Though Taylor is earnest about the meaningful nature of online life, she is also at pains to say that people still experience virtual worlds differently, in ways that make coming and going not only easy, but expected:

> That people can slip into and out of complex social networks that cross not only online and offline space, but genres within the online world is a fact often underacknowledged. The journalistic anecdotes that circulate, of identity deceptions for example, hide a much less sensational, even mundane, integration of technology into people's everyday lives. People are very adept at moving back and forth between on- and offline spaces and relationships, even while being ambivalent or unsure of how to frame the experience online life produces.[174]

The point seems to be that while people form connections in virtual communities just as they do in real space, there may be something different about virtual worlds (as opposed to reality) that makes entering and exiting those communities easier.

A possible response might be found in something related to the power to leave—the power to re-enter. Entering a virtual world often preserves a level of anonymity and allows a person transformative power of self-reinvention and creation. The traditional real-space bases for unequal treatment (such as race, gender, class, and identity politics) are all fluid in virtual worlds. As celebrated in many cyber-cultural works, cyberspaces can liberate a person from his offline persona and allow creative self-invention and transformation.[175] This power to change identities allows someone feeling marginalized and destined to remain within a fixed social class to leave and anonymously re-enter later, free of the stigma from the past identity. Put another way, virtual worlds can let people begin their virtual lives anew, with a fresh start. While this is not an ideal answer, it does show how someone whose ties to a virtual community are strong enough can leave, but later re-establish those ties albeit in different form. The power to leave and the power to re-enter mean there is less need for real-world authorities—governments and law-makers—to intervene, thus leaving virtual inequalities to virtual communities to address on their own.

C. Code, Real-Space Inequality, and the Problem of Enforcement

A final set of reasons for online community autonomy concerns the means of enforcing equality norms in this context. To begin with, if real-space laws are used to

---

[173] *See* Lastowka & Hunter, *Virtual Worlds*, *supra* note 82, at 52 n.280 (describing the growing numbers of people who inhabit virtual worlds and the importance of these virtual communities to their lives).
[174] TAYLOR, *supra* note 171, at 18.
[175] *See, e.g.*, DAVID BELL, AN INTRODUCTION TO CYBERCULTURES 6–29 (2002); LISA NAKAMURA, CYBERTYPES: RACE, ETHNICITY, AND IDENTITY ON THE INTERNET (2002).

enforce equality rights in virtual communities, such laws would almost certainly apply across multiple virtual communities. It would simply be impossible to pass an equality law for every virtual world where equality may or may not be a concern. Such general equality laws would have a hard time keeping up with the dynamism and innovative development of virtual worlds. Although courts could work this out on a case-by-case basis, it may be preferable to allow each community to formulate its own rules by itself or consult with virtual world operators and designers, given the newness of virtual law. Doing so certainly would provide more bright lines for virtual community members.

Second, even if equality norms are imposed by real-space regulators on virtual worlds to deal with problems of unequal treatment between emergent social classes, much of the problems would remain because real-world issues of distributive justice play a central role in perpetuating inequalities in virtual communities; they bleed from the real world to the virtual world. As long as real-world inequalities persist, so will virtual-world inequalities. A better approach, then, would be to let each virtual community address these problems as it sees fit with consensus and compromise, rather than passing laws to force them to eliminate a real-world problem they cannot possibly cure.

In the end, the most effective means to promote equality in virtual worlds is not necessarily any real-space law, contract, or constitutional norm; rather, as Lessig teaches, it is code.[176] It is application coders, virtual world designers, game world developers, and the members of online communities who best understand the code's impact on members in terms of inequality.

VI. DIRECTIONS FORWARD

Cyberlaw scholarship heralds the importance of freedom in cyberspace, but it has seriously neglected the issues of equality. This neglect is not justified—equality, as much as liberty and freedom, is an original foundational value of cyberspace. As such, it too should be studied and promoted. This Article aims to fill the void of scholarship on the issue of equality in cyberspace, in particular virtual worlds, by examining different forms of virtual inequality and their causes; here, most real-world issues of distributive inequality figured predominantly. It also argues that dealing with virtual inequalities is a challenge best left to virtual communities themselves.

This argument raises questions beyond the scope of this work. For example, this Article does not offer concrete proposals that would allow online communities to govern equality concerns. What such self-governance would look like should also be explored. Virtual inequalities cannot be battled in virtual worlds alone. The impact of real-world disparities in access to technology looms large and can only be defeated with hard work and advocacy offline to raise awareness about distributive justice and the digital divide. In terms of virtual communities, two possible models come to mind. First, virtual worlds could have complete autonomy to deal with issues like equality. For the reasons already discussed, this might be optimal depending on the circumstances. In practice, equality and other social concerns could be dealt with by a democratic formula.[177]

---

[176] See generally LESSIG, supra note 31.
[177] POST, supra note 17, at 185 ("It doesn't seem so crazy to me because there's a 'place-ness' to these virtual places—not just in the way they look but in the way they persist through time, and in the way they present opportunities for an infinite variety of repeated interactions between individuals, for collective

A second possibility is a form of what this author calls cyberspace federalism, which incorporates the use of national laws to promote equality but respects the autonomy of virtual communities. Under such a system, legislatures would pass generally applicable equality laws, such as laws recognizing a general right to equality. Courts enforcing equality rights would be required to interpret these rights in accordance with the local norms of the virtual world.[178] The term cyberspace federalism is appropriate because the system incorporates two levels of government: national or state level (generating generally applicable laws) and virtual level (establishing local norms, customs, and rules). However such a governance structure is accomplished, the main point is that equality can no longer be neglected. As a foundational value of cyberspace, it should to be explored further. That is the task ahead. And the conversation is only now beginning.

---

decision-making, and for common enterprise—that enables us to think about them and talk about them the way that the people who spend lots of time there often do: as true communities, with shared norms and customs and expectations characteristic of each and continually being created and re-created by the members within each. I don't see why they are somehow inherently less deserving of less respect [sic] than the other communities . . . within the international legal order.").

[178] This is something like what Joshua Fairfield has suggested concerning contractual interpretation. *See* Joshua A.T. Fairfield, *Anti-social Contracts: The Contractual Governance of Virtual Worlds*, 53 McGILL L.J. 427 (2008) (arguing for, among other things, judicial deference to virtual community norms when interpreting contract provisions).

Copyright 2012 by Northwestern University School of Law
Northwestern Journal of Technology and Intellectual Property

Volume 10, Number 3 (January 2012)

When the Software We Buy Is Not Actually Ours: An Analysis of *Vernor v. Autodesk* on the First Sale Doctrine and Essential Step Defense

By Terence Leong[*]

I. INTRODUCTION

While software copyright owners generally have broad discretion to license and protect their copyrighted software, there are several affirmative defenses that an alleged infringer can invoke, including the first sale doctrine[1] and the essential step defense.[2] A threshold issue to invoke either defense requires the infringer to be an "owner" of the software in question.

Circuits are split regarding whether software licensees are owners of their licensed software. The recent Ninth Circuit decision in *Vernor v. Autodesk, Inc.* holds that a user of software under a restrictive licensing scheme is not an owner of the software and therefore cannot invoke affirmative copyright infringement defenses.[3] Contrary to *Vernor*, decisions in the Second and Federal Circuits, and even decisions in the Ninth Circuit before *Vernor*, suggest that software licensees' rights are like those of an owner of the software.

This Note asks the question of how software licensing fits within the copyright regime, focusing on an investigation of *Vernor* and the implications on affirmative defenses for copyright infringement. Part II provides an overview of the first sale doctrine, the essential step defense, and the copyrightability of software in general. Part III investigates the issue of ownership versus licensee in the circuits prior to the *Vernor* decision. Part IV discusses the facts in *Vernor* and analyzes the decisions of both the district court and the Ninth Circuit. Part V explores the policy arguments of each party to the case. In Part VI, this Note compares *Vernor* to decisions in other circuits, specifically the split with the Second Circuit. Finally, Part VII concludes with a proposal to resolve the split.

II. OVERVIEW OF LIMITS ON THE RIGHTS OF SOFTWARE COPYRIGHT HOLDERS

The federal copyright regime finds its origin in the Copyright Clause of the U.S. Constitution, which grants Congress the power "[t]o promote the Progress of Science and useful Arts, by securing for limited Times to Authors and Inventors the exclusive Right

---

[*] Candidate for Juris Doctor, Northwestern University School of Law, 2012. Thanks to my parents, Chris and Kai-Jen, and my sister, Katrina, for their wisdom and guidance. Special thanks to Carol, for her unwavering and cheerful support throughout my career.
[1] *See* 17 U.S.C. § 109(a) (2006).
[2] *See id.* § 117(a)(1).
[3] Vernor v. Autodesk, Inc., 621 F.3d 1102, 1113 (9th Cir. 2010).

to their respective Writings and Discoveries."[4]   The Copyright Clause incentivizes the production of creative works by serving the interests of two opposing parties: authors and consumers of the works. It serves the interests of the author and incentivizes creation by granting authors exclusive rights in their works. The Copyright Act codifies this goal by enumerating copyright owners' exclusive rights, enabling the copyright owners to control their works.[5]   An individual is liable for damages for violating these exclusive rights.[6]   One way in which the Copyright Clause serves consumers and fosters the widespread dissemination of knowledge is by limiting those exclusive rights to "limited [t]imes." Additionally, there are several provisions of the Copyright Act that limit the exclusive rights of authors, two of which are discussed below.

A. Limit on the Exclusive Distribution Right: The First Sale Doctrine

The first sale doctrine, which allows owners of copies of a copyrighted work to resell that work after the initial purchase, represents a balance struck in common law between the conflicting interests of copyright holders and the public. Copyright holders possess the exclusive right to distribute copies of their work, including selling, renting, leasing, and lending the work.[7] This exclusive distribution right aims to protect the rights of copyright owners, but often it conflicts with the overall copyright goal of promoting information exchange.[8] If the distribution right were unchecked, copyright owners would be the only individuals who could authorize *any* distribution of their works. Not surprisingly, copyright holders historically have attempted to place restrictions on the alienability of copyrighted items.

The first sale doctrine developed in common law in response to this difficulty. The Supreme Court, articulating the first sale doctrine in *Bobbs-Merrill Co. v. Straus*, recognized that

> copyright statutes, while protecting the owner of the copyright in his right to multiply and sell his production, do not create the right to impose . . . a limitation at which the [copyrighted work] shall be sold at retail by future purchasers, with whom there is no privity of contract.[9]

The first sale doctrine was later codified in § 109 of the Copyright Act in much the same form articulated in *Bobbs-Merrill*.[10] A major limitation on the first sale doctrine under § 109 is that only the owner of a particular copy of a copyrighted work may raise the defense.[11]

---

[4] U.S. CONST. art. I, § 9, cl. 8.
[5] 17 U.S.C. § 106.
[6] *Id.* § 501(a).
[7] 17 U.S.C. § 106(3).
[8] H.R. REP. NO. 94-1476, at 62 (1976).
[9] 210 U.S. 339, 350 (1908).
[10] 17 U.S.C. § 109(a) ("[T]he owner of a particular copy or phonorecord lawfully made under this title, or any person authorized by such owner, is entitled, without the authority of the copyright owner, to sell or otherwise dispose of the possession of that copy or phonorecord.").
[11] Vernor v. Autodesk, Inc., 621 F.3d 1102, 1112 n.13 (9th Cir. 2010).

B. *Limit on the Exclusive Reproduction Right: The Essential Step Defense*

Copyright owners have the exclusive right to reproduce their copyrighted work.[12] The exclusive reproduction right grants copyright owners the exclusive right to make copies of their copyrighted work.[13] The essential step defense, like the first sale doctrine, limits an exclusive right of copyright owners. The essential step defense, as codified in § 117(a), is an exception to the reproduction right. It provides that the owner of a copy of a computer program can copy a copyrighted computer program if that copy is necessary to operate the computer.[14] The essential step defense arose in response to the common practice of computers making temporary cached copies of software during the ordinary running of that computer.[15] Without this defense, each computer user could potentially be liable for copyright infringement.

C. *Software Copyrightability*

Courts as well as Congress have struggled to determine the appropriate mode of protection for software. Courts have generally broadened the scope of software protected by copyright law, including operating systems[16] and nonliteral elements of software.[17] However, largely because of the intrinsically functional nature of software, courts have declined to apply copyright protection to other aspects of software, such as menu hierarchies.[18]

III. PRE-*VERNOR* DECISIONS

To assert a defense under either the first sale doctrine or the essential step defense, an alleged infringer must be an owner of the software.[19] Prior to the Ninth Circuit's decision in *Vernor*, there were two views on whether a software licensee is an owner for purposes of the first sale doctrine and the essential step defense. The first view, articulated by the Ninth Circuit, favors software copyright owners' rights to contract and limit the scope of end-user licenses. The second view, adopted by the Second Circuit, the Federal Circuit, and even in some Ninth Circuit decisions, sees the rights of software licensees as analogous to the rights of owners.

---

[12] *Id.* § 106(1).

[13] *Id.*; *see also* H.R. REP. NO. 94-1476, at 61 (indicating the exclusive reproduction right is intended to give the owner of a copyright "the right to produce a material object in which the work is duplicated . . . in a fixed form from which it can be 'perceived, reproduced, or otherwise communicated'").

[14] 17 U.S.C. § 117(a)(1) (indicating such copying is not infringement provided "that such a new copy or adaptation is created as an essential step in the utilization of the computer program in conjunction with a machine and that it is used in no other manner").

[15] *See* 2 MELVILLE B. NIMMER & DAVID NIMMER, NIMMER ON COPYRIGHT § 8.08 (2009).

[16] Apple Computer, Inc. v. Franklin Computer Corp., 714 F.2d 1240 (3d Cir. 1983).

[17] Computer Assocs. Int'l, Inc. v. Altai, Inc., 982 F.2d 693 (2d Cir. 1992).

[18] Lotus Dev. Corp. v. Borland Int'l, Inc., 49 F.3d 807 (1st Cir. 1995), *aff'd*, 516 U.S. 233 (1996).

[19] The first sale doctrine requires that a claimant be an "owner of a particular copy" of the copyrighted work. 17 U.S.C. § 109(a). Likewise, the essential step defense requires that an alleged infringer be the "owner of a copy" of copyrighted software. *Id.* § 117(a).

A. The Ninth Circuit: Software Licensees Do Not Have Owner Rights

The Ninth Circuit, generally seen as favorable to copyright owners, has considered software purchasers to be licensees rather than owners. In *United States v. Wise*, a criminal infringement case, the Ninth Circuit took one of the earliest looks at the relationship between the first sale doctrine and licenses.[20] The defendant in *Wise* operated a mail-order film business that sold copyrighted full length motion picture reels to film collectors throughout the country.[21] The issue was whether the defendant had the right under the first sale doctrine to re-sell the films that he obtained. None of the films that Wise sold were "subject to an outright sale" in their first transactions.[22] Instead, the transfers looked a lot more like licenses because the film studios licensed the films "for limited purposes and for limited periods of time," "reserved title to the films in the studios[,] and required [the films'] return at the expiration of the license period."[23] Interpreting the first sale doctrine, the court stated that the "statute requires a transfer of title before a 'first sale' can occur."[24] The court held that these film licenses were not first sales because "on their face and by their terms they were restricted licenses and not sales."[25]

However, the *Wise* court distinguished two licenses as sales—the *Funny Girl* and *Camelot* films. Wise sold a display license for *Funny Girl* to ABC that allowed ABC to retain, at its election and cost, a file-screening copy of the film.[26] In the absence of any evidence that ABC exercised its right to retain a copy, the court found that the government had not proven the absence of a first sale.[27] The *Camelot* license, which Wise granted to a collector named Vanessa Redgrave, stipulated that Redgrave pay Warner Brothers, the owner of the *Camelot* copyright, for the print and that the print was limited to home use.[28] Therefore, the court held that there was a first sale with regard to *Camelot*, as well, because Redgrave was given control of the copy of *Camelot* for an unlimited amount of time.[29]

The Ninth Circuit dealt with the licensee versus owner issue in the context of software sales in what the *Vernor* court deemed the *MAI* trio of cases.[30] The *MAI* trio consists of: *MAI Systems Corp. v. Peak Computer, Inc.*,[31] *Triad Systems Corp. v. Southeastern Express Co.*,[32] and *Wall Data Inc. v. Los Angeles County Sheriff's Department*.[33] In each of these cases, the Ninth Circuit discussed both the essential step defense and the first sale doctrine. While the cases involve different software licensing

---

[20] 550 F.2d 1180 (9th Cir. 1977).
[21] *Id.* at 1183–84.
[22] *Id.* at 1184.
[23] *Id.*
[24] *Id.* at 1187.
[25] *Id.* at 1190.
[26] *Id.* at 1191.
[27] *Id.* at 1191–92 ("[T]he government ha[d] failed in its burden of proving the absence of first sale . . . .").
[28] *Id.* at 1192.
[29] *Id.*
[30] Vernor v. Autodesk, Inc., 621 F.3d 1102, 1109 (9th Cir. 2010).
[31] 991 F.2d 511 (9th Cir. 1993).
[32] 64 F.3d 1330 (9th Cir. 1995).
[33] 447 F.3d 769 (9th Cir. 2006).

situations, the Ninth Circuit ultimately found that customers who use software under restrictive licenses are not owners for purposes of §§ 109 and 117.

The trio's namesake case, *MAI*, found no ownership where the alleged infringer utilized software licensed under a restrictive licensing agreement.[34] The defendant in *MAI*, Peak Computer, was a computer maintenance and repair firm that, in the course of servicing its clients' computers, made copies of MAI's copyrighted software into the memory of the computers they were servicing.[35] MAI licensed its software to its customers under a restrictive license that "d[id] not allow for the use or copying of MAI software by third parties such as Peak."[36] Thus, the court held that "any 'copying' done by Peak [wa]s 'beyond the scope' of the license" and therefore not covered by the essential step defense.[37] On the ownership versus licensee issue, the court stated that "[s]ince MAI licensed its software, the Peak customers do not qualify as 'owners' of the software and are not eligible for protection under § 117."[38] While *MAI* remains good law, it should be noted that Congress explicitly legislated around *MAI* when it revised § 117 to include a specific exception for computer maintenance.[39]

The second case of the *MAI* trio, *Triad*, illustrates the Ninth Circuit's distinction between a sale and a license.[40] *Triad* involved a company that initially sold auto maintenance software under a purchase regime, but then switched to a licensing regime.[41] Much like in *MAI*, the *Triad* defendants sought service from a third party not authorized by Triad, the copyright holder. The court held that under the purchase regime, the customers owned their software and therefore had the right under § 117 to "authorize the making of copies in the operation of their computers."[42]

However, customers under the licensing regime were subject to a strict license that stipulated that they "may not duplicate the software or allow it to be used by third parties."[43] Furthermore, if customers wished to sell their computer systems with Triad's software on it, the license required them to pay Triad a transfer fee.[44] The *Triad* court held that this license was like the license in *MAI* and that the majority of customers under the licensing agreements were licensees.[45] Because licensees could not authorize the

---

[34] *MAI*, 991 F.2d 511, 518 n.5.

[35] *Id.* at 517.

[36] *Id.*

[37] *Id.*

[38] *Id.* at 519 n.5.

[39] Section 117(c) of the copyright act creates an explicit exception to the exclusive reproduction right for purposes of computer maintenance. 17 U.S.C. § 117(c) (2006). The legislative history indicates that § 117(c) was passed in response to courts such as the *MAI* court that interpreted the running of software as a § 106 "reproduction." H.R. REP. NO. 105-551, pt. 1, at 27 (1998) ("This legislation has the narrow and specific intent of relieving independent service providers . . . from liability under the Copyright Act when, solely by virtue of activating the machine in which a computer program resides, they inadvertently cause an unauthorized copy of that program to be made.").

[40] *See* Triad Sys. Corp. v. Se. Express Co., 64 F.3d 1330 (9th Cir. 1995).

[41] *Id.* at 1333.

[42] *Id.*

[43] *Id.*

[44] *Id.*

[45] *Id.* at 1337 n.18 ("This arrangement is also appropriate because it appears that the majority of Triad computer owners are subject to license agreements and do not own their software outright . . . .").

making of copies that would be made in the course of repairs, they therefore could not use § 117 to authorize repairs.[46]

The final case in the *MAI* trio, *Wall Data*, involved a volume license sale where the defendant purchased a license to operate 3,663 copies of the plaintiff's software but installed 6,007 copies of the software by using disk-imaging software.[47] The defendants argued that the essential step defense covered their use of the software "because the hard drive imaging process was a necessary step of installation."[48] The court held, however, that the defendant was not an owner of the software, stipulating that "if the copyright owner makes it clear that she or he is granting only a license to the copy of software and imposes significant restrictions on the purchaser's ability to redistribute or transfer that copy, the purchaser is considered a licensee, not an owner, of the software."[49]

B. The Federal and Second Circuits: Software Licensees Have Owner Rights

The Federal and Second Circuits have taken conflicting views of the licensee versus ownership issue. The Federal Circuit, which does not normally deal with copyright issues, addressed whether software licensees were owners of software in *DSC Communications Corp. v. Pulse Communications, Inc.*[50] In *DSC*, the plaintiff manufactured telecommunications infrastructure equipment and copyrighted the software required to run the equipment.[51] The defendant manufactured hardware that served the same function as DSC's hardware but required the use of DSC's copyrighted software to properly function.[52] Regional bell operating companies (RBOCs), which had licensed DSC's software, installed the software on equipment that the defendant manufactured. The plaintiffs objected, claiming such use was a violation of the software licensing agreement.[53]

The Federal Circuit criticized the Ninth Circuit's decision in *MAI*, indicating it established an "overly simplistic" rule.[54] It claimed that the Ninth Circuit's rule "fail[ed] to recognize the distinction between ownership of a copyright, which can be licensed, and ownership of copies of the copyrighted software."[55] As a result, the Federal Circuit declined to "adopt the Ninth Circuit's characterization of all licensees as non-owners," adopting instead a test that looks at the incidents of ownership.[56] However, despite its criticism of the *MAI* rule, the *DSC* court ultimately held that the RBOCs were not owners

---

[46] *Id.* at 1333 (stating that licensees of the software could not repair their software due to a restrictive license).

[47] Wall Data Inc. v. L.A. Cnty. Sheriff's Dep't, 447 F.3d 769, 773 (9th Cir. 2006).

[48] *Id.* at 776.

[49] *Id.* at 785.

[50] 170 F.3d 1354 (Fed. Cir. 1999).

[51] *Id.* at 1358.

[52] *Id.*

[53] *Id.* at 1360.

[54] *Id.* at 1362.

[55] *Id.* at 1360 (citing 2 MELVILLE B. NIMMER & DAVID NIMMER, NIMMER ON COPYRIGHT § 8.08[B][1], at 8-119 to 1-121 (3d ed. 1997)).

[56] *Id.* Although it declined to follow *MAI*, the *DSC* court acknowledged the similarity in finding a mere license where the software agreement "imposed more severe restrictions on Peak's rights with respect to the software than would be imposed on a party who owned copies of software subject only to the rights of the copyright holder under the Copyright Act." *Id.*

of the software. Therefore, they were not entitled to the § 117 defense because the license stipulated that "[a]ll rights, title, and interest in the Software are and shall remain with seller, subject ... to a license to Buyer to use the Software solely in conjunction with" DSC's equipment.[57]

The Second Circuit is often at odds with the Ninth Circuit on copyright issues.[58] Taking the Federal Circuit's view of *MAI* as a cue, the Second Circuit's decision in *Krause v. Titleserv, Inc.* further fleshed out the distinction between licenses and sales for the purposes of § 117.[59] In *Krause*, the plaintiff, software developer Krause, developed and copyrighted software under a consulting arrangement for defendant Titleserv.[60] Before terminating the consulting relationship with Titleserv, Krause entered into an oral agreement with the CEO of Titleserv that the software Krause developed would remain his.[61] Instead of transferring title to the software, Krause granted Titleserv a license to use, but not modify, the software.[62]

Discussing the appropriate standard for determining ownership for the purposes of § 117, the *Krause* court considered two possible standards: (1) a standard like that articulated in *MAI* under which § 117 benefits are restricted to title owners and (2) the standard articulated in *DSC*, which "attache[s] less importance to formal title, looking rather at the various incidents of ownership."[63] The *Krause* court ultimately decided to adopt the *DSC* standard for two reasons. First, whether a party possesses formal title is generally a matter of state law, and "[i]f § 117(a) required formal title, two software users, engaged in substantively identical transactions might find that one is liable for copyright infringement while the other is protected" simply because they live in different states and are subject to different state laws.[64] Second, the court found it "anomalous" for a user whose ownership of a copy was so complete that he may lawfully use it and keep it forever to be unable to fix or make an archival copy of the software.[65] Applying this standard, the court found that Titleserv was an owner of the copies of the software that Krause authorized it to use, stating multiple factors that suggest ownership rather than restrictive license.[66]

---

[57] *Id.* at 1361 (internal quotation mark omitted).
[58] For example, the Second Circuit has a different analysis of substantial similarity than the Ninth Circuit. *Compare* Castle Rock Entm't, Inc. v. Carol Publ'g Grp., Inc., 150 F.3d 132, 138 (2d Cir. 1998) (stating there is a "qualitative" and "quantitative" view, requiring at least a *de minimis* amount of copying), *with* Cavalier v. Random House, Inc., 297 F.3d 815, 825 (9th Cir. 2002) (using a much broader "total concept and feel" test).
[59] *See* Krause v. Titleserv, Inc., 402 F.3d 119 (2d Cir. 2005).
[60] *Id.* at 120.
[61] *Id.* at 124.
[62] *Id.* at 121.
[63] *Id.* at 123.
[64] *Id.*
[65] *Id.*
[66] *Id.* at 124 ("Titleserv paid Krause substantial consideration to develop the programs for its sole benefit. Krause customized the software to serve Titleserv's operations. The copies were stored on a server owned by Titleserv. Krause never reserved the right to repossess the copies used by Titleserv and agreed that Titleserv had the right to continue to possess and use the programs forever, regardless whether its relationship with Krause terminated. Titleserv was similarly free to discard or destroy the copies any time it wished.").

IV. *VERNOR V. AUTODESK*

A. The Facts

In *Vernor*, the plaintiff used eBay to sell copies of the defendant Autodesk's copyrighted software program AutoCAD in 2005 and 2007.[67] However, the versions of AutoCAD that Vernor sold were not packaged and approved by Autodesk; rather, he sold what the district court deemed "AutoCAD packages."[68] These AutoCAD packages consisted of an "Autodesk-commissioned box" with a "jewel case" and a compact disc copy of AutoCAD inside it, sealed with a sticker claiming the software was "subject to the license agreement that appears during the installation process or is included in the package."[69] The packages also included a copy of the Autodesk Software License Agreement (SLA) and "possibly other documentation."[70] Vernor obtained the 2007 packages from an architecture firm that held a sale of office equipment. Although the architecture firm had broken the seal on the jewel case in each AutoCAD package, the parties agreed that the packages themselves were authentic.[71]

The SLA for AutoCAD places significant restrictions on the use and transfer of users of AutoCAD software. The SLA (1) states that Autodesk retains title to all copies, (2) grants the customer a nonexclusive and nontransferable license to use the software, (3) prohibits customers from renting, leasing, or transferring the software without Autodesk's prior consent, (4) imposes "significant use restrictions" that, among other things, prohibit the licensee from disassembling the software, removing any notices, and defeating the copy protection, (5) provides for a license termination for unauthorized copying or use, and (6) provides that if the licensee chooses to upgrade the software, the licensee must destroy any previous copies of the software.[72]

Autodesk invoked the "take-down" provisions of the Digital Millennium Copyright Act (DMCA) upon discovering Vernor's eBay operation in both 2005 and 2007.[73] Both takedowns resulted in delayed sales for Vernor, and in the 2007 takedown, eBay barred Vernor from selling anything on its site for a month.[74] Believing that the first sale doctrine applied to his software sales and that he therefore did not violate § 106, Vernor filed suit for a declaratory judgment, intending to bar further DMCA takedown actions against his operation. Autodesk, on the other hand, claimed that it never transferred title of the AutoCAD software packages to the architecture firm.[75] Rather, Autodesk claimed that the architecture firm breached its license to operate AutoCAD when it upgraded to a newer version of the software and sold the copies to Vernor.[76] Whether Vernor was

---

[67] Vernor v. Autodesk, Inc., 93 U.S.P.Q.2d (BNA) 1336, 1337 (W.D. Wash. 2009), *vacated*, 621 F.3d 1102 (9th Cir. 2010).
[68] *Id.*
[69] *Id.* (internal quotation mark omitted).
[70] *Id.*
[71] *Id.*
[72] Vernor v. Autodesk, Inc., 621 F.3d 1102, 1104 (9th Cir. 2010).
[73] *Id.* at 1105 & n.3 (citing 17 U.S.C. § 512(c)(1)(C) (2006)).
[74] *Id.*
[75] *Id.*
[76] *Id.*

entitled to declaratory judgment hinged on whether the architecture firm purchased AutoCAD software in sales or licenses.[77]

B. *The District Court: There Was a Sale, Not Simply a License*

The district court held that first sale doctrine applied to software, observing two different lines of binding precedent: *Wise* and the *MAI* trio.[78] The court interpreted *Wise* to hold that a transfer of copyrighted works under restrictive licenses that allow for the physical transfer of media, but do not specify a date to return the media, could be seen as a sale.[79] The district court held that Autodesk granted a license to the architecture firm similar to the Redgrave license in *Wise* because the AutoCAD license and the Redgrave license were both subject to terms that vested "title in the copy to the copyright holder, but made no provision for the copyright holder to regain possession of the copy."[80] Because Autodesk transferred the copies of AutoCAD to the architectural firm with no expectation that it would regain control of the copies, the district court found that under *Wise*, the AutoCAD license would transfer ownership of the software copy despite the restrictions present in the license.[81]

The district court then analyzed the facts under the rule adopted by the *MAI* trio. It admitted that under the *MAI* cases, Autodesk would prevail because the AutoCAD copies were transferred pursuant to a restrictive license.[82] Despite expert testimony on Autodesk's behalf by David Nimmer, author of the leading copyright treatise[83] suggesting otherwise, the court held that *Wise* and *MAI* articulated conflicting rules.[84] It then chose to apply *Wise*, following the admittedly weak rule that it "must follow the oldest precedent among conflicting opinions from three-judge Ninth Circuit panels."[85]

C. *The Ninth Circuit: There Was Simply a License, Not a Sale*

The Ninth Circuit took a significantly different view of *Wise* and the *MAI* trio than the district court. Instead of determining that the cases were irreconcilable, as the district court did, the Ninth Circuit reviewed its precedent regarding the ownership versus licensee issue and synthesized a "three consideration" test to determine whether a software user is a licensee rather than an owner: "First, we consider whether the copyright owner specifies that a user is granted a license. Second, we consider whether the copyright owner significantly restricts the user's ability to transfer the software. Finally, we consider whether the copyright owner imposes notable use restrictions."[86]

---

[77] *Id.* at 1107.
[78] Vernor v. Autodesk, Inc., 93 U.S.P.Q.2d (BNA) 1336, 1341–46 (W.D. Wash. 2009), *vacated*, 621 F.3d 1102 (9th Cir. 2010).
[79] *Id.* at 1342. The district court's decision was based primarily on the *Wise* court's discussion of the license attached to the Redgrave sale of *Camelot.*
[80] *Id.*
[81] *Id.* at 1343–44.
[82] *Id.* at 1344–45.
[83] NIMMER & NIMMER, *supra* note 15.
[84] *Vernor*, 93 U.S.P.Q.2d (BNA) at 1346 ("With two sets of conflicting precedent before the court, the question becomes which to follow.").
[85] *Id.* (citing United States v. Rodriguez-Lara, 421 F.3d 932, 943 (9th Cir. 2005)).
[86] Vernor v. Autodesk, Inc., 621 F.3d 1102, 1110–11 (9th Cir. 2010).

The Ninth Circuit explicitly stated that one of its goals in synthesizing the new three-consideration test was to "reconcile[] the *MAI* trio and *Wise*, even though the *MAI* trio did not cite *Wise*."[87] Under its newly formulated rule, the Ninth Circuit found first that "Autodesk retained title to the software," as stipulated in the SLA.[88] With regard to the second consideration, it found that Autodesk "imposed significant transfer restrictions" as "the software could not be transferred or leased without Autodesk's written consent."[89] Finally, with regard to the third consideration, the SLA imposed many usage restrictions.[90] Because Autodesk sold AutoCAD pursuant to the SLA and the architecture firm was bound by the SLA, the court held that the firm was a licensee rather than an "owner of a particular copy" of AutoCAD.[91]

D. The Ninth Circuit's Vernor Test Is Contrary to the Second Circuit's Krause Test

The three-factor test articulated by the Ninth Circuit in *Vernor* grants much more power to software copyright holders and makes it more likely that a modern software purchase will be a license rather than a first sale. However, in dismissing plaintiff Vernor's counterarguments, the Ninth Circuit claimed that it was not creating a circuit split with the Federal Circuit's decision in *DSC* or the Second Circuit's decision in *Krause* when it articulated its new rule.[92] The Ninth Circuit's characterization of the allegedly contrary authority in the other circuits is at least partially true. With its recasting of the rule articulated by the *MAI* trio, the Ninth Circuit effectively brought *DSC* into the fold of its framework, as *DSC* hinged on whether the software copyright holder retained title to the work.[93]

While it was appropriate for the Ninth Circuit to distinguish *DSC* given the facts of the case and relevant case law, the Ninth Circuit dismissed the Second Circuit's decision in *Krause* too quickly. The Ninth Circuit gave little weight to the restrictive license in *Krause* because the parties did not have a written license agreement, and Titleserv paid Krause "significant consideration" to develop software for its sole benefit.[94] It then, without much analysis, concluded that "the facts and the analysis in *Krause* are not contrary to our determination that [the architecture firm] is a licensee rather than an owner."[95] In dismissing *Krause*, the Ninth Circuit ignored the restrictive nature of the license at issue in *Krause*.

In fact, if the Ninth Circuit applied its test to the facts in *Krause*, it would have reached a contrary result. The first *Vernor* consideration is "whether the copyright owner specifies that the user is granted a license."[96] Krause explicitly made an oral contract

---

[87] *Id.* at 1111.

[88] *Id.*

[89] *Id.*

[90] *Id.* at 1111–12 ("The SLA also imposed use restrictions against the use of the software outside the Western Hemisphere and against modifying, translating, or reverse-engineering the software, removing any proprietary marks from the software or documentation, or defeating any copy protection device.").

[91] *Id.* at 1112.

[92] *Id.* at 1114.

[93] DSC Commc'ns Corp. v. Pulse Commc'ns, Inc., 170 F.3d 1354, 1360 (Fed. Cir. 1999).

[94] *Vernor*, 621 F.3d at 1114.

[95] *Id.*

[96] *Id.* at 1110.

with the CEO of Titleserv that the company would merely have a license to his copyrighted software, not ownership.[97] This is analogous to the AutoCAD license in *Vernor*, which explicitly stipulates that Autodesk retains all title to AutoCAD software.[98] The second *Vernor* consideration is "whether the copyright owner significantly restricts the user's ability to transfer the software."[99] While Krause may not have explicitly forbade Titleserv from selling the software to another individual, this consideration is moot because the software Krause wrote was only applicable to Titleserv's internal company operations and not readily adaptable to another business.[100]

The third *Vernor* consideration is whether the agreement imposes notable use restrictions.[101] This consideration would have weighed heavily in Krause's favor, as Krause was very explicit in his terms that his software was not to be modified or decompiled; he went to great lengths to remove all source code from the Titleserv offices.[102] Krause's intentions were analogous to the significant use restrictions in the AutoCAD License, which restrict the user from decompiling or otherwise modifying the software.[103] Therefore, under the *Vernor* test, Krause would have easily meet a burden of proving that Titleserv was not an owner of the software who was entitled to the § 117(a) essential step defense.

While the Second Circuit in *Krause* addressed the ownership issue for the purposes of the § 117(a) essential step defense, the Ninth Circuit in *Vernor* considered the ownership issue for the purposes of the § 109 first sale doctrine. Although courts have held that the two meanings of ownership are the same, the Ninth Circuit's *Vernor* test for ownership has not yet been applied to a fact pattern concerning the essential step defense. While the Ninth Circuit is not obligated to follow the Second Circuit's different reading of the ownership–licensee dichotomy, the split between the two circuits shows that the distinction between licensees and owners is far from settled on the national scale.

V. POLICY ARGUMENTS BEHIND *VERNOR*

A. *Finding First Sales in Software Purchases*

In formulating its rule in *Vernor*, the Ninth Circuit considered, but did not afford any weight to, a number of amici briefs that weighed on each side of the issue. Vernor's brief and those of the amici who sided with Vernor, eBay and the American Library Association (ALA), emphasized traditional property rights that favor alienability and the constitutional purpose behind copyright that favors dissemination of copyrighted works. Vernor emphasized the "law's aversion to restraints on alienation of personal property."[104] In light of this aversion, Vernor argued that the Ninth Circuit's decision "ignores the economic realities of the relevant transactions, in which the copyright owner permanently released software copies into the stream of commerce without expectation of

---

[97] Krause v. Titleserv, Inc., 402 F.3d 119, 124 (2d Cir. 2005).
[98] *Vernor*, 621 F.3d at 1104.
[99] *Id.* at 1111.
[100] *Krause*, 402 F.3d at 129.
[101] *Vernor*, 621 F.3d at 1111.
[102] *Krause*, 402 F.3d at 121.
[103] *See Vernor*, 621 F.3d at 1111.
[104] *Id.* at 1115.

return in exchange for upfront payment of the full software price."[105] Additionally, Vernor argued the decision would place an unworkable standard for those who wish to participate in secondary markets, as it would "force everyone purchasing copyrighted property to trace the chain of title to ensure that a first sale occurred."[106] In the same vein, eBay argued that

> a broad view of the first sale doctrine is necessary to facilitate the creation of secondary markets for copyrighted works, which contributes to the public good by (1) giving consumers additional opportunities to purchase and sell copyrighted works, often at below-retail prices; (2) allowing consumers to obtain copies of works after a copyright owner has ceased distribution; and (3) allowing the proliferation of businesses.[107]

Finally, the ALA argued that the court's decision would "(1) undermine[] 17 U.S.C. § 109(b)(2), which permits non-profit libraries to lend software for non-commercial purposes, and (2) would hamper efforts by non-profits to collect and preserve out-of-print software."[108] Additionally, "[t]he ALA fear[ed] that the software industry's licensing practices could be adopted by other copyright owners, including book publishers, record labels, and movie studios."[109]

Those who argue in favor of finding ownership in software licenses, such as Vernor and eBay, find support in the scholarly community. Scholars, looking at the district court's decision in *Vernor* and the Second Circuit's decision in *Krause*, are more willing to construe a license as a sale.[110] Some commentators have even advocated for a legislative modification of the copyright regime to extend the first sale doctrine to most transfers that are normally seen as licenses.[111]

B. Finding Licenses in Software Purchases

A number of parties, including Autodesk, the Software and Information Industry Association, and the Motion Picture Association of America (MPAA), filed briefs with policy arguments in support of the Ninth Circuit's result in *Vernor*. Autodesk argued that such restrictive licensing agreements "allow[] for tiered pricing for different software markets, such as reduced pricing for students or educational institutions," thus increasing access for users of its software.[112] Additionally, Autodesk argued that requiring all users of the software to license the software and not resell the software "lowers prices for all

---

[105] *Id.*
[106] *Id.*
[107] *Id.*
[108] *Id.*
[109] *Id.*
[110] *See, e.g.,* Ted Claypoole, *How a License Becomes a Sale: Software Applications of the First Sale Doctrine,* 2008 EMERGING ISSUES 2823 (analyzing how first sale doctrine is turning licensees into purchasers).
[111] *See, e.g.,* Joshua W. Newman, Note, *Selling the Right to License: Examination of the First Sale Doctrine Through the Lens of* UMG Recordings & Quanta Computer, 35 J. CORP. L. 849 (2010) (arguing that Congress should embrace the recent decisions that extend the first sale doctrine and legislatively revise those principles to protect consumer privileges).
[112] *Vernor,* 621 F.3d at 1114.

consumers by spreading costs among a large number of purchasers."[113]   Finally, Autodesk maintained that the decision would "reduce[] the incidence of piracy by allowing copyright owners to bring infringement actions against unauthorized resellers."[114]   The MPAA had a more practical policy reason to disfavor granting licensees ownership status, stating "there is often no practically feasible way for a consumer to return a copy [of software] to the copyright owner."[115]

Scholars who advocate for the licensing view over ownership focus on the changing nature of intellectual property and technology on and how the older precedent of § 109 does not apply in a modern context. Despite several attempts to bring it into compliance with modern technology, commentators argue that the copyright statute has not captured the proper level of protection for non-physical copyrighted works.[116] Ultimately, affirmative defenses and the current copyright regime make sense when consumers obtain *physical* manifestations of the intellectual property; unfortunately for copyright holders and Congress, the regime falls short in determining how to deal with non-physical media.[117]

VI. RECONCILING *VERNOR* AND *KRAUSE*: SEPARATING THE FIRST SALE DOCTRINE FROM THE ESSENTIAL STEP DEFENSE

There are now two ways to address the ownership issue for §§ 109 and 117(a): the Ninth Circuit's three consideration test presented in *Vernor* and the Second Circuit's incidences of ownership test presented in *Krause*. The Second Circuit's incidence of ownership test grants users broader rights to use and adapt software, which is in line with the Copyright Clause's goal of dissemination of copyrighted work. The Ninth Circuit's test, however, falls on the other side of the copyright policy debate, granting more protection to copyright owners to foster the creation of their works.

One way to reconcile the Second and Ninth Circuits' tests is to limit each to the affirmative defense that raised it. Each test serves different purposes and is an exception to a different exclusive right of the copyright holder. The essential step defense, at issue in *Krause*, is a modern element of the copyright regime that has been adapted to reflect the needs of software consumers and copyright holders. The first sale doctrine, on the other hand, is largely unchanged from the standard originally articulated by the Supreme

---

[113] *Id.* at 1114–15.
[114] *Id.* at 1115.
[115] *Id.*
[116] *See, e.g.*, Robert H. Rotstein et al., *The First Sale Doctrine in the Digital Age*, 22 INTELL. PROP. & TECH. L.J. 23 (2010) (arguing that the nature of intangible property requires a re-assessment of how intellectual property transactions and usage should be viewed); Diane L. Zimmerman, *Living Without Copyright in a Digital World*, 70 ALB. L. REV. 1375 (2007) (arguing that the current copyright legal regime is ill-equipped to deal with non-physical media, and that new copyright regimes should be imposed, most likely in the digital space, to effectively regulate non-physical intellectual property).
[117] Nika Aldrich, Note, *An Exploration of Rights Management Technologies Used in the Music Industry*, 2007 B.C. INTELL. PROP. & TECH. F. 051001 *available at* http://bciptf.org/wp-content/uploads/2011/07/25-AN-EXPLORATION-OF-RIGHTS-MANAGEMENT-TECHNOLOGIES-USED-IN-THE-MUSIC-INDUSTRY.pdf (tracking the development of digital rights management in the music industry, and the inadequacy of the current copyright regime to properly cover).

251

Court in *Bobbs-Merrill* in 1908, a time when intellectual property was still inextricably tied to physical media.

A. The Essential Step Defense Warrants Reading Software Sales as Purchases

The essential step defense was created to protect the interests of both software buyers and copyright holders. The Second Circuit came to its decision in *Krause* because it found that limiting the essential step defense to those who were owners of the software would lead to an absurd result, a sentiment shared by Congress when it amended § 109 in the wake of *MAI*. One need not look further than the facts of *MAI*, where copyright law barred a computer owner from hiring an individual of his choice to service his own computer.[118]   If the court had refused to read ownership into *Krause*, an even more absurd result would surface: a company that commissioned someone to write software for it, yet failed to properly contract to retain title to the software, would be unable to repair or adapt its systems to a changing world.

Such a reading of the owner requirement places too much power in the hands of software copyright owners. Instead of just controlling the reproduction of copyrighted software, the exclusive reproductive right would also preclude software customers from allowing any other entity but the copyright holder from servicing the software. Such power does not serve the creation or dissemination incentives of the copyright regime. Therefore, interpreting the owner requirement in the essential step defense makes sense in the context the essential step defense serves.

B. The First Sale Doctrine Warrants Reading Software Transfers as Licenses

The first sale doctrine, on the other hand, makes less sense in the context of medium-less intellectual property, such as digital music files, eBooks, and software purchased on the Internet. Often, such purchases are linked to a user who is a real person, rather than a physical manifestation of the copyrighted work (e.g., a book or a CD). The policy reasons behind the first sale doctrine established in *Bobbs-Merrill* are rooted in a copyright regime that assumes the existence of physical media and the higher cost to distribute and disseminate physical media.

One policy rationale behind the first sale doctrine is based on the difference between ownership of a copyrighted work and ownership of a particular copy of that work.[119]   While this distinction is as relevant now as it was when copyrighted works were disseminated at bookstores on books and records, the idea of the first sale doctrine as a proper limit to the exclusive distribution right makes less sense with media-less sales of intellectual property. When a consumer had to buy a physical copy of a copyrighted work to access the work, there was a tangible property right in the copy of the book purchased. This model of ownership of a copy of a copyrighted work falls short in today's world of digital distribution, for there oftentimes are no physical, tangible objects

---

[118] MAI Sys. Corp. v. Peak Computer, Inc., 991 F.2d 511, 517 (9th Cir. 1993).

[119] *See, e.g.*, United States v. Moore, 604 F.2d 1228, 1232 (9th Cir. 1979) ("[W]here a copyright owner parts with title to a particular copy of his copyrighted work, he divests himself of his exclusive right to vend that particular copy."); *see also* Bobbs-Merrill Co. v. Straus, 210 U.S. 339, 350 (1908) ("The purchaser of a book, once sold by authority of the owner of the copyright, may sell it again, although he could not publish a new edition of it.").

that a consumer owns. At some extremes, such as online gaming or video streaming subscriptions, such purchases are better seen as purchases of the ability to access a specific service rather than the purchase of a copy of a particular piece of intellectual property.[120] The traditional property rule against limiting alienability makes little sense if the property at issue is a monthly subscription to an online gaming service. With the increasing digital distribution of all forms of copyrighted work, the distinction of ownership between the copyrighted work and that of the copy of the work is breaking down. While it is clear that the copyright owner still owns the fruits of his creative labor, it less clear that the copyright consumer owns the MP3 file on her iPod, the eBook on her Kindle, or the app on her iPhone in the same way that a purchaser of a physical book *owns* the paper that the book is printed on.

Another policy rationale behind the first sale doctrine is that it exists to further the public dissemination of copyrighted works by allowing for secondary markets.[121] In much of the twentieth century, there were extremely high barriers to the dissemination of creative works due to the fact that a work had to be disseminated on physical media. As Internet-based services such as iTunes and YouTube show, it is much easier now for individuals to disseminate their creative works.[122] To protect their intellectual property in today's age of free information sharing on the Internet, software companies are shifting to medium-less sales and focusing more on server–client based systems.[123] Google built its entire business without ever distributing one box of software, Blizzard and Microsoft embraced the social gaming paradigm shift and built their models on selling clients to their game systems, and Apple, having revolutionized the mobile space by creating the first viable application store for mobile phones, is moving to create an entirely virtual market for computer applications.[124]

VII.   CONCLUSION

The copyright regime is best understood as balancing two competing incentives of consumers and producers. First, it grants authors exclusive rights to their works to

---

[120] *See, e.g., World of Warcraft Terms of Use*, BLIZZARD ENT., http://us.blizzard.com/en-us/company/legal/wow_tou.html (last updated Dec. 9, 2010) ("The Game includes two components: (a) the software program along with any accompanying materials or documentation (collectively, the 'Game Client'), and (b) Blizzard's proprietary World of Warcraft online service (the 'Service').").

[121] *See, e.g.,* R. Anthony Reese, *The First Sale Doctrine in the Era of Digital Networks*, 44 B.C. L. REV. 577, 586 (2003) ("The first sale doctrine also provides many consumers the chance to purchase a copy of the work at a price lower than that charged by the copyright owner or by the initial retailer . . . by allowing the development of secondary markets for the sale of copies."); Niva Elkin-Koren, *Cyberlaw and Social Change: A Democratic Approach to Copyright Law in Cyberspace*, 14 CARDOZO ARTS & ENT. L.J. 215, 277 (1996) ("The first sale doctrine restricts the power of distributors to control secondary markets for their works.").

[122] *See, e.g.,* Ryan Nakashima, *YouTube Offers Venue for Indie Filmmakers*, ASSOCIATED PRESS, June 19, 2008, *available at* http://www.msnbc.msn.com/id/25268434/ns/technology_and_science-internet/.

[123] *See, e.g.,* Andrew Webster, *The Future of Gaming: Up the Beanstalk and into the Cloud*, ARS TECHNICA (Apr. 4, 2010, 11:30 PM), http://arstechnica.com/business/future-of-cloud/2010/04/cloud-gaming.ars.

[124] *See, e.g.,* Earnest Cavalli, *Blizzard Adds Digital Distribution to Online Store*, WIRED (May 6, 2008, 12:06 PM), http://www.wired.com/gamelife/2008/05/blizzard-adds-d/; Mike Snider, *Social Media, Mobile Devices Help Video Games Grow*, USA TODAY (Feb. 28, 2011, 8:33 PM), http://www.usatoday.com/tech/news/2011-03-01-videogames01_CV_N.htm.

incentivize the creation of artistic works. Second, the copyright regime limits the rights of copyright holders so that copyrighted works can be widely disseminated. The first sale doctrine and essential step defense are exceptions to the exclusive rights of copyright holders that serve to strike the proper balance between the competing incentives of copyright holders and consumers. While both exceptions enable consumers to perform acts that are normally reserved to copyright authors, both the essential step and first sale doctrine require that any individual invoking the defense be an owner of the particular copy at issue; the implication being that those using copyrighted works under restrictive licenses cannot enjoy the defenses in the same way that an owner can.

As technology has progressed and the nature of copyrighted material has shifted from physical media to software, courts have struggled to strike the proper balance between incentivizing authors to create works and allowing the widespread dissemination of those works. At the same time, software authors have increasingly attempted to protect their creations by using licenses to contract around the essential step defense and first sale doctrine. As a result, different circuit courts have interpreted the ownership versus licensee debate differently, resulting in differing standards. One way to reconcile the difference in conflicting standards in the circuits is to restrict each standard to the defense in which the standard was articulated; the Ninth Circuit's standard was created in a first sale case, while the Second Circuit's standard was created in an essential step case. Such a solution would not only reconcile the split between the circuits, but would also recognize that the essential step defense and first sale doctrine address different exclusive rights, each of which requires a different balance between authors and consumers.

Copyright 2012 by Northwestern University School of Law
Northwestern Journal of Technology and Intellectual Property

Volume 10, Number 3 (January 2012)

The Continuing Viability of the Hot News Misappropriation Doctrine in the Age of Internet News Aggregation

By John C. McDonnell[*]

I. INTRODUCTION

On March 18, 2010, the United States District Court for the Southern District of New York released an opinion in *Barclays Capital Inc. v. Theflyonthewall.com* (*Barclays I*)[1] that many journalists, newspaper owners, and other content producers likely found reassuring. The opinion held that the hot news misappropriation doctrine prohibits a financial news aggregation website from sending subscribers stock recommendations that were researched and developed by analysts from various other financial firms.[2] The court found that the website, Theflyonthewall.com, was liable under the hot news misappropriation doctrine for disseminating time-sensitive information[3] gathered by the firms in direct competition with the website.[4] While the firms gathered the information at a cost,[5] the website was free-riding on those efforts,[6] potentially reducing the incentive to produce the information. The court found this free-riding substantially threatened the existence or quality of the gathered information.[7]

There are many similarities between the facts of this case and the situations many content producers face with news aggregators. This resemblance suggests that the hot news misappropriation doctrine may be a viable legal tool to protect these content producers from news aggregators which rely on them for content, yet may be responsible for a decline in the content producers' revenues.

The hot news misappropriation doctrine states that while the facts and ideas produced by a content producer may not be copyrightable, the content producer invested time and resources in obtaining this content and should retain some right to derive revenue from that content until its commercial value has passed.[8] For a competitor to take that content and resell it, without incurring the costs associated with gathering it, unfairly injures the content producer.[9] While created as part of the federal common law, the hot news misappropriation doctrine is currently only recognized in five states as part

---

[*] J.D. Candidate 2012, Northwestern University School of Law.
[1] 700 F. Supp. 2d 310 (S.D.N.Y. 2010), *rev'd*, 650 F.3d 876 (2d Cir. 2011).
[2] *Id.* at 313.
[3] *Id.* at 336.
[4] *Id.* at 339–41.
[5] *Id.* at 334.
[6] *Id.* at 335–40.
[7] *Id.* at 341–45.
[8] *See* Int'l News Serv. v. Associated Press, 248 U.S. 215, 245 (1918).
[9] *See id.*

of state unfair competition law.[10] The rise over the past decade of news aggregator websites, such as Google News and the Huffington Post, and the concurrent downfall of traditional news media makes the question of the applicability of this doctrine to the current news environment a important and necessary inquiry.

On June 20, 2011, the United States Court of Appeals for the Second Circuit handed down an opinion in *Barclays Capital Inc. v. Theflyonthewall.com, Inc.* (*Barclays II*).[11] The court held that federal copyright law preempted the financial firms' hot news misappropriation claim under the facts at issue,[12] but did not reject the hot news misappropriation doctrine in general.[13] Although the court clarified the doctrine[14] and in some ways limited it,[15] the remaining hot news misappropriation doctrine may still be sufficient to protect content producers.

This Comment explores why the hot news misappropriation doctrine is the most effective tool currently available to protect the journalism industry and why it is superior to other proposals. However, this Comment does not take a position as to whether pursuing action under the doctrine is in the best interest of content producers. In some circumstances, the public's increased familiarity with the producer, as acquired through aggregation, may be more valuable to the producer than any resulting decrease in revenue. This Comment simply discusses whether content producers can successfully sue Internet aggregators under the hot news misappropriation doctrine for aggregating the producer's content to its detriment.

Part II of this Comment discusses the district court's opinion in *Barclays I*. Part III delves into the history of the hot news misappropriation doctrine and its transformation into its modern form. Part IV discusses the Second Circuit Court of Appeal's opinion in *Barclays II* and how it affects the hot news misappropriation doctrine. Part V focuses on the current relationship between the journalism industry and news aggregators. Part VI explains why copyright law alone is insufficient to protect the journalism industry. Part VII applies the hot news misappropriation element test to news aggregators. Part VIII explains why other proposals to save the journalism industry are inadequate. Finally, Part IX explains why the hot news misappropriation doctrine, as it is currently recognized, is sufficient to protect journalism.

II. *BARCLAYS CAPITAL INC. V. THEFLYONTHEWALL.COM*

Barclays I is predicated on a fact pattern where a number of financial services firms expended considerable resources in developing and marketing research on publicly traded stocks for their most significant clients and making recommendations on whether to buy or sell those stocks.[16] The firms' reputations for reliable and valuable stock

---

[10] KIMBERLY ISBELL, CITIZEN MEDIA LAW PROJECT, THE RISE OF THE NEWS AGGREGATOR: LEGAL IMPLICATIONS AND BEST PRACTICES 16 (2010), *available at* http://papers.ssrn.com/sol3/papers.cfm?abstract_id=1670339.
[11] 650 F.3d 876 (2d Cir. 2011).
[12] *Id.* at 896–903.
[13] *Id.* at 890.
[14] *See id* at 898–901.
[15] *See id.*
[16] 700 F. Supp. 2d 310, 315 (S.D.N.Y. 2010), *rev'd*, 650 F.3d 876 (2d Cir. 2011).

recommendations was the basis for attracting and retaining their clients.[17]   Most recommendations were issued each day between midnight and 7:00 a.m. and may have affected the market price of a stock significantly.[18]   Such movement usually happened within hours of the market opening, so timely access to the recommendations was a valuable benefit to each firm's clients.[19]

Theflyonthewall.com (Fly) collects financial news and rumors and publishes them to its clients via a subscription newsfeed.[20]   A chief component of its business is its online newsfeed, which is updated continuously between 5:00 a.m. and 7:00 p.m. each day and presents a constant stream of financial headlines, none of which are independently researched.[21]   It was on this newsfeed that Fly posted the recommendations of the various financial firms.[22] Generally, the posts included the name of the firm making the recommendation.[23]   Frequently, Fly obtained its information directly from employees of the financial firms, who did not have authorization to disseminate this information.[24]   Other times, Fly obtained the information legitimately from firms or through various independent sources.[25]   Fly's subscribers consist of individual investors, institutional investors, and brokers.[26]   The client bases of the financial firms are similar.[27]

The firms sued Fly for hot news misappropriation in New York federal court.[28]   In deciding the case, the district court looked to the previously established elements of a hot news misappropriation claim. It described them as:

> (i) a plaintiff generates or gathers information at a cost; (ii) the information is time-sensitive; (iii) a defendant's use of the information constitutes free riding on the plaintiff's efforts; (iv) the defendant is in direct competition with a product or service offered by the plaintiffs; and (v) the ability of other parties to free-ride on the efforts of the plaintiff or others would so reduce the incentive to produce the product or service that its existence or quality would be substantially threatened.[29]

The court had no trouble finding that generating the stock recommendations involves substantial cost and that the information was time-sensitive.[30]   It also found that the core business of Fly involved free-riding on the sustained, costly efforts of the firms and that, since it made no investment of its own in equity research, it could sell the

---

[17] Id.
[18] Id. at 316.
[19] Id.
[20] Id. at 322.
[21] Id. at 323.
[22] Id.
[23] Id.
[24] Id. at 325.
[25] Id. at 326.
[26] Id. at 325.
[27] Id. at 339–40.
[28] Id. at 313. The firms also sued for damages, fees, and an injunction related to a few instances of copyright infringement. Id. at 328.
[29] Id. at 334–35 (quoting Nat'l Basketball Ass'n v. Motorola, Inc., 105 F.3d 841, 845 (2d Cir. 1997)).
[30] Id. at 335–36.

reworded stock recommendations at a cut-rate price to its subscribers and still make a profit.[31] The court did not find attributing the recommendation to the financial firm to be a mitigating factor, since it is the firm's expert reputation that gives the recommendation value.[32] Despite Fly's claims that it only competed directly with other financial news aggregators,[33] the court found that it directly competed with the firms to the extent that it disseminated recommendations to investors for making investment decisions.[34] Finally, the court found that the firms supplied ample evidence that allowing such conduct to continue "would so reduce [the firms'] incentive to invest the resources necessary to produce equity research reports that the continued viability of plaintiffs' research business is and 'would be substantially threatened.'"[35]

The court enjoined Fly from releasing the firms' recommendations until one half-hour after the New York Stock Exchange opens each day or 10:00 a.m., whichever is later.[36] The purpose of this injunction was to allow the financial firms to exploit benefit from the information they generate until its commercial value to the firms passes.[37]

The relationship between the financial services firms and Fly in *Barclays I* has some similarity to the relationship between news content producers and various news aggregation websites currently in existence. For the most part, the content on news aggregator websites is generated or gathered by content producers and then selected, summarized, commented upon, or linked to by the aggregators.

As more and more news content producers suffer from decreased revenue, news aggregation sites frequently draw upon the same news-reading clientele. While the aggregators provide readers with content that was gleaned from these producers and receive ad revenue in the process, they do not incur similar substantial costs in obtaining that content.

Before examining the legal consequences of the relationship between content producers and news aggregators, a review of the development of the hot news misappropriation doctrine is in order.

III. THE HOT NEWS MISAPPROPRIATION DOCTRINE

A. A Brief History[38]

The hot news misappropriation doctrine originated with the U.S. Supreme Court's decision in *International News Service v. Associated Press.*[39] International News Service (INS) and the Associated Press (AP) were competitors in the gathering and distribution of news to newspapers and other media sources throughout the United States and other

---

[31] *Id.* at 336.
[32] *See id.*
[33] *Id.* at 340.
[34] *Id.* at 339.
[35] *Id.* at 341.
[36] *Id.* at 347.
[37] *Id.* at 345.
[38] For a differing account of the facts behind this case, see Douglas G. Baird, *Property, Natural Monopoly, and the Uneasy Legacy of* INS v. AP (Univ. of Chi. Law Sch., John M. Olin Law & Economics, Working Paper No. 246, 2005), *available at* http://ssrn.com/abstract=730024.
[39] 248 U.S. 215 (1918).

nations.[40] This news would not have otherwise been accessible to the papers in a timely manner due to the expense associated with setting up their own foreign bureaus.[41] The most important news in 1916 related to World War I, which the United States had not yet entered.[42] American journalists covering the war in Europe sent back news via cable.[43] During the early part of the war, the owner of INS sympathized with Germany.[44] As a result, British censors prevented INS correspondents from sending back dispatches from the war, thus hindering INS from reporting on war developments.[45]

    To continue providing its subscriber papers with war news, INS bribed AP employees, employees of newspapers using the AP service, and telegraph operators for war news before AP member papers printed it.[46] More importantly, INS also copied AP news from early editions of papers in the eastern United States, as well as from bulletin boards outside of the offices of AP newspapers.[47] INS would rewrite the stories using the facts obtained from AP and distribute them to its member papers across the United States, in some cases scooping AP member papers on the west coast.[48] AP sued for an injunction.[49] After the district court granted the injunction, the case made its way to the U.S. Supreme Court.[50]

    The Court recognized that this case was a question of unfair competition rather than copyright.[51] It found that while individual newspaper buyers have the right to disseminate the news non-commercially, a competitor's transmission for commercial purposes is a different matter.[52] Between news-gathering competitors that concurrently expend labor, skill, and money to make profits, the news becomes a "quasi-property," regardless of either competitor's rights against the public.[53] The Court held that by selling a competitor's material that required organization and expenditure as its own, INS committed an unauthorized interference with the normal operation of AP's business "precisely at the point where the profit is to be reaped, in order to divert . . . profit from those who have earned it to those who have not."[54] This gave INS a special advantage because it was not burdened with the expense of gathering the news.[55] Thus, the Supreme Court created the hot news misappropriation doctrine. The underlying justifications for creating this doctrine include the labor (or "sweat of the brow") theory

---

[40] *Id.* at 229.
[41] ISBELL, *supra* note 10, at 14.
[42] Andrew L. Deutsch, *Protecting News in the Digital Era: The Case for a Federalized Hot News Misappropriation Tort, in* ADVANCED SEMINAR ON COPYRIGHT LAW 2010, at 511, 545 (PLI Patents, Copyrights, Trademarks, & Literary Prop., Course Handbook Series No. 1003, 2010).
[43] *Id.*
[44] Ryan T. Holte, *Restricting Fair Use to Save the News: A Proposed Change in Copyright Law to Bring More Profit to News Reporting,* 13 J. TECH. L. & POL'Y 1, 23 (2008).
[45] ISBELL, *supra* note 10, at 14.
[46] Deutsch, *supra* note 42, at 546.
[47] *Id.*
[48] ISBELL, *supra* note 10, at 14.
[49] Deutsch, *supra* note 42, at 546.
[50] *Id.* at 547.
[51] Int'l News Serv. v. Associated Press, 248 U.S. 215, 234–35 (1918).
[52] *Id.* at 239.
[53] *Id.* at 236.
[54] *Id.* at 240.
[55] *Id.*

of property, commercial immorality, and the preservation of an incentive to invest in information gathering.[56]

B. The Doctrine Shifts to the States

Because the Supreme Court created the hot news misappropriation doctrine in a diversity jurisdiction case, it became part of federal common law. Thus, the doctrine ceased to be formal precedent in 1938 when *Erie Railroad Co. v. Tompkins* overruled *Swift v. Tyson*, which had established federal common law.[57] Nonetheless, *INS* greatly influenced state common law development, and a number of states adopted the doctrine *INS* created.[58] A number of state decisions subsequently expanded the misappropriation doctrine from the narrow hot news fact pattern to other instances where a party reaped what it had not sown, frequently restraining any commercial activity of which the court disapproved.[59] Thus, the doctrine expanded to include many misappropriation claims involving "commercial immorality."[60]

C. Copyright Preemption Concerns

While some states eagerly adopted the misappropriation doctrine in the years following *Erie*, it was not clear whether federal intellectual property law preempted the doctrine. After New York adopted the misappropriation doctrine in 1950,[61] the Second Circuit Court of Appeals held in 1955 that the 1909 Copyright Act did not preempt the state misappropriation doctrine.[62] However, in 1964 the Supreme Court ruled in two cases that the federal patent law preempted Illinois state unfair competition law.[63] Broad application of the language in these decisions suggests that federal copyright and patent law would preempt state intellectual property protection if the state law conflicts, even indirectly, with the objectives of the federal protection.[64] Applied to copyright law, this indicates that state misappropriation claims would be preempted unless the misappropriating party had not cited the original source of information.[65] A decade later, the Court clarified its position in two rulings,[66] holding that states can protect certain

---

[56] Holte, *supra* note 44, at 24 (citing Rex Y. Fujichaku, Comment, *The Misappropriation Doctrine in Cyberspace: Protecting the Commercial Value of "Hot News" Information*, 20 U. HAW. L. REV. 421, 442 (1998)).

[57] *Barclays I*, 700 F. Supp. 2d 310, 332 (S.D.N.Y. 2010) (noting that *Erie* abrogated federal common law and ended *INS*'s formal precedent), *rev'd*, 650 F.3d 876 (2d Cir. 2011); Erie R.R. Co. v. Tompkins, 304 U.S. 64, 78 (1938) ("Except in matters governed by the Federal Constitution or by Acts of Congress, the law to be applied in any case is the law of the State. And whether the law of the State shall be declared by its Legislature in a statute or by its highest court in a decision is not a matter of federal concern.").

[58] *See* Deutsch, *supra* note 42, at 551.

[59] *See id.* at 551–53.

[60] *Id.* at 552.

[61] *See* Metro. Opera Ass'n v. Wagner-Nichols Recorder Corp., 101 N.Y.S.2d 483 (N.Y. Sup. Ct. 1950).

[62] *See* Capitol Records, Inc. v. Mercury Records Corp., 221 F.2d 657, 661–63 (2d Cir. 1955).

[63] *See* Compco Corp. v. Day-Brite Lighting, Inc., 376 U.S. 234 (1964); Sears, Roebuck & Co. v. Stiffel Co., 376 U.S. 225 (1964).

[64] Holte, *supra* note 44, at 27.

[65] *Id.*

[66] *See* Kewanee Oil Co. v. Bicron Corp., 416 U.S. 470 (1974); Goldstein v. California, 412 U.S. 546 (1973).

intellectual property rights under state copyright law, as long as the laws do not interfere with federal copyright laws.[67] They also held that states can make trade secret legislation in any area that Congress does not regulate.[68]

The 1976 Copyright Act directly addresses the issue of state law preemption.[69] Section 301 "explicitly preempts all state causes of action that protect any right equivalent to any of the exclusive rights protected by the Copyright Act, including copying and distribution."[70] This preempts many of the "commercial immorality" misappropriation claims that were essentially the same as wrongful copying.[71] However, the legislative history of the Act indicates that a hot news misappropriation claim survives preemption.[72]

D. The Modern Hot News Misappropriation Doctrine

The landmark case of *National Basketball Ass'n v. Motorola, Inc.*[73] also addressed whether the hot news misappropriation doctrine survived preemption. In this case, the National Basketball Association (NBA) brought an action against the manufacturer and the promoter of pagers that provided real-time information about professional basketball games.[74] A group of employees who watched basketball games on television or listened to them on the radio updated this information, entering data on a computer. Motorola then compiled and analyzed the data and transmitted it to the pagers.[75] In addition to misappropriation claims, the NBA asserted claims for false advertising, false representation of origin, copyright infringement, and unlawful interception of communications.[76] The district court found for the NBA on the misappropriation claim, dismissed all the other claims, and granted a permanent injunction against the defendants, who appealed to the Second Circuit Court of Appeals.[77]

The Second Circuit reversed and lifted the injunction.[78] However, it also held that a narrow hot news misappropriation claim survives preemption by the 1976 Copyright Act.[79] Looking back to *INS*, the court set out the elements central to a hot news

---

[67] Holte, *supra* note 44, at 27.

[68] *Id.*

[69] *Id.* at 28.

[70] *Barclays I*, 700 F. Supp. 2d 310, 333 (S.D.N.Y. 2010), *rev'd*, 650 F.3d 876 (2d Cir. 2011); *see also* 17 U.S.C. § 301 (2006).

[71] Deutsch, *supra* note 42, at 555.

[72] H.R. REP. NO. 94-1476, at 132 (1976) ("'Misappropriation' is not necessarily synonymous with copyright infringement, and thus a cause of action labeled as 'misappropriation' is not preempted if it is in fact based neither on a right within the general scope of copyright . . . nor on a right equivalent thereto. For example, state law should have the flexibility to afford a remedy . . . against a consistent pattern of unauthorized appropriation by a competitor of the facts . . . constituting 'hot' news, whether in the traditional mold of *International News Service v. Associated Press* or in the newer form of data updates from scientific, business, or financial data bases.") (internal citation omitted).

[73] 105 F.3d 841 (2d Cir. 1997).

[74] *See id.* at 843–44.

[75] *Id.* at 844.

[76] *Id.*

[77] *Id.* The NBA also appealed the dismissal of the false advertising claim. The court affirmed the district court's dismissal of the claim. *Id.* at 855.

[78] *Id.*

[79] *Id.* at 852.

misappropriation claim that would survive preemption.[80] It stated that the rationale for the doctrine is that protecting property rights in time-sensitive information incentivizes profit-seeking entrepreneurs to make information available to the public.[81] Without an incentive for private actors to collect "hot news," the general public would suffer.[82] The court found that it was the time-sensitive nature of the information's value, the defendant's free-riding, and "the threat to the very existence of a product or service provided by the plaintiff" that allows a hot news misappropriation claim to survive preemption.[83]

In addition to New York, Pennsylvania,[84] Missouri,[85] California,[86] and Illinois[87] have each adopted the hot news misappropriation tort as part of state unfair competition law.[88] The claim has also been asserted in Massachusetts[89] and Washington D.C.,[90] though not ruled on.

IV. BARCLAYS ON APPEAL

In holding that the financial firms' hot news misappropriation claim against Fly was preempted by the 1976 Copyright Act, the Second Circuit extensively examined its previous *NBA* opinion. After first noting that it was bound by the conclusion of the *NBA* court that the hot news misappropriation tort survives,[91] the court moved on to its preemption analysis.[92] In short, under § 301 of the Copyright Act,[93] federal copyright law preempts a state law claim that "seeks to vindicate 'legal or equitable rights that are equivalent' to one of the bundle of exclusive rights already protected by copyright law" (the "general scope requirement") "if the work in question is of the type of works protected by the Copyright Act" (under the "subject matter requirement").[94] It is not determinative that the material at issue is itself uncopyrightable—such as facts or ideas— if the material is contained in a work of the type that is generally protected.[95] However, if the state law claim requires an "extra element" instead of or in addition to the rights

---

[80] *Id.* at 845; *see also supra* Part II.

[81] *NBA*, 105 F.3d at 853.

[82] *Id.*

[83] *Id.*

[84] *See, e.g.*, Pottstown Daily News Publ'g Co. v. Pottstown Broad. Co., 192 A.2d 657 (Pa. 1963).

[85] *See, e.g.*, Fred Wehrenberg Circuit of Theaters, Inc. v. Moviefone, Inc., 73 F. Supp. 2d 1044 (E.D. Mo. 1999).

[86] *See, e.g.*, Pollstar v. Gigmania Ltd., 170 F. Supp. 2d 974 (E.D. Cal. 2000).

[87] *See, e.g.*, McKevitt v. Pallasch, 339 F.3d 530 (7th Cir. 2003).

[88] ISBELL, *supra* note 10, at 16.

[89] *See, e.g.*, Complaint, GateHouse Media Mass. I, Inc. v. N.Y. Times Co., No. 08-cv-12114-WGY (D. Mass. Dec. 22, 2008).

[90] *See, e.g.*, First Amended Complaint, Agence France Presse v. Google, Inc., No. 05CV00546 (GK) (D. D.C. Apr. 29, 2005).

[91] *Barclays II*, 650 F.3d 876, 890 (2d Cir. 2011).

[92] *See id.* at 890–94.

[93] 17 U.S.C. § 301 (2006).

[94] *Barclays II*, 650 F.3d at 892.

[95] *Id.* at 893 (citing Nat'l Basketball Ass'n v. Motorola, Inc.,, 105 F.3d 841, 849 (2d Cir. 1997)).

protected by federal copyright law, then there is no preemption because the claim is not covered by the general scope of copyright.[96]

The court then went on to discuss the elements of the hot news misappropriation claim that *NBA* laid out and the district court relied on.[97] Noting some slight inconsistencies in the wording of multiple reiterations of the free-riding element in *NBA*, the court held that *NBA*'s five-element hot news misappropriation claim test was not binding because it essentially amounted to dicta.[98]

Applying its review of the law to the facts of *Barclays*, the court found it determinative that the information that Fly distributed to clients was the fact that the firms were making certain recommendations and that Fly attributed the recommendations to the source firms.[99] Fly was not repackaging the research and recommendations as its own.[100] Rather, the court found that Fly was merely reporting on the fact that the firms made the recommendations.[101]

The court first held that the claim met the requirements for preemption, as the recommendations met the subject matter requirement as "original works of authorship fixed in a[] tangible medium of expression."[102] The general scope requirement was met—the violated right was the right of reproduction, which the Copyright Act addresses.[103] However, the court held that the claim at issue did not have the extra element required to avoid preemption because it found that Fly did not "free-ride" on the efforts of the firms.[104] In addressing this finding, the court noted that the firms were only seeking to protect their recommendations, not the underlying research conducted to reach those recommendations, and that the recommendations were a product of the firms' expertise and experience rather than information acquired through efforts akin to reporting.[105] The court also noted that, while Fly may be interfering with the firms' business at a point where the firms' profits are to be reaped, it was not clear that profit was being diverted to Fly.[106] While the firms earned revenue through commissions on trades placed through their brokers after their clients received the recommendations,[107] Fly received its revenue through subscribers to its information bulletins.[108] The court felt that instead of diverting profits to itself, Fly was most likely diverting profits to "whatever broker happens to execute a trade placed by the recipient of news of the [r]ecommendation from Fly."[109] Furthermore, the court made note of the fact that Fly has a staff dedicated to collecting the recommendations and reporting on them, a "substantial

---

[96] *Id.* at 893 (citing *NBA*, 105 F.3d at 850).
[97] *See id.* at 898.
[98] *See id.* at 899–901.
[99] *See id.* at 903–04.
[100] *Id.* at 904.
[101] *See id.* at 903.
[102] *Id.* at 902 (alteration in original) (internal quotation marks omitted) (citing 17 U.S.C. § 102 (2006)).
[103] *Id.*
[104] *See id.*
[105] *Id.* at 903.
[106] *Id.* at 904.
[107] *Id.* at 879, 882.
[108] *Id.* at 883.
[109] *Id.* at 904.

organizational effort" bearing its own costs of collecting factual information, thus weighing against a determination of "free-riding."[110]

Reflecting on what sort of hot news misappropriation case would survive preemption, the court stated that it was mindful of the facts before the *INS* court: "news, data, and the like, gathered and disseminated by one organization as a significant part of its business, taken by another entity and published as the latter's own in competition with the former."[111] Finally, the court noted that the firms might have had a hot news misappropriation claim against Fly if they "were to collect and disseminate to some portion of the public facts about securities recommendations in the brokerage industry" and were to "copy the facts contained in the [f]irms' hypothetical service" and distribute them as their own research.[112]

As a result of this opinion, it appears that for a hot news misappropriation claim to survive federal preemption, one party must expend resources collecting news or information as part of its business, while another party copies that news or information and distributes it as its own research in competition with the first party. Fortunately, this standard may be applicable to many situations involving news aggregators.

V. THE JOURNALISM INDUSTRY AND NEWS AGGREGATION

A. The Current State of the Journalism Industry

The journalism industry in the United States is changing. Newspaper daily print circulation decreased thirty percent since 1990.[113] More importantly, print and online advertising revenue for newspaper organizations has fallen nearly forty-eight percent since 2006.[114] Circulation revenues have fallen ten percent since 2003.[115] While radio, magazines, and cable, network, and local television news have each suffered from declining audiences over the past year, advertising revenue for each has actually increased.[116] However, only Internet news providers grew both in audience and revenue over the past year, with more people now getting their news online than through newspapers for the first time and more money being spent on online advertising than print newspaper advertising for the first time as well.[117]

More importantly, the changes that have affected the journalism industry over the past decade have led to a significant decline in investment in news gathering. Newspaper newsroom jobs are down almost a third since 2000.[118] Network news staffs are roughly half the size they were in the 1980s.[119] The trend is similar at news magazines.[120]

---

[110] *Id.* at 905.
[111] *Id.*
[112] *Id.* at 905–06.
[113] Rick Edmonds et al., *Newspapers: By the Numbers*, STATE NEWS MEDIA, http://stateofthemedia.org/2011/newspapers-essay/data-page-6/ (last visited Nov. 21, 2011).
[114] *Id.*
[115] *Id.*
[116] *Key Findings*, State News Media, http://stateofthemedia.org/2011/overview-2/key-findings/ (last visited Dec. 18, 2011).
[117] *Id.*
[118] Edmonds et al., *supra* note 113.
[119] *Id.*

264

Newspapers are now devoting $1.6 billion less annually to news gathering than they did four years ago.[121] However, there are some signs that online news entities are starting to invest more in news gathering.[122]

B. The Rise of Internet News Aggregation

Coinciding with this change in traditional journalism is the rise of the Internet news aggregator. Generally speaking, a news aggregator is a website that displays information from multiple sources in a single place.[123] News aggregators take on a number of forms, including what are commonly referred to as feed aggregators, specialty aggregators, user-curated aggregators, and blog aggregators.[124] For the purposes here, this Comment only discusses feed aggregators and blog aggregators.

1. Feed Aggregators

Feed aggregators are websites that contain material from a number of other sources—generally arranged by source, topic, or story—and are closest to the traditional conception of a news aggregator.[125] They generally display the headline of a story and link back to the original source.[126] Sometimes the first few lines of a story's lead are included, and the name of the originating website is often listed.[127] Google News[128] is an example of a feed aggregator.

The problem with feed aggregators is that readers receive a significant proportion (or "heart") of the story from the story's headline and lead without ever having to click on the link to the source. Thus, while the aggregator receives ad revenue for the views, the source website does not. This problem is significant. A recent study indicated that forty-four percent of people who visit Google News scan headlines without accessing the source websites.[129]

2. Blog Aggregators

Blog aggregators, such as the Huffington Post,[130] use third-party content to create a blog about a particular topic.[131] Posts frequently consist either of synthesizing third-party

---

[120] Katerina-Eva Matsa et al., *Magazines: By the Numbers*, State News Media, http://stateofthemedia.org/2011/magazines-essay/data-page-4/ (last visited Dec. 18, 2011).
[121] Rick Edmonds, *Shrinking Newspapers Have Created $1.6 Billion News Deficit*, Poynter Biz Blog (Oct. 10, 2009, 12:00 PM), http://www.poynter.org/latest-news/business-news/the-biz-blog/98784/shrinking-newspapers-have-created-1-6-billion-news-deficit/.
[122] *See* Tom Rosenstiel & Amy Mitchell, *Key Findings*, STATE NEWS MEDIA, http://stateofthemedia.org/2011/overview-2/key-findings/ (last visited Nov. 21, 2011).
[123] ISBELL, *supra* note 10, at 2.
[124] *Id.*
[125] *Id.*
[126] *Id.*
[127] *Id.*
[128] GOOGLE NEWS, http://news.google.com (last visited Nov. 21, 2011).
[129] Robin Wauters, *Report: 44% of Google News Visitors Scan Headlines, Don't Click Through*, TECHCRUNCH (Jan. 19, 2010), http://techcrunch.com/2010/01/19/outsell-google-news/.
[130] HUFFINGTON POST, http://www.huffingtonpost.com/ (last visited Nov. 21, 2011).
[131] ISBELL, *supra* note 10, at 5.

content from multiple sources into a single story and linking to the original content, either in the article or at the end of the article, or of a two or three sentence summary of a third-party article with a link to the original.[132] In linking to the original content, blog aggregators either use the original headline or create a new one.[133] Unlike feed aggregators, blog aggregators take original content and generally add new content or interpretation.

With this understanding of the current state of journalism and news aggregation, this Comment next looks to the legal remedies available to protect the journalism industry and other content producers.

VI. WHY COPYRIGHT LAW IS INSUFFICIENT TO PROTECT CONTENT PRODUCERS

The chance of recovery by a content producer against a news aggregator's infringement under current federal copyright law is poor. A major reason for this is that news aggregators primarily take the "heart" of the source content and reword it, instead of copying and reprinting large portions of it. For instance, blog aggregators will frequently only summarize the original content. To the extent that blog aggregators print small sections of the source headline or content and feed aggregators print source headlines and leads, the copyright doctrines of the idea/expression merger and fair use become important factors in the determination of copyright infringement.

A. The Idea/Expression Merger

Under U.S. copyright law, while the expression of a particular fact or idea is generally copyrightable, the underlying fact or idea is not.[134] Thus, if an aggregator copies a full paragraph of source content and prints it verbatim, the aggregator will most likely be liable for copyright infringement. However, if a blogger rewrites a story, using the underlying facts but putting them in his own words, it is not copyright infringement. This is the theoretical underpinning in the *INS* decision. Copyright infringement was not found in *INS* because most of the stories were rewritten. Therefore, the court created the misappropriation doctrine to alleviate what it perceived to be an unfair business practice.

The concept of the idea/expression merger comes into play when there is essentially only one way to express an idea. In such cases, the idea and the expression are considered to have merged, and the expression is not copyrightable.[135] Under similar reasoning, titles and short phrases generally do not receive copyright protection.[136]

Aggregators will thus not be liable for copyright infringement for any underlying facts or ideas that they take from a source. They will also not be liable for any expression they take when that expression is the only way of expressing the underlying fact or idea. This concept is especially relevant to feed aggregators. Generally, the source headlines or leads express the facts of the story in as few words as possible. Using fewer words

---

[132] *Id.*

[133] *Id.*

[134] *See* 17 U.S.C. § 102(b) (2006).

[135] *See* ATC Distrib. Grp., Inc. v. Whatever It Takes Transmission & Parts, Inc., 402 F.3d 700, 707–08 (6th Cir. 2005).

[136] *See* CMM Cable Rep, Inc. v. Ocean Coast Props., Inc., 97 F.3d 1504, 1519–20 (1st Cir. 1996).

leads to fewer ways of expressing particular facts, thus leading to a higher likelihood of a merger. The aggregators' case is only strengthened when one considers that headlines are generally just titles or short phrases. For all of these reasons, a successful copyright infringement case against a feed aggregator is unlikely.

B. Fair Use

Even when a blog aggregator reprints a portion of copyrighted material, it has an argument against infringement due to the fair use doctrine. To comport with First Amendment concerns regarding free expression, the Copyright Act contains a Fair Use clause, which sets forth four nonexclusive factors for a court to consider when determining whether a use qualifies as fair. Fair use precludes a finding of infringement. The fair use factors include:

(1) the purpose and character of the use, including whether such use is of a commercial nature or is for nonprofit educational purposes;

(2) the nature of the copyrighted work;

(3) the amount and substantiality of the portion used in relation to the copyrighted work as a whole; and

(4) the effect of the use upon the potential market for or value of the copyrighted work.[137]

1. The Purpose and Character of the Use

The first thing that courts look to when evaluating this factor is whether the use is commercial in nature.[138] As almost every aggregator relies on ad revenue to one extent or another, this factor should weigh in favor of the content producers. However, courts then look to whether the use is transformative—whether it adds something to the content, by either repurposing it or adding some new meaning or expression.[139]

Both feed and blog aggregators may have an advantage on this factor. Courts have found that the categorization and indexing functions generally performed by feed aggregators qualify as transformative uses.[140] While this transformative use may not be sufficient to overcome the free-riding aspect of a hot news misappropriation claim,[141] it appears that it is sufficient for this factor of a fair use claim. Blog aggregators have an even stronger claim, as they generally add their own thoughts and expressions to the original content.

---

[137] 17 U.S.C. § 107.

[138] ISBELL, *supra* note 10, at 10.

[139] *Id.*

[140] *See generally* Perfect 10, Inc. v. Amazon.com, Inc., 508 F.3d 1146 (9th Cir. 2007); Kelly v. Arriba Soft Corp., 336 F.3d 811 (9th Cir. 2003).

[141] *See Barclays I*, 700 F. Supp. 2d 310, 337 (S.D.N.Y. 2010), *rev'd*, 650 F.3d 876 (2d Cir. 2011).

2. The Nature of the Copyrighted Work

For this factor, courts generally look to whether the work is expressive or creative, or more factual.[142] Fair use claims receive more deference when they involve factual works.[143] The court also looks to whether the work is published, giving more deference to usage of published works.[144] The fact that the content at issue in this Comment is published work of a factual nature leads to a fair use finding on this factor in favor of feed and blog aggregators.

3. The Amount and Substantiality of the Portion Used in Relation to the Copyrighted Work as a Whole

For this factor, courts look to the amount of the source work that is reproduced— both quantitatively and qualitatively.[145] Quantitatively, most aggregators only use a small amount of the source work—just a few sentences and maybe a headline for a blog aggregator and just the headline and maybe a few sentences of lead for a feed aggregator. But examined from a qualitative perspective, the borrowing of content is greater. In general, the headlines and lead contain the heart of the source content. The remaining information is frequently mere detail to flesh out the story. The same is frequently true for blog aggregators. The Supreme Court has held that reprinting a short excerpt can weigh against fair use if the excerpt is the heart of the source work.[146] Thus, this factor could easily go for the content producers.

4. The Effect of the Use on the Potential Market for the Copyrighted Work

As in the misappropriation test, the fact that forty-four percent of Google News readers do not click through to the source content indicates that feed aggregators frequently function as a substitute for the source, thus hindering the potential market for the source material. The case with blog aggregators is less clear, but it is certainly conceivable that this factor will weigh in favor of the content producers.

While content producers are likely to be favored in the last two factors of the test, aggregators have much stronger arguments for the first two factors. Thus, depending on the facts of each case, a finding of fair use is certainly possible. Consequently, content producers cannot rely on copyright law alone to protect their content.

VII.   APPLYING THE HOT NEWS MISAPPROPRIATION DOCTRINE TO NEWS AGGREGATORS

A. Intent of the Doctrine

Courts can apply the same fundamental factors at the base of the opinions in *INS*, *NBA*, *Barclays I* and *Barclays II* to protect the news gathered by content producers from misappropriation by news aggregators. While the "sweat of the brow" theory of property

---

[142] ISBELL, *supra* note 10, at 11–12.
[143] *Id.* at 12.
[144] *Id.*
[145] *Id.*
[146] *See* Harper & Row, Publishers, Inc. v. Nation Enters., 471 U.S. 539, 564–65 (1985).

is no longer a viable factor in copyright law,[147] it is still a valid justification for unfair competition law. In the news aggregator setting, traditional news media and other content producers are expending significant amounts of labor, skill, and money to gather hot news from around the world and distribute it to their paying customers. However, precisely at the point where profits are to be reaped—via the viewing of an ad on a content producer's site as the reader views the news or through the sale of a physical paper—news aggregators are diverting the profit to themselves by displaying the heart of the news and receiving ad revenue on their sites instead. As in *INS*, news aggregators do not bear the expense of gathering the news they are reporting and, thus, are reaping what they did not sow.

The same principles of commercial immorality that support the hot news doctrine in *INS* are present in these current practices. Most importantly, the need to preserve an incentive to invest in information gathering is readily apparent. As the gathering and dissemination of news is a benefit to the public as a whole, the journalism industry should be protected and given the opportunity to receive a return on its investment in news gathering. This incentivizes industry members to continue gathering and disseminating news. Thus, courts should follow the lead of *INS*, *NBA*, and *Barclays I* and apply the test for a hot news misappropriation claim to news aggregators.

While the court in *Barclays II* seemed to dismiss the *NBA* element test as dicta, it is not clear from the opinion that the test is completely incompatible with the court's federal preemption analysis or its conception of a valid hot news misappropriation claim. As such, it is possible that the test is still valid and that future courts will use it. The following analysis assumes that courts will continue to apply the *NBA* element test in deciding hot news misappropriation claims.

B. Applying the NBA *Element Test to News Aggregators*

1. The Plaintiff Generates or Gathers Information at a Cost

News media and other content producers are likely to satisfy this element.[148] There is no doubt that the journalism industry expends great sums of money in gathering the news that it distributes. This element should thus be easy to meet. There is a slight chance that feed aggregators may be able to escape this element if the part of the headline or lead reproduced was not costly to gather.[149] For instance, if a feed aggregator uses a headline or lead from a content producer that says a particular politician won an election, the content producer probably did not incur significant costs to gather that particular piece of information.

2. The Information Is Time-Sensitive

This factor is determined on a case-by-case basis,[150] but it is not difficult to see that the information most relevant to this test is the information that is most in demand. As

---

[147] *See* Feist Publ'ns, Inc. v. Rural Tel. Serv. Co., 499 U.S. 340, 359–60 (1991).
[148] *See* ISBELL, *supra* note 10, at 18.
[149] *See id.*
[150] *Id.* at 19.

the "hotness" of the news is fleeting, it is the time-sensitive news that is most in demand and would be the subject of this examination.

3. Free-Riding on the Plaintiff's Efforts

While feed aggregators may argue that they add their own effort to that of content producers by selecting and collecting certain information in one place, a court may consider such aggregation activities insufficient to overcome the fact that the aggregator expended no effort to produce the information and did not contribute to the underlying research and analysis. While blog aggregators do add additional information and analysis to a story, courts may follow similar logic and hold that contribution insufficient to counter the amount of free-riding. It is not clear at what point courts would find that the level of additional contribution outweighs the level of free-riding.

4. Direct Competition

The fact that a significant proportion of the viewers of feed aggregators never click through to the source material is a strong indication that the aggregator serves as a replacement for the source and, thus, qualifies as direct competition. Due to the content added by a blog aggregator, it seems there would be less of a chance of direct competition between online newspapers and blog aggregators, but it is not difficult to imagine a case where there would be direct competition for readers between the two. For instance, some readers might consider the analysis provided by the Huffington Post to be a sufficient substitute for that provided by the New York Times.

5. Reduce the Incentive to Produce

The burden for this element is low. The content producer does not even have to show that the defendant "caused them actual, quantifiable damage"—as may be possible with news aggregators—just that "the free-riding, if left unrestrained, '*would* so reduce the incentive to produce the product or service that its existence or quality *would be* substantially threatened.'"[151] A content provider should be able to meet this element by showing a correlation between reduced media revenues due to aggregation and reduced investment in news gathering.

C. Applying the Hot News Misappropriation Doctrine Under Barclays II

If courts follow the lead of *Barclays II* and limit application of the hot news misappropriation doctrine to cases with facts similar to *INS*—i.e., where the copying party passes the information off as the result of its own research—aggregators will gain a significant advantage. An aggregator would be able to avoid all liability for a hot news misappropriation claim by giving credit for the content to the content producer. Currently, many aggregators provide attribution or link to the original source of their material. Thus, applying this interpretation of the doctrine is not likely to help content producers as much as the doctrine under *NBA*. Nonetheless, the doctrine will likely still

---

[151] *Barclays I*, 700 F. Supp. 2d 310, 342 (S.D.N.Y. 2010) (quoting Nat'l Basketball Ass'n v. Motorola, Inc., 105 F.3d 841, 845 (2d Cir. 1997)), *rev'd*, 650 F.3d 876 (2d Cir. 2011).

be a useful tool for content producers in some instances to address improper misappropriation.

VIII.   OTHER PROPOSALS FOR PROTECTING JOURNALISM

There have been a number of proposals for other methods of protecting journalism.[152]   While breach of contract as a cause of action and proposals to modify copyright law to cover news and to restrict fair use each have their benefits, only a proposal to create a federal hot news misappropriation tort is a viable solution to the problems journalism currently faces.

A.   Breach of Contract

Both Andrew Deutsch and Ryan Holte have discussed protecting information through a breach of contract claim.[153]   A content producer could include contractual terms on its website expressly prohibiting the usage of the content for aggregation purposes.[154]   If the terms of the agreement were violated, the content producer would have a breach of contract claim, which would not be federally preempted by § 301 of the Copyright Act.[155]

However, there are problems with this method.   Consent to the terms and conditions of a website is judged by the visibility of those terms and a clear method for expressing consent.[156]   To take advantage of a breach of contract cause of action, many content producers will have to change their practices to make their terms and conditions more obvious to aggregators, which may include making those terms and conditions more prominent on the website and, ideally, requiring the user to express affirmative consent to the terms and conditions (such as by clicking some sort of "I consent" link before they have access to the content).[157]   Many content producers may not like to put that many hurdles between their content and their readers.   In addition, it is unclear how difficult it would be to track down violators.[158]

B.   Modify Copyright Law to Close Gaps

Alfred Yen discusses proposals to protect newspapers by aggressively closing gaps in current copyright law through legislation.[159]   Specifically, this would require: "(1) defining newspaper headlines and lead sentences as copyrightable subject matter even if

---

[152] *See generally, e.g.,* Deutsch, *supra* note 42; Eric B. Easton, *Who Owns 'The First Rough Draft of History?': Reconsidering Copyright in News,* 27 COLUM. J.L. & ARTS 521 (2004); Holte, *supra* note 44; Alfred C. Yen, *A Preliminary First Amendment Analysis of Legislation Treating News Aggregation as Copyright Infringement,* 12 VAND. J. ENT. & TECH. L. 947 (2010).
[153] *See* Deutsch, *supra* note 42, at 558; Holte, *supra* note 44, at 31.
[154] *See* Deutsch, *supra* note 42, at 558.
[155] *See* Holte, *supra* note 44, at 31; *see also* 17 U.S.C. § 301 (2006).
[156] Deutsch, *supra* note 42, at 559.
[157] *Id.* at 559–61.
[158] Holte, *supra* note 44, at 31.
[159] *See* Yen, *supra* note 152, at 959.

they lack originality or represent the merger of idea and expression, (2) curtailing the scope of fair use, and (3) treating linking as a form of infringement."[160]
        As Yen himself points out, this proposal immediately runs afoul of the First Amendment. As it is, the Copyright Act already infringes on free speech to some extent.[161] It is only through the safety valves of fair use and the idea/expression dichotomy that courts have determined the Copyright Act does not violate free speech rights.[162] In addition, the protections guaranteed by the Copyright Act incentivize the creation of new speech, which helps overcome any concern over restrictions.[163] The proposed changes to copyright law would alter the traditional contours of copyright protection, eliminating some of the safety valves that prevent copyright law from unduly restricting speech.[164] These proposals would also prevent aggregators from distributing their own speech regarding news stories by not allowing them to provide information on articles or where they can be found.[165] In addition, the proposals would impermissibly extend copyright protection to material already in the public domain by automatically defining headlines and leads as copyrightable, regardless of whether they contain protectable material.[166] Due to these constitutional violations, these proposals are unfeasible.

C. Restricting Fair Use

        Ryan Holte proposes a slight change in fair use to protect the journalism industry.[167] He proposes changing fair use to extend a twenty-four hour monopoly to content producers on their content so that they can reap profits from it.[168] After that period, the story can be reproduced freely to allow the dissemination of ideas.[169] Holte believes that giving content producers these additional limited rights would allow them to find additional profits in news gathering. This would incentivize the gathering and dissemination of information to the public benefit.[170] To lessen the negative consequences of this proposal, such as reduced dissemination of information among the public, Holte suggests not extending this additional protection to news headlines so that other websites may advertise and link to the story.[171] He also proposes a loophole that would allow non-profit entities to post the content.[172] To further lessen the negative impact of this proposal, he suggests limiting damages for violations to "the cost of litigation plus the amount of profits the defendant gained from publishing the story during the time the plaintiff had monopoly rights to it."[173]

---

[160] Id. at 959–60 (footnote omitted).
[161] Id. at 960.
[162] See id. at 961.
[163] See id. at 959–61.
[164] Id. at 963–64.
[165] Id. at 969–70.
[166] Id. at 964, 969.
[167] See Holte, supra note 44, at 32–33.
[168] Id. at 33.
[169] Id.
[170] Id.
[171] Id.
[172] Id.
[173] Id.

This proposal is far superior to the one Yen discusses, as it alters the traditional contours of copyright protection much less significantly. However, while the negative consequences are far less severe, they still raise similar First Amendment concerns. Holte acknowledges this issue, but argues that the exception for not-for-profit entities and the limitation on damages are sufficient to mitigate any free speech concerns.[174] Yet these qualifications are unlikely to sufficiently mitigate these concerns because this proposal would still restrict fair use. Courts have found that the safety valves of fair use and the idea/expression dichotomy are necessary to protect free speech amidst copyright law's inherent free speech restrictions. Given this tenuous balance, it seems unlikely that a restriction on one of these safety valves would survive judicial scrutiny.

D. A Federal Hot News Misappropriation Tort

Andrew Deutsch makes a convincing case for a federal hot news misappropriation tort.[175] While he supports the logical underpinnings for the state cause of action, he expresses some concern for their uneven application and reliability.[176] His main concern is choice of law.[177] For a hot news misappropriation claim to succeed, the parties and the relevant facts must have a sufficient nexus to a state that has recognized the doctrine or is likely to recognize it.[178] Furthermore, he is concerned that the various states may not apply the third and fourth elements of the misappropriation claim uniformly.[179]

Deutsch believes the answer to this problem is a well-crafted federal hot news statute that provides uniform law across all states.[180] It would provide plaintiffs access to federal courts and federal rules of procedure and would theoretically provide clear elements for the claim, including the amount of competition between the parties and the threat to the plaintiff that is required.[181] Such legislation could also undo any limitations that *Barclays II* places on the doctrine and properly balance the rights of content producers with the benefit to society that aggregators provide. Legislators could also address free speech issues that the doctrine presents.

For these reasons, Deutsch's proposal would indeed be the best option for protecting journalism and other content producers. Unfortunately, there is currently no indication that Congress is considering this sort of legislation.[182] As such, content producers must turn to the current hot news misappropriation doctrine for protection.

---

[174] *Id.* at 36.
[175] *See generally* Deutsch, *supra* note 42.
[176] *See id.* at 579.
[177] *Id.* at 580.
[178] *Id.*
[179] *Id.* at 580–81.
[180] *Id.* at 581.
[181] *Id.* at 581–82.
[182] The House had previously considered applying the *NBA* five-element test to databases in the Consumer Access to Information Act of 2004, H.R. 3872, 108th Cong. (2004).

IX. WHY THE CURRENT HOT NEWS MISAPPROPRIATION DOCTRINE IS STILL A VIABLE
TOOL IN PROTECTING JOURNALISM

¶67   While the hot news misappropriation doctrine currently possesses a fraction of the
strength it held ninety years ago, the journalism industry can still use this doctrine to
protect itself, even after the *Barclays II* decision.   Although misappropriation is not
currently recognized in every state, eight of the top nine newspapers (by circulation) are
located in jurisdictions that recognize the doctrine or have been presented with it.[183]
Assuming that *USA Today* would be able to show substantial ties to a state that
recognizes the doctrine, such as by demonstrating significant readership and resulting
economic damage in New York, all nine papers are covered by the doctrine. Out of the
top one hundred papers, a third are located in jurisdictions that recognize the doctrine or
have been presented with it but have not ruled on it.[184]   These figures suggest that if these
content producers start enforcing their rights under the hot news misappropriation
doctrine, the resulting damages and expenses that aggregators would be forced to pay
could lead to a fundamental change in the way aggregators source content. New York in
particular has embraced the doctrine. It is home to four of the top seven newspapers by
circulation and nine of the top one hundred.[185] Furthermore, AP is based in New York.[186]
These organizations have the potential to be powerful players in how the relationship
between content producers and aggregators progresses.

¶68   Like with *INS*, AP is starting to fight back against aggregators. In a fact pattern
eerily similar to *INS*, AP filed suit against All Headline News (AHN) in the Southern
District of New York for hot news misappropriation and other claims.[187] AP alleged that
AHN had no actual reporters, but instead prepared stories by having employees copy
news reports off the Internet—some of which belonged to AP—and rewrite them.[188]
These rewritten stories were then sold to newspapers, web portals, websites, and other
news redistributors.[189] AHN filed a motion to dismiss most of the claims against it, but
the court refused to dismiss the hot news misappropriation claim.[190]   Before the case
could go to trial, the parties settled, and AHN agreed to cease using AP content.[191] This
is a strong indicator of the power that content producers still wield in jurisdictions that
recognize the hot news misappropriation doctrine. The *Barclays II* opinion even alluded
to this case as being an example of the hot news misappropriation tort that would survive
its preemption analysis.[192]

---

[183] *See eCirc for US Newspapers*, AUDIT BUREAU CIRCULATIONS,
http://abcas3.accessabc.com/ecirc/newstitlesearchus.asp (last visited Nov. 21, 2011).
[184] *See id.*
[185] *See id.*
[186] *About AP*, ASSOCIATED PRESS, http://www.ap.org/pages/about/about.html (last visited Nov. 6, 2011).
[187] Associated Press v. All Headline News Corp., 608 F. Supp. 2d 454 (S.D.N.Y. 2009).
[188] ISBELL, *supra* note 10, at 6.
[189] *Id.* at 7.
[190] *Id.*
[191] *Id.*
[192] *Barclays II*, 650 F.3d 876, 905–06 (2d Cir. 2011).

X. Conclusion

The current state of the hot news misappropriation doctrine is not the perfect tool for content producers to use against news aggregators to protect themselves from improper free-riding. It is currently only recognized in five states and has not been used extensively. Furthermore, *Barclays II* somewhat limits the doctrine. However, the currently available alternatives to the doctrine are insufficient to protect producers. The idea/expression merger, fair use doctrine, and limited amount of word-for-word copying by aggregators renders copyright law largely ineffective for this purpose. Breach of contract claims are hindered by consent requirements and the difficulty of tracking down violators. Finally, while proposals to modify copyright law could solve some of the problems that content producers are facing, they are unlikely to survive judicial scrutiny due to free speech concerns.

As the hot news misappropriation doctrine is available in states with a high percentage of content producers, it is still a viable tool that content producers can use to protect themselves. It is important to see how courts will apply the doctrine in light of *Barclays II*. Nonetheless, until a federal hot news misappropriation tort is created, the state hot news misappropriation doctrine is the best option that content producers have.

Copyright 2012 by Northwestern University School of Law
Northwestern Journal of Technology and Intellectual Property

Changing Tides in Music Licensing? *BMI v. DMX* and *In re THP*

By Carly Olson[*]

In cafés, restaurants, bars, and stores, music creates an ambience to keep customers happy. But this music is not free. Most businesses that play music must pay royalties to the copyright holders or else risk liability for copyright infringement. Traditionally, proprietors have protected themselves by entering into blanket agreements with performing rights organizations (PROs), which give licensees the unlimited right to play any music from the PRO's catalog in return for an annual fee.[1]

Recently, however, one company that plays such background music has entered into a different kind of licensing agreement. It makes direct payments to copyright holders to license music and then deducts those payments from its annual fee to the PRO. Last year this arrangement led to two lawsuits in the Southern District of New York which could significantly impact the music business:[2] *Broadcast Music, Inc. v. DMX, Inc.*[3] and *In re THP Capstar Acquisition Corp.*[4]

The first case involves a dispute between Broadcast Music, Inc. (BMI), one of the two major PROs in the United States, and DMX, Inc. (DMX), a commercial music services provider (CMSP) that provides background music for public spaces. The two companies disagreed over the fees for an adjustable-fee blanket license (AFB license), a method of payment that allows a licensee to reduce the fees it owes the PRO by licensing music directly from the copyright holder.[5] Both parties agreed that DMX should pay BMI an annual "per-location rate," but they had vastly different views of what the rate should be. BMI requested $41.81 per location, while DMX proposed $11.32 per location.[6]

The case *In re THP* covered largely the same issues as *BMI v. DMX*, but involved the other major PRO, the American Society of Composers, Authors and Publishers (ASCAP). In this case, DMX offered ASCAP the same general fee structure that BMI proposed.[7] ASCAP contended that an AFB license was unreasonable and that it was not required to issue a license.[8] Therefore, ASCAP refused to suggest a reasonable AFB

---

[*] Carly Olson is a third-year student at Northwestern University School of Law. She would like to thank her family, friends, professors, and peers for all of their support and assistance.
[1] *See, e.g.*, United States v. Broad. Music, Inc. (*In re AEI Music Network, Inc.*), 275 F.3d 168, 172 (2d Cir. 2001); United States v. Am. Soc'y of Composers, Authors & Publishers, 831 F. Supp. 137, 166–67 (S.D.N.Y. 1993).
[2] Ed Christman, *Licensed to Ill: U.S. Appeals Court's BMI Rate Decision Could Signal Other Changes for PROs*, BILLBOARD, Sept. 18, 2010, at 8.
[3] 726 F. Supp. 2d 355 (S.D.N.Y. 2010).
[4] 756 F. Supp. 2d 516 (S.D.N.Y. 2010).
[5] *BMI v. DMX*, 726 F. Supp. 2d at 355.
[6] *Id.* at 355, 357.
[7] *In re THP*, 756 F. Supp. 2d at 535.
[8] *Id.* at 539.

license fee structure and instead offered two proposals: a blanket license with no carve-outs and a blanket license with a static carve-out.[9]

An AFB license is essentially a blanket license, from which CMSPs can subtract a proportional credit reflecting the performances of the PRO's music it has directly licensed. CMSPs still have to contract with large PROs because it is not feasible for them to directly license a PRO's entire catalog, which can consist of millions of musical works and hundreds of thousands of copyright holders.[10] An AFB license allows CMSPs to protect themselves from liability for copyright infringement while still trying to save money by directly licensing music from specific copyright holders.

This issue has arisen only recently because in past years blanket licenses with PROs were the only practicable way for CMSPs to license musical works. It used to be too laborious and time-consuming for a CMSP to contact individual music publishers or copyright holders to attempt to directly license their works. Now, however, it is relatively quick and easy to contact multiple businesses around the country. Technological advances allow CMSPs to directly license music and to keep track of how much directly licensed music it plays. Therefore, AFB licenses are not only feasible in a way they were not before, but are also an attractive way for CMSPs to try to save money.

The *BMI v. DMX* and *In re THP* courts came to conclusions that conform to the government's model and further the government's goal of maintaining reasonable music licensing fees. These decisions provide a means by which CMSPs can directly license music from copyright holders and deduct the fees from their blanket licenses. The decisions also recognize that the blanket fees BMI offered were unreasonable.[11] This helps fulfill the original intent of the consent decrees under which BMI and ASCAP are allowed to operate: to "provid[e] a mechanism for the setting of reasonable license fees in a unique market in which ASCAP [and BMI] indisputably exercise[] market power."[12] BMI is resisting this decision in court, attempting to thwart the terms of its consent decree to retain its near monopoly on the music licensing industry.[13]

In Part I, this Note examines the historical developments in music licensing that led to the *BMI v. DMX* and *In re THP* cases. Part II examines how DMX sought direct licenses from copyright holders. Parts III and IV discuss the recent *BMI v. DMX* and *In re THP* decisions, respectively. Part V discusses the decisions' potential future effects on the music licensing industry as well as other industries that use similar licensing practices. Part VI concludes by examining BMI and ASCAP's opposition to the decisions, explaining that the Second Circuit should uphold the decisions of the district court to conform with government intent.

---

[9] *Id.*

[10] *See e.g.*, *Search the Repertoire*, BROADCAST MUSIC, INC., http://www.bmi.com/search/ (last visited Nov. 14, 2011).

[11] *BMI v. DMX, Inc.*, 726 F. Supp. 2d at 359.

[12] *In re THP*, 756 F. Supp. 2d at 541.

[13] *See, e.g.*, *BMI Appeals DMX Rate-Court Decision*, BROADCAST MUSIC, INC. (Aug. 24, 2010), http://www.bmi.com/news/entry/549016.

I. HISTORICAL DEVELOPMENTS

DMX considers itself an "international leader" in multi-sensory branding that has been "creating unforgettable brand experiences for commercial environments" since 1971.[14] This branding includes providing music for clients to play in their places of business. DMX delivers music to customers by satellite transmission, disc, and electronically transmitted programming data.[15] DMX has licenses with both BMI and ASCAP.[16] DMX uses technology that allows it to accurately report music use and to directly license with publishers "representing a total of more than 7,000 catalogs."[17]

BMI and ASCAP are the two major PROs that license the public performance rights for most copyrighted music in the United States.[18] They "grant[] licenses to music users, collect[] license fees from them, and distribute[] the royalties among [their] affiliated copyright holders."[19] BMI was founded in 1939 as a not-for-profit organization representing the owners of copyrighted music to issue non-exclusive licenses to music users.[20] ASCAP was formed in 1914 as a means to enforce the copyrights for works performed for profit, which were too difficult for the individual copyright owners to manage.[21] The two organizations have come to dominate the field of music licensing, meaning that nearly anyone who wishes to play music in public has to contract with both.[22]

The U.S. government, concerned that this two-party control of music publishing could be anti-competitive, brought antitrust suits against each company in 1941.[23] To settle both suits, the court approved consent decrees[24] that allowed BMI and ASCAP to operate under regulations designed to limit the likelihood of the companies engaging in monopolistic behavior.[25] The government believed that the "rate court" mechanism would protect bulk music users from PROs' attempts to exert their market power in setting blanket licensing fees,[26] foster competition, and further the antitrust goals of the consent decrees.[27]

The consent decrees allow BMI and ASCAP to license music through non-exclusive blanket licenses, which the Supreme Court has held is not per se invalid under

---

[14] *About Us*, DMX, http://www.dmx.com/about (last visited Nov. 14, 2011).
[15] *BMI v. DMX*, 726 F. Supp. 2d at 364.
[16] *See In re THP*, 756 F. Supp. 2d. at 518, 541.
[17] *Id.* at 532.
[18] United States v. Broad. Music, Inc. (*Music Choice IV*), 426 F.3d 91, 93 (2d Cir. 2005).
[19] *In re* AEI Music Network, Inc., 275 F.3d 168, 171 (2d Cir. 2001).
[20] United States v. Broad. Music, Inc. (*Music Choice II*), 316 F.3d 189, 190 (2d Cir. 2003).
[21] United States v. Am. Soc'y of Composers, Authors & Publishers, No. 13-95 (WCC), 1993 WL 60687, at *3 (S.D.N.Y. Mar. 1, 1993).
[22] *See* William Sloan Coats et al., *Surfacing from the Depths: Submarine Issues in Copyright and Rights of Publicity Licensing*, *in* UNDERSTANDING THE INTELLECTUAL PROPERTY LICENSE 2008, at 195, 216–18 (PLI Patents, Copyrights, Trademarks, & Literary Prop., Course Handbook Ser. No. 950, 2008); *see also* Chris Bosman, *ASCAP, BMI, SESAC Hurting Musicians*, PREFIX (Nov. 19, 2009, 7:19 PM), http://www.prefixmag.com/news/ascap-bmi-sesac-hurting-musicians/34969/.
[23] *In re AEI*, 275 F.3d at 171–72.
[24] *Id.* at 172; *Music Choice IV*, 426 F.3d 91, 93 (2d Cir. 2005).
[25] *In re AEI*, 275 F.3d at 175.
[26] *Id.* at 176.
[27] *Id.* at 172–73.

antitrust law.[28]   BMI and ASCAP have traditionally conducted business using such blanket licenses, which allow licensors access to the PRO's entire catalog for a flat fee. ASCAP's consent decree, effective since 1950, provides that, in the event that ASCAP and its customers cannot agree on reasonable license fees, a court could determine the rate.[29] Since 1994, BMI has been subject to the same regulation.[30] The goal of the rate court is to identify a rate that two similarly situated parties, operating willingly, would agree on in an arm's-length transaction.[31] To determine the rate, the rate court identifies a benchmark—a previous deal reached between similarly situated parties—and then contemplates differences between the parties in the instant case and those in the benchmark deal.[32]

BMI's consent decree places various restrictions on the company. It requires BMI to make licenses of its music available to any applicant, affiliate, or broadcaster.[33] It prohibits BMI from discriminating between similarly situated licensees and bars BMI from preventing the writers or publishers of a musical work from licensing their work directly.[34] When BMI negotiated its agreements with CMSPs for blanket fees starting in 2004, seventy-five percent of the CMSPs had been operating for years without a blanket fee agreement.[35] This gave BMI bargaining power. The first agreement BMI negotiated in 2004 was with Muzak, one of DMX's fellow CMSPs. Muzak had not had a negotiated blanket fee agreement with BMI since 1994.[36] The agreement reached by BMI and Muzak accounted for the difference between the rates Muzak had been paying for the past decade and the rates BMI viewed as reasonable.[37] This difference came to between $4.5 and 5.5 million.[38] Instead of retroactively paying the difference, the parties simply made the future rates higher to make up for the past debt; the per-location rate had previously ranged between $14 and $15, but the 2004 agreement set each at $36.36.[39] This rate was understood to be a compromise between BMI and Muzak, but was not explicitly stated in the agreement.[40]

BMI then offered the same rate to the other members of the CMSP industry, including DMX.[41] BMI declared it was unwilling to negotiate the per-location rate of

---

[28] Broad. Music, Inc. v. Columbia Broad. Sys., Inc., 441 U.S. 1, 24 (1979); *see also* Buffalo Broad. Co. v. Am. Soc'y of Composers, Authors & Publishers, 744 F.2d 917, 918 (2d Cir. 1984) (finding that because there are feasible alternatives to blanket licenses, such as direct licensing, blanket licenses are not per se an unreasonable restraint on trade).

[29] *In re AEI*, 275 F.3d at 172.

[30] *Music Choice IV*, 426 F.3d 91, 93 (2d Cir. 2005).

[31] *See Music Choice II*, 316 F.3d 189, 194 (2d Cir. 2003).

[32] *See* Broad. Music, Inc. v. DMX, Inc., 726 F. Supp. 2d 355, 357 (S.D.N.Y. 2010).

[33] *In re AEI*, 275 F.3d at 171–72.

[34] *Id.* at 172.

[35] *BMI v. DMX*, 726 F. Supp. 2d at 359.

[36] *Id.* at 358.

[37] *Id.*

[38] *Id.* at 358–59.

[39] *Id.* The $36.36 rate was merely the $6 million annual fee Muzak had agreed to pay divided by the amount of locations Muzak had (165,000). The license also provided for increased annual fees in the event that Muzak experiences growth. *Id.*

[40] *Id.* at 358–59 ("In fact, the $36.36 per-location figure in the BMI/Muzak 2004–2009 license is no more than an arithmetical allocation of the $30 million flat fee, and as an economic matter must be understood as including a significant component for the $4.5 to $5.5 million 'retroactive' claim.").

[41] *Id.*

$36.36 because to do so would violate its consent decree's prohibition of discriminating between licensees similarly situated.[42]   In order to challenge the $36.36 rate, CMSPs would have to appeal to the rate court. However, if they did so, BMI could exert its reserved right to seek retroactive payments for the period in which they had operated without a blanket agreement.[43] The CMSPs could not realistically negotiate with BMI, and nearly all of them accepted the form agreement containing the $36.36 per-location rate set by Muzak's agreement.[44] In this way, BMI forced the rates for the entire CMSP industry up and inverted the purpose of the consent decree. Instead of protecting CMSPs from BMI's exerting its market force, the consent decree had become a restriction that forced the whole industry to pay the same increased rate.

In 2001, the Second Circuit decided in *United States v. Broadcast Music, Inc.* (*In re AEI Music Network, Inc.*) that BMI's consent decree required the company to issue an AFB license with a reasonable fee structure upon request.[45] The purpose was to "check, to some degree, the market power of the BMI rights holder collective" by "plac[ing] an upper limit on the price that BMI can charge for the blanket license" because direct licensing would act as a market-based constraint on BMI.[46] Despite this decision, and despite multiple requests for AFB licenses, BMI had not issued a single AFB license at the time that this case was decided.[47]

II. DMX's Direct Licensing

In 2005, after DMX had been purchased out of bankruptcy, the company found that the rates BMI and ASCAP were charging it were too high for the difficult economy and the competition in the CMSP industry.[48] New competitors had entered the marketplace, such as music consultants and streaming Internet-based services, which caused both DMX's fees and its revenues to decrease.[49] Because the fees DMX pays PROs constitute one of the company's largest costs of sale,[50] DMX attempted to license performance rights directly from copyright holders to control its costs.[51] It offered copyright holders an annual fee of $25 multiplied by the number of locations for which DMX provided music.[52] DMX believed that this rate was reasonable given the market.[53] By the time of

---

[42] *Id.*
[43] *Id.*
[44] *Id.*
[45] *In re* AEI Music Network, Inc., 275 F.3d 168, 177 (2d Cir. 2001) ("[W]hen an applicant . . . requests a blanket license with a fee structure that reflects such alternative licensing, BMI must advise the applicant of the fee it deems reasonable . . . . Failure to do so will empower the district court to set a reasonable fee.").
[46] Memorandum of the United States on Decree Construction Issues at 2, BMI v. DMX, 726 F. Supp. 2d 355 (S.D.N.Y. 2010) (No. 08 Civ. 216 (LLS)), *available at* http://www.justice.gov/atr/cases/f257700/257736.pdf.
[47] *Id.* at 1–2.
[48] *BMI v. DMX*, 726 F. Supp. 2d at 359.
[49] *In re* THP Capstar Acquisition Corp., 756 F. Supp. 2d 516, 527–28 (S.D.N.Y. 2010). DMX's rates declined by twenty-five percent from July 2008 to September 2010. *Id.* at 528.
[50] *Id.* at 528.
[51] *BMI v. DMX*, 726 F. Supp. 2d at 359.
[52] *Id.*
[53] *Id.*

the December 2010 trial, DMX had secured approximately 850 direct licenses covering over 7,000 catalogs, which accounts for thirty percent of the company's programming.[54]

For the direct licensing effort to pay off, DMX calculated that it needed to secure direct licenses with one or two of the four major music publishers.[55] DMX realized that this would be difficult, as the practice of blanket licensing was an agreement the music licensing industry was accustomed and dedicated to, and most of the major publishers sat on the board of ASCAP.[56] To overcome this obstacle, DMX decided to offer incentives: advances of fifty percent over what BMI and ASCAP had been paying the major music publishers for the music DMX played.[57]

This approach worked to secure a direct license with Sony/ATV Music Publishing, Inc. (Sony), one of the four major music publishers.[58] This agreement between DMX and Sony was an important factor in persuading other music publishers to enter into direct licenses with DMX.[59] DMX also attempted to secure a direct license with another major publisher, Universal Music Publishing Group (Universal).[60] Universal, however, informed BMI of the negotiations to leverage advances from BMI.[61] Universal accepted BMI's offer of a $1,875,000 guarantee for the years 2008–2010 and did not enter into a direct license agreement with DMX.[62]

III. *BMI v. DMX*

Because the court already declared in 2001 that BMI had to offer AFB licenses,[63] the issue in *BMI v. DMX* was not whether DMX is entitled to an AFB license, but what the basis is for the rate of such a license.[64] Even though DMX already succeeded in licensing directly with several music publishers, it had not yet agreed how the fees it owed to BMI would be determined. The two parties had very different ideas as to what constitutes a reasonable market rate to calculate the fees DMX owed.[65] It was, therefore, the court's duty, as declared in BMI's consent decree, to determine a reasonable rate. The court noted at the outset of its discussion of the issues that, under its consent decree, BMI bore the burden of proof in establishing the reasonableness of the fees it proposed.[66]

The parties agreed that DMX should owe BMI a per-location rate and that the AFB license should include three components: (1) a "blanket fee," the fee DMX would pay if it did not directly license any of BMI's music it performs; (2) a "floor fee," the lowest fee DMX could pay to BMI, even if it directly licensed all of BMI's music; and (3) a "direct license ratio," which determines the percentage of BMI songs that DMX played that it

---

[54] *In re THP*, 756 F. Supp. 2d at 528, 532.
[55] *BMI v. DMX*, 726 F. Supp. 2d at 360.
[56] *Id.*
[57] *Id.*
[58] *Id.*
[59] *Id.*
[60] *Id.*
[61] *Id.*
[62] *Id.*
[63] *In re* AEI Music Network, Inc., 275 F.3d 168, 171 (2d Cir. 2001).
[64] *BMI v. DMX*, 726 F. Supp. 2d at 355–56.
[65] *Id.* at 358, 362–63.
[66] *Id.* at 357.

directly licensed.[67] The parties disagreed, however, on what reasonable blanket and floor fees would be and how to calculate the direct license ratio.[68]

A. Blanket Fee

Each party proposed a different benchmark to establish the blanket fee.[69] BMI argued that the blanket license agreement reached with Muzak in 2004 is the most appropriate benchmark,[70] given DMX's other competitors accepted the same rate in their blanket licenses.[71] Therefore, since the goal of the rate court is to determine "the price that a willing buyer and a willing seller would agree to in an arm's length transaction,"[72] BMI argued that the price other CMSPs paid in their transactions with BMI represents the fair market value of the licenses. Therefore, BMI declared that the benchmark rate should be $36.36 annually per location. BMI also demanded to increase the annual per location rate by fifteen percent to compensate BMI for the additional cost it would incur and for the benefit DMX would gain under an AFB license instead of a blanket license.[73] DMX's blanket fee should thus, BMI argued, be $41.81 annually per location.[74]

The United States took the "unusual step" of submitting a memorandum on the issue of BMI's proposed blanket fee increase for the "option value" of the AFB license while the case was still active.[75] The memorandum declared that "[t]he United States believes that this proposed increased fee undermines the BMI Consent Decree. BMI's approach would deter users from engaging in direct licensing with rights holders—a critical component of the structures created under the decree."[76] The government further asserted that agreeing to BMI's proposed "option value premium" for the AFB license would subvert the consent decree as well as *In re AEI Music Network, Inc.* by making directly licensing performance rights economically impractical for BMI licensees.[77] The government clearly opposed the increased fee BMI advocated.

The court, examining the $41.81 blanket fee proposed by BMI, found that the competing CMSPs "had no realistic opportunity freely to negotiate the future fees for their licenses," and, therefore, that the $36.36 fee they agreed to did not really reflect fair market value.[78] Therefore, the blanket agreement between BMI and Muzak, as well as all the agreements reached pursuant to that agreement, were "not reliable benchmarks" to use in determining DMX's blanket fee.[79] Instead, the court found that DMX's proposal of using its direct licenses as a benchmark was appropriate because the 550 direct

---

[67] *Id.* at 355–56.

[68] *Id.* at 356, 364.

[69] *Id.* at 357.

[70] *Id.*

[71] *Id.*

[72] *Music Choice II*, 316 F.3d 189, 194 (2d Cir. 2003) (quoting Am. Soc'y of Composers, Authors & Publishers v. Showtime/The Movie Channel, Inc., 912 F.2d 563, 569 (2d Cir. 1990)) (internal quotation marks omitted).

[73] *BMI v. DMX*, 726 F. Supp. 2d at 357.

[74] *Id.*

[75] Memorandum of the United States on Decree Construction Issues, *supra* note 46, at 1.

[76] *Id.*

[77] *Id.* at 2.

[78] *BMI v. DMX*, 726 F. Supp. 2d at 359.

[79] *Id.*

licenses DMX acquired were "sufficiently representative of the performance rights BMI provides through its blanket licenses."[80] The court therefore found that $25 per location annually was an appropriate benchmark for the blanket fee,[81] and that the blanket fee should be $10.25 more than the floor fee.[82]

B. Floor Fee

¶24   As the court explained, "[t]he Floor Fee represents the value to DMX of the portion of the [AFB license] that is independent of the value of the music performing rights."[83] This fee remains constant, no matter how much of the BMI catalog that DMX has directly licensed.[84] In determining the floor fee, the court attempted to ensure that BMI would not lose money by administering an AFB license for DMX.[85]

¶25   Both BMI and DMX agreed that the floor fee should include the PRO's overhead costs.[86] The rate for the overhead costs was an issue of contention, however; BMI wanted to use its domestic rate of 17% and DMX wanted to use the 11.7% rate BMI had announced in a press release in 2008, which included international performances.[87] The court found that because this case involved domestic performances, and because BMI monitors and distributes the license fees for domestic performances, the higher rate was appropriate.[88] Thus, the court included 17% of BMI's $36.36 per-location rate, or $6.18, in the floor fee for overhead costs.[89]

¶26   The court agreed that DMX's AFB license would be more expensive for BMI to administer than a regular blanket fee.[90] The court undertook the duty to determine how much of those increased costs should be added to the floor fee. Despite DMX's objections that the increased costs were unproven, the court accepted BMI's estimates for the additional cost BMI would incur as a result of the AFB license.[91]

¶27   The district court divided the incremental costs into two groups: the one-time costs required to set up the AFB license and the regular costs associated with administering the AFB license.[92] The court ruled that DMX should be completely responsible for the latter

---

[80] *Id.* at 360.

[81] *Id.* at 361.

[82] In determining the appropriate blanket fee, the court ruled that ten percent of the incremental costs, or $0.25, should be included in the per-location blanket fee for the "return on investment in the incremental costs." *Id.* at 364. It also found that the $10 "music fee" DMX proposed should be included in the blanket fee. *Id.*

[83] *Id.* at 361. The value "includes the convenience of gaining access to the entire BMI repertoire in one license, the immediate right to access new BMI works, and protection against copyright infringement." *Id.* at 361–62.

[84] *Id.* at 355.

[85] *Id.* at 362–63.

[86] *Id.* at 362.

[87] *Id.* BMI applies this 17% overhead rate to each of its commercial music service industry licenses. *Id.*

[88] *Id.*

[89] *Id.* at 364.

[90] *Id.* at 362.

[91] Since BMI had not administered any AFB licenses at the time, the estimates submitted were sufficient because they expressed BMI's costs associated with administering per-program licenses in the television industry (which also involves direct licensing). *Id.*

[92] *Id.*

costs, but should only be responsible for its share of the former costs.[93] BMI calculated the costs associated with implementing systems to administer the AFB license to be $339,875.[94] But since other CMSPs are likely to use these systems in the future, the court found that "[c]harging all the initial costs to DMX would be unfair. Simply being the first licensee to take advantage of the [AFB license] . . . should not require DMX to bear all the developmental costs associated with it."[95] Instead, it found that the costs of developing the AFB license system should be spread over all the licensees who take advantage of the AFB license.[96] Since it is impossible to determine how much of the initial implementation costs will be attributable to DMX before they are incurred, the court found it reasonable for DMX to bear the percentage of the implementation costs that corresponded to its market share of CMSP locations.[97] The court calculated that this amounted to a $0.10 annual per-location fee for implementation costs.[98]

As stated above, the court declared that DMX should pay the routine costs necessary to administer its AFB license.[99] The court accepted the bulk of BMI's estimates of the routine expenses associated with administering the AFB license.[100] The court determined the routine costs to be $2.38 per location.[101] The floor fee that the rate court determined comprised $6.18 for overhead costs, $0.10 for implementation costs, and $2.38 for routine costs, for a total of $8.66.[102] The court set the blanket fee at $18.91, adding $10.25 to the floor fee.[103] This was significantly less than BMI's proposed blanket fee (which was $41.81), but more than DMX's proposed blanket fee (which was $11.32).[104]

IV. *In re THP*

There were two issues at play in *In re THP*: (1) whether ASCAP was required to grant DMX an AFB license, and (2) what constituted a reasonable rate structure for their agreement.

---

[93] *Id.* at 362–63.

[94] The initial incremental costs will be incurred by BMI's IT and Operations Departments. *Id.* at 363.

[95] *Id.*

[96] *Id.*

[97] *Id.*

[98] The court found that DMX's market share of CMSP locations was approximately 16.6%. *Id.* at 364. BMI estimates the initial costs at $339,875, arguing DMX should pay for $56,419.25 of the implementation costs (16.6% of $339,875). *Id.*

[99] *Id.* at 362.

[100] The court said that the $10,000 BMI claimed it would incur for travel would be used for industry conventions and publisher meetings, and should thus not be included. *Id.*

[101] *Id.* at 364. These costs will be incurred by BMI's Licensing, Performing Rights, IT, and Operations Departments. *Id.* at 362. BMI estimated that the Licensing and Performing Rights Departments would incur $151,000 in routine costs and the IT and Operations Departments would incur $37,073 in annual costs. *Id.*

[102] *Id.* at 364.

[103] *Id.*

[104] There was also a determination of the direct license ratio needed to calculate fees, but an examination of the disagreements surrounding that factor is not pertinent to this Note. *See id.* at 364–67.

DMX requested an AFB license from ASCAP at the same time it did so from BMI.[105] It proposed a rate structure nearly identical to that deemed reasonable and adopted by the court in *BMI v. DMX*.[106] DMX suggested the same benchmark Judge Stanton adopted in that former case.[107] Unlike BMI, however, ASCAP refused to suggest a reasonable fee for an AFB license.[108] It argued that an AFB license is not a reasonable fee structure "because no willing seller would ever offer such a license," and, therefore, ASCAP should not be required to offer it.[109]

Instead, ASCAP requested a blanket license that charged DMX a flat fee of $15,677,777 for June 2005 to December 2009 and $49 per location for January 2010 to December 2012.[110] The court found this unacceptable for several reasons. First, it found that a reasonable licensing fee would have to consider DMX's "well-developed direct licensing program"[111] and that an AFB license was not only appropriate, but also justified.[112] It also noted that DMX had shown that such a license would further the government's original goal in granting ASCAP a consent decree by adding competition to the marketplace.[113] Finally, the court found that the rates proposed by ASCAP were "far above any yet paid by a licensee" and unreasonable.[114]

The court deemed ASCAP's second proffered option, a blanket license with a static carve-out, to be unacceptable.[115] ASCAP proposed that DMX pay a flat fee of $3,420,606 per year for the period from June 2005 to December 2009, less direct licenses, plus $25,000 per year for "additional administrative expense[s]."[116] For January 2010 to December 2012, ASCAP proposed a $49 per location annual blanket rate with a $230,000 carve-out credit each year plus an administrative charge of $25,000 per year.[117] ASCAP derived the $49 rate, similar to BMI's proposal in *BMI v. DMX*, from an agreement with Muzak; as in the previous case, the court found that the Muzak agreement was "not a reliable benchmark."[118]

The court noted that the proposed shift from the 2005–2009 fee structure to the 2010–2012 fee structure was highly suspect. The switch coincided suspiciously with DMX's entry into an agreement with DirecTV to take over the satellite television company's music channels, which raised DMX's locations from 70,000 to 95,000.[119] The increase in locations would have brought the per-location rate below the flat fee per-location rate in 2010, meaning that ASCAP would not make as much money as it would if it charged per location. The court observed that "ASCAP simply abandons the flat fee

---

[105] *In re* THP Capstar Acquisition Corp., 756 F. Supp. 2d 516, 535 (S.D.N.Y. 2010).
[106] *Id.* at 536.
[107] *Id.*
[108] *Id.* at 539.
[109] *Id.* at 541.
[110] *Id.* at 539.
[111] *Id.* at 540.
[112] *Id.* at 541.
[113] *Id.*
[114] *Id.* at 539.
[115] *See id.* at 541–47.
[116] *Id.* at 541–42.
[117] *Id.*
[118] *Id.* at 543.
[119] *Id.* at 521, 543.

when it no longer benefits from it and proposes a different method of calculating an annual fee for this latter period."[120]

The court also found the proposal unreasonable because "it [did] not allow DMX to reduce its payments to ASCAP based on the proportion of directly licensed music that it performs."[121] If allowed, this would remove any incentive for DMX to enter direct licenses because any time DMX enters into a new direct licensing agreement it will be paying more in total licensing fees.[122] ASCAP's proposal would have forced DMX to either reduce the amount of music it directly licenses below the ASCAP-granted credit or not have an ASCAP blanket license at all.[123]

ASCAP also failed to provide evidence supporting the $25,000 annual administrative costs fee and, in fact, "did no formal analysis or study to arrive at th[at] figure."[124] The court found ASCAP's proposals "extraordinarily aggressive"[125] and "strongly anti-competitive."[126] Instead, the court opted to accept DMX's proposal, referring to *BMI v. DMX*: "[I]t is noteworthy that BMI did not contest that its licensing fee arrangement with DMX should be structured in a manner very similar to this. Also, Judge Stanton recently approved this structure in setting the blanket license fee that DMX owes to BMI."[127] The court noted that Judge Stanton's judgment on issues similar to those present in *BMI v. DMX* affirmed the reasonableness of DMX's proposal in *In re THP.*[128]

V. FUTURE EFFECTS

This section examines the effects these decisions may have. It discusses the potential positive and negative effects on current industry players, as well as the effects on outside industries, and the potential they create for new industries.

A. Negative Effects for Rights Holders

In a press release on its website, BMI announced that it had filed an appeal on behalf of its songwriters, composers, and music publishers.[129] The release asserts that the decision would cause BMI's copyright holders to lose "more than half of their income from DMX."[130] It characterizes the fees established by DMX's direct licenses as "deeply discounted," asserting that the market rate for both BMI and ASCAP before the decision was $77 per location.[131] BMI, a not-for-profit company, declares that more than eighty-

---

[120] *Id.* at 544.
[121] *Id.*
[122] *Id.*
[123] *Id.*
[124] *Id.* at 545.
[125] *Id.* at 539.
[126] *Id.* at 544.
[127] *Id.* at 548 (citing Broad. Music, Inc. v. DMX, Inc., 726 F. Supp. 2d 355, 367 (S.D.N.Y. 2010)).
[128] *Id.* at 552.
[129] *See, e.g., BMI Appeals DMX Rate-Court Decision, supra* note 13.
[130] *Id.* (internal quotation marks omitted).
[131] *Id.*

seven percent of all the fees paid to BMI go to the affiliated copyright owners.[132]   The overarching theme of the press release is that the decision reached in *BMI v. DMX* will result in rights holders receiving a fraction of what they previously received for the right to perform their works.   Some media outlets estimate that "the decision could cost BMI songwriters and publishers about $9 million per year, as well as $17 million in retroactive adjustments."[133]   ASCAP stated in its 2010 Annual Report that it is appealing the district court decision.[134]

B. Positive Effects for Rights Holders

Despite claims to the contrary, this decision may benefit rights holders. DMX's general counsel claims that direct licensing "presents an opportunity for [music] publishers—and the writers they represent—to receive greater royalties through DMX'[s] increased use of their musical compositions."[135]   Since DMX aims "to construct programs that rely heavily on music covered by its direct licenses," direct licensors are likely to experience increased royalties from DMX due to increased numbers of performances.[136]

DMX's general counsel also touts the direct licenses' transparency, which allows licensors to see exactly how many times DMX has performed any given song, as well as the resulting royalty payments.[137]   Many users have criticized PROs' lack of transparency because the PROs are unable to offer such an accurate representation of the exact number of times a song has been performed for purposes of royalty calculation. BMI describes its method for determining how frequently commercial radio plays affiliates' music as such:

> All licensed stations are requested to log performances for a three-day period each year, with different stations logging each day of the year. This sample is then factored to create a statistically reliable projection of all feature performances on all commercial music format radio stations throughout the country. In addition to the sample, BMI includes data provided by proprietary pattern-recognition technology, which identifies performances from any source containing audio, achieving extraordinary accuracy, even in high-noise environments, after detecting audio for as little as one to two seconds.[138]

---

[132] *Music Licensing General FAQs*, BROADCAST MUSIC, INC., http://www.bmi.com/licensing/faq (last visited Nov. 14, 2011) (follow "Q: What Happens to the Fees We Pay and How Much Profit Does BMI Make?" hyperlink).

[133] Christman, *supra* note 2, at 8.

[134] John A. LoFrumento, *You Can Count on ASCAP*, *in* AM. SOC'Y OF COMPOSERS, AUTHORS & PUBLISHERS, 2010 ANNUAL REPORT 4–5 (2011), *available at* http://www.ascap.com/about/annualReport/annual_2010.pdf.

[135] Jesse Greenspan, *DMX Wins 1st-of-a-Kind Blanket License from BMI*, LAW360 (July 28, 2010, 6:18 PM EST), http://www.law360.com/articles/183728 (second alteration in original) (internal quotation marks omitted).

[136] *In re* THP, 756 F. Supp. 2d 516, 528 (S.D.N.Y. 2010).

[137] Greenspan, *supra* note 135.

[138] *Royalty Policy Manual*, BROADCAST MUSIC, INC., http://www.bmi.com/creators/royalty_print/detail (last updated Nov. 11, 2011).

BMI then calculates a "unique royalty rate" for each work using the licensing fees collected from the radio stations that performed that work and the amount of times the work was performed on the stations.[139]   BMI calculates royalties for television performances using "a census of program information from music cue sheets and performance information provided to BMI by BMI television licensees, the TV Data Corporation, and other qualified sources."[140] The company calculates a "unique royalty rate" for television as well, "based upon the license fees available . . . in combination with the duration of the performance, the weighted royalty value for each usage type and television audience measurement data provided by Nielsen Media Research for each program aired on that network."[141] For sources that it does not monitor, BMI states that it may distribute the fees it collects "against performances from a source or sources where sufficient data is available."[142] BMI may add or remove a distribution source that was previously unmonitored "if the availability of accurate performance data changes."[143]

To keep track of licensed performances, ASCAP conducts a "census survey," counting performances in a medium, so long as "the cost of collecting and processing accurate performance information is a low enough percentage of the revenues generated by that medium."[144] ASCAP conducts census surveys of major television stations, general entertainment cable networks, live concerts, and CMSPs.[145] When the cost of a census survey is too great, ASCAP conducts a "sample survey designed to be a statistically accurate representation of performances in a medium."[146] Sample surveys are designed to account for "[a]ll times of the day, all days of the year, every region of the country and all types and sizes of stations."[147] ASCAP surveys in proportion to the amount of fees a licensee pays; the more a station pays ASCAP in licensing fees, the more (proportionately) it is sampled.[148] DMX, on the other hand, gives copyright holders counts of each time a given work was played.[149] With these direct counts, copyright holders can be certain they are receiving royalties for each and every performance of their work.

The payment schedule DMX offers is also preferable to that which BMI and ASCAP currently use for their blanket licensing. BMI distributes royalties to writers and publishers quarterly;[150] however, "BMI does not distribute payments to its affiliates for CMS industry performances until approximately seven to nine months after the

---

[139] Id.
[140] Id.
[141] Id.
[142] Id.
[143] Id.
[144] ASCAP Payment System: Keeping Track of Performances, AM. SOC'Y COMPOSERS, AUTHORS & PUBLISHERS, http://www.ascap.com/members/payment/keepingtrack.aspx (last visited Nov. 14, 2011) [hereinafter Keeping Track of Performances].
[145] ASCAP Payment System: The ASCAP Surveys, AM. SOC'Y COMPOSERS, AUTHORS & PUBLISHERS, http://www.ascap.com/members/payment/surveys.aspx (last visited Nov. 14, 2011).
[146] Keeping Track of Performances, supra note 144.
[147] Id.
[148] Id.
[149] Mark Northam, DMX Wins Major Direct Licensing Royalties Case; May Fundamentally Change Performance Royalty Landscape, FILM MUSIC MAG. (July 28, 2010), http://www.filmmusicmag.com/?p=5992.
[150] Royalty Policy Manual, supra note 138.

performance dates."[151]   ASCAP distributes royalty checks eight times a year.[152]   ASCAP
states that it has worked to quicken the process of domestic royalty payments so that
copyright holders receive royalty payments "approximately six months after a
performance quarter."[153]   In contrast, DMX accounts to publishers and writers for its
direct licensed works quarterly, forty-five days after the end of each quarter.[154]   It goes
without saying that copyright holders would prefer to receive royalties sooner rather than
later, and, thus, DMX's method is the preferred one for them.

C. Negative Effects on PROs and Positive Effects on CMSPs

These two recent decisions will definitely affect PROs such as BMI and ASCAP.
Understandably, PROs dislike these decisions because such decisions decrease the fees
PROs receive from CMSPs. The court's decisions also allow other CMSPs to seek AFB
licenses, which will further decrease the amount of fees BMI and ASCAP receive.

The amount a PRO makes under a finding such as Judge Stanton's is significantly
lower than that which it made from CMSPs previously. As discussed above, under
BMI's standard blanket license agreement, for instance, it would receive approximately
$36.36 per location from a CMSP.[155]   If BMI were to have its way in determining the
AFB license, it would have received $41.81 per location from DMX.[156]   Yet, in light of
Judge Stanton's decision, the most it will ever receive from DMX is $18.91 per location
(the blanket fee).[157]   So, theoretically, the most BMI can make now from DMX is fifty-
two percent of what it received previously. Given that DMX had already directly
licensed with approximately 5,500 rights holders at the time of the trial, the blanket fee is
certain to be reduced further, so BMI will not even recover fifty-two percent in
practice.[158]   Many CMSPs, observing this result, may seek AFB licenses without directly
licensing at all, as they will be able to spend approximately half of what they had
previously for PRO licenses without exerting any extra effort.

At the time of the trial, two other CMSPs had already requested an AFB license.[159]
Music industry specialists expect that many more CMSPs will request similar AFB
licenses from PROs.[160]   Other industries, such as local television and commercial
broadcast radio, have already requested AFB licenses as well.[161]

Based on the court's analysis of the agreements BMI entered into pursuant to the
2004 Muzak agreement, CMSPs who continue contracting with BMI using the traditional
blanket license may also look to negotiate for a lower annual per-location fee which more
accurately reflects fair market value.[162]   The court's decision in BMI v. DMX may

---

[151] Broad. Music, Inc. v. DMX, Inc., 726 F. Supp. 2d 355, 367 (S.D.N.Y. 2010).
[152] The ASCAP Advantage, AM. SOC'Y COMPOSERS, AUTHORS, & PUBLISHERS,
http://www.ascap.com/about/ascapadvantage.aspx (last visited Nov. 14, 2011).
[153] Id.
[154] Northam, supra note 149.
[155] BMI v. DMX, 726 F. Supp. 2d at 357.
[156] Id.
[157] Id. at 364, 367.
[158] Id. at 360.
[159] Id. at 363.
[160] Christman, supra note 2.
[161] BMI v. DMX, 726 F. Supp. 2d at 363.
[162] Id. at 355, 359.

encourage CMSPs to challenge the form licenses offered by BMI in rate court, whereas previously they had no realistic option but to accept the form agreement modeled on that entered into with Muzak.[163]

D. Positive Effects on PROs

Despite the negative effect these decisions may have on the fees PROs receive, these decisions may provide PROs some benefits. For instance, Trusonic, a small CMSP that also deals in direct licensing, refused to "pay ASCAP anything for locations that only play music within the ASCAP repertory that Trusonic has directly licensed from publishers, or that play no ASCAP music."[164] In light of these two decisions, which assert that PROs should at least receive a floor fee, Trusonic would not be able to simply refuse to pay ASCAP anything.

This idea of carve-out licensing "could potentially be applied to public performance areas beyond in-store play, such as terrestrial radio."[165] If radio stations were to directly license with copyright holders, they may opt to purchase the performance rights for hit songs they play frequently. This would decrease the performance fees CMSPs pay PROs, as those fees would be deducted from the blanket fee.

E. Effects on Radio and Songwriters

If radio stations were to begin direct licensing with copyright holders, it could have varying effects on songwriters. Radio stations might play the songs they directly license more frequently, hoping to reduce the fees owed to PROs, which could lead to decreased diversity in the songs played on radio stations. This would be particularly likely if radio stations directly licensed for artists' complete catalogs. One artist would likely be played repeatedly, leaving less airtime for artists who are not directly licensed. On the other hand, if lesser-known artists were willing to directly license performance rights to radio stations at discounted rates to gain entry into the radio market, that could promote new artists and add to the diversity of music played on radio stations.

F. New Industries

Other sub-industries may also evolve to service the needs of the burgeoning direct licensing system. For instance, DMX hired Music Reports, Inc. (MRI), a company which specializes in "high-volume music license administration," to help in the development of its direct licensing campaign.[166] MRI was founded in 1989 with the aim "to help radio and television broadcasters take advantage of the per-program license available under the PRO consent decrees."[167] MRI identified the publishers whose works were most often played by DMX and developed a generic direct license agreement that would help DMX avoid in-depth individual negotiations with publishers and to negotiate and administer

---

[163] Id. at 359.
[164] In re THP Capstar Acquisition Corp., 756 F. Supp. 2d 516, 527 (S.D.N.Y. 2010).
[165] Christman, supra note 2, at 8.
[166] In re THP, 756 F. Supp. 2d at 528.
[167] Id.

deals en masse.[168] These decisions will allow companies such as MRI to develop to meet the changing needs of CMSPs and others seeking AFB licenses.

VI. CONCLUSION

BMI vehemently opposes the decision reached by the court in *BMI v. DMX*, and has already filed an appeal with the Second Circuit.[169] The argument BMI has offered against the decision is that it "ignores the long history of [PRO] licensing agreements in the background music industry."[170] BMI argues that because PROs have traditionally contracted for performance rights for CMSPs using blanket licenses, it should always stay that way. The company is demanding deference due to the powerful position it has held in the CMS industry. However, that is exactly what the government has been trying to combat since 1941, when it filed antitrust suits against BMI and ASCAP.

In its memorandum on this case, the government stated that "[t]he United States supported blanket carve-out licenses in [*In re*] *AEI* because they check, to some degree, the market power of the BMI rights holder collective," creating a competitive constraint more realistic than the court's ratemaking power.[171] Allowing music users to directly license from copyright holders places a limit on how high a fee PROs can charge for their blanket licenses because "[i]f the [PRO] collective charged more for a blanket license than users would pay if they licensed directly, users would forego a blanket license from [the PRO]."[172] Thus, direct licensing creates a more competitive market.

BMI's attempt to combat CMSPs from opting for AFB licenses was to increase the blanket fee for AFB licenses.[173] The government worried that such an "option value premium" would work against BMI's Consent Decree and the decision in *In re AEI*, taking away constraints on the PRO's market power because "[t]he greater the 'option value premium,' the fewer licensees will find the carve-out license mandated by [*In re*] *AEI* to be economically viable."[174]

Both BMI and ASCAP took ethically questionable steps in attempting to thwart DMX's direct licensing campaign. The CEO of ASCAP, John LoFrumento, attempted to dissuade both Sony and Universal from entering into AFB licenses with DMX.[175] Sony signed with DMX, but Universal used DMX's offer as leverage to secure from BMI a nearly $2 million "guarantee" in royalty payments for agreeing not to directly license with DMX.[176] BMI also strong-armed some music publishers into refusing to renew their direct licenses with DMX. Only fourteen of seventy-eight publishers have refused to renew their direct licenses with DMX.[177] BMI contacted three of those fourteen who controlled significant catalogs, telling one publisher that "if it renewed its direct license agreement with DMX, BMI would force [the publisher] to repay BMI the payments BMI

---

[168] *Id.* at 529.

[169] *BMI Appeals DMX Rate-Court Decision*, *supra* note 13.

[170] Northam, *supra* note 149 (internal quotation marks omitted).

[171] Memorandum of the United States on Decree Construction Issues, *supra* note 46, at 2.

[172] *Id.*

[173] *Id.* at 1.

[174] *Id.* at 3.

[175] *In re* THP Capstar Acquisition Corp., 756 F. Supp. 2d 516, 535 (S.D.N.Y. 2010).

[176] Broad. Music, Inc. v. DMX, Inc., 726 F. Supp. 2d 355, 360 (S.D.N.Y. 2010).

[177] *In re THP*, 756 F. Supp. 2d at 533.

had made to it during the direct license period."[178] The extralegal actions taken by BMI to prevent direct licensing demonstrates both the fear that PROs have of the change in licensing and their acknowledgement that the law is not on their side on this issue.[179]

The *BMI v. DMX* and *In re THP* decisions further the government's goals of creating a competitive marketplace within CMS licensing and checking the market power of PROs like BMI and ASCAP. Creating a competitive market for CMS licensing will force PROs to compete for customers in a way they have not before experienced. This competition will force the PROs to lower their blanket fees and increase the transparency of their operations to make licensing an attractive option to customers.[180]

As unpopular as the decision may be with PROs, it is not improper. It is merely a shift away from the traditional method of blanket licensing, one that was set in motion when the government first instituted antitrust suits against BMI and ASCAP in 1941.

When the *BMI v. DMX* case goes to the Second Circuit on appeal, the court should find that the district court was correct in not granting BMI the $41.81 per-location rate it requested, which represented the per-location rate determined by Muzak's 2004 blanket fee negotiation plus fifteen percent for the "option value" of the AFB license.[181] As the blanket license fee is the result of a misuse of BMI's consent decree and the high option value premium would deter CMSPs from seeking AFB licenses, granting the blanket fee BMI seeks is impermissible. This is why the Second Circuit should uphold the bulk of the district court's decision. Though certain figures may need to be reconsidered, the heft of the decision is well founded and furthers the government's interests in combating anticompetitive behavior in music licensing.

---

[178] *Id.*

[179] *Id.* at 533–35.

[180] Peter Cronin, *DMX Wins Rate Court Lawsuit Against BMI*, MUSIC ROW (July 28, 2010), http://www.musicrow.com/2010/07/dmx-wins-rate-court-lawsuit-against-bmi/.

[181] Broad. Music, Inc. v. DMX, Inc., 726 F. Supp. 2d 355, 357 (S.D.N.Y. 2010).

Copyright 2012 by Northwestern University School of Law
Northwestern Journal of Technology and Intellectual Property

Volume 10, Number 3 (January 2012)

Correcting Bayh-Dole's Inefficiencies for the Taxpayer

By Michael Sweeney[*]

I. INTRODUCTION

By transferring ownership rights of federally funded inventions to non-government contractors and their subsequent licensees, the University and Small Business Patent Procedures Act of 1980[1] (Bayh-Dole Act) gives private actors unprecedented rights to intellectual property that was cultivated with public money. This Comment discusses how shifting ownership rights for federally funded inventions from public agencies to the private sector affects what the taxpaying public receives in return for its investment. It also pinpoints ways to improve returns where inefficiencies exist through income sharing, open-licensing regimes, and a national tech transfer office.[2]

II. THE BAYH-DOLE ACT: PURPOSE AND PROBLEMS

The United States government invests many billions of dollars almost every year in scientific research.[3] By most metrics, federal funding is the largest bulwark for the United States' advancements in technology, medicine, and other vital fields. In 2007, the government funded roughly twenty-seven percent of basic research in the United States.[4]

The Bayh-Dole Act, passed three decades ago, was intended to promote the utilization of inventions arising from federally funded research or development.[5] Prior to Bayh-Dole, ownership rights of federally funded inventions predominantly went to the federal agency funding the research (such as the National Institute of Health (NIH) or the National Science Foundation (NSF)). However, federal agencies often left patents undeveloped and did not disseminate researchers' findings.[6] To ameliorate the agencies'

---

[*] Many thanks to the tireless JTIP student editors. While I didn't always know who was providing the anonymous editorial comments, I do know they were greatly appreciated and helped immensely. Also, thank you to my constant inspirations: my parents, my three sisters, my girlfriend, and anyone else I'm lucky enough to call a close friend.

[1] University and Small Business Patent Procedures Act of 1980 (Bayh-Dole), 35 U.S.C. §§ 200–212 (2006).

[2] See discussion *infra* Parts V-A through V-C.

[3] Michael Yamaner, *Federal Funding of Basic and Applied Research Increases in FY 2009*, NAT'L CTR. FOR SCI. & ENG'G STATISTICS (Nat'l Sci. Found., Arlington, Va.), July 2011, *available at* http://www.nsf.gov/statistics/infbrief/nsf11324.pdf.

[4] *See* MARK BOROUSH, NAT'L SCI. FOUND., NATIONAL PATTERNS OF R&D RESOURCES: 2008 DATA UPDATE 28, tbl.6 (2010), *available at* http://www.nsf.gov/statistics/nsf10314/pdf/nsf10314.pdf.

[5] Patent and Trademark Amendments (Bayh-Dole Act), Pub. L. No. 96-517, 94 Stat. 3015 (1980) (codified as amended at 35 U.S.C. §§ 200–212).

[6] *See* Rebecca S. Eisenberg, *Public Research and Private Development: Patents and Technology Transfer in Government-Sponsored Research*, 82 VA. L. REV. 1663, 1664, 1702 (1996).

neglect, Bayh-Dole provides a uniform system allowing the recipients of federal research funding, such as universities, to take title to inventions created using federal funds. To facilitate the transfer of ownership to funding recipients, Bayh-Dole requires that the inventor assign any inventions made using federal funds to the organization with which the inventor is affiliated (predominantly universities). From there, that organization can grant exclusive or non-exclusive licenses for these inventions at its discretion. In the 1980s, President Reagan issued both an executive memorandum[7] and an executive order[8] that extended this allowance for the assignment of rights to include large businesses.

Overall, scholars generally agree that Bayh-Dole is a clear improvement over the prior set of complex and non-uniform agency rules, simply because it created a standardized system of determining intellectual property ownership for federally funded research. Universities have certainly had some technology-transfer successes. The number of technology transfer offices at universities—which are in charge of registering and licensing researchers' patents—has increased substantially, and the number of patents they have filed has gone up at an even faster rate.[9]

However, this increase in private patent protection for federally funded inventions has also had some drawbacks. Since its passage in 1980, there have been highly critical reviews of Bayh-Dole's problems, countered by staunch defenses from its advocates. The disputes have led to extensive legislative tinkering by public officials.[10]

This debate has brought to light evidence which shows that universities are not always responsible caretakers of their intellectual property. Judge Lorelei Ritchie de Larena of the Trademark Trial and Appeal Board—and former Intellectual Property Manager at the University of California, Los Angeles—pinpoints the most common university missteps: "They get embroiled in research scandals without proper faculty monitoring; they regularly underreport technology-transfer activities to their federal sponsors; and they tend to drop even windfall income into a bureaucratic black hole."[11] Large percentages of tech-transfer revenue are directed towards university administration and do not go back to the researchers or entrepreneurs who actually commercialize the invention.[12] These critiques are not localized to any one type of tech-transfer office; mismanagement occurs at both public and private universities. Proponents argue that the Bayh-Dole Act has led to economic growth, particularly in the biotechnology industry.[13]

---

[7] Memorandum on Government Patent Policy, 1 PUB. PAPERS 248 (Feb. 18, 1983).

[8] Exec. Order No. 12,591, 3 C.F.R. 220 (1988), *reprinted as amended in* 15 U.S.C. § 3710.

[9] *See* Richard R. Nelson, *Observations on the Post-Bayh-Dole Rise in University Patenting*, *in* INNOVATION POLICY IN THE KNOWLEDGE-BASED ECONOMY 165 (Maryann P. Feldman & Albert N. Link eds., 2001); *FAQs: Has There Been Growth in Academic Technology Transfer Programs*, ASS'N U. TECH. MANAGERS, http://www.autm.net/FAQs/2186.htm#4 (last visited Dec. 28, 2011).

[10] *See, e.g.*, National Technology Transfer and Advancement Act of 1995, Pub. L. No. 104-113, 110 Stat. 775 (1996) (codified as amended in scattered sections of 15 U.S.C.); Cooperative Research and Technology Enhancement (CREATE) Act of 2004, Pub. L. No. 108-453, 118 Stat. 3596 (amending 35 U.S.C. § 103(c) to address joint research agreements); Technology Transfer Commercialization Act of 2000, Pub. L. No. 106-404, 114 Stat. 1742 (amending the Stevenson-Wydler Technology Innovation Act of 1980 and the Bayh-Dole Act).

[11] Lorelei Ritchie de Larena, *The Price of Progress: Are Universities Adding to the Cost?*, 43 HOUS. L. REV. 1373, 1438 (2007).

[12] *Id.* at 1441.

[13] *See* Chester G. Moore, *Killing the Bayh-Dole Act's Golden Goose*, 8 TUL. J. TECH. & INTELL. PROP. 151, 155–57 (2006).

Critics counter that Bayh-Dole has negatively affected the practice and norms of science,[14] created "anticommons" problems, contributed to patent hold-ups,[15] and led to unnecessary increases in consumer prices.[16]

While university tech-transfer patent practices often line up with the intent of Bayh-Dole—helping to develop markets where federal agencies do not have the expertise or resources—these "contractors"[17] also often leave certain vital markets underserved, or completely neglected. Entire lines of inventions and products that could be of great use to taxpayers, such as green technologies,[18] are often owned by private players who may or may not find their development to be economically prudent. Meanwhile, many of the inventions that are developed are sold at a higher cost than they might have been if not for Bayh-Dole, when they would have automatically gone into the public domain.

This Comment does not intend to deride Bayh-Dole as a whole. It is readily apparent that the Act's underlying philosophy is sound. The point, rather, is to recognize where it has strayed from that philosophy and to help optimize its effectiveness going forward.

III. RIGHTS AND RESPONSIBILITIES UNDER BAYH-DOLE

A. Contractors' Rights and Responsibilities

Bayh-Dole applies to all research performed under a federal funding agreement, whether funded entirely or partially by the government.[19] The Act requires a written agreement between the federal agency and the contractor that contains the terms for the funding.[20] Under these terms, as stated above, Bayh-Dole allows recipients of federal research aid to choose to retain title to federally funded inventions. However, if exercising this option, the contractor must then abide by concomitant responsibilities. One responsibility is that funding recipients choosing to take title, including universities, are required to file a patent application in the United States and grant the government a "nonexclusive, nontransferable, irrevocable, paid-up license to practice . . . any subject invention throughout the world."[21] Bayh-Dole also requires that contractors take steps to commercialize any discoveries or inventions resulting from federally funded research, with the right to grant nonexclusive, partially exclusive, or exclusive licenses.[22] It further

---

[14] See Arti Kaur Rai, Regulating Scientific Research: Intellectual Property Rights and the Norms of Science, 94 NW. U. L. REV. 77, 109 (1999).

[15] These are both problems attributable to transaction costs: an anticommons occurs when too many intellectual property rights in basic research create obstacles for future research, and hold-ups occur when a patent holder impedes a product's development by demanding royalties.

[16] See Clifton Leaf, The Law of Unintended Consequences, FORTUNE, Sept. 19, 2005, available at http://money.cnn.com/magazines/fortune/fortune_archive/2005/09/19/8272884/index.htm.

[17] This term is used to refer to recipients of federal aid under Bayh-Dole.

[18] See generally Lisa Larrimore Ouellette, Comment, Addressing the Green Patent Global Deadlock Through Bayh-Dole Reform, 119 YALE L.J. 1727 (2010).

[19] See 35 U.S.C. § 201(b) (2006).

[20] See id. § 202.

[21] Id. § 202(c)(4); JENNIFER A. HENDERSON & JOHN J. SMITH, ACADEMIA, INDUSTRY, AND THE BAYH-DOLE ACT: AN IMPLIED DUTY TO COMMERCIALIZE 3 (2002), available at http://www.cimit.org/news/regulatory/coi_part3.pdf.

[22] See 35 U.S.C. § 202(c)(4); HENDERSON & SMITH, supra note 21, at 3.

demands that contractors preference United States industry for the manufacture of their inventions and favor small businesses for granting of exclusive licenses. Contractors are also required to report to the funding agency periodically, divide royalties or income generated from inventions with the inventors, and apply any undistributed income toward further research or educational ventures.[23]

B. Federal Agencies' Rights and Responsibilities

The Bayh-Dole Act, while giving contractors the option to elect rights to subject inventions, also grants the funding agencies significant rights. The Act grants federal agencies the power to "use rights [to the inventions] concurrently; [to] require or place restrictions on use by others; and [to], if provisions are not followed, actually require that title revert back to the government sponsor."[24]

1. March-in Rights

If the grantee does not adequately commercialize its federally funded inventions, Bayh-Dole includes provisions for the government to expropriate the invention. These provisions allow the funding agency to "march in" and assume ownership rights of intellectual property when certain parts of the Act have not been followed.[25] For example, if the contractor fails to "achieve practical application of the subject invention,"[26] the government may invoke the march-in right. Under the march-in provision, federal funding agencies can "require the contractor, an assignee or exclusive licensee" to grant a license, which can be either "nonexclusive, partially exclusive, or exclusive" and may be limited to a particular "field of use"[27] or the agency can grant the license itself.[28] To qualify and moderate these broad powers, the Act makes sure that any such compulsory license must be made "upon terms that are reasonable under the circumstances."[29]

2. Grant-back Rights

Funding agencies also maintain a grant-back of rights on every invention developed using federal research funds.[30] The grant-back secures government rights to "practice" the subject invention or have someone else practice the invention on the government's behalf. "The government's license under section 202(c)(4) does not provide the same ability to use the invention as the march-in authority. It is limited to practice 'for or on behalf of the United States,' whereas march-in authority is not so limited."[31]

---

[23] See 35 U.S.C. § 202; HENDERSON & SMITH, supra note 21, at 3.
[24] Ritchie de Larena, supra note 11, at 1391 (footnotes omitted); see also 35 U.S.C. §§ 202(c)(4), 203, 204.
[25] 35 U.S.C. § 203.
[26] Id. § 203(a)(1).
[27] Id. § 203(a).
[28] Id.
[29] Id.
[30] See id. § 202(c)(4).
[31] Barbara M. McGarey & Annette C. Levey, Patents, Products, and Public Health: An Analysis of the CellPro March-in Petition, 14 BERKELEY TECH. L.J. 1095, 1114 (1999).

IV. DRAWBACKS ASSOCIATED WITH PRIVATE RIGHTS TO FEDERALLY FUNDED INVENTIONS

For better or worse, Bayh-Dole has led to a re-balancing of rights. When universities and other private contractors underutilize or improperly apply their Bayh-Dole responsibilities, taxpayers are often left footing the bill or are deprived of a potentially vital new technology (or both). The costs are varied and not always monetary. This Part discusses some of the ways in which the taxpaying public is not receiving sufficient returns on their investment in basic research.

A. Double Taxation

Double taxation occurs when the government spends tax dollars to develop an invention and then spends additional tax dollars (in the form of royalties) to use the invention in subsequently funded research.[32] While some inventions that would otherwise have gone unused in the hands of federal agencies are now developed because of the Act, "other inventions that would have been developed anyway are now being developed under the auspices of the Act."[33] Because of this, "these latter inventions now carry a 'tax' in the form of a royalty that subsequent researchers must pay to the patent holder, and this royalty is then passed on to the ultimate consumer, the public."[34] Insofar as these inventions would have been commercialized without the incentives provided by Bayh-Dole, the Act requires that the public pay more for something it otherwise would have obtained without private intermediaries.[35] In Committee debates, preceding passage of the Act, Senator Russell Long belabored this point, asking,

> Is this bill providing a limitation on just how much the successful contractor can charge the public for what the public has already paid for?
>
> . . . .
>
> . . . . Is there any limitation in this proposal as to how much he could charge the public to have the benefit of what the public had already paid for when they paid for the research?[36]

Some acknowledge that before the Act the public was forced to pay once and received nothing, but disagree with Senator Long's position on the ground that at least now the public receives some benefit, in the form of commercial products, even though they pay twice.[37] Still, there are better alternatives, as discussed below.

---

[32] *See* Gary Pulsinelli, *Share and Share Alike: Increasing Access to Government-Funded Inventions Under the Bayh-Dole Act*, 7 MINN. J.L. SCI. & TECH. 393, 443 (2006).

[33] *Id.* at 395.

[34] *Id.*

[35] *Id.*

[36] *Patent Policy: Hearings on S. 1215 Before the Subcomm. on Sci., Tech., & Space of the S. Comm. on Commerce, Sci., & Transp.*, 96th Cong. 392 (1979) [hereinafter *Patent Policy Hearings*] (statement of Sen. Russell B. Long, Member, S. Comm. on Commerce, Sci., & Transp.).

[37] *See* Pulsinelli, *supra* note 32, at 443.

B. Anticommons

Under a theory of anticommons, a property may be underused if too many people have the right to exclude others from using it. In Bayh-Dole's tech transfer context, anticommons occur when too many patent rights are being awarded in certain fields to universities and other non-governmental entities, and these patents are interfering with the progress of research in these areas.[38]

In many ways the same problem that occurred before Bayh-Dole—underutilization of vital products—still occurs, only now the inventions are monopolized in private hands rather than disregarded by public agencies. According to Stanford Law Professor and intellectual property specialist Mark Lemley, "While in theory patents spur innovation, they can also interfere with it. Broad patents granted to initial inventors can lock up or retard improvements needed to take a new field from interesting lab results to commercial viability."[39] Developers increasingly pass over "follow-on" inventions[40] because universities locked up the foundational inventions.[41] These collections of over-patented technologies are known as "patent thickets."[42] Although the Act provides important incentives for getting many inventions developed, some inventions would have been developed even without the incentives of the Bayh-Dole Act and are now less available because of it.[43]

Universities have licensing practices particular to their needs that can often exacerbate anticommons.[44] For example, universities rarely cross-license, whereas manufacturing entities typically do. When two manufacturers cross-license with each other and one competitor sues the other manufacturer for infringement, the other manufacturer can often countersue. However, because universities are non-manufacturing entities, they do not trade their patents away for cross-licenses. Universities are not concerned with receiving licenses to other people's patent rights because they do not need to develop competing technologies. Therefore, technology developers interested in licensing from universities can only respond to a suit, with little ability to countersue.

Secondly, universities generally grant exclusive licenses over non-exclusive licenses.[45] Because exclusive licenses allow tech transfer offices to charge higher fees to licensees who want to have sole ownership rights to an invention, they generate higher revenue and enable universities to pay the costs of patent prosecution.[46] However, exclusive licenses also block competitors from developing the invention.

Finally, universities are increasingly enforcing their patents:

---

[38] See Michael A. Heller & Rebecca S. Eisenberg, *Can Patents Deter Innovation? The Anticommons in Biomedical Research*, 280 SCIENCE 698, 698 (1998).

[39] Mark A. Lemley, *Patenting Nanotechnology*, 58 STAN. L. REV. 601, 618–19 (2005) (footnote omitted).

[40] *Id.* at 627.

[41] Jacob H. Rooksby, *University Initiation of Patent Infringement Litigation*, 10 J. MARSHALL REV. INTELL. PROP. L. 623, 637 (2011).

[42] *See id.*

[43] *See* Arti K. Rai & Rebecca S. Eisenberg, *Bayh-Dole Reform and the Progress of Biomedicine*, 66 LAW & CONTEMP. PROBS. 289 (2003).

[44] *See id.*

[45] Lemley, *supra* note 39, at 626.

[46] However, there is debate as to whether exclusive licenses lead to higher *long-term* revenue. *See* Mark A. Lemley, *Are Universities Patent Trolls?*, 18 FORDHAM INTELL. PROP. MEDIA & ENT. L.J. 611, 617 (2008).

Recent years have seen high-profile cases litigated to judgment by the University of California, the University of Rochester, Harvard, MIT, Columbia, Stanford, and suits filed by many other universities. . . .

Universities, recognizing patent licensing and litigation as an important revenue source in the modern environment, have been active in politics . . . in opposing most of the effective pieces of draft patent reform legislation.[47]

In the end, these licensing practices lead to patent hold-ups, wherein "a patent-holder impedes [a product's] development by demanding royalties."[48] Although the purpose of patents *is* to give the patent-holder the right to impede others' use of the invention (i.e., a monopoly), this result seems questionable when taxpayers funded the invention and universities are left with the monopoly.

C. High Cost

One econometric analysis, using data on academic licensing revenues from 1998–2002, suggests that after subtracting the high costs of patent management, net revenues earned by U.S. universities from patent licensing were "on average, quite modest"[49] nearly three decades after Bayh-Dole took effect. Seeing this trend, some commentators have suggested that heavily patent-leaning "universities should form a more realistic perspective of the possible economic returns from patenting and licensing activities."[50]

Because of this high cost, only a handful of universities make substantial profits from their tech-transfer offices.[51] While this might suggest that the universities outside of these few that profit handsomely should be doing *more* patenting, trying to squeeze as many inventions out of their intellectual property portfolios as possible, it is just as likely a sign that they are *over*-patenting, spending significant time and resources managing patents that do not generate enough revenue to cover their overhead.

D. Under-reporting

Under § 202 of Bayh-Dole, the funding recipient must comply with various disclosure and reporting requirements to retain rights to the invention, including reporting the existence of the invention to the government agency[52] and keeping the agency apprised of progress toward patenting and utilizing the invention.[53]

---

[47] *Id.* at 618.
[48] Lisa Larrimore Ouellette, Note, *How Many Patents Does It Take to Make a Drug? Follow-on Pharmaceutical Patents and University Licensing*, 17 MICH. TELECOMM. & TECH. L. REV. 299, 308 n.58 (2010).
[49] Harun Bulut & GianCarlo Moschini, *U.S. Universities' Net Returns from Patenting and Licensing: A Quantile Regression Analysis* 13 (Ctr. for Agric. & Rural Dev., Iowa State Univ., Working Paper No. 06-WP 432, 2006), *available at* http://www.card.iastate.edu/publications/DBS/PDFFiles/06wp432.pdf.
[50] *Id.* at 14; *see also* Anthony D. So et al., *Is Bayh-Dole Good for Developing Countries? Lessons from the US Experience*, 6 PUB. LIBR. SCI. BIOLOGY 2078, 2079 (2008).
[51] Bulut & Moschini, *supra* note 49, at 2.
[52] 35 U.S.C. § 202(c)(1) (2006).
[53] *Id.* § 202(c)(5).

In reality, many recipients of federal funding do not abide by these reporting requirements.[54] While the U.S. Department of Commerce is in charge of policing tech-transfer activity, sanctions for failing to report inventions lack clarity, and their enforceability is difficult.[55] The U.S. Government Accountability Office (GAO) has concluded that, under the current structure, it is not logistically possible to decipher whether universities are fulfilling their obligations under the Act and that government agencies must rely on universities to report their findings, since there are no established enforcement mechanisms.[56]

It is, therefore, up to each university to let the federal government know whether they are fulfilling their duty to commercialize. So far, they have failed to do so adequately. Under Bayh-Dole, the U.S. Patent and Trademark Office "should have two independent records of the government's rights to a federally sponsored invention—the government interest statement on the patent and the confirmatory license recorded in the Government Register."[57] According to the GAO's findings, research contractors complied with both reporting requirements *only six percent* of the time.[58]

The importance of reporting compliance should not be understated. When research institutions do not disclose their federally funded inventions, it is impossible for the respective agencies to utilize grant-back or march-in rights on taxpayers' behalf.[59] As stated above, a grant-back allows government researchers to freely utilize federally funded inventions without paying for licenses. However, without access to or knowledge of which university inventions federal agencies should have rights to, a grant-back is toothless.

E. Conflicts of Interest

Since Bayh-Dole heavily incentivized academic ties between federally funded researchers and private industry, "academic commercialism" has been much more prevalent in higher learning. Professors and other researchers commonly have financial incentives interwoven with their purely academic pursuits.[60] Because of this trend, there

---

[54] *See* U.S. GOV'T ACCOUNTABILITY OFFICE, GAO-99-242, TECHNOLOGY TRANSFER: REPORTING REQUIREMENTS FOR FEDERALLY SPONSORED INVENTIONS NEED REVISION 14 (1999) [hereinafter REPORTING REQUIREMENTS], *available at* http://www.gao.gov/archive/1999/rc99242.pdf.

[55] Scott D. Locke, Esq., *Patent Litigation over Federally Funded Inventions and the Consequences of Failing to Comply with Bayh-Dole*, 8 VA. J.L. & TECH. 3, 5, 27 (2003).

[56] *See* U.S. GOV'T ACCOUNTABILITY OFFICE, GAO-98-126, TECHNOLOGY TRANSFER: ADMINISTRATION OF THE BAYH-DOLE ACT BY RESEARCH UNIVERSITIES 5 tbl.1, 16 (1998), *available at* http://www.gao.gov/archive/1998/rc98126.pdf.

[57] *See* REPORTING REQUIREMENTS, *supra* note 54, at 6.

[58] *See id.*

[59] Ritchie de Larena, *supra* note 11, at 1398 ("While underreporting may seem relatively innocuous, and merely due to benign neglect, it means that federal taxpayers are not even getting basic governmental access to many of the inventions they fund.").

[60] JENNIFER WASHBURN, CTR. FOR AM. PROGRESS, BIG OIL GOES TO COLLEGE: AN ANALYSIS OF 10 RESEARCH COLLABORATION CONTRACTS BETWEEN LEADING ENERGY COMPANIES AND MAJOR U.S. UNIVERSITIES 12, 36 (2010), *available at* http://www.americanprogress.org/issues/2010/10/pdf/big_oil_Jf.pdf ("Today it is common for both U.S. universities and their professors to have direct financial interests in their own campus-based research (through patents, licenses, equity stakes in new companies, and royalty agreements). Many individual

are concerns that the ethos of academic institutions may be shifting, depriving students and the public of the objective, independent research usually expected in a university environment.

This increased commercialism is often paradoxically in unison with some parts of Bayh-Dole, while being in direct conflict with other provisions. For example, the Act directly promotes partnerships between academia and industry, but, as stated above, it also requires recipients of federal aid to "favor U.S. industry for the manufacture of inventions, and small businesses for the granting of exclusive licenses."[61] Yet, despite this requirement, many universities have increasingly shown a desire to partner with large, foreign corporations for research grants.[62] These partnerships, which are often intermingled with federally funded grant projects, raise questions about who should own the resulting invention—the university or the corporation. If the parties agree to give full ownership to the corporations, then they are directly violating the Act's provisions favoring "small businesses" and "U.S. industry."

The largest (and possibly most contentious) deal of this kind is British Petroleum's (BP) $500 million renewable energy research initiative.[63] The initiative partners two of the largest and most venerable public research institutions, UC Berkeley and the University of Illinois, with an oil conglomerate, BP. Deals like these between academia and large profit-driven corporations, while not specifically encouraged by Bayh-Dole, are much more common since its passage and raise a great deal of ire amongst research traditionalists. BP's recent oil spill has made the project's goals even more opaque and added an even higher level of public scrutiny.[64]

V. CASE STUDY: THE PHARMACEUTICAL INDUSTRY

A real-life example may best illustrate some of the drawbacks to Bayh-Dole stated in Part IV. In 1990, Mary-Claire King, a cancer expert at UC Berkeley, published research stating that there was a "breast cancer susceptibility gene" on Chromosome 17.[65] A number of research groups simultaneously began sifting through more than thirty million base pairs of nucleotides, trying to help locate the exact location of this gene.[66] In the spring of 1994, a team led by Mark Skolnick at the University of Utah was able to identify the gene's exact location—marginally beating out its competitors—finding a gene with 5,592 base pairs and codes for a protein that was 1,900 amino acids long.[67]

---

professors also have extensive personal financial ties to companies that sponsor their own academic research . . . .").

[61] HENDERSON & SMITH, *supra* note 21, at 3.

[62] *See generally* WASHBURN, *supra* note 60, at 31.

[63] *See* Robert Sanders, *BP Selects UC Berkeley to Lead $500 Million Energy Research Consortium with Partners Lawrence Berkeley National Lab, University of Illinois*, UC BERKELEY NEWS (Feb. 1, 2007), http://berkeley.edu/news/media/releases/2007/02/01_ebi.shtml.

[64] Terence Chea, *UC Berkeley's BP Deal Tainted by Oil Spill: $500 Million Research Agreement at Stake*, HUFFINGTON POST (July 31, 2010, 3:27 PM), http://www.huffingtonpost.com/2010/07/31/uc-berkeleys-bp-deal-tain_n_666355.html.

[65] Leaf, *supra* note 16.

[66] *Id.*

[67] *Id.*

Skolnick's team immediately filed a patent application and obtained sole title to the discovery in 1997.

The science leading to Skolnick's discovery was very much a collective effort. There is evidence that the "NIH had funded scores of investigative teams around the country and given nearly 1,200 separate research grants to learn everything there was to learn about the genetics of breast cancer."[68] Yet, after Skolnick's team received the patent, they refused to license the necessary technology to other cancer treatment companies and insisted on doing all U.S. testing for the presence of mutations in the gene, even though patients with the mutation have as high as an eighty-six percent chance of getting cancer.[69] They maintained their screening price at $2,975 for the analysis.[70]

This type of restrictive licensing occurs regularly, despite the fact that many of the companies reaping the profits are highly dependent on research performed by government-funded scientists. The end result is vastly higher drug prices and health insurance. In 2003, Americans spent $179 billion on prescription drugs, up from $12 billion in 1980.[71] This amounts to a thirteen percent increase *each year* for two decades. These costs apply to individuals not only as patients, but also as taxpayers, because "[t]he U.S. government picks up the tab for [the healthcare of] one in three Americans by way of Medicare, Medicaid, the military, and other programs."[72]

American pharmaceuticals have profited greatly from the government benefits provided under Bayh-Dole.   Coupled with their preferential tax treatment, pharmaceuticals are receiving double doses of federal aid. One analysis concluded "that pharmaceutical makers have one of the lowest effective tax rates and one of the highest after-tax profit rates of any industry."[73]

Meanwhile, the American public has received poor returns on their direct financial investments in health care research and development:

> Indeed, in the years 1985 through 1994, NIH received slightly less than $76 million in royalties, $40 million of which came from a single license for the HIV antibody test kit. From 1993 through 1999, royalties reached a total of nearly $200 million, reaching $45 million in 1999. But that figure still represents less than one percent of NIH's funding for 1999.[74]

Yet, for some reason, despite these skyrocketing costs and poor returns on investment, government agencies refuse to exercise their royalty-free use rights for federally funded inventions.

---

[68] *Id.*
[69] *Id.*
[70] *Id.*
[71] *Id.*
[72] *Id.*
[73] David Halperin, *The Bayh-Dole Act and March-In Rights*, OFF. TRANSFER TECH. 10 (Mar. 2001), http://www.ott.nih.gov/policy/meeting/David-Halperin-Attorney-Counselor.pdf.
[74] *Id.*

VI. STRATEGIES FOR GETTING THE TAXPAYERS A BETTER RETURN ON THEIR INVESTMENT

A. Alternative (but Unworkable) Proposals

A number of different proposals have attempted to counteract the increasingly private monopolization of scientific findings funded by public money. Some have argued for expanding copyright's fair use doctrine to patent law.[75] Others have argued for the expansion of the experimental use exception (particularly in the wake of *Madey v. Duke*[76]). A few have argued for prohibiting certain upstream patents or for ex ante, "reach-through" compulsory licenses to counteract patent thickets.[77] This debate is particularly acute today in relation to the patentability of genes.[78] Another proposal suggests that Congress should amend Bayh-Dole to "t[ie] socially responsible licensing practices to federal research grants," especially for the dissemination of green technologies in developing nations.[79] One more proposal, by Rochelle Dreyfuss, suggests a system in which non-profit researchers can use any patented technology if they sign a waiver requiring their "institution to promptly publish the results of work conducted with the patented technology and to refrain from patenting discoveries made in the course of that work."[80]

However, while these proposals may each have merit in certain contexts, they are all over- or under-inclusive in addressing the inequalities created by Bayh-Dole. Take, for example, Dreyfuss's proposal. While it recognizes the significant difference between public and private sector science and counteracting the special treatment universities receive as non-profits, the proposal would likely meet heavy industry resistance and create disincentives for firms wanting to develop vital technologies.[81]

B. Optimal Solutions

The ensuing discussion combines three preferred strategies for recovering research costs for the taxpayer. These proposals are specifically tailored to Bayh-Dole and are more viable than the alternatives discussed above.

---

[75] *See* Maureen A. O'Rourke, *Toward a Doctrine of Fair Use in Patent Law*, 100 COLUM. L. REV. 1177, 1198–1211 (2000).

[76] Madey v. Duke Univ., 307 F.3d 1351 (Fed. Cir. 2002).

[77] *See* Richard Li-dar Wang, *Biomedical Upstream Patenting and Scientific Research: The Case for Compulsory Licenses Bearing Reach-Through Royalties*, 10 YALE J.L. & TECH. 251 (2008).

[78] *See* Ass'n for Molecular Pathology v. United States Patent & Trademark Office, 702 F. Supp. 2d 181, 232 (S.D.N.Y. 2010); *see also* Andrew Pollack, *In a Policy Reversal, U.S. Says Genes Should Not Be Eligible for Patenting*, N.Y. TIMES, Oct. 30, 2010, at B1.

[79] Ouellette, *supra* note 18, at 1735.

[80] Rochelle Dreyfuss, *Protecting the Public Domain of Science: Has the Time for an Experimental Use Defense Arrived?*, 46 ARIZ. L. REV. 457, 471 (2004).

[81] Aaron Miller, *Repairing the Bayh-Dole Act: A Proposal for Restoring Non-Profit Access to University Science*, 2005 B.C. INTELL. PROP. & TECH. F. 093001, http://www.bc.edu/bc_org/avp/law/st_org/iptf/articles/content/2005093001.html.

1. Universities Share a Percentage of Federally Funded Licensing Income with Their
    Federal Sponsors

Universities that make "windfall" profits with the help of federal aid should be required to pay some of that revenue back to their sponsoring agency. This practice existed prior to Bayh-Dole and still exists in some forms today.[82] For example, as recently amended in the new Leahy-Smith America Invents Act, "Government-owned-contractor-operated facilities" are expected to pay 15% of any excess in profits over 5% of their annual budget back to the Treasury.[83] However, the provisions in Section 202(c)(7) currently do not apply to universities.[84] Moreover, section 204 of the original Bayh-Dole bill allowed the government to recoup part or all of its investment in research and development after the invention generated specified amounts of profit.[85] Senator Thurmond, an original sponsor of the bill, considered this provision "[p]erhaps the most significant feature of th[e] bill."[86] Although this provision does not appear in the final version of the bill, it was in the Senate-passed version and is directly in concert with much of the Act's overall intent.

Further legislative testimony directly "link[s] the invocation of march-in rights to the existence of 'windfall profits' on a subject invention."[87] The U.S. Comptroller General at the time, in a written response to the Senate, relayed that the Department of Energy "said that march-in rights to protect the public's interest were developed to take care of and address the patent policy issues of *contractor windfall profits*, suppression from granting contractors rights to inventions."[88] Former General Patent Counsel for General Electric testified as to march-in rights, "We think it is part of the answer to the so-called windfall situation."[89]

Except for approximately ten tech-transfer hotbeds,[90] most universities do not generate enough tech-transfer income to be significantly burdened by a larger "windfall sharing" requirement. Further, the most profitable universities that would be taxed the most heavily are also the ones with the largest endowments[91]—endowments fueled, in

---

[82] *See* Peter S. Arno & Michael H. Davis, *Why Don't We Enforce Existing Drug Price Controls? The Unrecognized and Unenforced Reasonable Pricing Requirements Imposed upon Patents Deriving in Whole or in Part from Federally Funded Research*, 75 TUL. L. REV. 631, 663 (2001).

[83] Leahy-Smith America Invents Act, Pub. L. 112-29, § 13, 125 Stat. 327, (2011) (amending 35 U.S.C. § 207(c)(7)(E)(i)).

[84] Ritchie de Larena, *supra* note 11, at 1388.

[85] *See* S. REP. NO. 96-480, at 34 (1979).

[86] *The University and Small Business Patent Procedures Act: Hearings on S. 414 Before the S. Comm. on the Judiciary*, 96th Cong. 34 (1979) [hereinafter *University and Small Business Patent Hearings*] (statement of Sen. Strom Thurmond, Member, S. Comm. on the Judiciary).

[87] Halperin, *supra* note 73, at 7.

[88] *University and Small Business Patent Hearings*, *supra* note 86, at 56 (statement of Elmer B. Staats, Comptroller Gen. of the United States) (emphasis added).

[89] *Patent Policy Hearings*, *supra* note 36, at 317 (statement of Harry F. Manbeck, Jr., General Patent Counsel, General Electric Co.).

[90] Leaf, *supra* note 16.

[91] NAT'L ASS'N OF COLL. & UNIV. BUSINESS OFFICERS, U.S. AND CANADIAN INSTITUTIONS LISTED BY FISCAL YEAR 2009 ENDOWMENT MARKET VALUE AND PERCENTAGE CHANGE IN ENDOWMENT MARKET VALUE FROM FY 2008 TO FY 2009 (2010), *available at* http://www.nacubo.org/Documents/research/2009_NCSE_Public_Tables_Endowment_Market_Values.pdf.

part, by licensing revenues from their tech-transfer activities.[92]   Although it is true that they would be taxed the most heavily because of their relative success, there should be little concern about their ability to withstand giving back some of the profits generated off the public dole.

2.   Researchers Supported by Federal Funds Should Have Licenses to Make and Use for Research Purposes All Inventions Developed with Federal Funds

This proposal, first suggested by Professor Gary Pulsinelli,[93] essentially embodies and animates the grant-back rights in Bayh-Dole's § 202(c)(4).   Regardless of commercial licensing status, government contractors should utilize the access Bayh-Dole gives them to every publicly funded invention for undertaking government research or procurement. This would help to "realiz[e] the government's Bayh-Dole grant-back to its fullest potential."[94]

This grant-back proposal could be used to benefit the public in three important ways.[95] First, government scientists could use the license to conduct research without the need for a paid license.[96]   Second, other government contractors, such as university recipients of federal funds, could use the license in follow-on research, or even independent research, where rights to an underlying invention might be particularly useful.[97] Third, the government could use the grant-back to procure inventions on its behalf.   For example, it could receive less expensive versions of pharmaceuticals administered through the Medicare or Department of Veterans Affairs programs.[98]

Another positive effect of this proposal is that under-reporting of inventions by tech-transfer offices would be less of a concern. Rather than waiting for universities to report their findings and monitor the by-products of their efforts, the impetus would fall on universities to *stop* government researchers from using their inventions. There would be a presumption in favor of government workers using any university inventions to which they can get access.   Further, it would cut back on the "double-taxation" phenomenon—when government agencies fund an invention and then pay for the rights to use that invention in subsequent research, as discussed above. If government funded researchers had a royalty-free license to use all government-developed technology for research purposes, then this "tax" would be substantially eliminated.

3.   Underutilized Patents Should Be Placed in the Public Domain and a National Technology Transfer Office Should Monitor Their Usage To Facilitate Partnerships

Anticommons are the result of over-patenting, where private actors have rights beyond their needs. Therefore, the best way to counteract the deleterious effects of

---

[92] Press Release, U.S. Patent & Trademark Office, USPTO Releases List of Top 10 Universities Receiving Most Patents in 2005 (Apr. 6, 2006), http://www.uspto.gov/news/pr/2006/06-24.jsp.
[93] Pulsinelli, *supra* note 32, at 442.
[94] Ritchie de Larena, *supra* note 11, at 1443.
[95] *Id.* at 1395.
[96] *Id.*
[97] *Id.*
[98] *Id.*

under-used, privatized patent pools would be to place those patents that are not being commercialized into the public domain.

Judge Ritchie de Larena wrote one of the seminal articles illustrating this plan.[99] In § 202(c)(5), the Act already gives federal agencies the right to require "periodic reporting on the utilization or efforts at obtaining utilization that are being made by the contractor or his licensees or assignees."[100] This reporting requirement implies that contractors must take necessary steps to commercialize any discoveries or inventions resulting from federally funded research. Failure to do so should result in cession of the patent over to public use. This should not adversely affect the patent owners in the long run, because if the patent has true potential, the private owner will certainly take steps to cultivate it, and, if it does not, the private owner should not mind that it is being ceded to public use.

Although it initially will cause tech-transfer offices to lose some sunk costs for those patents that they have already spent money procuring, they should quickly develop ways to tell if a patent is marketable and, if not, leave their findings open to royalty-free licensing. This could look something like a creative commons license,[101] wherein credit for the initial discoveries would still go to the researchers and institutions that made the breakthrough, but others could simultaneously use and develop the information free of charge.

In conjunction with the placement of underused patents in the public domain, a national technology transfer office should be established to act as a clearinghouse for parties that may be interested in developing them. As such, the national office could facilitate joint partnerships between research institutions looking to commingle their patent pools. Where many patents for minor inventions are relatively useless in the hands of one institution, many pools of minor inventions could become quite valuable if coalesced and opened up to every type of government researcher.

The U.S. GAO is in charge of monitoring Bayh-Dole implementation and determining when to allow the government to assert ownership control over federally funded inventions.[102] Because the GAO already monitors and periodically reports on the Act's implementation, maintaining a database of underutilized, federally funded inventions should be entirely within its purview.

If not administered by the GAO, then a national, independent tech-transfer office could also lend increased accountability and monitoring of existing patent portfolios, acting as a watch dog to ensure that universities are fulfilling their contractual Bayh-Dole responsibilities. For example, an independent, national tech-transfer office could monitor incoming revenue from university licensing deals to make sure it is funneled back into research, as required under § 202(c)(7). This could also help combat many of the conflicts of interest that currently exist by preventing revenue from improperly going back to the university's administration, endowment, or partnered corporations. A

---

[99] *Id.* at 1437–44.
[100] 35 U.S.C. § 202(c)(5) (2006).
[101] *See About the Licenses,* CREATIVE COMMONS, http://creativecommons.org/licenses/ (last visited Dec. 28, 2011).
[102] U.S GOV'T ACCOUNTABILITY OFFICE, GAO-09-742, FEDERAL RESEARCH: INFORMATION ON THE GOVERNMENT'S RIGHT TO ASSERT OWNERSHIP CONTROL OVER FEDERALLY FUNDED INVENTIONS 1 (2009), *available at* http://www.ott.nih.gov/PDFs/GAOreportTT.pdf.

national tech-transfer office could also open the door to more extensive use of march-in rights.

VII.   COUNTER ARGUMENTS

A. Fifth Amendment Takings

Patent owners might counter that invoking the grant-back or "march-in" provisions and seizing a patent on behalf of the public would constitute an unjust taking under the Fifth Amendment.[103]   The owners might argue that their research added value after receiving federal funds, and, by putting in the necessary work, they should receive full rights to the inventions. However, the counter to this is that Bayh-Dole firmly establishes both march-in and grant-back rights, and, because patent owners are bound to the Act's provisions by virtue of their willful contractual agreement, they essentially concede that the Fifth Amendment should not apply.

B. Deference to the Private Sector

Another critique of these proposals is that once the government disburses funds, development should be left to the private sector; allowing government researchers and the public free access to inventions disincentivizes private research and development investments. However, that too is an unfounded concern.

First of all, the vast majority of funding recipients are universities or research institutions whose fundamental priorities should not be enhancing their patent pool, but advancing their respective fields of endeavor. With or without endless patent portfolios, universities will perform research. They did so before Bayh-Dole was enacted, and they have continued to do so. Invoking march-in and other provisions of the Act for the public benefit likely will not change that.

Second, as stated above, many tech-transfer offices do not garner huge returns for their universities. Patent management nowadays—in contrast to the practice prior to Bayh-Dole, when most discoveries passed into the public domain—is very much a "lottery" based system: "[e]ven though most university inventions are never picked up by a licensee, and even fewer generate big income, there is the constant 'lottery' effect whereby technology-transfer offices take a risk in paying patent expenses on what they hope will be the big winner."[104]   Therefore, the vast majority of patents are applied for in the hopes that they will "win" big. However, it should be relatively clear within a short period of time that an invention will not be the big winner every tech-transfer office hopes for. By extracting those patents and turning them over to the public, tech-transfer revenues will likely suffer little to no effect, and the offices may learn to better utilize scarce funds to only apply for patents on those inventions they truly *know* are valuable.

Finally, the two proposals stated in Part VI do not take away the big "winners" in tech-transfer. The first proposal simply grants government researchers or their affiliates

---

[103] *See* U.S. CONST. amend. V.
[104] Ritchie de Larena, *supra* note 11, at 1381–82 (footnotes omitted); *see also* Gideon Parchomovsky & R. Polk Wagner, *Patent Portfolios*, 154 U. PA. L. REV. 1, 24 (2005).

the right to *use* an invention, not take it away, and the second proposal would only affect the "loser" patents, those that are left undeveloped.

C. Tech-Transfer Offices Actually Save Taxpayers Money

Some argue that revenue from university-owned patents often goes toward funding more research, reducing the need for government funding and thereby funding research by taxing those using the technology, rather than the population in general.

For one, the truth of this argument is debatable. While it is true that greater revenue from tech-transfer could be used to fund more research and decrease the need for taxpayer money, there is little evidence this actually occurs in practice. A large percentage of the indirect costs and Bayh-Dole income "go[es] into a black hole of university administration, which may or may not provide any clear payback to the funding public, or for that matter, to the university community including students who see rising tuition every year."[105] Nothing provides universities with instructions on how to spend their licensing income; university administrators frequently do not even know how this money is spent.[106] Therefore, to trust universities to abide by the Act's requirement that licensing income be earmarked for "scientific research or education"[107] without providing any way to monitor that this is actually occurring, is wishful thinking.

Secondly, taken to its extreme, this argument basically implies that if tech-transfer offices were successful enough, federal funding would not be necessary—an argument universities would likely never make. Federal aid is too much of a cash-cow, and too engrained in their cost structure, for them to claim that they can go it on their own.

D. Sharing Income with Funding Agencies Could Influence Future Research Grants

If universities were forced to share their Bayh-Dole licensing revenue with their funding agencies, one concern is that this might incentivize the agencies to only fund research that can be commercially licensed and neglect basic research that cannot be monetized.[108] However, "if that were the case then [agencies like] the NIH would already have an incentive to fund more applied rather than basic research today, since applied research tends to get more press and public attention in licenses."[109] However, there is evidence to the contrary, showing that, while NIH funding for both basic applied research increased in the last few decades, basic had a greater actual and proportional increase.[110]

---

[105] Ritchie de Larena, *supra* note 11, at 1411 (footnotes omitted).

[106] Jeffrey Brainard, *The Ghosts of Stanford: Have Federal Constraints on Reimbursing Overhead for Research Grants Gone Too Far?*, CHRON. HIGHER EDUC., Aug. 5, 2005, at A16.

[107] 35 U.S.C. § 202(c)(7)(C) (2006).

[108] Ritchie de Larena, *supra* note 11, at 1441 n.460.

[109] *Id.*

[110] *Compare* RONALD L. MEEKS, NAT'L SCI. FOUND., FEDERAL FUNDS FOR RESEARCH AND DEVELOPMENT: FISCAL YEARS 1973–2003; FEDERAL OBLIGATIONS FOR RESEARCH TO UNIVERSITIES AND COLLEGES BY AGENCY AND DETAILED FIELD OF SCIENCE AND ENGINEERING 65 tbl.2G (2004), *available at* http://www.nsf.gov/statistics/nsf04332/pdf/nsf04332.pdf (detailing basic research), *with id.* at 101 tbl.3G (detailing applied research).

VIII. CONCLUSION

The legislative intent behind Bayh-Dole was to promote an "Academic-Industrial Complex."[111] Much like the infamous military-industrial complex, Bayh-Dole was meant to foster ties between vital sectors of the U.S. economy—universities and federal agencies—and stimulate scientific advancement in the process. There is no doubt that "the importance of linking our unparalleled network of over 700 Federal laboratories and our Nation's universities with United States industry continues to hold great promise for our future economic prosperity."[112]

However, federal agencies have not always received adequate compensation for their investments in this relationship, and, in an era like the present, where federal deficits are a cause of great consternation, the U.S. government literally cannot afford to throw money at projects without receiving any return. As discussed above, there are a number of technology sectors where increased federal funding has not led to the anticipated public benefit.

To quote Judge Ritchie de Larena:

> [I]f universities misuse research funds, bungle licensing deals, or simply overlook important technologies that are vested in them by the Bayh-Dole Act, then taxpayers are not receiving that deserved benefit.
>
>   . . . .
>
>   From an equity perspective, surely partial, if not full, payback to the funding public seems eminently fair. If indeed the intent of the patent system at large is to reward—and thereby encourage—investment in the creation of new inventions, then it naturally follows that the reward for inventions created with federal research funds should inure to the federal taxpayers who paid for them. However, under the current regime, universities have no incentive—or even any mechanism—to try to recover any costs for their government sponsors.[113]

A rebalancing of ownership rights, licensing revenues and experimental use towards the federal side of the university–federal agency ledger could substantially benefit the taxpayers and would steer closer to the intended purpose of the Bayh-Dole Act.

Three suggestions, espoused in some form by a number of tech-transfer academics, are proffered here. First, a percentage of Bayh-Dole tech-transfer income should be sent back to federal funding agencies. Second, any researcher receiving federal funds should be allowed to use, for research purposes, all inventions developed with federal money. Finally, underutilized patents should be placed in the public domain to be monitored and exchanged through a national tech-transfer office. Implementing these three changes could go a long way to giving the taxpayer direct returns on some of the many billions of dollars spent every year on research in the United States.

---

[111] Felicia R. Lee, *Academic Industrial* Complex, N.Y. TIMES, Sept. 6, 2003, at B9; *see generally* Eyal Press & Jennifer Washburn, *The Kept University*, ATLANTIC, Mar.2000, at 39–40, *available at* http://www.theatlantic.com/magazine/archive/2000/03/the-kept-university/6629/.
[112] Technology Transfer Commercialization Act of 2000, Pub. L. No. 106-404, § 2(1), 114 Stat. 1742.
[113] Ritchie de Larena, *supra* note 11, at 1387, 1389 (footnotes omitted).

www.ingramcontent.com/pod-product-compliance
Lightning Source LLC
Chambersburg PA
CBHW031832170526
45157CB00001B/271

9 7 8 1 1 0 5 4 3 2 3 1 6